P9-DVO-353

Footprint Handbook
Delhi &
North

VANESSA BE

CALGARY PUBLIC LIBRARY

SEP 2016

This is Delhi &
Northwest India

Capped by the mightiest mountain range on earth, the northwest region of India encompasses the most dramatic and beautiful terrain in all the country. Many travellers come to experience the great outdoors. But the region is equally rich in cultural heritage, with Buddhism the dominant religion in mellow Ladakh, and pockets of Tibetan refugees scattered throughout the Himalayan foothills. The Kashmir Valley is another experience entirely, with remarkable tiered mosques and sufi shrines covered in colourfully painted papier mâché. A visit to the sublime Golden Temple at Amritsar – the holiest place of the Sikhs – further enriches a journey to or from the hills.

Perhaps the most striking landscapes are Ladakh's high-altitude plateaux and Spiti's narrow gorges – contrasting desert dust with sharp blue skies and snowy peaks, and where monasteries perch by ribboned rivers. The apple orchards and pine-clad hills of Himachal Pradesh and the lotus-fringed lakes of Kashmir are a verdant antidote to these harsh terrains.

The delightful houseboats in Srinagar hark back to the colonial era, and staying aboard for couple of nights is a highlight of any visit to the northwest. Relics of the Raj can also be seen in Himachal Pradesh, especially in quaint Dalhousie and Mussoorie or the capital, Shimla, where churches, clubs and promenades now throng with Indian tourists escaping Delhi's heat.

But be sure to leave some time for the plains – to discover the unique architecture of Chandigarh and the inspiring Mughal monuments and ancient cities of Delhi. And the road from Leh, either via Manali or Srinagar, might leave you in need of a rooftop beer in Hauz Khas or high tea at the Imperial Hotel.

Vanessa Betts

Victoria McCulloch

Best of
Delhi &
Northwest India

top things to do and see

❶ Qawwali singing at Nizamuddin's Tomb

Venture to the east of Delhi to the atmospheric Nizamuddin Tomb. Dating back 700 years, the rich Sufi tradition of *qawwali* singing – essentially a love song to God – can be heard at Sufi shrines and dargahs across the country. Page 42.

❷ Heritage walk at Qutb Minar

You can view the architectural changes of Delhi in a visit to the Qutb Minar, where Hindu temples were sacked to make the 73-m Victory Tower. Qutb Minar is close to the site of the first of Delhi's seven cities. Take a walking tour for an insight into the city's history. Page 43.

❸ Morning prayer at the Golden Temple

The Amritvela is the nectar of the dawn and a sublime time to visit the heart of the Sikh faith. Visitors pour in to see the temple 24 hours a day, but morning is a magical time as prayers are chanted and the sun warms the golden façade. Page 75.

❹ A dip in the hot springs at Vashisht Temple

High in the hills above the Beas River, this temple, dedicated to Rama, has bathing tanks fed by natural hot springs. Come here for a therapeutic dip after long mountain walks. Page 118.

❺ Walking the Kora in McLeodganj

Since 1959, when His Holiness the Dalai Lama made his home in McLeodganj, Buddhists, followers and travellers have walked the Kora – a clockwise circumambulation of His Holiness' residence and the temple. Enjoy epic mountain views and fluttering prayer flags. Page 133.

❻ Sleeping on a houseboat in Srinagar

This lakeside city has inspired poets and kings. You can sleep on a wooden houseboat, try a *wazwan* banquet and saunter through 17th-century Mughal gardens, in the shadow of the Pir Panjal's snow-covered peaks. Pages 162, 164 and 169.

❼ See the restoration of Leh Palace

Ladakh's laid-back capital, with flower-filled gardens and far-reaching views, is the perfect places to acclimatize before a high-altitude trek. Leh Palace and Tsemo Fort loom dramatically on a ridge above the city with bustling markets, mud-brick houses, stupas and monasteries. Page 182.

❽ Nubra Valley's remote villages

Spectacular scenery, remote and friendly villages, sand dunes and isolated Buddhist *gompas* characterize the northernmost Nubra-Shyok region. It's recommended you spend at least three days exploring these isolated valleys by jeep. Page 202.

Snow leopard

Route planner

By exploring this área you are rewarded with epic mountain views, high-altitude retreats, valleys full of flowers, lakes dotted with houseboats and also the rolling plains of the breadbasket of India – the agricultural lands of Punjab and Haryana. The region offers insights into Buddhist culture, the Sikh Faith, Hindu traditions and Islamic thought. From the stunning Golden Temple in Amritsar to the high-altitude Buddhist gompas in Spiti Valley or the impressive Hindu Mata Vishno Devi temple in Kashmir. You can immerse yourself in Buddhist culture in McLeodganj – home to His Holiness the Dalai Lama – or at the Alchi Monastery in Ladakh. It is a perfect invitation to experience nature and clear air as you travel high up in the Himalaya to experience the elements while trekking the valleys and mountain passes, whitewater rafting or simply sitting and enjoying the expansive view. Around McLeodganj and Manali there are great opportunities to consider our relationship with our own true nature during meditation courses.

Two weeks

Delhi–Sarahan–Spiti Valley–Pin Valley–Manali–Delhi

This two-week alternative route from Delhi is richly rewarding and takes you to some often overlooked spots in southern and eastern Himachal on the way to Manali. Bypass the tourist-friendly Shimla and head to the pretty orchards around **Narkanda** (page 91) en route to the stunning Bhimakali Temple, surrounded by mountain peaks at **Sarahan** (page 93). There is good trekking around **Kalpa** (page 98) or the beautiful Sangla village in the **Baspa Valley** (page 97) with epic views all the way across to the mountain range that runs between Manali and Dharamsala. From here, you can venture deeper into the Buddhist region of **Spiti Valley** (page 99) which is more similar to the terrain of Ladakh than its neighbouring valleys. The main towns of Spiti Valley are Kaza and Tabo, atmospheric villages with Mongol heritage. You can trek to Hikim gompa and explore the **Pin Valley National Park** (page 102), home to the snow leopard. At Tabo, the Chos Khor gompa is one of the oldest living Buddhist establishments. Travelling through the Rohang Pass, you reach **Manali** (page 117) and its creature comforts. **Naggar** (page 115) is a more relaxed place to stay than Manali; don't miss the beautiful Naggar Castle and the Nikolas Roerich Gallery, an hour south of Manali. Hailing from Russia, Nikolas Roerich painted evocative pictures of the ever-changing mountain terrain. If you have longer, you can explore the **Parvati Valley** (page 112) and the hot springs at **Manikaran** (page 112) as you drop down from Manali. If travelling to the Spiti Valley, check road and weather conditions before setting out.

Three weeks

Delhi–Amritsar–Dharamsala–Srinagar–Leh–Manali–Spiti Valley–Shimla–Delhi

This three-week itinerary is all-encompassing and takes you from the country's capital to the majestic Himalaya and high-altitude deserts. **Delhi** (page 24) deserves at least two days, however tight your schedule. Don't miss Qutb Minar in the south, the first of Delhi's seven cities, where the Mughals used existing Hindu temples to make their 73-m minaret – the tallest in India. Then explore the Old City and the bustle of Chandni Chowk and Kinari Bazar, where you'll find traditional craftsmen and *jalebi wallas* (sweet makers). Hop on a cycle rickshaw through the labyrinthine streets to reach the Jama Masjid mosque and the Red Fort.

The next destination is **Amritsar** (page 74) and the magical Golden Temple where you can easily spend a whole day soaking up the atmosphere. You can sample food from the langar (community kitchen) and even take a dip. From Amritsar, you can move on to the relaxed atmosphere of **Dharamsala** (page 132) and **McLeodganj** (page 132). The latter is home to His Holiness the Dalai Lama and a large Tibetan community; some people stay here for months to enjoy the great views, short treks, conversation classes with monks, meditation and yoga courses, or cookery classes that teach you to make momos (Tibetan dumplings). Make time to visit Norbulingka which is an institute preserving Tibetan handicrafts and Tangka painting or even catch an IPL cricket match in the Dharamsala stadium.

Travel onto **Srinagar** (page 162) and the **Kashmir Valley** (page 157). Spend some time on one of the hundreds of houseboats moored on the lakes, and being paddled around in a *shikara* or simply watching the birdlife from the veranda as the sun goes down. From Srinagar you can easily make a day or overnight trip to the hill station of **Pahalgam** (page 173) or the snow resort of **Gulmarg** (page 173).

It's a long road on to Leh but one of the most spectacular and unforgettable, winding over mountain passes and criss-crossing the Indus River. After **Kargil** (page 176), the culture abruptly changes from Muslim to Buddhist, and the wild mountain valleys are home to tiny villages and active monasteries poised on peaks. There is accommodation dotted throughout the villages, so if you want to slow things down, **Lamayuru** (page 198), **Alchi** (page 197), **Lekir** (page 196) and **Phyang** (page 195) are all possible night-stops.

Leh (page 181) is the perfect antidote to a gruelling journey. The new museum, the old bazar, relaxing garden restaurants and the impressive palace keep you busy in the city, while day trips can be made to the famous monasteries nearby, such as Hemis and Thikse. A three-day trek can be arranged when you've acclimatized, as can an excursion to the remote **Nubra Valley** (page 202).

Those who have plenty of time might choose to take the road back to Delhi, stopping in laidback **Manali** (page 117), dining on river trout and exploring India's honeymoon capital or doing some whitewater rafting in the **Kullu Valley** (page 109). From Manali, you could also venture to the stunning and often overlooked **Spiti Valley** (page 99). Dropping back down the mountains, via Kaza and Rekong Peo, you can visit Little England at **Shimla** (page 83) with beautiful hotels and scenic vistas. Check road and weather conditions before setting off.

Improve your travel photography

Taking pictures is a highlight for many travellers, yet too often the results turn out to be disappointing. Steve Davey, author of Footprint's *Travel Photography*, sets out his top rules for coming home with pictures you can be proud of.

Before you go

Don't waste precious travelling time and do your research before you leave. Find out what festivals or events might be happening or which day the weekly market takes place, and search online image sites such as Flickr to see whether places are best shot at the beginning or end of the day, and what vantage points you should consider.

Get up early

The quality of the light will be better in the few hours after sunrise and again before sunset – especially in the tropics when the sun will be harsh and unforgiving in the middle of the day. Sometimes seeing the sunrise is a part of the whole travel experience: sleep in and you will miss more than just photographs.

Stop and think

Don't just click away without any thought. Pause for a few seconds before raising the camera and ask yourself what you are trying to show with your photograph. Think about what things you need to include in the frame to convey this meaning. Be prepared to move around your subject to get the best angle. Knowing the point of your picture is the first step to making sure that the person looking at the picture will know it too.

Compose your picture

Avoid simply dumping your subject in the centre of the frame every time you take a picture. If you compose with it to one side, then your picture can look more balanced. This will also allow you to show a significant background and make the picture more meaningful. A good rule of thumb is to place your subject or any significant detail a third of the way into the frame; facing into the frame not out of it.

This rule also works for landscapes. Compose with the horizon two-thirds of the way up the frame if the foreground is the most interesting part of the picture; one-third of the way up if the sky is more striking.

Don't get hung up with this so-called Rule of Thirds, though. Exaggerate it by pushing your subject out to the edge of the frame if it makes a more interesting picture; or if the sky is dull in a landscape, try cropping with the horizon near the very top of the frame.

Fill the frame

If you are going to focus on a detail or even a person's face in a close-up portrait, then be bold and make sure that you fill the frame. This is often a case of physically getting in close. You can use a telephoto setting on a zoom lens but this can lead to pictures looking quite flat; moving in close is a lot more fun!

Interact with people

If you want to shoot evocative portraits then it is vital to approach people and seek permission in some way, even if it is just by smiling at someone. Spend a little time with them and they are likely to relax and look less stiff and formal. Action portraits where people are doing something, or environmental portraits, where they are set against a significant background, are a good way to achieve relaxed portraits. Interacting is a good way to find out more about people and their lives, creating memories as well as photographs.

Focus carefully

Your camera can focus quicker than you, but it doesn't know which part of the picture you want to be in focus. If your camera is using the centre focus sensor then move the camera so it is over the subject and half press the button, then, holding it down, recompose the picture. This will lock the focus. Take the now correctly focused picture when you are ready.

Another technique for accurate focusing is to move the active sensor over your subject. Some cameras with touch-sensitive screens allow you to do this by simply clicking on the subject.

Leave light in the sky

Most good night photography is actually taken at dusk when there is some light and colour left in the sky; any lit portions of the picture will balance with the sky and any ambient lighting. There is only a very small window when this will happen, so get into position early, be prepared and keep shooting and reviewing the results. You can take pictures after this time, but avoid shots of tall towers in an inky black sky; crop in close on lit areas to fill the frame.

Bring it home safely

Digital images are inherently ephemeral: they can be deleted or corrupted in a heartbeat. The good news though is they can be copied just as easily. Wherever you travel, you should have a backup strategy. Cloud backups are popular, but make sure that you will have access to fast enough Wi-Fi. If you use RAW format, then you will need some sort of physical back-up. If you don't travel with a laptop or tablet, then you can buy a backup drive that will copy directly from memory cards.

Recently updated and available in both digital and print formats, Footprint's Travel Photography by Steve Davey covers everything you need to know about travelling with a camera, including simple post-processing. More information is available at www.footprinttravelguides.com

When to go

... and when not to

Climate

The best time to visit Himachal Pradesh, Ladakh and Kashmir are the summer months from May to October, when trekking routes and the high mountain passes are open. Often people are waiting in areas like McLeodganj and Manali for the routes to Leh and Ladakh to open. The monsoon season lasts two to three months, from July to September, with the east seeing the strongest and longest rains in the Himalayan foothills. If you are travelling to Himachal Pradesh and Kashmir during the monsoon you need to be prepared for extended periods of torrential rain and disruption to travel. However, Ladakh, beyond the monsoon line, is almost always visited only in the summer season. You can visit many places in Himachal Pradesh during the winter, like Shimla, Manali and McLeodganj – where some places have a roaring fire; honeymooning couples and families flock to Manali for fun in the snow. If you are using Delhi as your gateway to the north, you will often be going from extreme heat to much cooler climes. Before the monsoon season in Delhi, Chandigarh and Amritsar, May and June see temperatures of around 40°C. Locals escape the heat of the plains by heading for the hills of Shimla, Manali and McLeodganj. It is best to visit Delhi and Chandigarh from October to May to avoid the worst of the heat.

Festivals

India has a wealth of festivals with many celebrated nationwide, while others are specific to a particular state or community or even a particular temple. Many fall on different dates each year depending on the Hindu lunar calendar so check with the tourist office, or see the thorough calendar of upcoming major and minor festivals at www.drikpanchang.com. There are many Buddhist festivities celebrated in this region as well. For public holidays and celebrations, see page 223.

What to do

The western Himalaya, and up into Kashmir and Ladakh, are rich in flora and fauna with contrasting environs from high-altitude desert life to flower meadows, crashing rivers to apple orchards. It is a great region to embrace nature, with activities from trekking and wildlife spotting to volunteering opportunities.

Birdwatching

Some common birds to be found in the western Himalaya are Himalayan griffons, crested serpent eagles, lammergeiers, forest owlets, golden orioles, rose finches and Himalayan blue magpies. You might even see the rare western tragopan – the state bird of Himachal Pradesh. The Great Himalayan National Park in the Kullu district is a good starting point for birdwatching. *A Birdwatcher's Guide to India*, by Krys Kazmierczak and Raj Singh (published by Prion Ltd, Sandy, Bedfordshire, UK, 1998), is well researched and comprehensive with helpful practical information and maps. For further information, **Bird Link**, biks@giasdl01.vsnl.net.in, is concerned with the conservation of birds and their habitat. Useful websites include www.delhibird.net, www.orientalbirdclub.org and www.sacon.org.

Creative activities

In Delhi there are photography courses and photography walks, as well as Travel Blogging workshops at **Kunzum Café**, Hauz Khas Village. Check out www.photographtours.in for chances to perfect your shot with tours in Himcahal and Kashmir, looking at spectacular views, tribal portraits and religious festivals.

Trekking

You can be on top of the world in Himachal Pradesh and Ladakh. Treks in this region vary widely, both in intensity and in the nature of the landscape. You can explore the high-altitude desert of Spiti for epic views and Buddhist gompas. There are some beautiful treks around the Baspa Valley in southern Himachal and some pretty walks around Shimla. In Ladakh, you can venture out on the highest motorable road to the Nubra Valley, or the more accomplished trekker can seek out the trails around Zanskar. For details of trekking in the Himachal and Ladakh regions, see the Footprint *Indian Himalaya* guide.

Volunteering

There are some fantastic opportunities to meet locals and get involved with the community. In McLeodganj you can volunteer within the Tibetan community by offering conversation and English language classes with Tibetan monks or work at the **Rogpa** day-care centre (see page 137). You will learn as much about Tibetan culture as they do about English – it offers a great insight. In Spiti, there is a fantastic group **Ecosphere Spiti** with volunteering options as well as there treks. You can invest your time helping with waste management, construction of greenhouses and passive solar structures.

Whitewater rafting

South of Manali, you can tackle the rapids of the Beas River winding its way through the Kullu Valley. There are numerous outfits plying the river but it's best to ask your hotel to recommend a responsible operator.

Wildlife spotting

The best opportunities are in Ladakh or the Great Himalayan National Park. From September to November the animals make their seasonal migration to lower climes, and it's a good time to spot them. The snow leopard (see box, page 207) and Himalayan musk deer are both endangered species and catching sight of them is a rare delight.

Shopping tips

India excels in producing fine crafts at affordable prices. Handicrafts are sold in the government emporia in major cities, which guarantee quality at fixed prices (no bargaining), but many are poorly displayed and staff can be reluctant. Private shops and top hotel arcades offer better quality and service but at a higher price. Vibrant and colourful local bazaars are often a great experience but you must be prepared to bargain. Worth a special mention is **Norbilingka** (see page 134), south of Dharamsala, an institute that preserves the tradition of Tibetan crafts. Also check out **Playclan** (see page 58), which has outlets in Delhi and across India, and **Purple Jungle** (see page 58), based in Haus Khaz Village. Crafts typical of Delhi and northwest India include:

Carpets and dhurries Flat woven cotton *dhurries* in subtle colours are found easily in Delhi and Chandigarh.
Jewellery Tibetan jewellery with heavy silver and turquoise is popular in Himachal Pradesh and Ladakh, while there are more delicate pieces available in Kashmir.
Metal work Stalls line the streets of McLeodganj with Tibetans selling beautiful artefacts and singing bowls. There is a good Tibetan Market in Janpath in Delhi, too.
Paintings *Thangkas* are stunning Buddhist paintings on fabric, which can be easily rolled and transported.
Textiles Sober handspun *khadi* and heavy shawls from the Kullu Valley are popular, as well as Tibetan-style silks in Ladakh and northern Himachal.

Where to stay

India has an enormous range of accommodation. You can stay safely and very cheaply by Western standards right across the country. In Delhi, there is a wide range of accommodation, from the backpacker enclave of Parhaganj to chic B&Bs and super-luxurious hotels. In Himachal Pradesh, you can stay in renovated 200-year-old houses, medieval castles, palaces and even a judge's house. Some hotels, although new, have been constructed in the traditional kathakuni style around Manali (layers of intricate stonework and wood), while in some remote locations you can even stay under canvas. In both Amritsar and Sarahan, you can have a very atmospheric stay in the temples or you can stay on a Punjabi farm near Chandigarh.

The mainstay of the budget traveller is the ubiquitous Indian 'business hotel': these are usually within walking distance of train and bus stations, anonymous but generally decent value, with en suite rooms of variable cleanliness and a TV showing 110 channels of cricket and Bollywood MTV. At the top end, alongside international chains like ITC Sheraton and Ramada, India boasts several home-grown hotel chains, best of which are the exceptional heritage and palace hotels operated by the Oberoi (Delhi and Shimla) and Taj groups.

Delhi hotels are naturally busy all year round. For Himachal Pradesh, Kashmir and Ladakh the peak season (June to September) prices rise and hotels get very booked up in popular destinations, especially when trekking routes and mountain roads are opened after the snows. It is advisable to book in advance

Price codes

Where to stay	Restaurants
$$$$ over US$150	$$$ over US$12
$$$ US$66-150	$$ US$6-12
$$ US$30-65	$ under US$6
$ under US$30	
For a double room in high season, excluding taxes.	For a two-course meal for one person, excluding drinks or service charge.

by phone or email, but double check your reservation. If you do not have a reservation try to arrive as early as possible in the day.

In Delhi, there is a wide range of accommodation, from the backpacker enclave of Parhaganj to chic B&Bs and super-luxurious hotels, while in Agra, predictably, rooms are an expensive affair whatever the quality. In the peak season (October to April) prices rise and hotels get very booked up in popular destinations, especially around Diwali. It is advisable to book in advance by phone or email, but double check your reservation. If you do not have a reservation try to arrive as early as possible in the day.

Hotels

Price categories

The category codes used in this book are based on the price of a double room excluding taxes. They are not star ratings and individual facilities vary considerably. The most expensive hotels charge in US dollars only. Modest hotels may not have their own restaurant but will often offer 'room service', bringing in food from outside. In temple towns, restaurants may only serve vegetarian food. Expect to pay more in Delhi and Chandigarh. Prices away from large cities tend to be lower for comparable hotels.

Off-season rates

Large reductions are made by hotels in all categories out of season. Always ask if any discount is available. You may also request the 10-15% agent's commission to be deducted from your bill if you book direct. Clarify whether the agreed figure includes all taxes. If travelling to Himachal and Ladakh out of season, check ahead of time that your hotel of choice is open as many close out of season.

Taxes

In general most hotel rooms rated at Rs 3000 or above are subject to a tax of 10%. Many states levy an additional luxury tax of 10-25%, and some hotels add a service charge of 10% on top of this. Taxes are not necessarily payable on meals, so it is worth settling your meals bill separately. Most hotels in the $$ category and above accept payment by credit card. Check your final bill carefully. Visitors have complained of incorrect bills, even in the most expensive hotels. The problem particularly afflicts groups, when last-minute extras appear mysteriously on some guests' bills. Check the evening before departure, and keep all receipts.

Hotel facilities

Be prepared for difficulties that are uncommon in the West. It is best to inspect the room and check that all equipment (air conditioning, TV, water heater, flush) works before checking in at a modest hotel. Many hotels try to wring too many years' service out of their linen, and it's quite common to find sheets that are stained, frayed or riddled with holes. Don't expect any but the most expensive or tourist-savvy hotels to fit a top sheet to the bed.

Power cuts are common, or hot water may be restricted to certain times of day. The largest hotels have their own generators but it is best to carry a good torch. The Wi-Fi connection may be intermittent.

In some regions water supply is rationed periodically. Keep a bucket filled to use for flushing the toilet during water cuts. Occasionally, tap water may be discoloured due to rusty tanks. In remote locations, hot water will be available at certain times of the day, sometimes in buckets, but is usually very restricted in quantity. Electric water heaters may provide enough for a shower but not enough to fill a bath tub. For details on drinking water, see page 21. Some hotels provide a turn down service, including a hot water bottle in the bed!

Hotels close to temples can be very noisy, especially during festivals. Music blares from loudspeakers late at night and from very early in the morning, often making sleep impossible. Mosques call the faithful to prayers at dawn. Earplugs can be helpful.

Some hotels offer 24-hour checkout, meaning you can keep the room a full 24 hours from the time you arrive – a great option if you arrive in the afternoon and want to spend the morning sightseeing.

Homestays

At the upmarket end, increasing numbers of travellers are keen to stay in private homes and guesthouses, opting not to book large hotel chains that keep you at arm's length from a culture. Instead, travellers get home-cooked meals in heritage houses and learn about a country through conversation with often fascinating hosts. Delhi has many new and smart family-run B&Bs springing up. Tourist offices have lists of families with more modest homestays. Companies specializing in homestays include **Home & Hospitality** ① *www.homeandhospitality.co.uk*, **MAHout** ① *www.mahoutuk.com*, and **Sundale Vacations** ① *www.sundale.com*.

Food
& drink

traditional *thalis* and Tibetan *momos*

Food

You find just as much variety in dishes crossing India as you would on an equivalent journey across Europe. Combinations of spices give each region its distinctive flavour. The larger hotels, open to non-residents, often offer buffet lunches with Indian, Western and sometimes Chinese dishes. Sunday brunch buffets are becoming increasingly popular in big cities such as Delhi, and you can find restaurants run by celebrity chefs. These can be good value (Rs 400-500; but Rs 1000 in the top grades, and some of the Sunday lunch buffets in Delhi are Rs 2500) and can provide a welcome, comfortable break in the cool. The health risks, however, of food kept warm for long periods in metal containers are considerable, especially if turnover at the buffet is slow. We have received several complaints of stomach trouble following a buffet meal, even in five-star hotels. It is essential to be very careful since food hygiene may be poor, flies abound and refrigeration in the hot weather may be inadequate and intermittent because of power cuts. It is best to eat only freshly prepared food by ordering from the menu (especially meat and fish dishes). Avoid salads and cut fruit, unless the menu advertises that they have been washed in mineral water.

If you are unused to spicy food, go slow. Food is often spicier when you eat with families or at local places. Popular local restaurants are obvious from the number of people eating in them. Try a traditional *thali*, which is a complete meal served on a large stainless steel plate. Several preparations, placed in small bowls, surround the central serving of wholewheat chapati and rice. A vegetarian *thali* would include *dhal* (lentils), two or three curries (which can be quite hot) and crisp poppadums. A variety of pickles are offered – mango and lime are two of the most popular. These can be exceptionally hot, and are designed to be taken in minute quantities alongside the main dishes. Plain *dahi* (yoghurt), or *raita*, usually act as a bland 'cooler'. Simple *dhabas* (rustic roadside eateries) are an alternative experience for sampling authentic local dishes.

Many city restaurants and backpacker eateries offer a choice of so-called European options such as toasted sandwiches, stuffed pancakes, apple pies, fruit crumbles and cheesecakes. Italian favourites (pizzas, pastas) can be very different from what you are used to. Ice creams, on the other hand, can be exceptionally good; there are excellent Indian ones as well as some international brands.

You can enjoy apples straight from the orchard, plums and apricots across Himachal Pradesh. Mangoes come into season in May and June across India and are available in the north

Regional specialities
There is a wonderful diversity in the foods of northwest India, with the butter rich Punjabi cusine, the delicate flavours of Kashmiri and Himachali dishes, and the Tibetan influences. In cities and larger towns, you will see all types of Indian food on the menus, with some restaurants specializing in regional cuisine. North Indian kebabs and the richer flavoursome cuisine of Delhi and the Punjab are popular. In the Punjab, many dishes feature butter (*desi ghee*) like *daal makhani* (the queen of lentils) and the ubiquitous butter chicken. You can also try *sarson ka saag*, a delicious spinach and mustard greens preparation. Traditional Himachali (*pahari*) dishes are flavoured with yoghurt, buttermilk and often cardamom. Try the delicious *dham* (lentil and bean preparation cooked in curd) and *chha gosht* (lamb cooked in curd and chickpea flour). Across Himachal and Ladakh, you will also find many Tibetan/Ladakhi dishes like *momos* or *kothey* as they are known in Ladakh (dumplings with vegetable, chicken or mutton) and *thukpa* (noodle soups). In Ladakh, you can sample butter tea and *chhaang* (fermented barley or millet based alcoholic brew). In Kashmir, try the *wazwan* style of food infused with the delicate spices of cardamom, clove and cinnamon and of course, the Kashmiri chilli. Mutton *rogan josh*, *dum aloo* (stuffed potatoes) and Kashmiri *naan* (bread stuffed with dried fruits and nuts) are delicious to try.

Drink

Drinking water used to be regarded as one of India's biggest hazards and it is still true that water from the tap or a well should never be considered safe to drink since public water supplies are often polluted. Bottled water is now widely available although not all bottled water is mineral water; most are simply purified water from an urban supply. Buy from a shop or stall, check the seal carefully and avoid street hawkers. When disposing of bottles puncture the neck, which prevents misuse but allows recycling.

There is growing concern over the mountains of plastic bottles that are collecting and the waste of resources needed to produce them, so travellers are being encouraged to carry their own bottles and take a portable water filter. It is important to use pure water for cleaning teeth.

Tea and coffee are safe and widely available. Both are normally served sweet, and with milk. If you wish, say 'no sugar' (*chini nahin*), 'no milk' (*dudh nahin*) when ordering. Alternatively, ask for a pot of tea and milk and sugar to be brought separately. Freshly brewed coffee is rare in north India; ordinary city restaurants will usually serve the instant variety. Even in aspiring smart cafés, espresso or cappuccino may not turn out quite as you'd expect in the West.

Bottled soft drinks such as Coke, Pepsi, Teem, Limca and Thums Up are universally available but always check the seal when you buy from a street stall. There are also several brands of fruit juice sold in cartons, including mango, pineapple and apple – Indian brands are very sweet. Don't add ice cubes as the water source may be contaminated. Take care with fresh fruit juices or lassis as ice is often added.

Travelling across Himachal, take advantage of the delicious bottled apple juice straight from the orchards.

Indians rarely drink alcohol with a meal. In the past wines and spirits were generally either imported and extremely expensive, or local and of poor quality. Now, the best Indian whisky, rum and brandy (IMFL or 'Indian Made Foreign Liquor') are widely accepted, as are good Champagnoise and other wines from Maharashtra. If you hanker after a bottle of imported wine, you will only find it in the top restaurants or specialist liquor stores for at least Rs 1000.

For the urban elite, refreshing Indian beers are popular when eating out and are widely available. 'Pubs' have sprung up in the major cities. Elsewhere, seedy, all-male drinking dens in the larger cities are best avoided for women travellers, but can make quite an experience otherwise – you will sometimes be locked into cubicles for clandestine drinking. If that sounds unsavoury then head for the better hotel bars instead; prices aren't that steep. In rural India, local rice, palm, cashew or date juice toddy and arak are deceptively potent. Most states have alcohol-free dry days or enforce degrees of prohibition. Some upmarket restaurants may serve beer even if it's not listed, so it's worth asking. In some states there are government approved wine shops where you buy your alcohol through a metal grille.

Menu reader

Styles of cooking

bhoona in a thick, fairly spicy sauce

chops minced meat, fish or vegetables, covered with mashed potato, crumbed and fried

cutlet minced meat, fish, vegetables formed into flat rounds or ovals, crumbed and fried (eg prawn cutlet, flattened king prawn)

dopiaza with onions (added twice during cooking)

dum pukht steam baked

jhal frezi spicy, hot sauce with tomatoes and chillies

kebab skewered (or minced and shaped) meat or fish; a dry spicy dish cooked on a fire

kima minced meat (usually 'mutton')

kofta minced meat or vegetable balls

korma in fairly mild rich sauce using cream/yoghurt

masala marinated in spices (fairly hot)

madras hot

makhani in butter rich sauce

mughlai rich North Indian style

nargisi dish using boiled eggs

navratan curry ('9 jewels') colourful mixed vegetables and fruit in mild sauce

peshwari rich with dried fruit and nuts (northwest Indian)

tandoori baked in a tandoor (special clay oven) or one imitating it

tikka marinated meat pieces, baked quite dry

Meat and fish

gosht, mas meat

jhinga prawns

macchli fish

murgh chicken

Vegetables (sabzi)

aloo potato

baingan aubergine

band gobi cabbage

bhindi okra, ladies' fingers

gajar carrots

khumbhi mushroom

phool gobi cauliflower

piaz onion

matar peas

sag spinach

Tibetan/Ladakhi dishes

momos dumplings steamed or fried with vegetable, chicken or mutton

thentuk flat noodle soup with vegetables or mutton

thukpa flat noodle soup

Rice

bhat/sada *chawal* plain boiled rice

biriyani partially cooked rice layered over meat and baked with saffron

khichari rice and lentils cooked with turmeric and other spices

pulao/pilau fried rice cooked with spices (cloves, cardamom, cinnamon) with dried fruit, nuts or vegetables. Sometimes cooked with meat, like a biriyani

Roti – breads

chapati (roti) thin, plain, wholemeal unleavened bread cooked on a *tawa* (griddle), usually made from *ata* (wheat flour). *Makkaikiroti* is with maize flour.

nan oven baked (traditionally in a tandoor) white flour leavened bread often large and triangular; sometimes stuffed with almonds and dried fruit

paratha fried bread layered with *ghi* (sometimes cooked with egg or with potatoes)

poori thin deep-fried, puffed rounds of flour

Delhi

Delhi can take you aback with its vibrancy and growth. Less than 70 years ago the spacious, quiet and planned New Delhi was still the pride of late colonial British India, while the lanes of Old Delhi resonated with the sounds of a bustling medieval market.

Old and new, simple and sophisticated, traditional and modern, East and West are juxtaposed in Old and New Delhi. Close to New Delhi Railway Station, the cheap hotels and guesthouses of Paharganj squeeze between cloth merchants and wholesalers. Old Delhi, further north, with the Red Fort and Jama Masjid, is still a dense network of narrow alleys, tightly packed markets, noise, smells and apparent chaos. Another area comprises the remorselessly growing squatter settlements (*jhuggies*), which provide shelter for more than a third of Delhi's population. To the south is a newer, chrome-and-glass city of the modern suburbs, where the rural areas of Gurgaon have become the preserve of the prosperous, with shopping malls, banks and private housing estates.

Whatever India you are looking for, the capital has it all: getting lost in warrens of crowded streets and spice markets, eating kebabs by the beautiful Jama Masjid, lazing among Mogul ruins, listening to Sufi musicians by a shrine at dusk or shopping in giant shining malls, drinking cocktails in glitzy bars and travelling on the gleaming Metro.

Essential Delhi

Finding your feet

Delhi is served by **Indira Gandhi International (IGI) Airport**, which handles both international and domestic traffic. The new T3 (International Terminal) is connected to the city centre by Metro, taking 20 minutes. It is about 23 km from the centre, taking 30-45 minutes from the Domestic Terminal and 45-60 minutes from the International Terminal by road in the day. A free shuttle runs between the terminals. Alternatively, take a pre-paid taxi (see Transport, page 63), an airport coach, or ask your hotel to collect you.

The **Inter State Bus Terminus (ISBT)** is at Kashmere Gate, near the Red Fort, about 30 minutes by bus from Connaught Place.

There are three main railway stations. The busy **New Delhi Station**, a 10-minute walk north of Connaught Place, can be maddeningly chaotic; you need to have all your wits about you. The quieter **Hazrat Nizamuddin** is 5 km southeast of Connaught Place. The overpoweringly crowded **Old Delhi Station** (2 km north of Connaught Place) has a few important train connections.

Orientation

The sights are grouped in three main areas. In the centre is the British-built capital of New Delhi, with its government buildings, wide avenues and Connaught Place: New Delhi's centre and a hub of colonial England with restaurants and shops. New Delhi

Railway Station and the main backpackers' area, Paharganj, are also here. Running due south of Connaught Place is Janpath, with hotels and small craft shops, and intersected by Rajpath with major state buildings at its western end. Immediately south is the diplomatic enclave, Chanakyapuri. Most upmarket hotels are scattered across the wide area between Connaught Place and the airport.

About 2 km north of Connaught Circus, the heart of Shahjahanabad (Old Delhi) has the Red Fort and Jama Masjid. Chandni Chowk, the main commercial area, heads west from the fort. Around this area are

➡ **Delhi maps**
1 Old Delhi, page 30
2 New Delhi, page 36
3 Connaught Place, page 40

Footprint
picks

narrow lanes packed with all different types of wares for sale.

As Delhi's centre of gravity has shifted southwards, new markets have emerged for the South Extension, Greater Kailash and Safdarjang Enclave housing colonies. This development has brought a major historic site, the Qutb Minar complex, within the city limits, about 10 km south of Connaught Place. The old fortress city of Tughluqabad is 8 km east of Qutb Minar.

East of the centre across Yamuna River is the remarkable new Akshardham Temple.

Getting around

Delhi is a vast city but the wide roads and new Metro has made it feel smaller. You can travel by Metro, taxi and bus (the latter only off peak). Hiring a car and driver saves much haggling with rickshaw drivers. The Metro has made the sprawling city very navigable: it's now possible to get from Connaught Place to Old Delhi in a cool five minutes; while Connaught Place to Qutb Minar takes 30 minutes, and all the way to the final stop in Gurgaon takes an hour. Auto-rickshaws and taxis are widely available. City buses are usually packed and have long queues. Fleets of radio taxis are the newest additions to Delhi's transport options.

When to go

October to March are the best months to visit, but December and January can get quite cold and foggy at night. Pollution can affect asthma sufferers and a lot of people develop respiratory problems and sore throats if they spend more than a few days in Delhi; echinacea can help. Monsoon lasts from the end of June to mid-September. May and June are very hot and dry and, with the whole city switching on its air-conditioning units, power cuts occur more frequently at this time.

Time required

At least three days to explore Old Delhi and the key museums and archaeological sites.

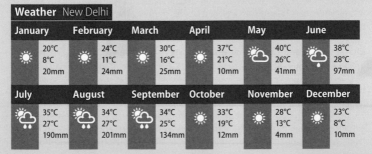

Weather	New Delhi					
January	**February**	**March**	**April**	**May**	**June**	
20°C 8°C 20mm	24°C 11°C 24mm	30°C 16°C 25mm	37°C 21°C 10mm	40°C 26°C 41mm	38°C 28°C 97mm	
July	**August**	**September**	**October**	**November**	**December**	
35°C 27°C 190mm	34°C 27°C 201mm	34°C 25°C 134mm	33°C 19°C 12mm	28°C 13°C 4mm	23°C 8°C 10mm	

narrow alleys, teeming bazars and impressive Mughal monuments

Shah Jahan (ruled 1628-1658) decided to move back from Agra to Delhi in 1638. Within 10 years the huge city of Shahjahanabad, now known as Old Delhi, was built. The plan of Shah Jahan's new city symbolized the link between religious authority enshrined in the Jama Masjid and political authority represented by the Diwan-i-Am in the Fort.

Shahjahanabad was laid out in blocks with wide roads, residential quarters, bazars and mosques. Its principal street, Chandni Chowk, had a tree-lined canal flowing down its centre which became renowned throughout Asia. The canal is long gone, but there is a jumble of shops, alleys crammed with craftsmen's workshops, food stalls, mosques and temples.

The city was protected by rubble-built walls, some of which still survive. These walls were pierced by 14 main gates. The Ajmeri Gate, Turkman Gate (often referred to by auto-rickshaw wallahs as 'Truckman Gate'), Kashmere Gate and Delhi Gate still survive.

Red Fort (Lal Qila)
Tue-Sun sunrise to sunset, Rs 250 foreigners, Rs 15 Indians, allow 1 hr. The entrance is through the Lahore Gate (nearest the car park) with the admission kiosk opposite; keep your ticket as you will need to show it at the Drum House. There are new toilets inside, best to avoid the ones in Chatta Chowk. You must remove shoes and cover all exposed flesh from your shoulders to your legs.

Between the new city and the River Yamuna, Shah Jahan built a fort. Most of it was built out of red *lal* (sandstone), hence the name **Lal Qila** (Red Fort), the same as that at Agra on which the Delhi Fort is modelled. Begun in 1639 and completed in 1648, it is said to have cost Rs 10 million, much of which was spent on the opulent marble palaces within. In recent years much effort has been put into improving the fort and gardens, but visitors may be saddened by the neglected state of some of the buildings, and the gun-wielding soldiers lolling around do nothing to improve the ambience. However, despite the modern development of roads and shops and the never-ending traffic, it's an impressive site.

The approach The entrance is by the Lahore Gate. The defensive barbican that juts out in front of it was built by Aurangzeb. A common story suggests that Aurangzeb built the curtain wall to save his nobles and visiting dignitaries from having to walk – and bow – the whole length of Chandni Chowk, for no one was allowed to ride in the presence of the emperor. When the emperor sat in the Diwan-i-Am he could see all the way down the chowk, so the addition must have been greatly welcomed by his courtiers. The new entrance arrangement also made an attacking army more vulnerable to the defenders on the walls.

Chatta Chowk and the Naubat Khana Inside is the **Covered Bazar**, which was quite exceptional in the 17th century. In Shah Jahan's time there were shops on both upper and lower levels. Originally they catered for the Imperial household and carried stocks of silks, brocades, velvets, gold and silverware, jewellery and gems. There were coffee shops too for nobles and courtiers.

The **Naqqar Khana** or **Naubat Khana** (Drum House or music gallery) marked the entrance to the inner apartments of the fort. Here everyone except the princes of the royal family had to dismount and leave their horses or *hathi* (elephants), hence its other name

BACKGROUND
Delhi

In the modern period, Delhi has only been India's capital since 1911. It is a city of yo yo-ing fortunes and has been repeatedly reduced to rubble. There have been at least eight cities founded on the site of modern Delhi.

According to Hindu mythology, Delhi's first avatar was as the site of a dazzlingly wealthy city, Indraprastha, mentioned in the Mahabharata and founded around 2500 BC. The next five cities were to the south of today's Delhi. First was Lalkot, which, from 1206, became the capital of the Delhi Sultanate under the Slave Dynasty. The story of the first Sultan of Delhi, Qutb-ud-din Aybak, is a classic rags-to-riches story. A former slave, he rose through the ranks to become a general, a governor and then Sultan of Delhi. He is responsible for building Qutb Minar, but died before its completion.

The 1300s were a tumultuous time for Delhi, with five cities built during the century. Siri, the first of these, has gruesome roots. Legend has it that the city's founder, Ala-ud-din, buried the heads of infidels in the foundation of the fort. Siri derives its name from the Hindi word for 'head'. After Siri came Tughlaqabad, whose existence came to a sudden end when the Sultan of Delhi, Muhammad Tughlaq, got so angry about a perceived insult from residents, he destroyed the city. The cities of Jahanpanah and Ferozebad followed in quick succession. Delhi's centre of gravity began to move northwards. In the 1500s Dinpanah was constructed by Humayun, whose wonderful tomb (1564-1573) graces Hazrat Nizamuddin. Shahjahanabad, known today as Old Delhi, followed, becoming one of the richest and most populous cities in the world. The Persian emperor Nadir Shah invaded, killing as many as 120,000 residents in a single bloody night and stealing the Kohinoor Diamond (now part of the British royal family's crown jewels).

The next destroyers of Delhi were the British, who ransacked the city in the wake of the Great Uprising/Mutiny of 1857. The resulting bloodbath left bodies piled so high that the victors' horses had to tread on them. For the next 50 years, while the port cities of Calcutta and Bombay thrived under the British, Delhi languished. Then, in 1911, King George, on a visit to India, announced that a new city should be built next to what remained of Delhi, and that this would be the new capital of India. The British architect Edwin Lutyens was brought in to design the city. You could argue that the building hasn't stopped since.

The central part of New Delhi is an example of Britain's imperial pretensions. The government may have been rather more reticent about moving India's capital, if it had known that in less than 36 years' time, the British would no longer be ruling India. Delhi's population swelled after the violence of partition, with refugees flooding to the city. In 10 years the population of Delhi doubled, and many well-known housing colonies were built during this period.

The economic boom that began in the 1990s has led to an explosion of construction and soaring real estate prices. Delhi is voraciously eating into the surrounding countryside. It is a city changing at such breakneck speed that shops, homes and even airports seem to appear and disappear almost overnight.

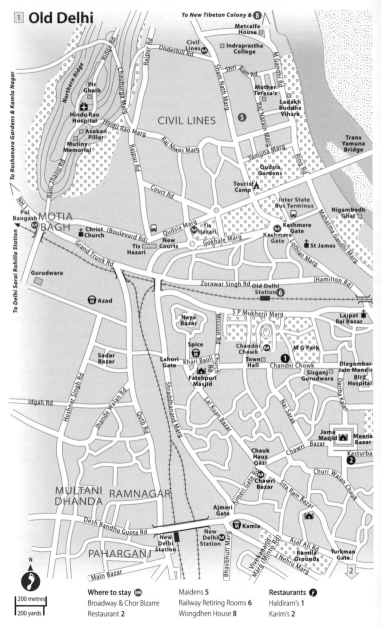

To New Tibetan Colony & 8

Metcalfe House

Civil Lines Ⓜ

Indraprastha College

Underhill Rd

Raipur Rd

Shri Ram Rd

Shyam Nath Marg

M Gandhi Rd

Mother Teresa's

Ladakh Buddha Vihara

Northern Ridge

Ridge Rd

Pir Ghaib

Chauburja Marg

CIVIL LINES 5

Hindu Rao Hospital

Hindu Rao Marg

Rai Narain Marg

Asokan Pillar

Trans Yamuna Bridge

Mutiny Memorial

Rajpur Rd

Rai Niwas Marg

Yamuna Marg

Qudsia Gardens

Ring Rd

Mahatma Gandhi Marg

Ram Chand Rd

Court Rd

Tourist Camp

Inter State Bus Terminus

Nigambodh Ghat

To Roshanara Gardens & Kamla Nagar

To Delhi Sarai Rohilla Station

Pul Bangash Ⓜ

MOTIA BAGH

Christ Church

(Boulevard Rd)

Qudsia Marg

Tis Hazari

Gokhale Marg

Kashmere Gate Ⓜ

Kashmere Gate

Lothian Marg

St James

New Courts

Tis Hazari

Grand Trunk Rd

Gurudwara

Azad Ⓜ

Zorawar Singh Rd

Old Delhi Station 6

(Hamilton Rd)

S P Mukherji Marg

Lajpat Rai Bazar

Naya Bazar

Mission Rd

Spice Ⓜ

Khari Baoli

Church Mission Rd

Chandni Chowk Ⓜ

M G Park

Lahori Gate

Town Hall 1

Chandni Chowk

Diagambar Jain Mandir

Sadar Bazar

Fatehpuri Masjid

Sisganj Gurudwara

Bird Hospital

Shradhanand Marg

Lal Kuan Bazar

Nai Sarak

Dariba Kalan

Idgah Rd

Hoshiari Singh Rd

Jhande Walan Rd

Qutb Rd

Chauk Hauz Qazi

Chawri

Jama Masjid

Meena Bazar

Kasturba

Chawri Bazar Ⓜ

Churi Walan Chauk

MULTANI DHANDA

RAMNAGAR

Ajmeri Gate

Ajmeri Gate Rd

Sita Ram Bazar

Churi Walan

Desh Bandhu Gupta Rd

New Delhi Station

New Delhi Station Ⓜ

Kamla Ⓜ

Asaf Ali Rd

Turkman Gate

PAHARGANJ

Main Bazar

Bhavbhuti Marg

Vivekananda Marg (Minto Rd)

Ramlila Grounds

Nehru Marg

N

2

200 metres
200 yards

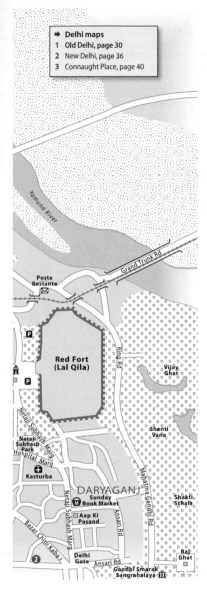

➡ Delhi maps
1 Old Delhi, page 30
2 New Delhi, page 36
3 Connaught Place, page 40

of **Hathi Pol** (Elephant Gate). Five times a day ceremonial music was played on the kettle drum, *shahnais* (a kind of oboe) and cymbals, glorifying the emperor. In 1754 Emperor Ahmad Shah was murdered here. The gateway with four floors is decorated with floral designs. You can still see traces of the original panels painted in gold or other colours on the interior of the gateway.

Diwan-i-Am Between the first inner court and the royal palaces at the heart of the fort, stood the **Diwan-i-Am** (Hall of Public Audience), the furthest point a normal visitor would reach. It has seen many dramatic events, including the destructive whirlwind of the Persian Nadir Shah in 1739 and of Ahmad Shah the Afghan in 1756, and the trial of the last 'King of Delhi', **Bahadur Shah II** in 1858.

The well-proportioned hall was both a functional building and a showpiece intended to hint at the opulence of the palace itself. In Shah Jahan's time the sandstone was hidden behind a very thin layer of white polished plaster, *chunam*. This was decorated with floral motifs in many colours, especially gilt. Silk carpets and heavy curtains hung from the canopy rings outside the building; such interiors were reminders of the Mughals' nomadic origins in Central Asia, where royal durbars were held in tents.

At the back of the hall is a platform for the emperor's throne. Around this was a gold railing, within which stood the princes and great nobles separated from the lesser nobles inside the hall. Behind the throne canopy are 12 marble panels inlaid with motifs of fruiting trees, parrots and cuckoos. Figurative workmanship is very unusual in Islamic buildings, and these panels are the only example in the Red Fort.

Shah Jahan spent two hours a day in the Diwan-i-Am. According to Bernie, the French traveller, the emperor would enter to a fanfare and mount the throne by a flight of movable steps. As well as matters of official administration, Shah Jahan would listen to accounts of illness, dream interpretations and anecdotes from his ministers and nobles. Wednesday was the day of judgement. Sentences were often swift and brutal and sometimes the punishment of dismemberment, beating or death was carried out on the spot. The executioners were close at hand with axes and whips. On Friday, the Muslim holy day, there would be no business.

Inner palace buildings Behind the Diwan-i-Am is the private enclosure of the fort. Along the east wall, overlooking the River Yamuna, Shah Jahan set six small palaces (five survive). Also within this compound are the Harem, the Life-Bestowing Garden and the Nahr-i-Bihisht (Stream of Paradise).

Life-Bestowing Gardens (Hayat Baksh Bagh) The original gardens were landscaped according to the Islamic principles of the Persian *char bagh*, with pavilions, fountains and water courses dividing the garden into various but regular beds. The two pavilions **Sawan** and **Bhadon**, named after the first two months of the rainy season (July-August), reveal something of the character of the garden. The garden used to create the effect of the monsoon and contemporary accounts tell us that in the pavilions – some of which were especially erected for the **Teej** festival, which marks the arrival of the monsoon – the royal ladies would sit in silver swings and watch the rains. Water flowed from the back wall of the pavilion through a slit above the marble shelf and over the niches in the wall. Gold and silver pots of flowers were placed in these alcoves during the day whilst at night candles were lit to create a glistening and colourful effect.

Shahi Burj From the pavilion next to the Shahi Burj (**Royal Tower**) the canal known as the **Nahr-i-Bihisht** (Stream of Paradise) began its journey along the Royal Terrace. The three-storey octagonal tower was seriously damaged in 1857 and is still unsafe. In Shah Jahan's time the Yamuna lapped the walls. Shah Jahan used the tower as his most private office and only his sons and a few senior ministers were allowed with him.

Moti Masjid To the right are the three marble domes of Aurangzeb's 'Pearl Mosque' (shoes must be removed). Bar the cupolas, it is completely hidden behind a wall of red sandstone, now painted white. Built in 1662 of polished white marble, it has some exquisite decoration. All the surfaces are highly decorated in a fashion similar to rococo, which developed at the same time as in Europe. Unusually the prayer hall is on a raised platform with inlaid outlines of individual *musallas* ('prayer mats') in black marble. While the outer walls were aligned to the cardinal points like all the other fort buildings, the inner walls were positioned so that the mosque would correctly face Mecca.

Hammam The **Royal Baths** have three apartments separated by corridors with canals to carry water to each room. The two flanking the entrance, for the royal children, had hot and cold baths. The room furthest away from the door has three basins for rose water fountains.

Diwan-i-Khas Beyond is the single-storeyed **Hall of Private Audience**, topped by four Hindu-style *chhattris* and built completely of white marble. The *dado* (lower part of the wall) on the interior was richly decorated with inlaid precious and semi-precious stones. The ceiling was silver but was removed by the Marathas in 1760. Outside, the hall used to have a marble pavement and an arcaded court. Both have gone.

This was the Mughal office of state. Shah Jahan spent two hours here before retiring for a meal, siesta and prayers. In the evening he would return to the hall for more work before going to the harem. The hall's splendour moved the 14th-century poet Amir Khusrau to write the lines inscribed above the corner arches of the north and south walls: *"Agar Firdaus bar rue Zamin-ast/Hamin ast o Hamin ast o Hamin ast"* (If there be a paradise on earth, it is here, it is here, it is here).

Royal palaces Next to the Diwan-i-Khas is the three-roomed **Khas Mahal** (Private Palace). Nearest the Diwan-i-Khas is the **Tasbih Khana** (Chamber for the Telling of Rosaries) where the emperor would worship privately with his rosary of 99 beads, one for each of the mystical names of Allah. In the centre is the **Khwabgah** (Palace of Dreams) which gives on to the octagonal **Mussaman Burj** tower. Here Shah Jahan would be seen each morning. A balcony was added to the tower in 1809 and here George V and Queen Mary appeared in their Coronation Durbar of 1911. The **Tosh Khana** (Robe Room), to the south, has a beautiful marble screen at its north end, carved with the scales of justice above the filigree grille. If you are standing with your back to the Diwan-i-Khas you will see a host of circulating suns (a symbol of royalty), but if your back is to the next building (the Rang Mahal), you will see moons surrounding the scales. All these rooms were sumptuously decorated with fine silk carpets, rich silk brocade curtains and lavishly decorated walls. After 1857 the British used the Khas Mahal as an officer's mess and sadly it was defaced.

The **Rang Mahal** (Palace of Colours), the residence of the chief *sultana*, was also the place where the emperor ate most of his meals. It was divided into six apartments. Privacy and coolness were ensured by the use of marble *jali* screens. Like the other palaces it was beautifully decorated with a silver ceiling ornamented with golden flowers to reflect the water in the channel running through the building. The north and south apartments were both known as **Sheesh Mahal** (Palace of Mirrors) since into the ceiling were set hundreds of small mirrors. In the evening when candles were lit a starlight effect would be produced.

Through the palace ran the **Life-bestowing Stream** and at its centre is a lotus-shaped marble basin which had an ivory fountain. As might be expected in such a cloistered and cosseted environment, the ladies sometimes got bored. In the 18th century the **Empress of Jahandar Shah** sat gazing out at the river and remarked that she had never seen a boat sink. Shortly afterwards a boat was deliberately capsized so that she could be entertained by the sight of people bobbing up and down in the water crying for help.

The southernmost of the palaces, the **Mumtaz Mahal** (Palace of Jewels) ⓘ *Tue-Sun 1000-1700*, was also used by the harem. The lower half of its walls are of marble and it contains six apartments. After the Mutiny of 1857 it was used as a guardroom and since 1912 it has been a museum with exhibits of textiles, weapons, carpets, jade and metalwork as well as works depicting life in the court. It should not be missed.

Chandni Chowk and the bazars

The impressive red sandstone façade of the **Digambar Jain Mandir** (temple) standing at the eastern end of Chandni Chowk, faces the Red Fort. Built in 1656, it contains an image of Adinath. The charity bird hospital (www.charitybirdshospital.org) within this compound releases the birds on recovery instead of returning them to their owners; many remain within the temple precincts. Outside the Red Fort, cycle rickshaws offer a trip to the spice market, Jama Masjid and back through the bazar. You travel slowly westwards down Chandni Chowk passing the town hall. Dismount at Church Road and follow your guide into the heart of the market on Khari Baoli where wholesalers sell every conceivable spice. Ask to go to the roof for an excellent view over the market and back towards the Red Fort. The ride back through the bazar is equally fascinating – look up at the amazing electricity system. The final excitement is getting back across Netaji Subhash Marg. Panic not, the rickshaw wallahs know what they are doing. Expect to pay about Rs 100 for a one-hour ride. The spice laden air may irritate your throat. Also ask a cycle rickshaw to take you to Naughara Street, just off Kinari Bazar; it's one of the most atmospheric streets in Delhi, full of brightly painted and slowly crumbling havelis.

Jama Masjid (Friday Mosque)
Visitors welcome from 30 mins after sunrise until 1215; and from 1345 until 30 mins before sunset, free, still or video cameras Rs 150, tower entry Rs 20.

The magnificent Jama Masjid is the largest mosque in India and the last great architectural work of Shah Jahan, intended to dwarf all mosques that had gone before it. With the fort, it dominates Old Delhi. The mosque is much simpler in its ornamentation than Shah Jahan's secular buildings: a judicious blend of red sandstone and white marble, which are interspersed in the domes, minarets and cusped arches.

The gateways symbolize the separation of the sacred and the secular, the threshold is a place of great importance where the worshipper steps to a higher plane. There are three huge gateways, the largest being to the east. This was reserved for the royal family who gathered in a private gallery in its upper storey. Today, the faithful enter through the east gate on Fridays and for **Id-ul-Fitr** and **Id-ul-Adha**. The latter commemorates Abraham's (Ibrahim's) sacrificial offering of his son Ishmael (Ismail). Islam (unlike the Jewish and Christian tradition) believes that Abraham offered to sacrifice Ishmael, Isaac's brother.

The courtyard The façade has the main *iwan* (arch), five smaller arches on each side with two flanking minarets and three bulbous domes behind, all perfectly proportioned. The *iwan* draws the worshippers' attention into the building. The minarets have great views from the top; well worth the climb for Rs 10 (women may not be allowed to climb alone). The **hauz**, in the centre of the courtyard, is an ablution tank placed as usual between the inner and outer parts of the building to remind the worshipper that it is through the ritual of baptism that one first enters the community of believers. The **Dikka**, in front of the ablution tank, is a raised platform. Muslim communities grew so rapidly that by the eighth century it sometimes became necessary to introduce a second *muballigh* (prayer leader) who stood on this platform and copied the postures and chants of the *imam* inside to relay them to a much larger congregation. With the introduction of the loudspeaker and amplification, the *dikka* and the *muballigh* became redundant. In the northwest corner of the mosque there is a small shed. For a small fee, the faithful are shown a hair from the beard of the prophet, as well as his sandal and his footprint in rock.

Civil Lines and Northern Ridge
Beyond Shahjahanabad to the north lies Kashmere Gate, Civil Lines and the Northern Ridge. The siting of the railway line which effectively cut Delhi into two unequal parts was done deliberately. The line brought prosperity, yet it destroyed the unity of the walled city forever. The Northern Ridge was the British cantonment and Civil Lines housed the civilians. In this area the temporary capital of the British existed from 1911-1931 until New Delhi came. The Northern Ridge is a paradise for birds and trees. Follow the **Mutiny Trail** by visiting Flagstaff Tower, Pir Ghaib, Chauburj, Mutiny Memorial. Around Kashmire Gate and Civil Lines, you can discover the Old Residency, St James Church, Nicholson's Cemetery and Qudsia Bagh.

Delhi's present position as capital was only confirmed on 12 December 1911, when George V announced at the Delhi Durbar that the capital of India was to move from Calcutta to Delhi. The new city, New Delhi, planned under the leadership of British architect Edwin Lutyens with the assistance of his friend Herbert Baker, was inaugurated on 9 February 1931. The city was to accommodate 70,000 people and have boundless possibilities for future expansion.

India Gate and around

A tour of New Delhi will usually start with a visit to this war memorial, situated at the eastern end of **Rajpath**. Designed by Lutyens, it commemorates more than 70,000 Indian soldiers who died in the First World War. Some 13,516 names of British and Indian soldiers killed on the Northwest Frontier and in the Afghan War of 1919 are engraved on the arch and foundations. Under the arch is the Amar Jawan Jyoti, commemorating Indian armed forces' losses in the Indo-Pakistan War of 1971. The arch (43 m high) stands on a base of Bharatpur stone and rises in stages. Similar to the Hindu *chhattri* signifying regality, it is decorated with nautilus shells symbolizing British maritime power. Come at dusk to join the picnicking crowds enjoying the evening. You may even be able to have a pedalo ride if there's water in the canal.

National Gallery of Modern Art

Jaipur House, near India Gate, T011-2338 4640, www.ngmaindia.gov.in, Tue-Sun 1000-1700, Rs 150 foreigners, Rs 40 Indians.

There is now a new air-conditioned wing of this excellent gallery and select exhibits in the old building are housed in a former residence of the Maharaja of Jaipur. The '*In the Seeds of Time...*' exhibition traces the trajectory of modern Indian art. Artists include: Amrita Shergil, with over 100 exhibits, synthesizing the flat treatment of Indian painting with a realistic tone; Rabindranath Tagore (ground floor) with examples from a brief but intense spell in the 1930s; and The Bombay School or Company School (first floor) which includes Western painters who documented their visits to India. Realism is reflected in Indian painting of the early 19th century represented by the schools of Avadh, Patna, Sikkim and Thanjavur; The Bengal School (the late 19th-century Revivalist Movement) showcases artists such as Abanindranath Tagore and Nandalal Bose have their works exhibited here. Western influence was discarded in response to the nationalist movement. Inspiration derived from Indian folk art is evident in the works of Jamini Roy and YD Shukla. Prints from the gallery shop are incredibly good value – up to Rs 80 for poster-size prints of famous works.

National Museum

Janpath, T011-2301 9272, www.nationalmuseumindia.gov.in, Tue-Sun 1000-1700, foreigners Rs 300 (including audio tour), Indians Rs 10, camera Rs 300; free guided tours 1030, 1130, 1200, 1400, films are screened every day (1430), marble squat toilets, but dirty.

The collection was formed from the nucleus of the Exhibition of Indian Art, London (1947). Now merged with the Asian Antiquities Museum it displays a rich collection of the artistic treasure of Central Asia and India including ethnological objects from prehistoric archaeological finds to the late Medieval period. Replicas of exhibits and books on Indian culture and art are on sale. There is also a research library.

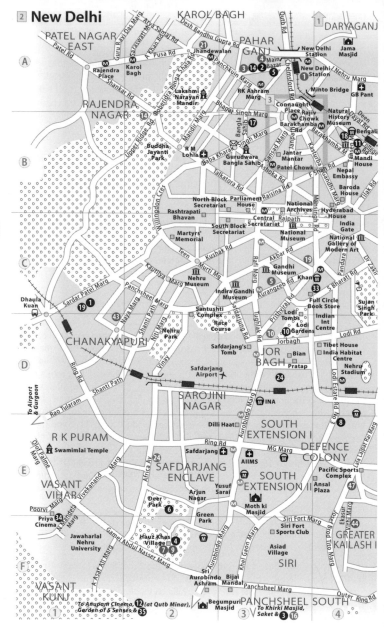

➡ **Delhi maps**
1 Old Delhi, page 30
2 New Delhi, page 36
3 Connaught Place, page 40

N

| 700 metres |
| 700 yards |

Where to stay

Amarya Villa **24** *E2*
Claridges &
  Sevilla restaurant **5** *C3*
Joyti Mahal **1** *A3*
K One One **28** *D4*
Life Tree **12** *E4*
Lutyens Bungalow **10** *D3*
Manor **13** *E5*
Master Guest House **14** *B2*
Oberoi **15** *C4*
Prince Polonia **3** *A3*
Rak International **4** *A3*
Taj Mahal & Rick's Bar **19** *C3*
Tree of Life **16** *F3*
Yatri Paying Guest House **21** *A2*

Restaurants

Baci **21** *C4*
Bukhara **1** *C1*
Café Sim Tok **2** *A3*
Desi Roots **3** *F3*
Diva **15** *F4*
Dum Pukht *19 C1*
Everest Bakery Café **5** *A3*
Indian Accent **13** *E5*
Kainoosh **34** *E1*
Khan Cha Cha **33** *C4*
Lodi **10** *D3*
Magique **35** *F2*
Naivedyam **4** *F2*
Nathu's & Bengali Sweet
  House **18** *B4*
Oh! Calcutta **16** *F5*

Olive at the Qutb **12** *F2*
Park Baluchi **6** *E2*
Ploof **24** *D3*
Sagar Ratna **8** *E4*
Sakura **17** *B3*
Tadka **14** *A3*
Triveni Tea Terrace **11** *B4*

Bars & clubs

Living Room **7** *F2*
Out of the Box **9** *F2*
Pegs-n-Pints **43** *D1*
Shalom **44** *F4*
Urban Pind **47** *E4*

Metro Stops (Yellow Line) Ⓜ
Metro Stops (Violet Line) Ⓜ

Ground floor **Prehistoric**: seals, figurines, toy animals and jewellery from the Harappan civilization (2400-1500 BC). **Maurya Period**: terracottas and stone heads from around the third century BC include the *chaturmukha* (four-faced) *lingam*. **Gandhara School**: stucco heads showing the Graeco Roman influence. **Gupta terracottas** (circa AD 400): including two life-size images of the river goddesses Ganga and Yamuna and the four-armed bust of Vishnu from a temple near Lal Kot. **South Indian sculpture**: from Pallava and early Chola temples and relief panels from Mysore. Bronzes from the Buddhist monastery at Nalanda. Some of Buddha's relics were placed in the Thai pavilion in 1997.

First floor **Illustrated manuscripts**: include the *Babur-i-nama* in the emperor's own handwriting and an autographed copy of Jahangir's memoirs. **Miniature paintings**: include the 16th-century Jain School, the 18th-century Rajasthani School and the Pahari schools of Garhwal, Basoli and Kangra. **Aurel Stein Collection** consists of antiquities recovered by him during his explorations of Central Asia and the western borders of China at the turn of the 20th century.

Second floor **Pre-Columbian and Mayan artefacts**: anthropological section devoted to tribal artefacts and folk arts. **Sharad Rani Bakkiwal Gallery of Musical Instruments**: displays over 300 instruments collected by the famous *sarod* player.

Rashtrapati Bhavan and Nehru Memorial Museum

Once the Viceroy's House, Rashtrapati Bhavan is the official residence of the President of India. The Viceroy's House, New Delhi's centrepiece of imperial proportions, was 1 km around the foundations, bigger than Louis XIV's palace at Versailles. It had a colossal dome surmounting a long colonnade and 340 rooms in all. It took nearly 20 years to complete, similar to the time it took to build the Taj Mahal. In the busiest year, 29,000 people were working on the site and buildings began to take shape. The project was surrounded by controversy from beginning to end. Opting for a fundamentally classical structure, both Baker and Lutyens sought to incorporate Indian motifs, many entirely superficial. While some claim that Lutyens achieved a unique synthesis of the two traditions, Tillotson asks whether "the sprinkling of a few simplified and classicized Indian details (especially *chhattris*) over a classical palace" could be called a synthesis. The Durbar Hall, 23 m in diameter, has coloured marble from all parts of India.

To the south is **Flagstaff House**, formerly the residence of the commander-in-chief. Renamed Teen Murti Bhawan it now houses the **Nehru Memorial Museum** ① *T011-2301 4504, Tue-Sun 1000-1500, planetarium Mon-Sat 1130-1500, library Mon-Sat 0900-1900, free*. Designed by Robert Tor Russell, in 1948 it became the official residence of India's first prime minister, Jawaharlal Nehru. Converted after his death (1964) into a national memorial, the reception, study and bedroom are intact. A *Jyoti Jawahar* (torch) symbolizes the eternal values he inspired and a granite rock is carved with extracts from his historic speech at midnight on 14 August 1947; an informative and vivid history of the Independence Movement.

The **Martyr's Memorial**, at the junction of Sardar Patel Marg and Willingdon Crescent, is a magnificent 26-m-long, 3-m-high bronze sculpture by DP Roy Chowdhury. The 11 statues of national heroes are headed by Mahatma Gandhi.

Eternal Gandhi Multimedia Museum
Birla House, 5 Tees Jan Marg (near Claridges Hotel), T011-3095 7269, www.eternalgandhi.org, closed Mon and 2nd Sat, 1000-1700, free, film at 1500.

Gandhi's last place of residence and the site of his assassination, Birla House has been converted into a whizz-bang display of 'interactive' modern technology. Over-attended by young guides eager to demonstrate the next gadget, the museum seems aimed mainly at those with a critically short attention span, and is too rushed to properly convey the story of Gandhi's life. However, a monument in the garden marking where he fell is definitely worth a visit. Other museums in the city related to Gandhi include: **National Gandhi Museum** ① *opposite Raj Ghat, T011-2331 1793, www.gandhimuseum.org, Tue-Sat 0930-1730*, with five pavilions – sculpture, photographs and paintings of Gandhi and the history of the *Satyagraha* movement (the philosophy of non-violence); **Gandhi Smarak Sangrahalaya** ① *Raj Ghat, T011-2301 1480, Fri-Wed 0930-1730*, displays some of Gandhi's personal belongings and a small library includes recordings of speeches; and the **Indira Gandhi Museum** ① *1 Safdarjang Rd, T011-2301 1358, Tue-Sun 0930-1700, free*, charting the phases of her life from childhood to the moment of her death. Exhibits are fascinating, if rather gory – you can see the blood-stained, bullet-ridden sari she was wearing when assassinated.

Parliament House and around
Northeast of the Viceroy's House is the **Council House**, now **Sansad Bhavan**. Baker designed this based on Lutyens' suggestion that it be circular (173 m diameter). Inside are the library and chambers for the Council of State, Chamber of Princes and Legislative Assembly – the **Lok Sabha**. Just opposite the Council House is the **Rakabganj Gurudwara** in Pandit Pant Marg. This 20th-century white marble shrine, which integrates the late Mughal and Rajasthani styles, marks the spot where the headless body of Guru Tegh Bahadur, the ninth Sikh Guru, was cremated in 1657. West of the Council House is the **Cathedral Church of the Redemption** (1927-1935) and to its north the Italianate Roman Catholic **Church of the Sacred Heart** (1930-1934), both conceived by Henry Medd.

Connaught Place and Connaught Circus *See map, page 40.*
Connaught Place and its outer ring, Connaught Circus (now officially named **Rajiv Chowk** and **Indira Chowk**, but still commonly referred to by their old names), comprise two-storey arcaded buildings, arranged radially around a circular garden that was completed after the Metro line was installed. Designed by Robert Tor Russell, they have become the main commercial and tourist centre of New Delhi. Sadly, the area also attracts bands of insistent touts.

Lakshmi Narayan Mandir
To the west of Connaught Circus is the Lakshmi Narayan **Birla Temple** in Mandir Marg. Financed by the prominent industrialist Raja Baldeo Birla in 1938, this is one of the most popular Hindu shrines in the city and one of Delhi's few striking examples of Hindu architecture. Dedicated to Lakshmi, the goddess of well-being, it is commonly referred to as **Birla Mandir**. The design is in the Orissan style with tall curved *sikharas* (towers) capped by large *amalakas*. The exterior is faced with red and ochre stone and white marble. Built around a central courtyard, the main shrine has images of Narayan and his consort Lakshmi while two separate cells have icons of Siva (the Destroyer) and Durga (the 10-armed destroyer of demons). The temple is flanked by a *dharamshala* (rest house) and a Buddhist *vihara* (monastery).

Gurudwara Bangla Sahib
Baba Kharak Singh Rd, free.

This is a fine example of Sikh temple architecture, featuring a large pool reminiscent of Amritsar's Golden Temple. The 24-hour reciting of the Guru Granth Sahib – the Sikh holy book – adds to the atmosphere. There's free food on offer from their community kitchen, although don't be surprised if you're asked to help out with the washing up! You must remove your shoes and cover your head to enter; suitable scarves are provided if you arrive without. It is very special to come here during sunset for evening prayers.

③ Connaught Place

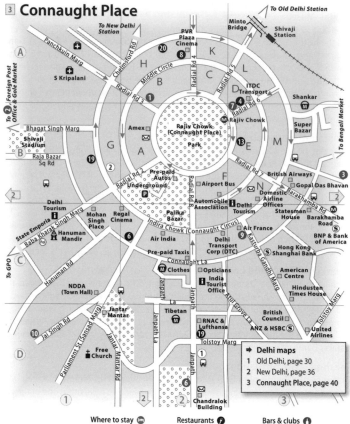

Where to stay 🛏
Asian Guest House **9** C3
Corus & Life Caffe **1** A2
Imperial, Spice Route
 Restaurant & 1911 Bar **6** D2
Palace Heights **7** B3
Sakura **2** B1
YMCA Tourist Hostel **10** D1

Restaurants 🍴
Embassy **4** A3
Kwality **6** C2
Nizam's Kathi Kebabs **8** A2
Saravana Bhavan **19** B1, D2
United Coffee House **13** B3
Veda **20** A2

Bars & clubs 🍸
Kitty Su **3** B3

Shopping ◯
Central Cottage Industries
 Emporium **1** D2
Hidesign **2** B1

➡ Delhi maps
1 Old Delhi, page 30
2 New Delhi, page 36
3 Connaught Place, page 40

100 metres
100 yards

Further northeast on Baba Kharak Singh Marg is **Hanuman Mandir**. This small temple was built by Maharaja Jai Singh II of Jaipur. **Mangal haat** (Tuesday Fair) is a popular market.

Jantar Mantar

Just to the east of the Hanuman Mandir in Sansad Marg (Parliament Street) is Jai Singh's **observatory** (Jantar Mantar) ① *sunrise to sunset, Rs 100 foreigners, Rs 5 Indians.* The Mughal Emperor Mohammad Shah (ruled 1719-1748) entrusted the renowned astronomer Maharaja Jai Singh II with the task of revising the calendar and correcting the astronomical tables used by contemporary priests. Daily astral observations were made for years before construction began and plastered brick structures were favoured for the site instead of brass instruments. Built in 1725 it is slightly smaller than the later observatory at Jaipur.

Memorial Ghats

Beyond Delhi Gate lies the **Yamuna River**, marked by a series of memorials to India's leaders. The river itself, a kilometre away, is invisible from the road, protected by a low rise and banks of trees. The most prominent memorial, immediately opposite the end of Jawaharlal Nehru Road, is that of Mahatma Gandhi at **Raj Ghat**. To its north is **Shanti Vana** (Forest of Peace), landscaped gardens where Prime Minister Jawaharlal Nehru was cremated in 1964, as were his grandson Sanjay Gandhi in 1980, daughter Indira Gandhi in 1984 and elder grandson, Rajiv, in 1991. To the north again is **Vijay Ghat** (Victory Bank) where Prime Minister Lal Bahadur Shastri was cremated.

South Delhi

modern commercial area with some of Delhi's best historic sights

South Delhi is often overlooked by travellers. This is a real pity as it houses some of the city's most stunning sights, best accommodation, bars, clubs and restaurants, as well as some of its most tranquil parks. However be warned, South Delhi can be hell during rush hour when the traffic on the endless flyovers comes to a virtual standstill. But with the Metro, you can explore all the way down to Gurgaon with relative ease.

Lodi Gardens

These beautiful gardens, with mellow stone tombs of the 15th- and 16th-century Lodi rulers, are popular for gentle strolls and jogging. In the middle of the garden facing the east entrance from Max Mueller Road is **Bara Gumbad** (Big Dome), a mosque built in 1494. The raised courtyard is provided with an imposing gateway and *mehman khana* (guest rooms). The platform in the centre appears to have had a tank for ritual ablutions.

The **Sheesh Bumbad** (Glass Dome, late 15th century) is built on a raised incline north of the Bara Gumbad and was once decorated with glazed blue tiles, painted floral designs and Koranic inscriptions. The façade gives the impression of a two-storey building, typical of Lodi architecture. **Mohammad Shah's Tomb** (1450) is that of the third Sayyid ruler. It has sloping buttresses, an octagonal plan, projecting eaves and lotus patterns on the ceiling. **Sikander Lodi's Tomb**, built by his son in 1517, is also an octagonal structure decorated with Hindu motifs. A structural innovation is the double dome which was later refined under the Mughals. The 16th-century **Athpula** (Bridge of Eight Piers), near the northeastern entrance, is attributed to Nawab Bahadur, a nobleman at Akbar's court.

Safdarjang's Tomb
Sunrise to sunset, Rs 100 foreigners, Rs 5 Indians.

Safdarjang's Tomb, seldom visited, was built by Nawab Shuja-ud-Daulah for his father Mirza Mukhim Abdul Khan, entitled Safdarjang, who was Governor of Oudh (1719-1748), and Wazir of his successor (1748-1754). Safdarjang died in 1754. With its high enclosure walls, *char bagh* layout of gardens, fountain and central domed mausoleum, it follows the tradition of Humayun's tomb. Typically, the real tomb is just below ground level. Flanking the mausoleum are pavilions used by Shuja-ud-Daulah as his family residence. Immediately to its south is the battlefield where Timur and his Mongol horde crushed Mahmud Shah Tughluq on 12 December 1398.

Hazrat Nizamuddin
Dress ultra-modestly if you don't want to feel uncomfortable or cause offence.

At the east end of the Lodi Road, Hazrat Nizamuddin Dargah (Nizamuddin 'village') now tucked away behind the residential suburb of Nizamuddin West, off Mathura Road, grew up around the shrine of Sheikh Nizamuddin Aulia (1236-1325), a Chishti saint. This is a wonderfully atmospheric place. *Qawwalis* are sung at sunset after *namaaz* (prayers), and are particularly impressive on Thursdays – be prepared for crowds. Highly recommended.

West of the central shrine is the **Jama-at-khana Mosque** (1325). Its decorated arches are typical of the Khalji design also seen at the Ala'i Darwaza at the Qutb Minar. South of the main tomb and behind finely crafted screens is the grave of princess Jahanara, Shah Jahan's eldest and favourite daughter. She shared the emperor's last years when he was imprisoned at Agra Fort. The grave, open to the sky, is in accordance with the epitaph written by her: "Let naught cover my grave save the green grass, for grass suffices as the covering of the lowly". Pilgrims congregate at the shrine twice a year for the Urs (fair) held to mark the anniversaries of Hazrat Nizamuddin Aulia and his disciple Amir Khusrau, whose tomb is nearby.

Humayun's Tomb
Sunrise to sunset, Rs 250 foreigners, Rs 10 Indians, video cameras Rs 25, located in Nizamuddin, 15-20 mins by taxi from Connaught Circus, allow 45 mins.

Eclipsed later by the Taj Mahal and the Jama Masjid, this tomb is the best example in Delhi of the early Mughal style of tomb. Superbly maintained, it is well worth a visit, preferably before visiting the Taj Mahal. Humayun, the second Mughal emperor, was forced into exile in Persia after being heavily defeated by the Afghan Sher Shah in 1540. He returned to India in 1545, finally recapturing Delhi in 1555. The tomb was designed and built by his senior widow and mother of his son Akbar, Hamida Begum. A Persian from Khurasan, after her pilgrimage to Mecca she was known as Haji Begum. She supervised the entire construction of the tomb (1564-1573), camping on the site.

The approach The tomb enclosure has two high double-storeyed gateways: the entrance to the west and the other to the south. A *baradari* occupies the centre of the east wall, and a bath chamber that of the north wall. Several Moghul princes, princesses and Haji Begum herself lie buried here. During the 1857 Mutiny Bahadur Shah II, the last Moghul emperor of Delhi, took shelter here with his three sons. Over 80, he was seen as a figurehead by Muslims opposing the British. When captured he was transported to Yangon (Rangoon) for the remaining four years of his life. The tomb to the right of the approach is that of Isa Khan, Humayun's barber.

The dome Some 38 m high, the dome does not have the swell of the Taj Mahal and the decoration of the whole edifice is much simpler. It is of red sandstone with some white marble to highlight the lines of the building. There is some attractive inlay work, and some *jalis* in the balcony fence and on some of the recessed keel arch windows. The interior is austere and consists of three storeys of arches rising up to the dome. The emperor's tomb is of white marble and quite plain without any inscription. The overall impression is that of a much bulkier, more squat building than the Taj Mahal. The cavernous space under the main tombs is home to great colonies of bats.

Hauz Khas village

South of Safdarjang's Tomb, and entered off either Aurobindo Marg on the east side or Africa Avenue on the west side, is Hauz Khas. This is a great area to explore at leisure. Here you will find the heritage buildings of the **madrasa** (Delhi's oldest university), a green oasis with the **Deer Park** and the small but lovely **Delhi Art Gallery**. Labyrinthine alleys lead to numerous design studios, boutiques and restaurants. Wandering the streets of Hauz Khas village, with its boho vibe, you can almost forget that you are in India.

Ala-ud-din Khalji (ruled 1296-1313) created a large tank at Hauz Khas for the use of the inhabitants of Siri, the second capital city of Delhi founded by him. Fifty years later Firoz Shah Tughluq cleaned up the silted tank and raised several buildings on its east and south banks which are known as Hauz Khas or Royal Tank.

Firoz Shah's austere **tomb** is found here. The multi-storeyed wings, on the north and west of the tomb, were built by him in 1354 as a *madrasa* (college). The octagonal and square *chhattris* were built as tombs, possibly to the teachers at the college. Hauz Khas is now widely used as a park for early-morning recreation – walking, running and yoga *asanas*. Classical music concerts, dance performances and a *son et lumière* show are held in the evenings when monuments are illuminated by thousands of earthen lamps and torches.

Qutb Minar Complex

Sunrise to sunset, Rs 250 foreigners, Rs 10 Indians. The Metro goes to Qutb Minar. Bus 505 from New Delhi Railway Station (Ajmeri Gate), Super Bazar (east of Connaught Circus) and Cottage Industries Emporium, Janpath. Auto Rs 110, though drivers may be reluctant to take you. This area is also opening up as a hub for new chic restaurants and bars.

Muhammad Ghuri conquered northwest India at the very end of the 12th century. The conquest of the Gangetic plain down to Benares (Varanasi) was undertaken by Muhammad's Turkish slave and chief general, Qutb-ud-din-Aibak, whilst another general took Bihar and Bengal. In the process, temples were reduced to rubble, the remaining Buddhist centres were dealt their death blow and their monks slaughtered. When Muhammad was assassinated in 1206, his gains passed to the loyal Qutb-ud-din-Aibak. Thus the first sultans or Muslim kings of Delhi became known as the **Slave Dynasty** (1026-1290). For the next three centuries the Slave Dynasty and the succeeding Khalji (1290-1320), Tughluq (1320-1414), Sayyid (1414-1445) and Lodi (1451-1526) dynasties provided Delhi with fluctuating authority. The legacy of their ambitions survives in the tombs, forts and palaces that litter Delhi Ridge and the surrounding plain. Qutb-ud-din-Aibak died after only four years in power, but he left his mark with the **Qutb Minar** and his **citadel**. Qutb Minar, built to proclaim the victory of Islam over the infidel, dominates the countryside for miles around. Visit the *minar* first.

Qutb Minar In 1199 work began on what was intended to be the most glorious tower of victory in the world and was to be the prototype of all *minars* (towers) in India. Qutb-ud-din-Aibak had probably seen and been influenced by the brick victory pillars in Ghazni in Afghanistan, but this one was also intended to serve as the minaret attached to the Might of Islam Mosque. From here the muezzin could call the faithful to prayer. Later every mosque would incorporate its minaret.

As a mighty reminder of the importance of the ruler as Allah's representative on earth, the Qutb Minar (literally 'axis minaret') stood at the centre of the community. A pivot of Faith, Justice and Righteousness, its name also carried the message of Qutb-ud-din's (Axis of the Faith) own achievements. The inscriptions carved in Kufi script tell that "the tower was erected to cast the shadow of God over both east and west". For Qutb-ud-din-Aibak it marked the eastern limit of the empire of the One God. Its western counterpart is the Giralda Tower built by Yusuf in Seville.

The Qutb Minar is 73 m high and consists of five storeys. The diameter of the base is 14.4 m and 2.7 m at the top. Qutb-ud-din built the first three and his son-in-law Iltutmish embellished these and added a fourth. This is indicated in some of the Persian and Nagari (North Indian) inscriptions which also record that it was twice damaged by lightning in 1326 and 1368. While repairing the damage caused by the second, Firoz Shah Tughluq added a fifth storey and used marble to face the red and buff sandstone. This was the first time contrasting colours were used decoratively, later to become such a feature of Mughal buildings. Firoz's fifth storey was topped by a graceful cupola but this fell down during an earthquake in 1803. A new one was added by a Major Robert Smith in 1829 but was so out of keeping that it was removed in 1848 and now stands in the gardens.

The original storeys are heavily indented with different styles of fluting, alternately round and angular on the bottom, round on the second and angular on the third. The beautifully carved honeycomb detail beneath the balconies is reminiscent of the Alhambra Palace in Spain. The calligraphy bands are verses from the Koran and praises to its patron builder.

Quwwat-ul-Islam Mosque The Quwwat-ul-Islam Mosque (The Might of Islam Mosque), the earliest surviving mosque in India, is to the northwest of the Qutb Minar. It was begun in 1192, immediately after Qutb-ud-din's conquest of Delhi and completed in 1198, using the remains of no fewer than 27 local Hindu and Jain temples.

The architectural style contained elements that Muslims brought from Arabia, including buildings made of mud and brick and decorated with glazed tiles, *squinches* (arches set diagonally across the corners of a square chamber to facilitate the raising of a dome and to effect a transition from a square to a round structure), the pointed arch and the true dome. Finally, Muslim buildings came alive through ornamental calligraphy and geometric patterning. This was in marked contrast to indigenous Indian styles of architecture. Hindu, Buddhist and Jain buildings relied on the post-and-beam system in which spaces were traversed by corbelling, ie shaping flat-laid stones to create an arch. The arched screen that runs along the western end of the courtyard beautifully illustrates the fact that it was Hindu methods that still prevailed at this stage, for the 16-m-high arch uses Indian corbelling, the corners being smoothed off to form the curved line.

Screens Qutb-ud-din's screen formed the façade of the mosque and, facing in the direction of Mecca, became the focal point. The sandstone screen is carved in the Indo-Islamic style, lotuses mingling with Koranic calligraphy. The later screenwork and other extensions (1230) are fundamentally Islamic in style, the flowers and leaves having been replaced by more arabesque patterns. Indian builders mainly used stone, which from the fourth century AD had been intricately carved with representations of the gods. In their first buildings in India the Muslim architects designed the buildings and local Indian craftsmen built them and decorated them with typical motifs such as the vase and foliage, tasselled ropes, bells and cows.

Iltutmish's extension The mosque was enlarged twice. In 1230 Qutb-ud-din's son-in-law and successor, Shamsuddin Iltutmish, doubled its size by extending the colonnades and prayer hall – 'Iltutmish's extension'. This accommodated a larger congregation, and in the more stable conditions of Iltutmish's reign, Islam was obviously gaining ground. The arches of the extension are nearer to the true arch and are similar to the Gothic arch that appeared in Europe at this time. The decoration is Islamic. Almost 100 years after Iltutmish's death, the mosque was enlarged again, by Ala-ud-din Khalji. The conductor of tireless and bloody military campaigns, Ala-ud-din proclaimed himself 'God's representative on earth'. His architectural ambitions, however, were not fully realized, because on his death in 1316 only part of the north and east extensions were completed.

Ala'i Minar and the Ala'i Darwaza To the north of the Qutb complex is the 26-m **Ala'i Minar**, intended to surpass the tower of the Qutb, but not completed beyond the first storey. Ala-ud-din did complete the south gateway to the building, the **Ala'i Darwaza**; inscriptions testify that it was built in 1311 (Muslim 710 AH). He benefited from events in Central Asia: since the early 13th century, Mongol hordes from Central Asia fanned out east and west, destroying the civilization of the Seljuk Turks in West Asia, and refugee artists, architects, craftsmen and poets fled east. They brought to India features and techniques that had developed in Byzantine Turkey, some of which can be seen in the Ala'i Darwaza.

The gatehouse is a large sandstone cuboid, into which are set small cusped arches with carved *jali* screens. The lavish ornamentation of geometric and floral designs in red sandstone and white marble produced a dramatic effect when viewed against the surrounding buildings.

Iltutmish's Tomb Built in 1235, Iltutmish's Tomb lies in the northwest of the compound, midway along the west wall of the mosque. It is the first surviving tomb of a Muslim ruler in India. Two other tombs also stand within the extended Might of Islam Mosque. The idea of a tomb was quite alien to Hindus, who had been practising cremation since around 400 BC. Blending Hindu and Muslim styles, the outside is relatively plain with three arched and decorated doorways. The interior carries reminders of the nomadic origins of the first Muslim rulers. Like a Central Asian *yurt* (tent) in its decoration, it combines the familiar Indian motifs of the wheel, bell, chain and lotus with the equally familiar geometric arabesque patterning. The west wall is inset with three *mihrabs* that indicate the direction of Mecca.

The tomb originally supported a dome resting on *squinches* which you can still see. The dome collapsed (witness the slabs of stone lying around) suggesting that the technique was as yet unrefined. From the corbelled squinches it may be assumed that the dome was corbelled too, as found in contemporary Gujarat and Rajput temples. The blocks of masonry were fixed together using the Indian technology of iron dowels. In later Indo-Islamic buildings lime plaster was used for bonding.

Tughluqabad

Sunrise to sunset, foreigners Rs100, Indians Rs 5, video camera Rs 25, allow 1 hr for return rickshaws, turn right at entrance and walk 200 m. The site is often deserted so don't go alone. Take plenty of water.

Tughluqabad's ruins, 7.5 km east from Qutb Minar, still convey a sense of the power and energy of the newly arrived Muslims in India. From the walls you get a magnificent impression of the strategic advantages of the site. **Ghiyas'ud-Din Tughluq** (ruled 1321-1325), after ascending the throne of Delhi, selected this site for his capital. He built a massive fort around his capital city which stands high on a rocky outcrop of the Delhi Ridge. The fort is roughly octagonal in plan with a circumference of 6.5 km. The vast size, strength and obvious solidity of the whole give it an air of massive grandeur. It was not until Babur (ruled 1526-1530) that dynamite was used in warfare, so this is a very defensible site.

East of the main entrance is the rectangular **citadel**. A wider area immediately to the west and bounded by walls contained the **palaces**. Beyond this to the north lay the **city**. Now marked by the ruins of houses, the streets were laid out in a grid fashion. Inside the citadel enclosure is the **Vijay Mandal tower** and the remains of several halls including a long underground passage. The fort also contained seven tanks.

A causeway connects the fort with the tomb of Ghiyas'ud-Din Tughluq, while a wide embankment near its southeast corner gave access to the fortresses of **Adilabad** about 1 km away, built a little later by Ghiyas'ud-Din's son Muhammad. The tomb is very well preserved and has red sandstone walls with a pronounced slope (the first Muslim building in India to have sloping walls), crowned with a white marble dome. This dome, like that of the Ala'i Darwaza at the Qutb, is crowned by an *amalaka*, a feature of Hindu architecture. Also Hindu is the trabeate arch at the tomb's fortress wall entrance. Inside are three cenotaphs belonging to Ghiyas'ud-Din, his wife and son Muhammad.

Ghiyas'ud-Din Tughluq quickly found that military victories were no guarantee of lengthy rule. When he returned home after a victorious campaign the welcoming pavilion erected by his son and successor, Muhammad-bin Tughluq, was deliberately collapsed over him. Tughluqabad was abandoned shortly afterwards and was thus only inhabited for five years. The Tughluq dynasty continued to hold Delhi until Timur sacked it and slaughtered its inhabitants. For a brief period Tughluq power shifted to Jaunpur near Varanasi, where the Tughluq architectural traditions were carried forward in some superb mosques.

Baha'i Temple (Lotus Temple)

1 Apr-30 Sep 0900-1900, 1 Oct-31 Mar Tue-Sun 0930-1730, free entry and parking, visitors welcome to attend services, at other times the temple is open for silent meditation and prayer. Audio-visual presentations in English are at 1100, 1200, 1400 and 1530, remove shoes before entering. Bus 433 from the centre (Jantar Mantar) goes to Nehru Place, within walking distance (1.5 km) of the temple at Kalkaji, or take a taxi or auto-rickshaw.

Fact...
The Baha'i faith was founded by a Persian, Baha'u'llah (meaning 'glory of God'; 1817-1892), who is believed to be the manifestation of God for this age. His teachings were directed towards the unification of the human race and the establishment of a permanent universal peace.

Architecturally the Baha'i Temple is a remarkably striking building. Constructed in 1980-1981, it is built out of white marble and in the characteristic Baha'i temple shape of a lotus flower – 45 lotus petals form the walls – which internally creates a feeling of light and space

(34 m high, 70 m in diameter). It is a simple design, brilliantly executed and very elegant in form. All Baha'i temples are nine-sided, symbolizing 'comprehensiveness, oneness and unity'. The Delhi Temple, which seats 1300, is surrounded by nine pools, an attractive feature also helping to keep the building cool. It is particularly attractive when flood-lit. Baha'i temples are "dedicated to the worship of God, for peoples of all races, religions or castes. Only the Holy Scriptures of the Baha'i Faith and earlier revelations are read or recited".

East of the Yamuna
stunning but ostentatious modern temple complex

Designated as the site of the athletes' village for the 2010 Commonwealth Games, East Delhi has just one attraction to draw visitors across the Yamuna.

Swaminarayan Akshardham
www.akshardham.com, Apr-Sep Tue-Sun 1000-1900, Oct-Mar Tue-Sun 0900-1800, temple free, Rs 170 for 'attractions', musical fountain Rs 20, no backpacks, cameras or other electronic items (bag and body searches at entry gate). Packed on Sun; visit early to avoid crowds.

Opened in November 2005 on the east bank of the Yamuna, the gleaming Akshardham complex represents perhaps the most ambitious construction project in India since the foundation of New Delhi itself. At the centre of a surreal 40-ha 'cultural complex' complete with landscaped gardens, cafés and theme park rides, the temple-monument is dedicated to the 18th-century saint Bhagwan Swaminarayan, who abandoned his home at the age of 11 to embark on a lifelong quest for the spiritual and cultural uplift of Western India. It took 11,000 craftsmen, all volunteers, no less than 300 million hours to complete the temple using traditional building and carving techniques.

The temple You enter the temple complex through a series of intricately carved gates. The Bhakti Dwar (Gate of Devotion), adorned with 208 pairs of gods and their consorts, leads into a hall introducing the life of Swaminarayan and the activities of BAPS (Bochasanwasi Shri Akshar Purushottam Swaminarayan Sanstha), the global Hindu sect-cum-charity which runs Akshardham. The main courtyard is reached through the Mayur Dwar (Peacock Gate), a conglomeration of 869 carved peacocks echoed by an equally florid replica directly facing it.

From here you get your first look at the central monument. Perfectly symmetrical in pink sandstone and white marble, it rests on a plinth encircled by 148 elephants, each sculpted from a 20-tonne stone block, in situations ranging from the literal to the mythological: mortal versions grapple with lions or lug tree trunks, while Airavatha, the eight-trunked mount of Lord Indra, surfs majestically to shore after the churning of the oceans at the dawn of Hindu creation. Above them, carvings of deities, saints and *sadhus* cover every inch of the walls and columns framing the inner sanctum, where a gold-plated *murti* (idol) of Bhagwan Swaminarayan sits attended by avatars of his spiritual successors, beneath a staggeringly intricate marble dome. Around the main dome are eight smaller domes, each carved in hypnotic fractal patterns, while paintings depicting Swaminarayan's life of austerity and service line the walls (explanations in English and Hindi).

Surrounding the temple is a moat of holy water supposedly taken from 151 sacred lakes and rivers visited by Swaminarayan on his seven-year barefoot pilgrimage. 108 bronze *gaumukhs* (cow heads) representing the 108 names of God spout water into the tank, which is itself hemmed in by a 1-km-long *parikrama* (colonnade) of red Rajasthani sandstone.

Tourist information

Most tourist offices are open
Mon-Fri 1000-1800.

Delhi Tourism

*N-36 Connaught Pl, T011-2331 5322 (touts
pester you to use one of many imposters; the
correct office is directly opposite 'Competent
House'), www.delhitourism.gov.in.*
Other branches at: **Coffee Home Annexe**
(Baba Kharak Singh Marg, T011-336 5358);
at the airport terminals; the Inter-State Bus
Terminal; and New Delhi Railway Station
(T011-2373 2374). The branch at **Coffee
Home Annexe** is close to Connaught Pl and
offers hotel, transport and tour bookings
(T011-2462 3782, open 0700-2100).

Government of India Tourist Office

*88 Janpath, T011-332 0005. Mon-Sat 0900-
1800; also at the international airport.*
Helpful and issues permits for visits to
Rashtrapati Bhavan and gardens.

Where to stay

Avoid hotel touts. Airport taxis may pretend
not to know the location of your chosen
hotel so give full details and insist on being
taken there. Around Paharganj particularly,
you might be followed around by your
driver trying to eek a commission out of the
guesthouse once you have checked in.

It really saves a lot of hassle if you make
reservations. Even if you change hotel
the next day, it is good to arrive with
somewhere booked especially if you
are flying in late at night.

Hotel prices in Delhi are significantly
higher than in most other parts of the
country. Smaller **$$** guesthouses away
from the centre in **South Delhi** (eg Kailash,
Safdarjang) or in **Sunder Nagar**, are quieter
and often good value but may not provide

food. **$** accommodation is concentrated
around **Janpath** and **Paharganj** (New
Delhi), and **Chandni Chowk** (Old Delhi); well
patronized but basic and usually cramped
yet good for meeting other backpackers.

Signs in some hotels warn against taking
drugs as this is becoming a serious cause
for concern. Police raids are frequent.

Old Delhi and beyond

$$$$ Maidens Hotel

*7 Sham Nath Marg, T011-2397 5464,
www.maidenshotel.com.*
Opened in 1903, this is one of Delhi's
oldest hotels packed full of colonial charm.
54 large well-appointed rooms, restaurant
(barbecue nights are excellent), characterful
bar, spacious gardens with excellent pool,
friendly welcome, personal attention.
Recommended.

$$$ Broadway

*4/15A Asaf Ali Rd, T011-4366 3600,
www.hotelbroadwaydelhi.com.*
Charming hotel with 36 rooms, some
wonderfully quirky. Interior designer
Catherine Levy has decorated some of
the rooms in a quirky kitsch style, brightly
coloured with psychedelic bathroom tiles.
The other rooms are classic design. **Chor
Bizarre** restaurant and 'Thugs' pub are
highly regarded. Great walking tours of
Old Delhi. Easily one of the best options.

$$-$ Wongdhen House

*15A New Tibetan Colony,
Manju-ka-Tilla, T011-2381 6689,
wongdhenhouse@hotmail.com.*
Very clean rooms, some with a/c and TV,
safe, cosy, convivial, good breakfast and
great Tibetan meals, an insight into Tibetan
culture, peacefully located by Yamuna River
yet 15 mins by auto-rickshaw north of Old
Delhi Station. Recommended.

Connaught Place

$$$$ Imperial
Janpath, T011-2334 1234,
www.theimperialindia.com.
Quintessential Delhi. 230 rooms and beautiful 'deco suites' in supremely elegant Lutyens-designed 1933 hotel. Unparalleled location, great bar, antiques and art everywhere, beautiful gardens with spa and secluded pool, amazing **Spice Route** restaurant. Highly recommended.

$$$ Hotel Corus
B-49 Connaught Pl, T011-4365 2222,
www.hotelcorus.com.
Comfortable hotel right at the heart of things. Good-value rooms. You get 15% discount in their onsite **Life Caffe.**

$$$ Palace Heights
D26-28 Connaught Pl, T011-4358 2610,
www.hotelpalaceheights.com.
Bright, modern rooms with good attention to detail, best choice in Connaught Pl in this price bracket. There's also an attractive glass-walled restaurant, **Zaffran**, overlooking the street.

$$$-$ YMCA Tourist Hostel
Jai Singh Rd, T011-2336 1915,
www.newdelhiymca.org.
120 rooms, for both sexes, common areas have been recently refurbished. Prices are creeping up here. Good location. Good pool, luggage storage, pay in advance but check bill, reserve ahead, very professional.

$ Asian Guest House
14 Scindia House, off Kasturba Gandhi Marg, the sign is hidden behind petrol pump, T011-2331 0229, www.asianguesthouse.com.
Great central location. Friendly faces greet you here, although it's a bit tricky to find – call ahead for directions. Clean basic rooms, some with a/c, some with TV.

Paharganj
Parharganj is where backpackers congregate. Sandwiched between the main sights and near the main railway station, it's noisy, dirty and a lot of hassle. Its chief virtues are economy and convenience, with plenty of shops, travel agents, budget hotels and cafés catering for Western tastes. Avoid **Hotel Bright**.

$$$$-$$$ Jyoti Mahal
2488 Nalwa St, behind Imperial Cinema, T011-2358 0524, www.jyotimahal.net.
An oasis in Paharganj with large and atmospheric rooms in a beautiful converted *haveli* and new deluxe rooms in a stylish new wing. Cool and quiet with antique pieces dotted around and bowls of floating rose petals lining the staircases. Top-notch rooftop restaurant serving Continental and Indian dishes. It's a very atmospheric place to dine. Nice boutique, **Pink Safari**, too. Highly recommended.

$$ Prince Polonia
2325-26 Tilak Gali (behind Imperial Cinema), T011-4762 6600, www.hotel princepolonia.com.
Very unusual for Paharganj in that it has a rooftop pool (small, but good for a cool down). Breezy rooftop café. Attracts a slightly more mature crowd. Safe, clean. Recently refurbished.

$ Rak International
820 Main Bazar, Chowk Bowli, T011-2358 6508, www.hotelrakinternational.com.
27 basic but clean rooms. Professionally run. Quiet, friendly hotel with a rooftop restaurant.

Karol Bagh and Rajendra Nagar
West of Paharganj on the Metro line, **Karol Bagh** is full of identikit modern hotels, albeit a degree more upmarket than Paharganj. There are plentiful good eating places, and the area is handy for Sarai Rohilla station. Nearby **Rajendra Nagar**, a residential suburb, this has one of Delhi's best homestays.

$$$ Yatri Paying Guest House
Corner of Panchkuin and Mandir margs, T011-2362 5563, www.yatrihouse.com.
A quiet, peaceful oasis with beautiful gardens. 6 large, attractive rooms all with 42-inch televisions, nice bathrooms, Wi-Fi, fridge and a/c. Free airport pick-up or drop off. Breakfast, tea/coffee and afternoon snack included.

$$$-$$ Master Guest House
R-500 New Rajendra Nagar (Shankar Rd and GR Hospital Rd crossing), T011-2874 1089, www.master-guesthouse.com.
3 beautiful rooms, a/c, Wi-Fi, rooftop for breakfast, *thalis*, warm welcome that makes you feel like Delhi is home. Each room has a different vibrant colour scheme and named after a god. Very knowledgeable, caring owners run excellent tours of 'hidden Delhi'. Recommended.

South Delhi
Most of the city's smartest hotels are located south of Rajpath, in a broad rectangle between Chanakyapuri and Humayun's Tomb. The southern residential suburbs are also peppered with homestays; a list is available from **Delhi Tourism**, BK Singh Marg (see Tourist information), or arrange with the reliable **Metropole** (see Car hire, page 61).

$$$$ Claridges
12 Aurangzeb Rd, T011-3955 5000, www.claridges.com.
138 chic rooms, art deco-style interiors, colonial atmosphere, attractive restaurants (**Jade Garden** and Sevilla), beautiful **Aura** bar, impeccable service, charming atmosphere. Recommended.

$$$$ Manor
77 Friends Colony, T011-2692 5151, www.themanordelhi.com.
Contemporary boutique hotel with 10 stylish rooms, heavenly beds, relaxing garden, a haven. Beautiful artwork and relaxed vibe. Award-winning restaurant **Indian Accent**. Charming service.

$$$$ Oberoi
Dr Zakir Hussain Marg, T011-2436 3030, www.oberoihotels.com.
300 rooms and extremely luxurious suites overlooking golf club, immaculate, quietly efficient, beautiful touches, carved Tree of Life in the lobby. 5-star facilities including 2 pools and a spa, superb business centre and good restaurants – 360° gets rave reviews for its Sun brunch.

$$$$ Taj Mahal
1 Mansingh Rd, T011-2302 6162, www.tajhotels.com.
1 of 3 **Taj** hotels in Delhi. 300 attractive rooms, comfortable, new club levels outstanding, excellent restaurants and service (**Haveli** offers a wide choice and explanations for the newcomer; **Ming House's** spicing varies; **Machan** overlooks palm trees and has a wildlife library), good Khazana shop, lavishly finished with 'lived-in' feel, friendly 1920s-style bar. There is also a **Vivanta by Taj** hotel close to khan with a more business mood.

$$$$-$$$ Amarya Villa
A2-20 Safdarjung Enclave, T011-4103 6184, www.amaryagroup.com.
Truly hip boutique guesthouse, run by 2 Frenchmen. Unique, bright, en suite rooms with TV and Wi-Fi. The decor is inspired by *Navratna* (nine gems). Fantastic roof garden. Great home-cooked food. Effortlessly chic. Highly recommended.

$$$ K One One
K11, Jangpura Extn, 2nd floor, T011-4359 2583, www.parigold.com.
Homely guesthouse in a quiet, central residential area. Run by wonderful ex-TV chef, who also gives cooking lessons. All rooms en suite with a/c, minibar, Wi-Fi, some with balconies. Wonderful roof terrace with views of Humayan's Tomb. Rooftop room is lovely. Book ahead.

$$$ Lutyens Bungalow
39 Prithviraj Rd, T011-2469 4523,
www.lutyensbungalow.co.in.
Private guesthouse in a bungalow that
has been running for more than 35 years –
it's looking a little faded around the edges.
Eccentric, rambling property with 15 a/c
rooms, a wonderful pool and beautiful
gardens with a garden accessory shop
on-site. Free airport pickup/drop off, full
services, used for long-stays by NGOs
and foreign consultants.

$$$-$$ Tree of Life B&B
D-193, Saket, T(0)9810-277699,
www.tree-of-life.in.
Stylish B&B with beautifully decorated
rooms, simple but chic. Kitchen access,
excellent on-site reflexology and yoga –
really good atmosphere. The owner also runs
Metropole Tourist Service (see page 61).
Close to Saket Metro station and to **PVR**
cinema and malls.

$$ Life Tree
*G 14 Lajpat Nagar Part II (near Central
Market), T(0)9910-460898, lifetreebnb@
gmail.com.*
A more simple but charming B&B from the
Tree of Life family – well located for Khan
Market and the centre.

Airport
Unless you can afford a 5-star, hotels around
the airport are overpriced and best avoided.

$$$-$$ Sam's Snooze at My Space
*T3 IGI Airport, opposite Gate 17, T(0)8800-
230013, www.newdelhiairport.in.*
You can book a snooze pod for US$12 per
hr – only if you are flying out of T3. There's
Wi-Fi, TV and DVD, work stations.

$$-$ Hotel Eurostar International
*A 27/1 Street No 1, near MTNL office,
Mahipalpur Extension, T011-4606 2300,
www.hoteleurostar.in.*
Good-value option near the airport.

Restaurants

The larger hotel restaurants are often the
best for cuisine, decor and ambience. Sun
buffets are very popular costing around
Rs 3000 or more. Some hotels may only
open around 1930 for dinner; some close
on Sun. Alcohol is served in most top hotels,
but only in some non-hotel restaurants.

The old-fashioned 'tea on the lawn' is still
served at **The Imperial**, **Claridges** and **Taj
Mahal** hotels (see Where to stay, pages 49
and 50). **Aapki Pasand**, at 15 Netaji Subhash
Marg, offers unusual tea-tasting in classy
and extremely professional surroundings;
it's quite an experience. Hauz Khas in South
Delhi is a great area where there are many
restaurants and bars in walking distance of
each other – there is a fast turnover of what is
hip in this area however so walk around and
see what you fancy.

Old Delhi
In **Paranthewali Gali**, a side street off
Chandni Chowk, stalls sell a variety of
paranthas including *kaju badam* (stuffed with
dry fruits and nuts). Other good places to try
local foods like *bedmi aloo puri* with spiced
potato are **Mahalaxmi Misthan Bhandhar**,
659 Church Mission St, and **Natraj Chowk**,
1396 Chandni Chowk, for *dahi balli* and *aloo
tikki*. For sweets you have to seek out **Old
Famous Jalebi Wala**, 1797 Dariba Corner,
Chandni Chowk – as they are old and famous!

$$$-$$ Chor Bizarre
*Broadway Hotel (see Where to stay, page 48),
T011-4366 3600.*
Tandoori and Kashmiri cuisine (Wazwan,
Rs 500). Fantastic food, quirky decor,
including salad bar that was a vintage car.
Well worth a visit.

$ Haldiram's
1454/2 Chandni Chowk.
Stand-up counter for excellent snacks and
sweets on the run (try *dokhla* with coriander
chutney from seller just outside), and more
elaborate sit-down restaurant upstairs.

$ Karim's
Gali Kababiyan (south of Jama Masjid), Mughlai.
Authentic, busy, plenty of local colour. The experience, as much as the food, makes this a must. Not a lot to tempt vegetarians though.

Connaught Place

$$$ Sakura
Hotel Metropolitan (see New Delhi map, page 36), Bangla Sahib Rd, T011-2334 0200.
Top Japanese royal cuisine in classic, uncluttered surroundings. One of the best in the city, priced accordingly.

$$$ Spice Route
Imperial Hotel (see Where to stay, page 49).
Award-winning restaurant charting the journey of spices around the world. Extraordinary temple-like surroundings (took 7 years to build), Kerala, Thai, Vietnamese cuisines, magical atmosphere.

$$$ Veda
27-H, T011-4151 3535,
www.vedarestaurants.com.
Owned by fashion designer Rohit Bal with appropriately beautiful bordello-style decor, done out like a Rajasthani palace with high-backed leather chairs and candles reflecting from mirror work on ceilings. Food is contemporary Indian. Great atmosphere at night. There is another branch at DLF Vasant Kunj.

$$ Embassy
D-11, T093-1108 5132.
International food. Popular with an artistic/intellectual/political crowd, good food, longstanding local favourite.

$$ Kwality
7 Regal Building, near Park Hotel, T011-2374 2310.
International. Spicy Punjabi dishes with various breads. Try *chhole bhature*.

$$ Life Caffe
Hotel Corus (see Where to stay, page 49), B49 Connaught Pl, T099-5896 6357.
Tranquil garden, imaginative, good-value food. Perfect for when you want to escape the noise of CP.

$$ United Coffee House
E-15 Connaught Pl, T011-2341 1697.
Recommended more for the colonial-era cake-icing decor than for the fairly average food. Often someone waxing lyrical over a Casio keyboard. Always attracts a mixed crowd, well worth a visit.

$ Nathu's and Bengali Sweet House
Both in Bengali Market (east of Connaught Pl, see New Delhi map).
Sweet shops also serving vegetarian food. Good *dosa, iddli, utthapam* and North Indian *chana bathura, thalis*, clean, functional. Try *kulfi* (hard blocks of ice cream) with *falooda* (sweet vermicelli noodles).

$ Nizam's Kathi Kebabs
H-5 Plaza, T011-2332 1953.
Very good, tasty filled *parathas*, good value, clean. There's another branch in Defence Colony.

$ Saravana Bhavan
P-15/90, near McDonalds, T011-2334 7755; also at 46 Janpath.
Chennai-based chain, light and wonderful South Indian, superb chutneys, unmissable *kaju anjeer* ice cream with figs and nuts. No reservations so can take ages to get a table at night or at weekends. Highly recommended.

$ Street stalls
At entrance to Shankar Market.
Stalls dish out *rajma chawal* (bean stew and rice) to an appreciative crowd on weekdays.

$ Triveni Tea Terrace
Triveni Kala Sangam, 205 Tansen Marg, near Mandi House Metro station (not Sun).
Art galleries, an amphitheatre and this little café in quite an unusual building close to CP – the tea terrace is a bit of an institution.

Paharganj

The rooftop restaurants at **Jyoti Mahal** and **Shelton** are great locations for a bite to eat.

$$-$ Café Sim Tok
Tooti Chowk, above Hotel Navrang, near Hotel Rak, T(0)9810-386717.
Tucked away little gem of a Korean restaurant. No signage, ask for **Hotel Navrang** and keep going up stairs to find delicious *kimbab* (Korean sushi), *kimchi* and all sorts of soups, in a sweet little café. You can always calm the spice with cold beer too.

$ Everest Bakery Café
Dal Mandi, near Star Palace Hotel.
Fantastic *momos*, cakes and pies, green teas, sociable. Recommended.

$ Tadka
Off Main Bazar (near veg market).
Good option for tasty food in this area. Great range of all the usual Indian favourites, with nice decor, friendly staff and good hygiene levels.

South Delhi

$$$ Baci
23 Sunder Nagar Market, near HDFC Bank, T011-4150 7445.
Classy, top-quality Italian food, run by gregarious Italian-Indian owners. There are also branches of her cheaper café **Amici** springing up in Khan Market and Hauz Khas.

$$$ Bukhara
ITC Maurya Sheraton, Sardar Patel Marg, T011-2611 2233, www.itcwelcomgroup.com.
Stylish Northwest Frontier cuisine amidst rugged walls draped with rich rugs (but uncomfortable seating). Outstanding meat dishes and dhal. Also tasty vegetable and *paneer* dishes, but vegetarians will miss out on the best dishes.

$$$ Desi Roots
G-16/17, Salcon Rasvilas Mall, near Saket City Walk, T011-4161 4008.
Expect the unexpected at this concept restaurant, where your mutton curry will be served in a toy truck and your chipotle chicken tikka in an old iron. Try the avocado raita or a kichdi made from quinoa. Fun and delicious.

$$$ Diva
M8, M-Block Market, Greater Kailash II, T011-2921 5673.
Superb Italian in minimalist space popular with celebrity crowd. Great fish dishes, inventive starters, dedicated vegetarian section, extensive wine list. Owner Ritu Dalmia has also opened **Latitude 28,** a delightful café in Khan Market.

$$$ Dum Pukht
ITC Maurya Sheraton, Sardar Patel Marg, T011-2611 2233, www.itcwelcomgroup.com. Open evenings; lunch only on Sun.
Voted one of the best restaurants in the world, it marries exquisite tastes and opulent surroundings.

$$$ Indian Accent
At The Manor, 77 Friends Colony West, T011-4323 5151.
With a menu designed by Manish Mehotra, who runs restaurants in Delhi and London, this acclaimed restaurant offers Indian food with a modern twist: *dosas* will reveal masala morel mushrooms; and rather than the traditional Goan prawns *balchao,* here you will find it with roasted scallops. Or how about toffee *chyawanprash* cheesecake with badam milk (*chyawanprash* is a health elixir from the amla fruit)? The menu reflects the changing of the seasons and there is live fusion music on Sat. Highly recommended.

$$$ Kainoosh
122-124 DLF Promenade Mall, Vasant Kunj, T(0)9560-715533.
Under the watchful eye of celebrity chef Marut Sikka, delicious *thalis* marry the traditional and modern faces of Indian food. This is *thali* with a difference – bespoke with giant morel mushrooms, sea bass mousse and chicken cooked in orange juice and saffron in a terracotta pot.

$$$ Lodi
Lodi Gardens, T098-1874 3232.
Excellent location; come here for fusion foods taking in tastes from around the globe. Mediterranean-style surroundings, nice terrace and garden.

$$$ Magique
Gate No 3, Garden of 5 Senses, Mehrauli Badarpur Rd, T(0)9717-535533.
Delicious fusion food, in a magical setting. Sit outside among the candles and fairy lights. One of Delhi's most romantic restaurants.

$$$ Olive at the Qutb
T011-2957 4444, www.olivebar andkitchen.com.
Branch of the ever popular Mumbai restaurant and some people say the Delhi version wins hands down. Serving up delicious platters of Mediterranean food and good strong cocktails.

$$$ Park Baluchi
Inside Deer Park, Hauz Khas Village, T011-2685 9369.
Atmospheric dining in Hauz Khas Deer Park. The lamb wrapped in chicken served on a flaming sword comes highly recommended. Can get crowded, book ahead.

$$$ Ploof
13 Main Market, Lodhi Colony, T099-5802 7772.
Billed as a Gourmet Kitchen, this is the place to come for seafood. Very popular. Bright, comfortable restaurant.

$$$ Sevilla
Claridges Hotel (see Where to stay, page 50).
Beautiful restaurant with lots of outdoor seating serving up specialities like tapas and paella as well as wood-fired pizza and the dangerous house special sangria.

$$ Naivedyam
Hauz Khas village, T011-2696 0426.
Very good South Indian, great service and very good value in a very beautiful restaurant. Highly recommended.

$$ Oh! Calcutta
E-Block, ground floor, International Trade Towers, Nehru Pl, T011-3040 2415.
Authentic Bengali cuisine, with excellent vegetarian and fish options in a somewhat odd location but not far from the Baha'i temple.

$ Khan Cha Cha
Khan Market, 75 Middle Lane.
This no-frills joint serves some of the best kebabs in the city from a window in the middle lane of Khan Market. Fantastic value. You can recognize the place from the crowd clamouring at the counter. There is another branch in CP.

$ Sagar Ratna
18 Defence Colony Market, T011-2433 3440.
Other branches in Vasant Kunj, Malviya Nagar and NOIDA. Excellent South Indian. Cheap and "amazing" *thalis* and coffee, very hectic (frequent queues). One of the best breakfasts in Delhi.

Bars and clubs

Many national holidays are 'dry' days. Delhi's bar/club scene has exploded over the last few years. Expect to pay a lot for your drinks and, when in doubt, dress up; some clubs have strict dress codes. Delhi's 'in' crowd is notoriously fickle. For more insight into Delhi check out the website www.bringhomestories.com and www.timeout.com/delhi.

Connaught Place

1911
Imperial Hotel (see page 49).
Elegantly styled colonial bar, good snacks.

Kitty Su
Lalit Hotel, Barakhamba Av.
Boasting molecular mixology with their cocktails and regular turns by prominent DJs and more alternative acts.

South Delhi

Out of the Box
9 Hauz Khas, T011-4608 0533.
Party place with themed nights and live music. Café and bar.

Pegs-n-Pints
Chanakya Lane, Chanakyapuri (tucked away behind Akbar Bhawan), T011-2687 8320.
On Tue evenings it hosts Delhi's only gay club. Western and Indian pop. It gets packed. A lot of fun.

Rick's
Taj Mahal Hotel, 1 Mansingh Rd, T011-2302 6162, www.tajhotels.com.
Suave Casablanca-themed bar with long martini list, a long-time fixture on Delhi's social scene.

Shalom
'N' Block Market, Greater Kailash 1, T011-4163 2280.
Comfortable, stylish lounge bar serving Lebanese cuisine; the resident DJ plays ambient music. Sufi and soul on Thu, House on Fri.

Urban Pind
N4, N-block market, GK1, T011-3951 5656.
Multi-level bar, with large roof terrace, popular – recently refurbished. Hosts a controversial expat/journalist night on Thu with an 'all-you-can-drink' entry fee, unsurprisingly this normally features a lot of drunk foreigners.

Entertainment

For advance notice of upcoming events see www.delhievents.com. Current listings and reviews can be found on *www.timeout. com* and www.brownpaperbag.in/delhi. For programmes see cinema listings in the daily *Delhi Times*.

Cinema
PVR is a multiplex chain with branches everywhere, mostly screening Hindi movies, including **PVR Plaza** in Connaught Pl. Now with the Metro, it's pretty easy to get to PVR Saket, for example, whereas previously it was extremely unlikely you would bother.

Music, dance and culture
Goethe Institute, *3 Kasturba Gandhi Marg, T011-2347 1100.* Recommended for arts, film festivals, open-air cinema, plays and events.
India Habitat Centre, *Lodi Rd, T011-2468 2022.* Good programme of lectures, films, exhibitions, concerts, excellent restaurant.
Indian International Centre, *40 Lodhi Estate, Max Mueller Marg, T011-2461 9431, www.iicdelhi.nic.in.* Some fantastic debates and performances, well worth checking the 'forth-coming programmes' section of their website.
Kingdom of Dreams, *Great Indian Nautanki Company Ltd. Auditorium Complex, Sector 29, Gurgaon, Metro IFFCO, T0124-452 8000, www.kingdomofdreams.in.* Ticket prices Rs 750-3000 depending on where you sit and more pricey at the weekend. The highlight is a much acclaimed all-singing, all-dancing Bollywood-style performance. A little like an Indian Disneyland showcasing Indian tastes, foods, culture, dress and dance all in one a/c capsule, but done impeccably.
Triveni Kala Sangam, *205 Tansen Marg (near Mandi House Metro station), T011-2371 8833.* Strong programme of photography and art exhibitions, plus an excellent North Indian café.

Son et lumière
Red Fort *(see page 28), Apr-Nov 1800-1900 (Hindi), 1930-2030 (English). Entry Rs 50. Tickets available after 1700.* Take anti-mosquito cream.

Festivals

For exact dates consult the weekly *Delhi Diary* available at hotels and many shops and offices around town. Muslim festivals of **Ramadan, Id-ul-Fitr, Id-ul-Zuha** and **Muharram** are celebrated according to the lunar calendar.

Jan

26 Jan Republic Day Parade, Rajpath.
A spectacular fly-past and military march-past, with colourful pageants and tableaux from every state, dances and music. Tickets through travel agents and most hotels, Rs 100. You can see the full dress preview free, usually 2 days before; week-long celebrations during which government buildings are illuminated.

29 Jan Beating the Retreat, Vijay Chowk, a stirring display by the armed forces' bands marks the end of the Republic Day celebrations.

30 Jan Martyr's Day, Marks the anniversary of Mahatma Gandhi's death; devotional *bhajans* and Guard of Honour at Raj Ghat.

Kite Flying Festival, Makar Sankranti above Palika Bazar, Connaught Pl.

Feb

2 Feb Vasant Panchami, celebrates the 1st day of spring. The Mughal Gardens are opened to the public for a month.

Thyagaraja Festival, South Indian music and dance, Vaikunthnath Temple.

Apr

Amir Khusrau's Birth Anniversary, a fair in Nizamuddin celebrates this with prayers and *qawwali* singing.

Aug

Janmashtami, celebrates the birth of the Hindu god Krishna. Special *puja*, Lakshmi Narayan Mandir.

15 Aug Independence Day, Impressive flag-hoisting ceremony and prime ministerial address at the Red Fort.

Oct-Nov

2 Oct Gandhi Jayanti, Mahatma Gandhi's birthday; devotional singing at Raj Ghat.

Dasara, with over 200 Ramlila performances all over the city recounting the *Ramayana* story.

Ramlila Ballet, the ballet, which takes place at Delhi Gate (south of Red Fort) and Ramlila Ground, is performed for a month

and is most spectacular. Huge effigies of Ravana are burnt on the 9th night; noisy and flamboyant.

Diwali, the festival of lights; lighting of earthen lamps, candles and firework displays.

National Drama Festival, Rabindra Bhavan.

Oct/Nov Dastkar Nature Bazar, working with over 25,000 crafts people from across India, **Dastkar's** main objective is to empower rural artisans and keep alive the traditional crafts of India. They hold many events each year, but this is the pinnacle. Knowing that shopping here will bring a difference to the lives of rural people.

Dec

25 Dec Christmas, Special Christmas Eve entertainments at major hotels and restaurants; Midnight Mass and services at all churches.

Shopping

There are several state emporia around Delhi including the **Cottage Industries Emporium (CIE)**, a huge department store of Indian handicrafts, and those along Baba Kharak Singh Marg (representing crafts from most states of India). In this stretch, there are several places selling products from women's collectives or rural artisans, like **Mother Earth** and **Hansiba**). Shops generally open 1000-1930 (winter 1000-1900). Food stores and chemists stay open later. Most shopping areas are closed on Sun.

Art galleries

Galleries exhibiting contemporary art are listed on www.timeout.com.

Delhi Art Gallery, *Hauz Khas Village, www.delhiartgallery.com.* A newly expanded gallery with a good range of moderately priced contemporary art.

Nature Morte, *A-1 Neethi Bagh, near Kamla Nehru College, www.naturemorte.com.* With a twin gallery in Berlin, you can expect the most profound and inspiring of contemporary art here.

Photo Ink, *Hyundai MGF building, 1 Jhandewalan Faiz Rd, www.photoink.net.* Close to Paharganj, this gallery offers up top notch contemporary photography.

Books and music

Serious bibliophiles should head to the Sunday book market in Daryaganj (Kabaadi Bazar), Old Delhi, when 2 km of pavement are piled high with books – some fantastic bargains to be had.

Bahri & Sons, *opposite Main Gate, Khan Market.* One among many in the booklovers' heaven of Khan Market. Wide choice.

Central News Agency, *P 23/90, Connaught Pl.* Carries national and foreign newspapers and journals.

Full Circle, *5 B, Khan Market, T011-2465 5641.* Helpful knowledgeable staff. Sweet café upstairs for a quick drink – food is hit and miss though.

Manohar, *4753/23 Ansar Rd, Daryaganj, Old Delhi.* A real treasure trove for books on South Asia and India especially, most helpful, knowledgeable staff. Highly recommended.

Rikhi Ram, *G Block Connaught Circus, T011-2332 7685.* This is the place to come if you've wondered about how easy it is to learn to play and travel with a sitar. Has a range of guitars and other stringed instruments too.

Carpets

Carpets can be found in shops in most top hotels and a number round Connaught Pl, not necessarily fixed price. If you are visiting Agra, check out the prices here first.

Clothing

For designer wear, try **Ogaan** and for more contemporary, less budget blowing try **Grey Garden** both in **Hauz Khas Village**, **Sunder Nagar Market** near the Oberoi hotel, or the Crescent arcade near the Qutab Minar. The new market of choice is Meherchand in South Delhi.

For inexpensive (Western and Indian) clothes, try shops along Janpath and between Sansad Marg and Janpath; you can bargain down 50%.

Fab India, *14N-Gt Kailash I (also in B-Block Connaught Pl, Khan Market and Vasant Kunj).* Excellent shirts, Nehru jackets, *salwar kameez*, linen, furnishing fabrics and furniture. The most comprehensive collection is in N block.

Earthenware

Unglazed earthenware *khumba matkas* (water pots) are sold round New Delhi Railway Station (workshops behind main road).

Emporia

Most open 1000-1800 (close 1330-1400).

Central Cottage Industries Emporium, *corner of Janpath and Tolstoy Marg.* Offers hassle-free shopping, gift wrapping, will pack and post overseas; best if you are short of time.

Dilli Haat, *opposite INA Market.* Rs 15, open 1100-2200. Well-designed open-air complex with rows of brick alcoves for craft stalls from different states; local craftsmen's outlets (bargaining obligatory), occasional fairs (tribal art, textiles, etc). Also good regional food – hygienic, safe, weighted towards non-vegetarian. Pleasant, quiet, clean (no smoking) and uncrowded, not too much hassle.

Khazana, *Taj Mahal and Taj Palace hotels (daily 0900-2000).* High class.

Jewellery

Traditional silver and goldsmiths in Dariba Kalan, off Chandni Chowk (north of Jama Masjid). Cheap bangles and accessories along Janpath; also at Hanuman Mandir, Gt Kailash I, N-Block. Also Sunder Nagar market. Bank St in Karol Bagh is recommended for gold.

Amrapali, Khan Market has an exceptional collection from affordable to mind-blowing.

Ashish Nahar, *1999 Naughara St, Kinari Bazar, Chandni Chowk, T011-2327 2801.* On quite possibly the prettiest street in Delhi, full of brightly painted and slowly crumbling *havelis*, you will find a little gem of a jewellery shop.

Leather

Cheap sandals from stalls on Janpath (Rs 150). **Yashwant Place Market** next to Chanakya Cinema Hall, Chanakyapuri. **Khan Market** (see below) sells leather goods and shoes. **Hidesign**, *G49, Connaught Pl*. Beautifully made leatherware.

Markets and malls

Beware of pickpockets in markets and malls. **Hauz Khas village**, *South Delhi*. Authentic, old village houses converted into designer shops selling handicrafts, ceramics, antiques and furniture in addition to luxury wear. Many are expensive, but some are good value. A good place to pick up old Hindi film posters with many art galleries and restaurants.

Khan Market, *South Delhi*. Great bookshops, cafés, restaurants and boutiques. Full of expats so expect expat prices.

Sarojini Nagar, *South Delhi*. Daily necessities as well as cheap fabric and clothing. Come for incredible bargains. This is where a lot of the Western brands dump their export surplus or end-of-line clothes. Haggle hard.

Select City Walk, *Saket*. An enormous, glitzy mall for the ultimate in upmarket shopping. Lots of chains, cinemas, etc.

Shahpur Jat, is a new up and coming shopping area, south of **South Extension**.

Tibetan Market, *North Delhi*. Stalls along Janpath have plenty of curios – most are new but rapidly aged to look authentic.

Unique souvenirs

Aap ki Pasand, *opposite Golcha cinema, Netaji Subhash Marg, Old Delhi*. Excellent place to taste and buy Indian teas.

Dastkari Haat, *39 Khan Market, www.indian craftsjourney.in*. Charming selection of conscious crafts from around India working with rural artisans and women's collectives.

Gulabsingh Johrimal Perfumers, *467 Chandni Chowk, T011-2326 3743*. Authentic *attars* (sandalwood based perfumes), perfumes and incense. High-quality oils are used.

Haldiram's, *Chandni Chowk near Metro*. Wide selection of sweet and salty snack foods.

Khazana India, *50A Hauz Khas village*. Little treasure trove of Bollywood posters, old photographs and all sorts of interesting bric-a-brac.

People Tree, *8 Regal Building, Connaught Pl*. Handmade clothing, mostly T-shirts with arty and people conscious slogans. Great posters made up of all those weird signs that you see around India and wide-range of ecological books. A real find.

Playclan, *17 Meherchand Market, www.the playclan.com*. Fantastic shop selling all manner of clothes, notebooks, lighters and pictures with great colourful cartoon designs created by a collective of animators and designers – giving a more animated view of India's gods, goddesses, gurus, Kathakali dancers and the faces of India.

Purple Jungle, *16 Hauz Khas Village, T(0)9650-973039, www.purple-jungle.com*. Offering up kitsch India with bollywood pictures and curious road signs refashioned onto bags, clothes, cushions, etc.

What to do

Body and soul

Integral Yoga, *Sri Aurobindo Ashram, Aurobindo Marg, T011-2656 7863*. Regular yoga classes (Tue-Thu and Sat 0645-0745 and 1700-1800) in *asana* (postures), *pranayama* (breathing techniques) and relaxation.

Laughter Club of Delhi, *various locations, T011-2721 7164*. Simple yogic breathing techniques combined with uproarious laughter. Clubs meet early morning in parks throughout the city.

Sari School, *Jangpura Extension, near Lajpat Nagar, T011-4182 3297*. Author of *Saris in India*, Rta Christi Kapur holds classes every Sat in different styles of sporting a sari.

Tree of Life Reflexology, *T(0)9810-356677*. Reflexology with acclaimed teacher Suruchi. She also does private and group yoga classes on the roof and in the park.

The Yoga Studio, *Hauz Khas, www.theyoga studio.in.* Regular yoga classes with Seema Sondhi, author of several yoga books, and her team. Sometimes they run outside classes.

Tours and tour operators
Delhi Tourism tours
Departs from **Delhi Tourism** (Baba Kharak Singh Mg near State Govt Emporia, T011-2336 3607, www.delhitourism.gov.in). Book a day in advance. Check time. Offers morning, afternoon and evening tours taking in various sites (Rs 258) – see website. **Evening Tour** (Tue-Sun 1830-2200): Rajpath, India Gate, Kotla Firoz Shah, Purana Qila, *son et lumière* (Red Fort), Rs 207.

Walking tours
Walking tours are a fantastic way to get an insight into the city.
Chor Bizarre, *Hotel Broadway, T011-2327 3821.* Special walking and cycle rickshaw tours of Old Delhi, with good lunch, 0930-1330, 1300-1630, Rs 350 each, Rs 400 for both.
Delhi Metro Walks, *T(0)9811-330098, www. delhimetrowalks.com.* With the charismatic Surekha Narain guiding your every step, informative heritage walks around Delhi. She offers group walks but can also do private tours. Highly recommended.
Master Guest House *(see Where to stay, page 50).* Highly recommended walking tours for a more intimate experience.
Salaam Baalak Trust, *T(0)9873-130383, www.salaambaalaktrust.com.* NGO-run tours of New Delhi station and the streets around it, guided by former street children. Your Rs 200 goes to support the charity's work with street children. Excellent.

Tour operators
There are many operators offering tours, ticketing, reservations, etc, for travel across India. Many are around Connaught Circus, Parharganj, Rajendra Pl and Nehru Pl. Most belong to special associations (IATA, PATA) for complaints.

Ibex Expeditions, *30 Community Centre East of Kailash, New Delhi, T011-2646 0244, www. ibexexpeditions.com.* Offers a wide range of tours and ticketing, all with an eco pledge. Recommended.
Kunzum Travel Café, *T-49 Hauz Khas village, T011-2651 3949.* Unusual travel centre and meeting place for travellers. Free Wi-Fi, walls lined with photos, magazines, and buzzing with people. Also hosts photography workshops and travel writing courses.
Namaste Voyages, *I-Block 28G/F South City, 2 Gurgaon, 122001, T0124-221 9330, www. namastevoyages.com.* Specializes in tailor-made tours, tribal, treks, theme voyages.
Royal Expeditions, *26 Community Center (2nd floor), East of Kailash, New Delhi 110065, T011-2623 8545, www.royalexpeditions. com.* Specialist staff for customized trips, knowledgeable about options for senior travellers. Owns luxury 4WD vehicles for escorted self-drive adventures in Himalaya, offers sightseeing in classic cars in Jaipur.
Shanti Travel, *F-189/1A Main Rd, Savitri Nagar, T011-4607 7800, www.shantitravel.com.* Tailor-made tours throughout India.
Wild Frontiers India, *D-131 (2nd floor), Mohammadpur, Bhakaji Cama Place, New Delhi, T011-2619 5950, www.wildfrontiers india.com.* Great local outfit that are a subsidiary of **Wild Frontiers UK**. Responsible tours offering an excellent insight into India.

Transport

For up-to-date transport contact numbers check out www.delhitourism.gov.in.

Air
Indira Gandhi International Airport (IGI), 20 km southwest of Connaught Pl, T0124-377 6000, www.newdelhiairport.in, has one of the longest runways in Asia. All international and some domestic flights arrive at the shiny new Terminal 3; Terminal 1 is now used mostly by low-cost domestic carriers. A free shuttle runs between the 2 terminals every 30 mins during the day (show your boarding

pass and onward ticket), every 20 mins, but can take more than an hour so allow plenty of time. At check-in, be sure to tag your hand luggage, and make sure it is stamped after security check, otherwise you will be sent back at the gate to get it stamped.

The domestic air industry is in a period of massive growth, so check a 3rd-party site such as www.cleartrip.com or www. makemytrip.com for the latest flight schedules and prices.

The most extensive networks are with **Air India**, T140/T011-2562 2220, www. airindia.com; and **Jet Airways**, T011-3989 3333, www.jetairways.com. **Indigo**, T(0)9910-383838, www.goindigo.in, has the best record for being on time, etc, and **Spicejet**, T(0)9871-803333, www.spicejet.com.

Transport to and from the airport

The **Metro** is up and running and it is now possible to travel between New Delhi Railway Station and the airport in just 20 mins (orange line).

By road, it can take 30-45 mins from the Domestic Terminal and 45-60 mins from the International Terminal to travel to the centre. There is a booth just outside 'Arrivals' at the International and Domestic terminals for the **bus** services. It is a safe, economical option. Some hotel buses leave from the Domestic terminal. **Bus 780** runs between the airport and New Delhi Railway Station.

Both terminals have **pre-paid taxi** counters outside the baggage hall (3 price categories) which ensure that you pay the right amount (give your name, exact destination and number of items of luggage). Most expensive are white '**DLZ' limousines** and then white '**DLY' luxury taxis**. Cheapest are '**DLT' ordinary Delhi taxis** (black with yellow top Ambassador/Fiat cars and vans, often very old). 'DLY' taxis charge 3 times the DLT price. A 'Welcome' desk by the baggage reclamation offers expensive taxis only. Take your receipt to the ticket counter outside to find your taxi and give it to the driver when you reach the destination; you don't

need to tip, although they will ask. From the International terminal DLT taxis charge about Rs 240 for the town centre (Connaught Pl area); night charges double 2300-0500.

Bus

Be on your guard from thieves around New Delhi Station. Also watch your change or cash interactions even at the pre-paid booths – sometimes they do a switch of a Rs 100 note for a Rs 10 for example.

Local

The city bus service run by the **Delhi Transport Corporation** (**DTC**) connects all important points in the city and has more than 300 routes. Information is available at www.dtc.nic.in, at DTC assistance booths and at all major bus stops. Don't be afraid to ask conductors or fellow passengers. Buses are often hopelessly overcrowded so only use off-peak.

State Entry Rd runs from the southern end of Platform 1 to Connaught Pl. This is a hassle-free alternative to the main Chelmsford Rd during the day (gate closed at night).

Long distance

The main **Inter-State Bus Terminal** (**ISBT**) is at Kashmere Gate (see below), from where buses run to most major towns in North India. Services are provided by **Delhi Transport Corporation** (**DTC**) and State Roadways of neighbouring states. Local buses connect it to the other ISBTs. Allow at least 30 mins to buy your ticket and find the right bus.

Kashmere Gate, north of Old Delhi near the Red Fort, T011-440 0400 (general enquiries), is accessible by Metro (yellow line; 15 mins from Connaught Pl) or bus. Facilities include a restaurant, left luggage, bank (Mon-Fri 1000-1400; Sat 1000-1200), post office (Mon-Sat 0800-1700) and telephones (includes international calls). The following operators run services to neighbouring states from here: **Delhi Transport Corp**, T011-2386 5181; **Haryana Roadways**, T011-2296

1262; daily to **Agra** (5-6 hrs, quicker by rail), **Chandigarh** (5 hrs), **Himachal Roadways**, T011-2296 6725; twice daily to **Dharamshala** (12 hrs), **Manali** (15 hrs), **Shimla** (10 hrs), etc. **J&K Roadways**, T011-2332 4511; **Punjab Roadways**, T011-2296 7892, to **Amritsar**, **Chandigarh**, **Jammu**, **Pathankot**. **UP Roadways**, T011-2296 8709, city office at Ajmeri Gate, T011-2323 5367; to **Almora** (5 hrs), **Dehradun**, **Haridwar**, **Mussoorie**, **Gorakhpur**, **Kanpur**, **Jhansi**, **Lucknow**, **Nainital**, **Varanasi**.

Sarai Kale Khan Ring Rd, smaller terminal near Nizamuddin Railway Station, T011-2469 8343 (general enquiries), for buses to Haryana, Rajasthan and UP: **Haryana Roadways**, T011-2296 1262. **Rajasthan Roadways**, T011-2291 9537. For **Agra**, **Mathura** and **Vrindavan**; **Ajmer**; **Alwar**; **Bharatpur** (5 hrs); **Bikaner** (11 hrs); **Gwalior**; **Jaipur**; **Jodhpur**; **Pushkar**; **Udaipur**, etc.

Anand Vihar, east side of Yamuna River, T011-2215 2431, for buses to Uttar Pradesh, Uttarakhand and Himachal Pradesh.

HPTDC, Chandralok Bldg, 36 Janpath, T011-2332 5320, hptdcdelhi@hub.nic.in, runs a/c Volvo and Sleeper buses to **Manali** and **Dharamshala**. Of the myriad private bus operators, **Raj National Express** has by far the best buses, and highest prices.

Car hire

Hiring a car is an excellent way of getting about town either for sightseeing or if you have several journeys to make. However, the main roads out of Delhi are very heavily congested; the best time to leave is in the very early morning.

Full-day local use with driver (non a/c) Rs 900 and for (a/c) is about Rs 13-1600, 80 km/8 hrs, driver overnight *bata* Rs 150 per day; to Jaipur, about Rs 6 to 8000 depending on size of car. The **Government of India** tourist office (see page 48), 88 Janpath, has a list of approved agents. We highly recommend **Metropole**, see below.
Cozy Travels, N1 BMC House, Middle Circle, Connaught Pl, T011-4359 4359, cozytravels@

vsnl.net.com. **Metropole Tourist Service**, 224 Defence Colony Flyover Market (Jangpura side), New Delhi, T011-2431 2212, T(0)9810-277699, www.metrovista.co.in. Car/jeep (US$45-70 per day), safe, reliable and recommended, also hotel bookings and can help arrange homestays around Delhi. Highly recommended.

Metro

The sparkling new Metro system (T011-2436 5202, www.delhimetrorail.com) has revolutionized transport within Delhi. For travellers, the yellow line is the most useful as it stops Chandni Chowk, Connaught Pl, Qutb Minar and the Kashmere Gate ISBT. The blue line connects to Parhaganj; the violet line runs to Khan Market; and the orange line links the airport with New Delhi Railway Station.
Line 1 (Red) Running northwest to east, of limited use to visitors; from Rithala to Dilshad Garden.
Line 2 (Yellow) Running north–south through the centre from Jahangipuri to Huda City via Kashmere Gate, Chandni Chowk, New Delhi Station, Connaught Pl (Rajiv Chowk), Hauz Khas, Qutb Minar and Saket – probably the most useful line for visitors.
Line 3 (Blue) From Dwarka 21 to Valshall or City Centre (splits after Yamuna Bank) Intersecting with Line 2 at Rajiv Chowk and running west through Paharganj (RK Ashram station) and Karol Bagh.
Line 4 (Orange) Just 4 stations for now including IGI Airport to New Delhi Railway Station.
Line 5 (Green) From Mundka to Inderlok.
Line 6 (Violet) From Central Secretariat to Badarpur, including Khan Market and Lajpat Nagar. Useful.

Trains run 0600-2200; rush hour is best avoided. Fares are charged by distance: tokens for individual journeys cost Rs6-19. **Smart Cards**, Rs 100, Rs 200 and Rs 500, save queuing and money. **Tourist Cards** valid for 1 or 3 days (Rs 70/200) are useful if you plan to make many journeys. Luggage is limited to 15 kg; guards may not allow big backpacks on board. At each Metro station you have to go through airport-like security and have your bag x-rayed.

Look out for the women-only carriages at the front of each train, clearly marked in pink; these are much less crowded. For an insight into the construction of the Metro, there is a Metro museum at **Patel Chowk** on the yellow line.

Motorcycle hire

Chawla Motorcycles, 1770, Shri Kissan Dass Marg, Naiwali Gali, T(0)9811-888913. Very reliable, trustworthy, highly recommended for restoring classic bikes. **Ess Aar Motors**, Jhandewalan Extn, west of Paharganj, T011-2353 4426, www.essaarmotors.com. Recommended for buying Enfields, very helpful. For scooter rentals try **U Ride**, T(0)9711-701932, www.uridescooters.com.

Rickshaw

Auto-rickshaws These are widely available at about half the cost of taxis. Normal capacity for foreigners is 2 people (3rd person extra); the new fare system is encouraging rickshaw wallahs to use the meter, even with foreigners. Expect to pay Rs 30 for the shortest journeys. Allow Rs 150 for 2 hrs' sightseeing/shopping. It is best to walk away from hotels and tourist centres to look for an auto. Try to use pre-paid stands at stations, airport terminals and at the junction of Radial Road 1 and Connaught Place if possible.

Cycle-rickshaws Available in the Old City. Be prepared to bargain. They are not allowed into Connaught Pl. When looking for a cycle-rickshaw, follow the advice under auto-rickshaws above.

Taxi

Yellow-top taxis, which run on compressed natural gas, are readily available at taxi stands or you can hail one on the road. Meters should start at Rs 13; ask for the conversion

card. Add 25% at night (2300-0500) plus Rs 5 for each piece of luggage over 20 kg. **Easy Cabs**, T011-4343 4343. Runs clean a/c cars and claim to pick up anywhere within 15 mins; Rs 20 per km (night Rs 25 per km). Waiting charges Rs 50/30 mins.

Also recommended are: **Mega Cabs**, T011-4141 4141; and **Quick Cab**, T011-4533 3333.

Avoid app-based companies like **Uber** and **Ola** which are not licensed by the government.

Train

The busy **New Delhi Station**, a 10-min walk north of Connaught Place, connects with most destinations; you need to have all your wits about you. The quieter **Hazrat Nizamuddin** is 5 km southeast of Connaught Place and has some southbound trains. The overpoweringly crowded **Old Delhi Station** (2 km north of Connaught Place) has a few important train connections. The smaller **Delhi Sarai Rohilla**, northeast of Connaught Place, serves Rajasthan. Trains that originate from Delhi stations have codes: **OD** – Old Delhi, **ND** – New Delhi, **HN** – Hazrat Nizamuddin, **DSR** – Delhi Sarai Rohilla.

New Delhi and Hazrat Nizamuddin stations have pre-paid taxi and rickshaw counters with official rates per km posted: expect to pay around Rs 25 for 1st km, Rs 8 each km after. Authorized *coolies* (porters), wear red shirts and white *dhotis;* agree the charge, there is an official rate, before engaging one. For left luggage, you need a secure lock and chain.

Buying tickets

The publication *Trains at a Glance* (Rs 30) lists important trains across India, available at some stations, book shops and newsagents. Each station has a computerized reservation counter where you can book any Mail or Express train in India. Train enquiries T131. Reservations T1330.

International Tourist Bureau (ITB), 1st floor, Main Building, New Delhi Station, T011-2340 5156, Mon-Fri 0930-1630, Sat

ON THE ROAD

Taxi tips

First-time visitors can be vulnerable to exploitation by taxi drivers at the airport. If arriving at night, you are very strongly advised to have a destination in mind and get a pre-paid taxi. Be firm about being dropped at the hotel of your choice and insist that you have a reservation; you can always change hotels the next day if you are unhappy. Don't admit to being a first-time visitor.

If you don't take a pre-paid taxi, the driver will demand an inflated fare. He may insist that the hotel you want to go to has closed or is full and will suggest one where he will get a commission (and you will be overcharged).

Some travellers have been told that the city was unsafe with street fighting, police barricades and curfews and have then been taken to Agra or Jaipur. In the event of taxi trouble, be seen to note down the licence plate number and threaten to report the driver to the police; if you need to do this, the number is T011-2331 9334.

0930-1430, provides assistance with planning and booking journeys, for foreigners only; efficient and helpful if slow. You need your passport; pay in US$, or rupees (with an encashment certificate/ATM receipt). Those with **Indrail** passes should confirm bookings here. Be wary of rickshaw drivers/travel agents who tell you the ITB has closed or moved elsewhere. (There are also counters for foreigners and NRIs at **Delhi Tourism**, N-36 Connaught Pl, 1000-1700, Mon-Sat, and at the airport; quick and efficient.)

Services

There are a couple of trains which get you to Agra at a good time to view the Taj Mahal – **Agra**: *Shatabdi Exp 12002*, ND, usually leaving 0600, 2 hrs; *Taj Exp 12280*, HN, around 0700, 2¾ hrs. The *Shatabdi Express* will also give you a breakfast. **Amritsar**: *Shatabdi Exp 12013*, ND, 6 hrs; *Shan-e-Punjab Exp 12497*, ND (early morning) 7½ hrs. **Bengaluru** (**Bangalore**): *Ktk Smprk K Exp 12650*, Mon, Tue, Sat, Sun, HN, 36 hrs; **Chandigarh**: *Shatabdi Exp 12011*, ND, 3½ hrs. **Chennai**: *Tamil Nadu Exp 12622*, ND, 33½ hrs. **Dehradun**: *Shatabdi Exp 12017*, ND, early morning 5¾ hrs; same train stops at **Haridwar** for **Rishikesh. Kolkata**: *Rajdhani Exp 12314*, ND, 17½ hrs. **Madgaon** (Goa): *Mngla Lksdp Exp 12618*, HN, 35 hrs, goes on to **Ernakulum (Kochi). Mumbai (Central)**: *Rajdhani Exp 12954*, ND, 17½ hrs; *Golden Temple Mail 12904*, ND, 22 hrs.

North
from Delhi

Tucked beneath the foothills of the mighty Himalaya are high-altitude deserts, flower-filled valleys and remote Buddhist and Hindu temples. Leaving behind the heat of Delhi and the chessboard grid of Chandigarh's streets, India becomes wilder and more relaxed.

Close to nature and close to the divine, you breathe in the air of the gods as tread the hills, mountains and valleys of this region. In the Dhualadar range, it is traditional to walk the Kora in McLeodganj – a ritual circuit of His Holiness the Dalai Lama's residence and beautiful Namgyal Temple. Similarly, it is auspicious to walk three times clockwise around the Golden Temple at Amritsar taking a dip in the Amrit Sarovar tank. Or spiral up the stairs of the stunning Bhimakali Temple in Sarahan – a remote temple with epic mountain vistas dedicated to Hindu goddess Kali.

The Spiti and Kullu valleys are great places to witness the diversity of birdlife and flowers in the mountains and plateaux, while in the small towns around Manali you can admire the beautiful kathakuni architecture and temples. Whether trekking or motorbiking, you can revive your achy bones with dips in the hot springs at Manikaran or Vashist.

Or try something completely different – venture out to the Pakistani border for the changing of the guard, help to install solar energy with Spiti Ecosphere, make Tibetan *momos* (dumplings) in McLeodganj, or try trout fishing or whitewater rafting in the Tirthan or Beas rivers.

Essential North from Delhi

Getting around

Chandigarh and Amritsar have frequent train connections with Delhi, as well as buses to Himachal Pradesh. The only way to get around most of mountainous Himachal Pradesh is by bus or car. There is also the Kalka–Shimla narrow-gauge train (see page 89) and the Kangra Valley Railway (see page 146).

Best scenic walks

Stroll through pink fields in the Baspa Valley, page 97
Hike to the Buddhist gompa close to Dankar in Spiti, page 101
Trek with Spiti Ecosphere, page 104
Walk the Kora around the Dalai Lama's residence, McLeodganj, page 133

When to go

Across the plains of Haryana and Punjab, it can get dry and dusty in the heat of summer, with numbingly cold winter mornings. Many Indian tourists escape the heat of the plains in May and June and head up to the mountain air of Shimla, Dharamsala and Manali making roads busy at the weekends. The hills are a mercifully cool retreat in April through June. At lower altitudes the summers can be very hot and humid whereas the higher mountains are permanently under snow. Monsoon rains can bring landslides and closed roads. In Shimla, the Kangra Valley, Chamba and the Kullu Valley, the monsoon arrives in July and lasts until mid-September, giving periods of very heavy rain; in the Kullu Valley there can be sudden downpours in March and early April. To the north, Lahaul and Spiti are beyond the influence of the monsoon, and consequently share the high-altitude desert climatic characteristics of Ladakh. It is best to avoid the heat of Chandigarh and Amritsar in the summer months, but if it is your gateway to the mountains, spend just one day seeing the sights and then head for the hills. It is possible to visit Himachal Pradesh in the winter, but do check what will be open. Dharamsala and Manali are popular winter destinations.

Time required

One day in Chandigarh is enough for most people. Allow at least a day for the Golden Temple in Amritsar and there are a few day trips locally, including the evening trip to the Wagah border. Himachal Pradesh (Himalayan Province) is wholly mountainous, with peaks rising to over 6700 m. The Dhaula Dhar range runs from the northwest to the Kullu Valley. The Pir Panjal is further north and parallel to it. High, remote, arid and starkly beautiful, Lahaul and Spiti are sparsely populated. They contrast strongly with the well-wooded lushness of those areas to the south of the Himalayan axis.

Shimla and Manali both warrant two or three days. Many people spend weeks in Dharamshala but a couple of days is enough to soak up the atmosphere and do some day treks. If you are heading off to the more remote places in the Baspa or Spiti valleys you will need a couple of weeks. Roads are slow and you want to enjoy the ride.

Best days out

Chandigarh's Rock Garden, page 70
Wagah border parade, page 80
Chadwick Falls, page 85
Bhimakali Temple, Sarahan, page 93
Roerich Art Gallery, Naggar, page 115
Traditional Tibetan craft-making, Norbulingka, page 134

Chandigarh
& around

In 1947 when Lahore, Punjab's former capital, was allocated to Pakistan, the Indian government decided to build a new capital for the Indian state of the Punjab. The result is Chandigarh, a planned city in the post-war modernist style, acting as the dual capital of Punjab and Haryana states. Some critics describe Chandigarh as soulless; anyone familiar with England may be reminded of Milton Keynes. Not quite the garden city it was meant to be, it is nevertheless a convenient stop en route to Himachal Pradesh, or before flying to Leh.

Ironically, many now seem to visit Chandigarh more for the quixotic delights of Nek Chand's Rock Garden than for its European architect's alien buildings.

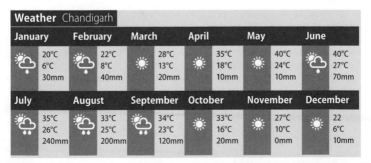

Weather Chandigarh					
January	**February**	**March**	**April**	**May**	**June**
20°C 6°C 30mm	22°C 8°C 40mm	28°C 13°C 20mm	35°C 18°C 10mm	40°C 24°C 10mm	40°C 27°C 70mm
July	**August**	**September**	**October**	**November**	**December**
35°C 26°C 240mm	33°C 25°C 200mm	34°C 23°C 120mm	33°C 16°C 20mm	27°C 10°C 0mm	22 6°C 10mm

BACKGROUND
North from Delhi

Haryana (population 21.1 million) and Punjab (population 24.9 million) occupy the strategic borderlands between the Indus and Yamuna Ganga river systems. Well over 1000 km from the sea, their gently sloping plains are less than 275 m above sea level. In the southwest, on the arid borders of Rajasthan, sand dunes form gentle undulations in the plain. Most major towns and cities of the region are close to the Grand Trunk Road, the great highway from Peshawar to Kolkata, which Rudyard Kipling described as "the backbone of all Hind". Today, the Grand Trunk Road is a multi-lane highway, lined not only with Punjabi *dhabas* but also drive-thru fast-food joints and coffee chains. And you can spy Audi dealerships as well as Maruti.

Himachal Pradesh (Himalayan Province) lies north of Haryana and Punjab and is wholly mountainous, with peaks rising to over 6700 m. The Dhaula Dhar range runs from the northwest to the Kullu Valley. The Pir Panjal is further north and parallel to it. High, remote, arid and starkly beautiful, Lahaul and Spiti are sparsely populated. They contrast strongly with the well-wooded lushness of those areas to the south of the Himalayan axis. Since 1966 Shimla has been the state capital. Dharamshala (McLeodganj) has been the home of His Holiness the Dalai Lama and the Tibetan government in exile since 1959, following the Chinese takeover of Tibet. With the long-term closure of routes through Kashmir, Himachal Pradesh has seen a sharp rise in tourism, and is the main land route to Ladakh. The new strategically important tunnel under the Rohtang Pass is scheduled for completion in 2019.

Delhi to Chandigarh through Haryana

historical and mythical battlefields

Panipat
Panipat is the site of three great battles which mark the rise and fall of the Mughal Empire. It stands on the higher ground made up of the debris of earlier settlements near the old bank of the River Yamuna. Today it is an important textile town with over 30,000 looms. A high proportion of the products – carpets, curtains and tablewear are exported.

The main old building in Panipat is a **shrine** to the Muslim saint Abu Ali Kalandar.

Kurukshetra
The battlefield where Arjuna learned the meaning of *dharma* has left no trace. The plain around Kurukshetra is described in Sanskrit literature as "Brahmavarta" (Land of Brahma). Like many other sacred sites it becomes the special focus of pilgrimage at the time of exceptional astronomical events. In Kurukshetra, eclipses of the sun are marked by special pilgrimages, when over one million people come to the tank. It is believed that the waters of all India's sacred tanks meet together at the moment of eclipse, giving extra merit to anyone who can bathe in it at that moment.

Chandigarh's major centres are the Capitol Complex, consisting of the Secretariat, Legislative Assembly and High Court in the northeast with the Shiwalik Hills as a backdrop; Sector 17, the central business district with administrative and state government offices, shopping areas and banks; a Cultural Zone in Sector 14 for education, which includes a museum and a campus university with institutions for engineering, architecture, Asian studies and medicine. A vast colonnaded shopping mall has opened in Sector 35, with hotels, restaurants, banks, a well-stocked supermarket and internet/international phones. Sector 7 also has a high density of shops.

Sights

The multi-pillared **High Court** stands nearby with a reflective pool in front. Primary colour panels break up the vast expanses of grey concrete but this classic work of modernist architecture looks stark and bleak. The **Legislative Assembly** has a removable dome and a mural by Le Corbusier that symbolizes evolution. In the same sector is the **Open Hand Monument**. The insignia of the Chandigarh Administration, it symbolizes "the hand to give and the hand to take; peace and prosperity, and the unity of humankind". The metal monument, 14 m high and weighing 50 tonnes, rotates in the wind and sometimes resembles a bird in flight. The geometrical hill nearby, known as the **Tower of Shadows** ① *tours 1030-1230 and 1420-1630, ask at Secretariat reception desk (you may need special permission to enter)*, was designed to beautify the complex, breaking its symmetrical lines.

The **Government Museum and Art Gallery** ① *Sector 10, Tue-Sun 1000-1630*, has a collection of stone sculptures dating back to the Gandhara period, as well as miniature paintings, modern art, prehistoric fossils and artefacts. The **Museum of Evolution of Life** ① *Sector 10, Tue-Sun 1000-1630*, has exhibits covering 5000 years from the Indus Valley Civilization to the present day. The **Fine Arts Museum** ① *Punjab University, Sector 14 (all the faculties of the university are in Gandhi Bhavan, Sector 14), Mon-Fri 1000-1700 (closed between 1300-1400)*, specializes in Gandhi studies. The **Chandigarh Architecture Museum** ① *Sector 10-C, Tue-Sun 1000-1645* charts the planning and creation of Chandigarh.

Essential Chandigarh

Finding your feet

The airport and railway stations are some distance from the centre with pre-paid auto rickshaws to town. From the large **Inter-State Bus Terminus (ISBT)** in the busy Sector 17, you can walk to several budget hotels and restaurants. See Transport, page 72.

Getting around

Buses serve the different sectors but if you are only here for a few hours, it is best to hire transport as there are long distances to cover in this widely spread out city and it is not always easy to find a taxi or auto-rickshaw for single journeys. Half-day tours 'Fun on Wheels' offer a hop-on hop-off service around the attractions; contact **CITCO** for information (see under Tourist information in Listings, below).

When to go

The best time to visit is November to March; monsoon season is June to August. See also the weather chart on page 67.

The **Rock Garden** or **Garden of Nek Chand** ① *Apr-Sep 0900-1900, Oct-Mar closes1800, Rs 15, allow 3 hrs*, an unusual place, is the creation of Nek Chand, a road inspector in the Capitol City project. The 'garden' comprises an extraordinary collection of stones from the nearby Shiwaliks (carried on his bike) and domestic rubbish transformed into sculptures. Nek Chand dreamed of "creating a temple to Gods and Goddesses" out of discarded items of everyday use, for example bottle tops, fluorescent lights, mud guards, tin cans, and by highly imaginative re-assembling made models of people and animals. These have been set out along a maze of paths, creating an amusing and enjoyable park. First opened in 1976 the park is still being extended. The low archways make visitors bow to the gods who have blessed the park. It definitely challenges the uniformity of the rest of Chandigarh.

Just below the rock garden is the man-made **Sukhna Lake**, the venue of the Asian rowing championships which is circled by a walk. It gets crowded on holidays and Sunday. There are cafés, boating and fishing (permits needed).

The **Rose Gardens** ① *Sector 16, until sunset*, are one of the largest in Asia (25 ha), contains over 1500 varieties of rose; well worth visiting in spring. There's a rose show in early March.

The **Zoological Park** ① *Chaat Bir, a few kilometres out of the city centre, Rs 30 per person*, has a lion and deer safari park.

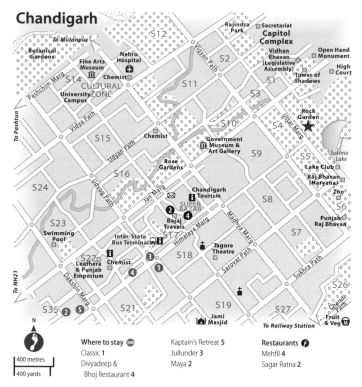

Chandigarh

Where to stay ⬤
Classic **1**
Divyadeep &
  Bhoj Restaurant **4**

Kaptain's Retreat **5**
Jullunder **3**
Maya **2**

Restaurants ⬤
Mehfil **4**
Sagar Ratna **2**

Tourist information

Chandigarh Tourism
ISBT, Sector 17, T0172-270 3839,
www.chandigarhtourism.gov.in.

Himachal Tourism
1st floor, ISBT, T0172-270 8569.

**Uttarakhand and Uttar
Pradesh Tourism**
ISBT, T0172-271 3988.

Where to stay

$$$$-$$$ Maya
SCO 325-28, S35-B, T0172-260 0547.
After quite the nip and tuck, Maya is a
stylish, boutique hotel with comfortable
rooms and chic restaurant. Definitely
worth checking out.

$$$ Deep Roots Retreat
Village Ranjitpur, 25 km from Chandigarh,
T(0)9878-430085, www.deeprootsretreat.com.
Out in the countryside beyond Chandigarh,
you get insight into the life of a Punjabi farm.
Stylish rooms, great home-cooked food
and good for dipping into Chandigarh for
sightseeing. Picnics, tractor rides and bonfires
can all be arranged. They have another fort
property close to Anandapur Sahib.

$$$ Kaptain's Retreat
303 S35-B, T0172-500 5599,
kaptainsretreat@hotmail.com.
Owned by the legendary cricketer, Kapil Dev,
this is Chandigarh's first boutique hotel. Each
room is named after one of the great man's
achievements, eg 'nine wickets', although
the interiors are more than cricket chic with
attractive decor and excellent attention to
detail. There's also an appealing bar and
restaurant. Good value. Recommended.

$$$-$$ Classic
S35-C, T0172-260 6092, www.
hotelclassicchandigarh.com.

Comfortable modern hotel (buffet breakfast
included), with a bar, lively bar and disco.
Reasonable value.

$$$-$$ Jullunder
S22, opposite ISBT, T0172-461 1121,
www.jullunderhotel.com.
17 average a/c rooms with restaurant on site.

$$-$ Divyadeep
S22-B, Himalaya Marg, T0172-270 5191.
15 rooms, some a/c, neat and clean, great
value, good **Bhoj** restaurant. Recommended.

Restaurants

$$$ Elevens
Kaptain's Retreat (see Where to stay, above).
Unusual combination of Pakistani, Indian and
Thai cuisines in Mediterranean-style interior.
Recommended.

$$$ Mehfil
183, S17-C, T0172-502 5599.
International. Upmarket, a/c, comfortable
seating, spicy meals.

$$ Bhoj
S22-B, Divyadeep (see Where to stay, above).
Indian Vegetarian. Good set *thalis* only,
pleasant, clean, busy at lunch, good value.

$$ Pashtun
S35-B.
Excellent frontier-style cuisine in pleasant
ground-floor restaurant plus 'Wild West' bar
in basement, complete with cowboy waiters.
Formerly called **Khyber**. Recommended.

$$ Sagar Ratna
S35-C.
High-quality South Indian. Well-presented,
nationwide chain, very professional.

Festivals

Apr All the Hindu festivals are celebrated
especially **Baisakhi**, celebrated by both
Hindus and Sikhs as **New Year's Day**

(13-14 Apr). Bhangra dancers perform, celebrating harvest.

What to do

Tour operators

Chandigarh Tourism, *T0172-505 5462, www.chandigarhtourism.gov.in, or book at ISBT (see Finding your feet, page 69)*. Local tours including good-value open-top bus and further afield to Pinjore Gardens, Bhakra Dam, Amritsar, Shimla, Kullu and Manali. They do half-day tours of the city in their double decker fun bus.

Transport

Air Airport, 11 km. Taxis charge Rs 300 to centre. **Air India**: reservations, S17, T0172-265 4941, airport, T0172-622 6029, 1000-1630. Daily to **Mumbai** and **Delhi**. **Jet Airways**, 14 S 9D Madhya Marg, T0172-3939 3333, daily to **Delhi**.

Bicycle hire Free to **CITCO** hotel guests.

Bus It is easier to get a seat on the **Shimla** bus from Chandigarh than from Kalka. Many buses daily from **ISBT**, S17. A 2nd terminal in S43 has some buses to **Himachal Pradesh**, **Jammu** and **Srinagar**; city buses connect the 2. Transport offices: ISBT, S17, 0900-1300, 1400-1600; Chandigarh, T0172-270 0006; Haryana, T0172-272 2980; Himachal, T0172-266 8943; Punjab, T0172-270 4023, you can also check out www.punbusonline.com. Buy bus tickets from the designated booths next to platforms before boarding. Seat numbers (written on the back of tickets) are often assigned. **Shimla** buses (via Kalka) leave from platform 10. To **Amritsar**, 6 hrs (from Aroma Hotel, T0172-270 0045); **Pathankot**, 7 hrs; **Dharamshala**, 10 hrs; **Kalka** (from Platform 10), Rs 11-28. Buses to **Shimla** also stop at **Kalka**; **Kullu** 12 hrs. Also **Himachal Tourism** coaches during the season, to **Delhi**, 5 hrs; **Manali**, 0800, 10 hrs; **Shimla**, 5 hrs.

Rickshaw Auto-rickshaws are metered with a minimum fare, but you can bargain. Stands at bus station, railway station and the Rock Garden. Cycle rickshaws are unmetered.

Taxi Private taxi stands in S22, S17, S35. **Mega Cabs**, T0172-414 1414. To **Kalka**, up to Rs 400.

Train The station (8 km) has a clean waiting room but a poor bus service to the city. Pre-paid auto-rickshaws, Rs 45 to S22; to bus stand Rs 34; to Kalka (for the brave) Rs 200. Enquiries/reservations, T1333, T0172-264 1651, 1000-1700; City Booking Office, 1st floor, Inter-State Bus Terminal (ISBT), S17, T0172-270 8573, Mon-Sat 0800-1345, 1445-2000, Sun 0800-1400. Tourist office, 0600-2030. **New Delhi**: *Shatabdi Exp 12006* (early morning), 3¾ hrs; *Shatabdi Exp 12012* (evening), 3½ hrs; **Shimla (via Kalka)**: *Himalayan Queen 14095*, 1 hr to **Kalka**, then 40 mins' wait for *Himalayan Queen 52455* to **Shimla** (1210, 6 hrs, book ahead). See also Kalka, page 89.

Pinjore (Pinjaur)

The **Yadavindra Gardens**, at Pinjore, 20 km on the Kalka road, were laid out by Aurangzeb's foster brother Fidai Khan, who also designed the Badshahi Mosque in Lahore. Within the Mughal *char bagh* gardens are a number of palaces in a Mughal-Rajasthani style: **Shish Mahal**, which has mirror-encased ceiling and is cooled by water flowing underneath (remove a slab to see!); **Rang Mahal**, a highly decorated pavilion; and **Jal Mahal**, set among fountains, cool and delightful. There are also camel rides and fairground attractions to tempt city dwellers. Keep a close eye on your belongings at all times; thefts have been reported.

Just beyond Pinjore is **Kalka**, the starting point for the mountain railway to Shimla. Two Britons were killed when the train derailed in September 2015 after leaving Kalka station. Services are now running at lower speeds.

Anandpur Sahib

Anandpur Sahib (City of Divine Bliss), in a picturesque setting at the foot of the Shiwaliks by the River Sutlej, was established by the ninth guru, Tegh Bahadur, in 1664, when the Sikhs had been forced into the foothills of the Himalaya by increasing Mughal opposition. Guru Tegh Bahadur himself was executed in Chandni Chowk, Delhi, and his severed head was brought to Anandpur Sahib to be cremated. The event added to the determination of his son, Guru Gobind Singh, to forge a new body to protect the Sikh community. The Khalsa Panth was thus created on Baisakhi Day in 1699. Anandpur Sahib became both a fortress and a centre of Sikh learning. **Hola Mohalla** is celebrated the day after **Holi** when battles are re-enacted by *nihangs* (Guru Gobind Singh's army) on horseback, dressed in blue and huge turbans, carrying old weapons.

The stunning blossom of **the Khalsa Heritage Complex** ⓘ *www.khalsaheritage complex.org*, is a dramatic addition to the architecture of Anandpur Sahib. It will house galleries, a state of the art museum, a research library, 400-seat auditorium, water gardens and restaurant.

Anandpur Sahib is also the home of **Dashmesh Sadan** ⓘ *www.dashmeshsadan.org*, the former residence of Yogi Bhajan and now popular with students of Kundalini Yoga as a retreat and training space.

Listings Chandigarh to Himachal Pradesh

Where to stay

Anandpur Sahib
It is possible to stay in one of the many *gurudwaras* in town.

$$-$ Kissan Haveli
Dashmesh Academy Rd, T01887-232 650.
10 rooms in this characterful heritage-style property.

$ Holy City
Dashmesh Academy Rd, T01887-232 330, www.hotelholycity.com.
Clean basic rooms and good value restaurant.

Transport

Anandpur Sahib
Bus From **Chandigarh** and **Ropar**.

Amritsar
& around

Amritsar ('Pool of the Nectar of Immortality') is named after the sacred pool in the Golden Temple, the holiest of Sikh sites. The temple itself, the city's singular attraction, is a haven of peace amidst an essentially congested city. The atmosphere is particularly powerful during *amritvela* (dawn to early light), when the surrounding glistening white-marble pavement is still cold under foot and the gold begins to shimmer on the lightening water. Sunset and evening prayers are also a special time to visit.

You cannot help but be touched by the sanctity and radiance of the place, the friendly welcome of the people and the community spirit. Music constantly plays from within the inner sanctum of the Hari Mandir.

Essential Amritsar

Finding your feet

Sri Guru Ram Das Jee International Airport is 11 km away with taxi or auto-rickshaw transfers. The railway is central, the bus station 2 km east; both are a 15-minute auto-rickshaw ride from the Golden Temple to the south. If you have a couple of hours to spare between connections, you can fit in a visit. See Transport, page 82.

Getting around

The city is quite spread out. Cycle-rickshaws squeeze through the crowded lanes. Auto-

Best Punjabi tastes

Guru Ram Das Langar community food, page 77
Free chai outside the Golden Temple at 0600, page 81
Food with a view from The Glass, page 81

rickshaws are handy for longer journeys unless you get a bike. The old city is south of the railway station encircled by a ring road, which traces the line of the city walls built during the reign of Ranjit Singh.

Every Sikh tries to make a visit and bathe in the holy water at the Golden Temple. It is immensely powerful, spiritual and welcoming to all, with an all-pervasive air of strength and self-sufficiency.

Visiting the temple

Shoes, socks, sticks and umbrellas can be left outside the cloakroom free of charge. Visitors should wash their feet outside the entrance. It is best to go early as for much of the year the marble gets too hot by noon. Dress appropriately and cover your head in the temple precincts. Head scarves are available during the day but not at night; a handkerchief suffices. Avoid sitting with your back towards the temple or with your legs stretched out. Tobacco, narcotics and intoxicants are not permitted. The community kitchen provides food all day, for a donation. The **information office** ① *near the main entrance, T0183-255 3954*, is very helpful.

1 Amritsar

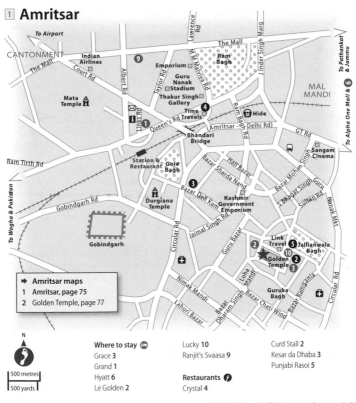

N

500 metres
500 yards

Where to stay 🛏
Grace **3**
Grand **1**
Hyatt **6**
Le Golden **2**

Lucky **10**
Ranjit's Svaasa **9**

Restaurants 🍴
Crystal **4**

Curd Stall **2**
Kesar da Dhaba **3**
Punjabi Rasoi **5**

BACKGROUND

Amritsar

The original site for the city was granted by the Mughal Emperor Akbar (ruled 1556-1605) who visited the temple, and it has been sacred to the Sikhs since the time of the fourth guru, Guru Ram Das (1574-1581). He insisted on paying its value to the local Jats who owned it, thereby eliminating the possibility of future disputes on ownership. Guru Ram Das then invited local merchants to live and trade in the immediate vicinity. In 1577 he heard that a cripple had been miraculously cured while bathing in the pool here. The pool was enlarged and named Amrit Sarovar (Immortality).

Guru Arjan Dev (1581-1601), Guru Ram Das' son and successor, enlarged the tank further and built the original temple at its centre from 1589-1601. The Afghan Ahmad Shah Durrani, desecrated the Golden Temple in 1757. The Sikhs united and drove him out, but four years later he defeated the Sikh armies, sacking the town and blowing up the temple. Later, the Sikhs reconquered the Punjab and restored the temple and tank. Under their greatest secular leader, Maharaja Ranjit Singh, the temple was rebuilt in 1764. In 1830 he donated 100 kg (220 lbs) of gold which was applied to the copper sheets on the roof and much of the exterior of the building, giving rise to the name the 'Golden Temple'.

Now Punjab's second largest town, Amritsar was a traditional junction of trade routes. The different peoples, Yarkandis, Turkomans, Kashmiris, Tibetans and Iranians indicate its connections with the Old Silk Road.

Worship

Singing is central to Sikh worship, and the 24-hour chanting at the Golden Temple adds greatly to the reverential atmosphere. After building the temple, Guru Arjan Dev compiled a collection of hymns of the great medieval saints and this became the *Adi Granth* (Original Holy book). It was installed in the temple as the focus of devotion and teaching. Guru Gobind Singh, the 10th and last Guru (1675-1708) revised the book and also refused to name a successor saying that the book itself would be the Sikh Guru. It thus became known as the *Guru Granth Sahib* (The Holy Book as Guru).

Tip...
Morning prayers at sunrise are beautiful.

The temple compound

Entering the temple compound through the main entrance or clock tower you see the **Harmandir** (the Golden Temple itself, also spelt Harimandir, and known by Hindus as the Durbar Sahib) beautifully reflected in the stunning expanse of water that surrounds it. Each morning (0400 summer, 0500 winter) the *Guru Granth Sahib* is brought in a vivid procession from the **Akal Takht** at the west end to the Harmandir, to be returned at night (2200 summer, 2100 winter). The former represents temporal power, the latter spiritual – and so they do not quite face each other. Some like to attend **Palki Sahib** (night ceremony).

All pilgrims walk clockwise round the tank, stopping at shrines and bathing in the tank on the way round to the Harmandir itself. The tank is surrounded by an 8-m-wide white marble pavement, banded with black and brown Jaipur marble.

East end

To the left of the entrance steps are the bathing ghats and an area screened off from public view for women to dip. Also on this side are the **68 Holy Places** representing 68 Hindu pilgrimage sites as referenced in Guru Nanak's Japji Sahib. When the tank was built, Guru Arjan Dev told his followers that rather than visit all the orthodox Hindu places of pilgrimage, they should just bathe here, thus acquiring equivalent merit.

A shrine contains a copy of the **Guru Granth Sahib**. Here and at other booths round the tank the Holy Book is read for devotees. Sikhs can arrange with the temple authorities to have the book read in their name in exchange for a donation. The *granthi* (reader) is a temple employee and a standard reading lasts for three hours, while a complete reading takes 48 hours. The tree in the centre at the east end of the tank is popularly associated with a healing miracle.

Dining Hall, Kitchen, Assembly Hall and Guesthouses

The surrounding *bunghas* (white arcade of buildings), are hostels for visitors. Through the archway a path leads to the **Guru Ram Das Langar** (kitchen and dining hall) immediately on the left, while two tall octagonal minarets, the 18th-century **Ramgarhia Minars**, provide a vantage point over the temple and inner city. At the far end of the path are a series of guesthouses including **Guru Ram Das Sarai**, where pilgrims can stay free for up to three nights.

Sikhs have a community kitchen where all temple visitors, regardless of their religious belief, can eat together. The third Guru, Guru Amar Das (1552-1574), abolished the custom of eating only with others of the same caste. He even refused to bless the Mughal Emperor Akbar unless he was prepared to eat with everyone else who was present. *Seva* (voluntary service), which continues to be a feature of modern Sikhism, extends to the kitchen staff and workers; visitors are also welcome to lend a hand. The Amritsar kitchen may feed up to 10,000 people a day, with 3000 at a sitting and up to 1 Lakh (100,000) visitors at the weekends. It is free of charge and vegetarian, though Sikhs are not banned from eating meat. Lunch is 1100-1500 and dinner 1900 onwards.

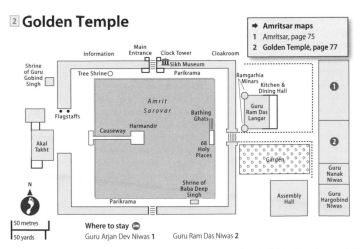

2 Golden Temple

→ Amritsar maps
1 Amritsar, page 75
2 Golden Temple, page 77

Where to stay
Guru Arjan Dev Niwas **1**   Guru Ram Das Niwas **2**

BACKGROUND
Jallianwala Bagh Massacre

Relations with the British had soured in 1919. *Hartals* (general strikes) became a common form of demonstration. The Punjab, which had supplied 60% of Indian troops committed to the First World War, was one of the hardest hit economically in 1918 and tension was high. The lieutenant governor of the province decided on a 'fist force' to repulse the essentially non-violent but vigorous demonstrations. Some looting occurred in Amritsar and the British called in reinforcements. These arrived under the command of General Dyer.

Dyer banned all meetings but people were reported to be gathering on Sunday 13 April 1919 as pilgrims poured into Amritsar to celebrate Baisakhi, the Sikh New Year and the anniversary of the founding of the *khalsa* in 1699. That afternoon thousands were crammed into Jallianwala Bagh, a piece of waste ground popular with travellers, surrounded on all sides by high walls with only a narrow alley for access. Dyer personally led some troops to the place, gave the crowd no warning and ordered his men to open fire leaving 379 dead and 1200 wounded. Other brutal acts followed.

The massacre was hushed up and the British government in London was only aware of it six months later at which time the Hunter Committee was set up to investigate the incident. It did not accept Dyer's excuse that he acted as he did in order to prevent another insurrection on the scale of the Mutiny of 1857. He was asked to resign and returned to England where he died in 1927. However, he was not universally condemned. A debate in the House of Lords produced a majority of 126 to 86 in his favour and the *Morning Post* newspaper launched a fund for 'The Man who Saved India'. More than £26,000 was raised to comfort the dying general.

India was outraged by Dyer's massacre. Gandhi, who had called the nationwide *hartal* in March, started the Non Co-operation Movement, which was to be a vital feature of the struggle for Independence. This was not the end of the affair. O'Dwyer, the governor of the province, was shot dead at a meeting in Caxton Hall, London, by a survivor of Jallianwala Bagh who was hanged for the offence. For a modern take on the whole story, check out the Bollywood movie *Rang de Basanti*.

Next to the Guru Amar Das Langar is the **residence of Baba Kharak Singh** who is hailed by Sikhs as a saint. His followers are distinguished by their orange turbans while temple employees and members of the militant Akali sect wear blue or black turbans.

Returning to the temple tank, the **shrine** on the south side is to Baba Deep Singh. When Ahmad Shah Durrani attacked Amritsar in 1758, Baba Deep Singh was copying out the *Guru Granth Sahib*. He went out to fight with his followers, vowing to defend the temple with his life. He was mortally wounded, 6 km from town; some say that his head was hacked from his body. Grimly determined and holding his head on with one hand he fought on. On his way back to the temple he died on this spot. The story is recounted in the picture behind glass.

West end

The complex to the west has the Akal Takht, the flagstaffs, and the Shrine of Guru Gobind Singh. The **flagstaffs** symbolize religion and politics, in the Sikh case intertwined. They are joined in the middle by the emblem of the Sikh nation, the two swords of Hargobind, representing spiritual and temporal authority. The circle is inscribed with the Sikh rallying call *Ek Onkar* (God is One).

Started when Arjan Dev was Guru (1581-1605), and completed by Guru Hargobind in 1609, the **Akal Takht** is the seat of the Sikhs' religious committee. It is largely a mixture of 18th- and early 19th-century building, the upper storeys being the work of Ranjit Singh. It has a first-floor room with a low balcony which houses a gilt-covered ark, central to the initiation of new members of the Khalsa brotherhood.

To the side of the flagstaffs is a **shrine** dedicated to the 10th and last guru, Gobind Singh (Guru 1675-1708). In front of the entrance to the temple causeway is a square, a gathering place for visitors.

Sometimes you may see Nihang (meaning 'crocodile') Sikhs, followers of the militant Guru Gobind Singh, dressed in blue and armed with swords, lances and curved daggers.

At the centre of the tank stands the most holy of all Sikh shrines, the **Harmandir** (The Golden Temple). Worshippers obtain the sweet *prasad* before crossing the causeway to the temple where they make their offering. The 60-m-long bridge, usually crowded with jostling worshippers, is built out of white marble like the lower floor of the temple. The rest of the temple is covered in copper gilt. On the doorways verses from the *Guru Granth Sahib* are inscribed in Gurumukhi script while rich floral paintings decorate the walls and excellent silver work marks the doors. The roof has the modified onion-shaped dome, characteristic of Sikh temples, but in this case it is covered in the gold that Ranjit Singh added for embellishment.

The ground floor of the three-storey temple contains the Holy Book placed on a platform under a jewel-encrusted canopy. *Guru Granth Sahib* contains approximately 3500 hymns. Professional singers and musicians sing verses from the book continuously from 0400-2200 in the summer and 0500-2130 in winter. An excited crowd of worshippers attempts to touch the serpent horn. Each evening the holy book is taken ceremonially to the Akal Takht and brought back the next morning; visitors are welcome. The palanquin used for this, set with emeralds, rubies and diamonds with silver poles and a golden canopy, can be seen in the treasury on the first floor of the entrance to the temple. Throughout the day, pilgrims place offerings of flowers or money around the book. There is no ritual in the worship or pressure from temple officials to donate money. The marble walls are decorated with mirror-work, gold leaf and designs of birds, animals and flowers in semi-precious stones in the Mughal style.

On the first floor is a balcony on which three respected Sikhs always perform the **Akhand Path** (Unbroken Reading). In order to preserve unity and maintain continuity, there must always be someone practising devotions. The top floor is where the gurus used to sit and here again someone performs the *Akhand Path*; this is the quietest part of the building and affords a good view over the rest of the complex.

On the edge of the tank just west of the entrance is the **Tree Shrine**, a gnarled, 450-year-old *jubi* tree, reputed to have been the favourite resting place of the first chief priest of the temple. Women tie strings to the ingeniously supported branches, hoping to be blessed with a son by the primaeval fertility spirits that choose such places as their home. It is also a favourite spot to arrange and sanctify marriages, despite the protests of the temple authorities. The **Sikh Museum** ① *at the main entrance to the temple (just before steps leading down to the parikrama)*, 0700-1830, free, is somewhat martial, reflecting the struggles against the Mughals, the British and the Indian Army. The **Sikh Library** ① *in the Guru Nanak Building, Mon-Sat 0930-1630*, has a good selection of books in English as well as current national newspapers.

Amritsar town

Jallianwala Bagh, noted for the most notorious massacre under British rule (see box, page 78), is 400 m north of the Golden Temple. Today the gardens are a pleasant enclosed park. They are entered by a narrow path between the houses, opening out over lawns. A **memorial plaque** recounts the history at the entrance, and a large memorial dominates the east end of the garden. There is an interesting museum. On the north side is a well in which many who tried to escape the bullets were drowned, and remnants of walls have been preserved to show the bullet holes.

The old town has a number of mosques and Hindu temples – the **Durgiana Temple** (16th century), and the new **Mata Lal Devi Temple**, which imitates the difficult access to the famous Himalayan Mata Vaishno Devi Cave Temple of Katra by requiring the worshipper to wade awkwardly through water and crawl through womb-like tunnels is well worth a visit. The whole temple area is Disneyesque with plastic grottoes and statues. Women who wish to have children come here to pray, there is community food and a charity hospital run from the temple's trust. It's a very popular and lively temple, and definitely worth a visit. Northeast of the railway station are the **Ram Bagh gardens**, the Mall and Lawrence Road shopping areas.

Trips from Amritsar

Wagah The changing of the guards and the ceremonial lowering of the flags ceremony at sundown on the border with Pakistan, carried out with great pomp and rivalry, are quite a spectacle. There is much synchronized foot stamping, gate slamming and displays of scorn by colourful soldiers! It is the ministry of funny walks. New viewing galleries have been built but crowds still clamour to get the best view. Women are allowed to get to the front, and there is a VIP section (open to foreign visitors) next to the gate. It is best to get there near closing time though photography is difficult with the setting sun.

Goindwal and Tarn Taran On the way from Amritsar to Jalandar, there are important *gurudwaras* where Sikhs on pilgrimage traditionally stop. There are separate bathing places for men and women at Goindwal, with a small market place outside the temple. The *gurudwara* at Taran Tarn is surrounded by a busy bazar. The *gurudwara* itself is very beautiful, with a very large water tank and cloisters providing welcome shade.

Tourist information

Tourist office
Opposite the railway station, T07837-613 500.
There is another branch outside the Golden
Temple (T07837-613200).

Where to stay

More chain hotels are opening up
in Amritsar.

$$$$ Hyatt
Next to Alpha One Mall, GT Rd,
T0183-287 1234, www.hyatt.com.
Formerly **Ista** hotel, this is a beautiful
boutique hotel. There is a stunning spa
with all the usual ayurvedic fare, but also
rose quartz and amethyst facials.

$$$$-$$$ Ranjit's Svaasa
47-A The Mall Rd, T0183-256 6618,
www.welcomheritage hotels.in.
Ramada hotel. Tastefully restored rooms
with huge windows in a 250-year-old red-
brick manor surrounded by palms and
lawns, elegant service, great food, beautiful
Spa Pavilion offering Ayurvedic and
international treatments. Recommended.

$$$-$$ Hotel Le Golden
Clock tower extension, outside Golden
Temple complex, T0183-255 6949,
www.hotellegolden.com.
Modern rooms close to the temple, with
views of Akal Takht. The rooftop restaurant
The Glass has views of Siri Harmandir Sahib.

$$ Grand
Queens Rd, opposite the train station,
T0183-256 2424, www.hotelgrand.in.
32 modern but characterful rooms, some
a/c, set around an attractive garden. There's
a popular restaurant and appealing bar with
Kingfisher on draught and good food. Very
friendly management.

$ Grace
35 Braham Buta Market, close to Golden
Temple, T0183-255 9355.
Good range of rooms, friendly management.

$ Lucky
Mahna Singh Rd, near Golden Temple and
Jallianwala Bagh, T0183-254 2175.
Basic rooms, some with a/c. Good value.

$ Rest Houses
In/near the Golden Temple, eg Guru Ram
Das Niwas and for foreigners especially
Guru Gobind Singh Niwas.
Some free (up to 3 nights), very simple food;
please leave a donation. Tobacco, alcohol
and drugs are prohibited. They can be noisy
sometimes because people stay in the
courtyard, but it's an eye-opening experience.

Restaurants

Eating with pilgrims in the *langar* (Golden
Temple community kitchen) can be a
great experience. Remember to hold
out both hands (palms upwards) when
receiving food. The corner of the Mall
and Malaviya Rd comes alive with
ice cream and fast-food stalls in the
evening. *Dhabas* near the station and
temple sell local *daal, saag paneer*
and mouthwatering stuffed *parathas*.

$$$ The Glass
At Le Golden Hotel close to Golden Temple.
Glass rooftop restaurant serves up range
of foods and great views of the temple.

$$ Crystal
Queens Rd, T0183-222 5555.
Good international food, excellent service,
pleasant ambience, huge portions. There
is **Crystal** on the ground floor proclaiming
that there is only 1 branch. And there is
Crystal on the 2nd floor proclaiming the
same thing – the 2 brothers have fallen
out and both refuse to change the name.

$$ Punjabi Rasoi
Near Jallianwala Bagh.
The best option near the Golden Temple.
Very good *thalis*, South Indian food and
traditional Punjabi fare. Internet café
upstairs too. Recommended.

$ Kesar da Dhaba
Passian Darwaza, near Durgiana Temple.
Serves extremely popular sweet *phirni* in
small earthenware bowls. Also Punjabi *thalis*.

Festivals

The birth anniversaries of the 10 gurus are
observed as holy days and those of Guru
Gobind Singh (Dec/Jan) and Guru Nanak
in Nov, which is also a National Holiday, are
celebrated as festivals with *Akhand Path*
and processions.

Apr Baisakhi, for Sikhs, the Hindu New
Year marks the day in 1699 Guru Gobind
Singh organized the Sikhs into the Khalsa,
see page 73. The vigorous *bhangra* dance
is a common sight in the villages and falls
on 13 or 14 Apr.

Oct/Nov Diwali Illumination of the Golden
Temple, fireworks.

What to do

Time Travels, *14 Kapoor Plaza, Crystal Sq,
T0183-240 0131, www.travelamritsar.com.*
Organizes homestays, tours to Dharamshala,
Manali, Shimla, etc, local villages, as well
as to important Gurudwaras in the state.
Very efficient, helpful. Recommended.

Transport

Air Raja Sansi Airport – taxi (Rs 550)
or auto-rickshaw (Rs 200) to town.

Domestic flights Daily flights to
New Delhi with **Air India**, T0183-220 4012,
Jet Airways, T0183-3939 3333.

International flights Weekly flights to/
from **London** and **Birmingham** on Air India.
Jet Airways, both via Delhi.

Bicycle hire A bicycle is worthwhile here;
available for hire from Hide Market.

Bus Daily services to **Delhi** (tiring
10 hrs); **Dharamshala** (7 hrs); **Dalhousie**
(8 hrs), **Jammu** (5 hrs); **Pathankot** (3 hrs);
Chandigarh (5 hrs); **Shimla** 0530 and
0730, 10 hrs. **Link Travels** and other private
operators leave for Delhi from outside railway
station, 2200; for **Jammu** and **Chandigarh**
from Hall Gate. Cross-border bus service
to **Lahore** (Tue, Wed, Fri and Sat). Contact
International Bus Terminal, T0183-255 1734.
Advance booking is necessary.

Rickshaw Auto-rickshaw/*tonga*: full day,
Rs 600, half day Rs 400.

Taxi Non-a/c car from **Time Travels** near
Crystal restaurant, Queens Rd, T0183-240
0131/4, www.travelamritsar.com, and **Link
Travels**, outside Golden Temple Clock Tower
Car Park: full day, Rs 1200, half day Rs 800,
Wagah Rs 900. To **Delhi** from Rs 7500,
Dharamshala Rs 4000.

Train Enquiries T131. There is a free shuttle
bus from the station to the Golden Temple.
Computerized reservations in the Golden
Temple Complex (far right of the office),
open until 2000 on weekdays. **New Delhi**:
Amritsar Shatabdi Exp 12014 (early morning),
6¼ hrs; *Shan-e-Punjab Exp 12498*, 8 hrs (HN).
Pathankot (for **Kangra** and **Dharamsala**);
Jammu Tawi Exp 18101/18601, 2¾ hrs,
continues to Jammu, 6 hrs.

From Pathankot, you can continue onto
Kangra for Dharamsala on the spectacular
narrow-gauge Kangra Valley Railway, built in
1928, which runs to **Jogindernagar**, 56 km
northwest of Mandi in HP or you can get a
taxi direct to Dharamsala and **McLeodganj**.

Southern
Himachal

Southern Himachal offers an intriguing mix of experiences. Shimla's colonial past, with its Little England architecture and anachronistic air, seems to be fighting for survival amidst the modern-day bustle of Himachal's capital city. The area around Shimla offers stunning views of the foothills of the Himalaya and plenty of attractive places to stay nestled amongst the cool pine forests. This area is also the gateway to the altogether more rugged landscapes of Kinnaur, a world far less affected by the advance of time.

Shimla

memories of British India haunt the state capital

Once a charming hill station and the summer capital of the British, Shimla (population 150,000, altitude 2213 m) now has an air of decay hanging over its many Raj buildings, strung out for 3 km along a ridge. Below them a maze of narrow streets, bazars and shabby 'local' houses with corrugated-iron roofs cling to the hillside. Some find it delightfully quaint and less spoilt than other hill stations. There are some lovely walks with magnificent pines and cedars.

Sights
Shimla is strung out on a long crescent-shaped ridge that connects a number of hilltops from which there are good views of the snow-capped peaks to the north: Jakhu (2453 m), Prospect Hill (2176 m), Observatory Hill (2148 m), Elysium Hill (2255 m) and Summer Hill (2103 m). For the British, the only way of beating the hot weather on the plains in May and June was to move to hill stations, which they endowed with mock-Tudor houses, churches, clubs, parks with bandstands of English county towns, and a main street invariably called The Mall.

Christ Church (1844), on the open area of The Ridge, dominates the eastern end of town. Consecrated in 1857, a clock and porch were added later. The original chancel window, designed by Lockwood Kipling, Rudyard's father, is no longer there. The mock Tudor **library** building (circa 1910) is next door. The Mall joins The Ridge at Kipling's '**Scandal Point**', where today groups gather to exchange gossip. Originally the name referred to the stir caused by the supposed 'elopement' of a lady from the Viceregal

Essential Shimla

Finding your feet

Despite the romance of the narrow-gauge railway from Kalka, see page 87, most arrive in Shimla by bus or taxi as it is so much quicker. The bus stand and the station are on Cart Road, where porters and hotel touts jostle to take your luggage up the steep hill; possibly the best few rupees you will ever spend. If you are staying on the western side of town it is worth getting off the bus at the railway station. Buses from the east, including Rampur and Kinnaur, stop at the Rivoli Bus Stand. Shimla (Jabbarhatti) airport has a coach (Rs 50) in season, and taxis (Rs 400-500) for transfer.

Getting around

The Mall can only be seen on foot; it takes about half an hour to walk from the Viceroy's Lodge to Christ Church. The main traffic artery is Cart Road, which continues past the station to the main bus stand, taxi rank and the two-stage lift which goes to The Mall above. The Victory Tunnel cuts through from Cart Road to the north side of the hill. A new ropeway (cable car system) to avoid congestion is in the works. See Transport, page 87.

When to go

October and November are very pleasant, with warm days and cool nights. December to February is cold and there are snowfalls. March and April are changeable; storms are not infrequent and the air can feel very chilly. Avoid May and June, the height of the Indian tourist season prior to the monsoon.

Lodge and a dashing Patiala prince after they arranged a rendezvous here.

The **Gaiety Theatre** (1887) and the **Town Hall** (circa 1910) are reminiscent of the arts and crafts style, as well as the timbered **General Post Office** (1886). Beyond, to the west, is the **Grand Hotel**. Further down you pass the sinister-looking **Gorton Castle**, designed by Sir Samuel Swinton Jacob, which was once the Civil Secretariat. A road to the left leads to the railway station, while one to the right goes to Annandale, the racecourse and cricket ground. The Mall leads to the rebuilt **Cecil Hotel**.

On Observatory Hill, the **Viceregal Lodge** (1888) is the most splendid of Shimla's surviving Raj-era buildings, built for Lord Dufferin in the Elizabethan style. Now the **Rashtrapati Niwas** ① *1000-1630, Rs 10 including a brief tour*, it stands in large grounds with good views of the mountains. Reminders of its British origins include a gatehouse, a chapel and the meticulously polished brass fire hydrants imported from Manchester. Inside, you can visit the main reception rooms and the library which are lined from floor to ceiling with impressive teak panelling. It is a long up the hill walk from the gate. It is now the Indian Institute of Advanced Study and there is a café on-site.

Himachal State Museum ① *near Chaura Maidan, www.himachalstatemuseum.in, Tue-Sun 1000-1330, 1400-1700, Rs 100*, is a 30-minute walk west from the GPO along The Mall; then it's a short climb from the Harsha Hotel. Small, with a good sculpture collection and miniatures from the Kangra School, it also houses contemporary art including work by Nicholas Roerich, costumes, jewellery, bronzes and textiles (everything is well labelled).

Walks

Jakhu Temple on a hill with excellent views (2455 m), dedicated to Hanuman the monkey god, is 2 km from Christ Church. Walking sticks (handy for warding off monkeys, which can be vicious – keep all food out of sight) are available at *chai* shops at the start of the ascent.

The Glen (1830 m), to the northwest, is a 4-km walk from the centre past the Cecil Hotel. Summer Hill (1983 m), a pleasant 'suburb' 5 km from town, is a stop on the Shimla–Kalka railway. Chadwick Falls (1586 m), 3 km further, drops 67 m during the monsoon season.

Prospect Hill (2175 m) is 5 km from The Ridge and a 20-minute walk from Boileauganj to the west. Tara Devi (1851 m), with a hilltop temple, 11 km southwest from the railway station, can also be reached by car or train.

Listings Shimla *maps p86 and p88*

Tourist information

Himachal Pradesh Tourism Development Corportation (HPTDC)
The Mall, T0177-265 2561, www.hptdc.nic.in. Open 0900-1800, in season 0900-1900; also at Cart Rd, near Victory Tunnel, T0177-265 4589, open 1000-1700.
Very informative and helpful. For details of their tours, see What to do, below.

Where to stay

Prices soar May-Jun when modest rooms can be difficult to find especially after midday, so book ahead. Some places close off-season; those that remain open may offer discounts of 30-50%. From the railway or bus station it is a stiff climb up to hotels on or near the Ridge. Porters are available (Rs 20 per heavy bag).

$$$$ The Oberoi Cecil
Chaura Maidan (qulet end of The Mall), T0177-280 4848, www.oberoihotels.com.
A beautifully renovated hotel, with 79 sumptuous rooms, stylishly furnished, and superb views. Colonial grandeur on the edge of town. There's a good restaurant and a special ultra-modern pool. Rates are full board. Recommended.

$$$$-$$$ Woodville Palace (Heritage)
Raj Bhavan Rd, The Mall, T0177-262 3919, www.woodvillepalacehotel.com.
A spacious hotel, one of the quietest in town, set in large grounds. It has 30 rooms of variable quality, including some good suites with period furniture (freezing in

winter). The dining hall is worth visiting for its eclectic mixture of portraits, weapons and hunting trophies (non-residents need to give advance notice), owned by the Raja of Jubbal's family and featured in *Jewel in the Crown*.

$$$ Combermere
2 entrances, next to the lift at top and bottom, T0177-265 1246, www.hotelcombermere.com.
In a good central location, this place has 40 decent rooms (including penthouses) on 6 levels (partly served by lift). Staff are friendly, efficient and very helpful. There's a pleasant terrace café and bar, games room and central heating/a/c; the super deluxe rooms worth spending a little extra on.

$$ Aapo Aap Homestay
Panthaghati Bazar, Sargheen Chowk, 10 km outside Shimla, T(0)8091-208353, www.aapoaapshimla.com.
In a beautiful location outside of Shimla with stunning views, this homestay has 3 lovely guest rooms. There is also Wi-Fi and a meditation room. Recommended.

$$ Dalziel
The Mall, above station, T0177-280 6725, www.dalzielhotel.com.
30 clean enough, comfy, creaky valley-facing rooms with bath (hot water) in a heritage building. Indian meals are served; prices depend on the size of TV.

$$-$ Mayur
Above Christ Church, T0177-265 2393, www.hotelmayur.com.
This modern, clean hotel is in a great central location. It has 30 rooms in 1970s style, some

with mountain views, some with tub. Good restaurant, but check the bill.

$$-$ Woodland
Daisy Bank, The Ridge, T(0)94180-21100, www.hotelwoodlandshimla.com.
An off-season bargain, this hotel has 21 rooms, some wood-panelled, some with great views, all with bath, although cleanliness varies. Avoid the noisy downstairs rooms near reception. Friendly staff, room service and safe luggage storage.

Restaurants

$$ Alfa's
The Mall.
Modern interior, range of continental dishes in addition to good *thalis*, courteous service.

$$ Café Sol
Hotel Combermere, see Where to stay, above.
Set in an airy glass building, this café serves decent Western and Indian foods.

$$ Wake & Bake
The Mall.
Up some rickety stairs, you will find good coffee, baked goods and international food; a cute place. There is an internet café below.

$ Guptajee's Vaishnav Bhojanalaya
62 Middle Bazar.
First-class Indian vegetarian fare including tasty stuffed tomatoes and great *thali*. Recommended.

$ Sagar Ratna
6/1 The Mall, upstairs, T0177-280 0526.
Good vegetarian South Indian food, including *dosas* and *idlis*; all good value.

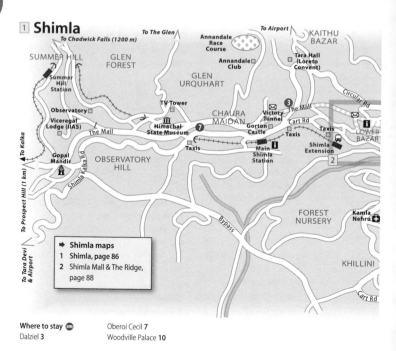

1 Shimla

To The Glen
To Chadwick Falls (1200 m)
To Airport
KAITHU BAZAR
Annandale Race Course
SUMMER HILL
GLEN FOREST
Annandale Club
Tara Hall (Loreto Convent)
Summer Hill Station
GLEN URQUHART
TV Tower
Circular Rd
Observatory
CHAURA MAIDAN
Victory Tunnel
The Mall
Viceregal Lodge (IIAS)
Himachal State Museum
Gorton Castle
Cart Rd
Taxis
LOWER BAZAR
The Mall
To Kalka
Taxis
Shimla Extension
Gopal Mandir
OBSERVATORY HILL
Shimla Kalka Rd
Taxis
Main Shimla Station
To Prospect Hill (1 km)
FOREST NURSERY
Kamla Nehru
Bypass
To Tara Devi & Airport
KHILLINI
Cart Rd

➡ Shimla maps
1 Shimla, page 86
2 Shimla Mall & The Ridge, page 88

Where to stay
Dalziel 3
Oberoi Cecil 7
Woodville Palace 10

Festivals

May-Jun Summer Festival includes cultural programmes from Himachal and neighbouring states, and art and handicrafts exhibitions.
25 Dec An **ice skating carnival** is held on Christmas Day.

What to do

Ice skating
Skating rink: below Rivoli, winter only, Rs 50 to skate all day to loud Indian film hits.

Tour operators
HPTDC, *see under Tourist information, above.* HPTDC organize well-run tours during the season, usually 1000-1700. All start from Rivoli, enquire when booking for other pick-up points. Return drop at Lift or Victory Tunnel. 2 tours visit Kufri, Chini Bungalow and Nature Park; 1 returns to Shimla via Fagu, Naldehra and Mashobra, the other by Chail and Kairighat. A further tour visits Fagu, Theog, Matiana and Narkanda. Book in advance at the HPTDC office on The Mall, where staff are very friendly and helpful.

Transport

Air Shimla (Jabbarhatti) airport (23 km from town) had flights with Kingfisher until their demise, and at the time of writing no other airline was operating flights.

Local bus From Cart Rd. Lift: 2-stage lift from the Taxi Stand on Cart Rd and near **Hotel Samrat** on The Mall, takes passengers to and from The Mall, 0800-2200. Porters at bus stand and upper lift station will ask anything from Rs 10 to Rs 50 per bag; lower prices mean hotel commission.

Long-distance bus From the main bus stand, Cart Rd, T01772-265 8765. Buy tickets from counter before boarding bus (signs are in Hindi so ask for help) some long-distance buses can be reserved in advance: HPTDC coaches during the season are good value and reliable. **Kalka**, 3 hrs quicker than the train but requires a strong stomach; **Chandigarh**, 4 hrs **Dehra Dun**, 9 hrs; **Delhi**, 10-12 hrs; overnight to **Dharamshala**, 10 hrs. **Manali**, departs outside the 'Tunnel', 8-10 hrs, tickets from main bus stand. HPTDC deluxe buses between Shimla and Delhi in the summer, 9 hrs.

From **Rivoli Bus Stand** (Lakkar Bazar): frequent buses to **Kufri**, **Rampur**, hourly from 0530, 8 hrs, and **Chitkul**, 2 daily; **Jeori** for **Sarahan** (8 hrs).

Car hire HPTDC (see under Tourist information, above), has a/c cars. **Shimla Taxis**, T(0)9418-082385, www.shimlataxis.in, have a wide range of cars.

Taxi Local taxis have fixed fares and run from near the lift on Cart Rd, T01772-657645. Long-distance taxis run from Union Stands near the lift, T01772-805164, and by the main bus stand on Cart Rd. **Chandigarh**, Rs 2500;

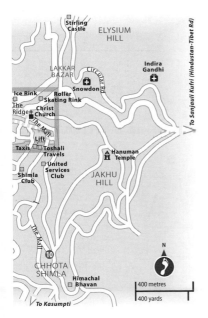

Kalka (90 km), Rs 1600; **Mussoorie**, Rs 5500, 8 hrs, including stops; **Rekong-Peo**, around Rs 7000 (11 hrs).

Train Enquiry T131. Computerized reservations at main station (T01772-652915), 1000-1330, 1400-1700, Sun 1000-1400, and by tourist office on The Mall. The newer extension station, where some trains start and terminate, is just below the main bus stand. Travel to/from Shimla involves a change of gauge to the slow and cramped but extremely picturesque 'toy train' at **Kalka**. To reach Shimla from **Delhi** in a day by train, catch the *Himalayan Queen* or *Shatabdi Exp 12011* leaving New Delhi station at 0740 to arrive in Kalka by 1200 (see below). In the reverse direction, the 1030 train from Shimla gets you to Kalka at 1600 in time to board the Delhi-bound *Himalayan Queen 14096*. Book

tickets for the toy train in advance; the 'Ticket Extension Booth' on Kalka station sells out by 1200 when the *Shatabdi* arrives, and the train often arrives on the Kalka platform already full of locals who board it while it waits in the siding. It's worth paying Rs 150-170 plus a reservation fee of Rs 20 to guarantee a seat on 1st class. **Kalka to Shimla**: *Kalka Shimla Passenger 52457*, 0400, 5½ hrs; *Shivalik Exp Deluxe 52451*, 4¾ hrs (has bigger windows and comfy seats); *Kalka Shimla Express 52453*, 5 hrs; *Himalayan Queen 52455*, 5 hrs. Extra trains in season (1 May-15 Jul; 15 Sep-30 Oct; 15 Dec-1 Jan): You can book a special train carriage which can be attached to regular trains with elegant furnishings and big windows which accommodates 8 people through IRCTC Chandigarh. **Shimla to Kalka**: *Himalayan Queen*, 5½ hrs; *Shivalik Exp Deluxe 52452*, 4¾ hrs.

2 Shimla Mall & The Ridge

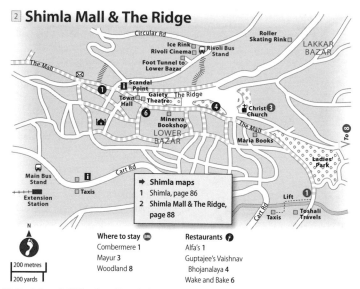

➡ **Shimla maps**
1 Shimla, page 86
2 Shimla Mall & The Ridge, page 88

200 metres
200 yards

Where to stay 🛏
Combermere 1
Mayur 3
Woodland 8

Restaurants 🍴
Alfa's 1
Guptajee's Vaishnav
Bhojanalaya 4
Wake and Bake 6

Kufri

About 16 km from Shimla, at 2500 m, Kufri hosts a winter sports festival in January which includes the **National Snow Statue Competition**. Don't expect European or American resort standards though. There are some attractions around and about the town. At **Danes Folly** (2550 m), 5 km away, is a government-run orchard. A 10-minute walk uphill takes you to a mini zoo of Himalayan wildlife. **Mahasu Peak** (bus, Rs 15) 20 minutes from a path behind the Kufri Resort cottages, offers fabulous mountain views on a clear day and there is a small but interesting temple at the start of the walk. The best time to visit is in January and February.

Chharabra

Chharabra is an enjoyable 3-km forest walk down from Kufri. The Wildflower Hall which once stood here was the residence of **Lord Kitchener**, commander-in-chief of the Indian Army. The original building was replaced; its successor was converted into a hotel which burnt down in 1993. **Oberoi** has opened a new luxury hotel (see Where to stay, below).

Naldera

Off the Hindusthan–Tibet road, 26 km north of Shimla, Naldera has a nine-hole golf course, possibly the oldest in India and one of the highest in the world, and the beautiful Mahung temple. The colourful **Sipi Fair** in June attracts handicraft sellers from surrounding villages.

Chail

In a superb forest setting with fine snow views, 45 km southeast of Shimla (2½ hours by bus), off the NH22, Chail was once the Maharaja of Patiala's summer capital. Built across three hills, it claims to have the country's highest cricket ground at 2444 m, a 2-km walk from the bus stand. The old palace on Rajgarh Hill has been converted to a hotel while the old residency, Snow View, and a Sikh temple stand on the other hills. The **Chail Sanctuary**, once a private hunting reserve, is popular with birders and has a Cheer pheasant-breeding programme. It is an idyllic spot until the weekend when day-trippers descend on the tiny resort.

Kalka

Kalka is the terminus for the **narrow-gauge railway** from Shimla. The Kalka–Shimla line (0.76 m), completed in 1903, runs 97 km from Kalka in the foothills to Shimla at over 2000 m. The magnificent journey takes just over five hours. The steepest gradient is 1:33; there are 107 tunnels covering 8 km and 969 bridges over 3 km. See also Transport, above.

Tragically, there was a derailment in September 2015 where several Britons were killed or injured. Investigations were continuing at the time of writing.

Nalagarh

The area around Nalagarh was once ruled by the Chandela Rajputs. The fort has wonderful views above an estate of forests and orchards and is built on five levels around manicured grassy courts. Originally built in the 15th century; the **Diwan-i-Khas** (1618) is now the Banquet Hall. The present raja has opened his home to guests. You can request the **Nalagarh Fort** hotel pickup from Ropar (20 km) or Kalka (40 km).

Where to stay

Kufri

$$$$ Kufri Holiday Resort
T0177-264 8341, www.kufriholidayresort.com.
30 rooms and 8 modern cottages
(2-3 bedrooms), limited hot water, cold in
winter, but attractive design and setting
with flower-filled gardens, outstanding
views from cottages above and good walks.

Chharabra

$$$$ Wildflower Hall
T0177-264 8585, www.oberoihotels.com.
Standing on the grounds of the former
residence of Lord Kitchener, this place retains
period exterior but has been completely
refurbished inside. 87 sumptuous rooms,
beautifully decorated, mountain views, good
restaurants and lovely gardens surrounded
by deodar forest with beautifully peaceful
walks, plus extensive spa, yoga classes under
pine trees, Ayurvedic treatments.

Naldera

$$$$ The Chalets Naldehra
*Durgapur Village, T0177-274 7715,
www.chaletsnaldehra.com.*
14 alpine-style pine chalets plus restaurant
and a wide range of outdoor activities
including world's highest golf course.

$$$ Koti Resort
T0177-274 0177, www.kotiresort.net.
A beautifully located hotel surrounded
by deodar forest with 40 modern, if
slightly spartan, rooms in. Friendly
manager, very relaxing.

$$-$ Mitwa Cottage
Near Koti Resort, T0177-201 2279.
Sweet little homestay with kitchens and
balconies. Lovely food as well and plenty
of nature walks around. Recommended.

Chail

$$$$-$$$ Toshali Royal View Resort
*Shilon Bagh (5 km outside Chail), T0177-
200 6470, www.toshaliroyalview.com.*
There are 77 modern rooms in this huge
alpine-style lodge, with great views from
dining terrace and friendly staff.

$ Himneel
T01792-248141, www.hptdc.nic.in.
The 16 rooms here are modest but full of
character. The **Kailash** restaurant serves
good-value breakfasts and lunches.

Kalka

If using your own transport, there are many
hotels, guesthouses and *dhabas* along the
Kalka–Shimla road. **Kasauli** is an attractive
hill resort with a distinctly English feel, 16 km
off the main road with a few hotels, notably:

$$$$ Baikunth
*Village Chabbal, near Kasauli, T(0)9857-
166230, www.baikunth.com.*
Red brick building in the hills. Lovely
airy, sunny rooms with all mod cons.
Recommended for its spa.

$$$-$$ Alasia
T01792-272008.
Hugely atmospheric Raj-era hotel with
13 rooms, remarkably authentic English
cuisine and impeccable staff.

Nalagarh

$$$ Nalagarh Fort
T01795-223179, www.nalagarh.com.
Set in rural surroundings, this hotel has
plenty of atmosphere and 15 comfortable
rooms (some suites), with modern baths
and traditional furniture. There's good food
(buffets only), a small pool and tennis. Book
ahead. Recommended.

What to do

Naldera
Golf
There is a 9-hole course in Naldera. Casual members: green fee and equipment, about Rs 100, see page 89.

Transport

Kalka
Bus or taxi Easily reached from **Shimla**, by bus or taxi (Rs 1600), and from **Chandigarh** by taxi (Rs 500).

Train To Delhi: *Shatabdi Exp 12006*, 4 hrs; *Shatabdi Exp 12012*, 4 hrs. All via Chandigarh, 45 mins. For information on the Kalka–Shimla train, see page 88.

Old Hindustan Tibet Road
lush valleys, snow-clad peaks and precipitous gorges

The Old Hindustan Tibet road runs east from Shimla to the Tibetan border, connecting a string of prosperous-looking farms, villages and towns. It passes through terraced slopes covered with orchards before entering the high-altitude deserts of Spiti. As the narrow road winds even deeper towards the Tibetan border its unprotected sides plunge hundreds of metres to the roaring monsoon-swollen River Sutlej below, grasping at huge boulders brought down by thundering landslides into the gloomy gorges. By bus or jeep, this road is not for the faint-hearted. The road may be severely damaged in the rains.

Narkanda
The small market town of Narkanda (altitude 2700 m) occupies a superb position. The town offers a base from which to ski but the skiing does not compare with that found in Western resorts. Enquire at the Marketing Office in Shimla for skiing in winter and the seven-day beginners' course.

Nirath
The road drops sharply through woodland interspersed with apple orchards from Narkanda, down to Kingel from where it zig-zags down to Sainj. The seasonal route is best by 4WD though buses cover this route very carefully. Some 5 km beyond Sainj there are superb views both across the valley, and of a wall of eroded outwash deposits at least 50 m thick. The main road passes through Nirath where there is a **Surya Temple** believed to date from the eighth century which still has some fine carving preserved on the outer walls and has carved wooden panels within. At an altitude of 800-900 m the Sutlej Valley towards Rampur has a subtropical summer climate, with mango trees and bananas replacing apples.

Rampur Bushahr
This is one of Himachal's most important market towns. **Padam Palace** (1920s), opposite the bus stand, once the residence of the raja, has interesting carved wooden panels and wall murals, but is difficult to enter. **Sat Narain Temple** in the main bazar (1926) has a beautiful but decaying façade. **Lavi Fair** (November) draws large crowds of colourful hill people who bring their produce – handicrafts, carpets, rugs, fruit and nuts and animals – to the special market. There are sporting competitions in the day, and dancing and making music around bonfires after dark.

Essential Old Hindustan Tibet Road

Permits

Inner Line Permits, which are needed for travel close to the Tibetan border (essentially the area between Kaza and Jangi), are easy enough to get. Permits are issued free to individuals for seven days from the date of issue (easily renewable for three days at Kaza or Recong Peo). Take your passport, two copies of the details and Indian visa pages, and three passport photos and complete the form from the **Sub-Divisional Magistrate's office (SDM)** in **Shimla**, T0177-265 5988; **Recong Peo**, T01786-222252; or **Kaza**, T01906-222202, where you need the additional 'No Objection' certificate from the chief of police (a mere formality of a stamp and signature). In Recong Peo, the whole process takes about an hour, which may include *chai* or breakfast with the SDM.

Permits are also available (in theory) from the **Resident Comissioner of Himachal Pradesh**, Himachal Bhavan, 27 Sikandra Road, New Delhi, T011-2371 6574, and other magistrates offices. In Shimla, travel agents charge Rs 150.

Permits are checked at Jangi if coming from Shimla and at Sumdo coming from Spiti. Carry about 10 photocopies as some checkpoints demand to keep one.

Tip...
It is virtually impossible to get foreign exchange in this area.

Where to stay

Rules regarding overnight stays have been relaxed considerably; it is now possible to sleep in Puh and Nako. Accommodation is limited to simple rest houses, lodges or tents. In some places enterprising local families are opening their modest homes to paying guests. Local village shops often stock canned food and bottled water.

Rampur to Sarahan

From Rampur the highway enters one of the most exciting (and geologically active) stretches of road in the region. During the rains, the Sutlej River is a surging torrent of muddy water, dropping over 450 m in under 30 km and passing through gorges and deeply incised valleys. Although an ancient trade route, the road is comparatively recent and is constantly being upgraded particularly in connection with the Nathpa-Jhakhri HEP scheme, with a 28-km-long tunnel from **Nathpa**, near Wangtu, to **Jhakhri**, about 10 km beyond Rampur. When completed this will be one of the largest Hydel schemes in the world. The blasting both for the shafts and for road widening has further destabilized the already landslide-prone hillsides and during the rains the road may be blocked. Blockages are usually cleared within hours, though travelling times are wholly unpredictable. You also need a strong stomach, both for the main road and for diversions, especially up the Baspa Valley to Sangla.

Some 9 km west of Jeori the river passes through a dramatic gorge. On the north side of the river isolated tiny pockets of cultivated land cling to the hillside. **Jeori** is the junction for Sarahan, 21 km south, an hour away. There are several provisions stores to pick up the basics here since Sarahan has very limited supplies.

Where to stay

Narkanda

$$$$ Banjara Orchard Retreat
Thanedar Village, 15 km from Narkanda
(80 km from Shimla), T(0)98167 47451,
www.banjaracamps.com.
6 double rooms, 2 suites and 2 lovely log
cabins, set in apple orchards with stunning
views down the Sutlej Valley. Evenings are
spent round the fire under the stars. There's
also trekking and excellent food available.
Recommended.

$$$$ Tethy's Narkanda Resort
T01782-242641.
Comfortable rooms and some swiss cottage
tents with stunning views. They organize
snow skiing, hiking, mountain biking, river
rafting and horse riding. Meals are included.

$$$-$$ The Hatu (HPTDC)
T01782-242430.
Typical government fare, but with great views.

Rampur Bushahr

$$ Bushehar Regency
2 km short of Rampur on NH22,
T01782-234103.
20 well-positioned rooms, some with a/c.
There's also a restaurant, a huge lawn and
a bar nearby.

What to do

Skiing

Early Jan to mid-Mar. Ski courses at Narkanda
organized by **HPTDC**, 7- and 15-day courses,
Jan-Mar, Rs 1700-3000; see page 91.

Transport

Rampur Bushahr

Bus Buses are often late and overcrowded.
To **Chandigarh**, **Delhi**; **Mandi** (9 hrs); **Recong
Peo** (5 hrs) and **Puh**; **Sarahan** (2-3 hrs), better
to change at Jeori; **Shimla**, several (5-6 hrs);
Tapri (and Kalpa) 0545 (3¼ hrs), change at
Karchham for Sangla and Chitkul.

Sarahan

An important market for traders of neighbouring regions, Sarahan (population
1200, altitude 2165 m) is an attractive town, surrounded by high peaks. The bazar
is interesting: friendly villagers greet travellers, and shops sell flowers, bright red
and gold scarves and other offerings for worshippers among local produce, fancy
goods, clothes and jewellery. It is also a stop on the trekkers' route.

Bhimakali Temple

Sarahan was the old capital of the local Rampur Bushahr rulers and has a palace complex
containing the strikingly carved wood-bonded Bhimakali Temple (rebuilt circa 1927), in
a mixture of Hindu and Buddhist styles.
The two temples stand on a slope among
apple and apricot orchards behind the
bazar. The Bhimakali is dedicated to Durga
as the destroyer of the *asuras* (demons) and
has a Brahmin priest in attendance. Plan
for an early morning visit to the temple to
see morning prayers; evening prayers are

Tip...
A pilgrimage route encircles Shrikhand
Mahadev peak (5227 m), which takes
pilgrims seven days to go round. On a
clear day you get fantastic panoramic
views of the snow-covered peaks.

around 1900. Leave shoes and leather objects with the attendant and wear the saffron cap offered to you before entering. You may only photograph the outside of the temples. It is worth climbing around the back of the complex for a picturesque view.

According to some sources the ancient temple on the right (closed for safety reasons) is many centuries old. Built in traditional timber-bonded style it has whitewashed dry stone and rubble masonry alternating with horizontal deodar or spruce beams to withstand earthquakes. The upper floors have balconies and windows with superb ornamental woodcarving; the silver repoussée-work doors are also impressive. The first floor has a 200-year-old gold image of goddess Bhimkali which is actively worshipped only during the **Dasara festival** when animals and birds are sacrificed in the courtyard, while on the second floor daily early-morning *puja* is carried out to a second image. The sacrificial altar and the old well are in the courtyard with three other shrines. The palace of the Rampur rajas behind the temple has a drawing room with ornate furniture and a painted ceiling; the caretaker may let you in.

Listings Sarahan

Where to stay

$$-$ Srikhand (HPTDC)
T01782-274234, www.hptdc.nic.in.
Superb hilltop site, overlooking the Sutlej Valley, Srikhand peak and beyond. The 19 rooms have bath and hot water (3 are large with a balcony, 8 are smaller with views, and the 4 in the annexe are cheaper), dorm (Rs 75), 2-bedroom royal cottage, restaurant but limited menu. It's also very close to the stunning temple.

$ Bhimakali Temple
You can stay in the temple itself. Rooms are very basic with clean bathrooms and shared balconies; it's highly atmospheric.

Transport

Bus Daily buses between **Shimla** (**Rivoli Bus Stand**) and **Jeori** on the Highway (6 hrs), quicker by car. Local buses between Jeori and the army cantonment below Sarahan.

Kinnaur
& Spiti

The regions of Kinnaur and Spiti lie in the rain shadow of the outer Himalayan ranges. The climate in Spiti is much drier than in the Kullu Valley and is similar to that of Ladakh. The temperatures are more extreme both in summer and winter and most of the landscape is barren and bleak. The wind can be bitingly cold even when the sun is hot. The annual rainfall is very low so cultivation is restricted to the ribbons of land that fringe rivers with irrigation potential. The crops include potatoes, wheat, barley and millet. The people are of Mongol origin and almost everyone follows a Tibetan form of Buddhism.

Kinnaur and Spiti are accessible only in the summer when the snow melts on the higher passes, meaning they can be crossed by road. They can be seen by following a circular route, first along the Old Hindustan Tibet Road by the Sutlej River, then crossing into the wild Spiti Valley, which has the evocative Tibetan Buddhist sites of Tabo and Kaza set against the backdrop of a rugged mountain landscape. The road continues round to the Rohtang Pass and Manali, or on up to Ladakh. It's also worth making a side trip up the Baspa Valley via Sangla to Chitkul for its views and landscapes, villages, pagodas and culture.

Along the Sutlej

An exciting mountain road runs through cliffside cuttings along the south bank of the Sutlej, which is frequently blocked by rockfalls and landslides during the monsoons. At **Choling** the Sutlej roars through a narrow gorge, and at **Wangtu** the road re-crosses the river where vehicle details are checked. Immediately after crossing the Wangtu bridge a narrow side road goes to **Kafnoo village** (2427 m), in the Bhabha Valley (a camping site and the start for an attractive 10-day trek to the Pin Valley). From Wangtu the road route runs to **Tapri** (1870 m) and **Karchham** (1899 m) both of which have hot springs. Here the Baspa River joins the Sutlej from the south.

Kinnaur & Spiti

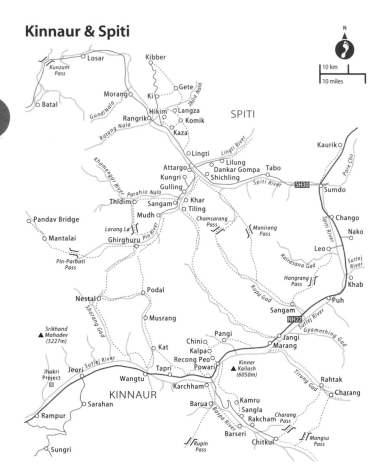

Baspa Valley

A hair-raising excursion by a precipitous winding rough road leads 16 km up the Baspa Valley to Sangla; buses take approximately 1½ hours. The valley carries the marks of a succession of glacial events which have shaped it, although the glaciers which formed the valley have now retreated to the high slopes above Chitkul at over 4500 m. Recently the valley has been terribly scarred by the Baspa Hydroelectric Project, with blasting, dust and truck logjams commonplace, but persevere and carry on up the valley and the rewards are worth it.

All villages in Baspa are characterized by exaggerated steeply sloping slate roofs, rich wood carving and elaborate pagoda temples. Although Kinner Kailash (sacred to Hindus and Buddhists) is not visible from here, the valley is on the circumambulating Parikrama/Kora route which encircles the massif. Fields of the pink coloured *ogla*, a small flower seed grown specifically in the Baspa Valley for grinding into grain, add a beautiful colouring in the season.

Sangla At 2680 m, is built on the massive buttress of a terminal moraine which marks a major glacial advance of about 50,000 years ago. The Baspa River has cut a deep trench on its south flank. Immediately above is the flat valley floor, formed on the dry bed of a lake which was once dammed behind the moraine. The village has excellent carving and is full of character. No foreign exchange is available but there are telephone facilities. Sangla is famous for its apples, while a saffron farm just north of the village is claimed to be better than that at Pampore in Kashmir.

The old seven-storey **Killa** (Fort) ① *0800-0900, 1800-1900*, where the Kinnaur rajas were once crowned, is 1 km north of new Sangla just before the road enters the village. It was occupied by the local rulers for centuries. It now has a temple to Kamakshi where the idol is from Guwahati, Assam.

Barseri Eight kilometres from Sangla, is situated on an outwash cone which has engulfed part of the Baspa's valley floor. This well-kept 'green village' is happy to show visitors its solar heaters, *chakkis* (water mills) and water-driven prayer wheels. The Buddha Mandir, with *Shakyamuni* and other images and a large prayer wheel, is beautiful inside. Villagers weave shawls and do woodcarving.

The beautifully carved pagoda-style Rakcham temple is dedicated to Shamshir Debta, Devi and Naga, combining Buddhist and Hindu deities. The ibex horns on the roof are ancient male fertility symbols. There is also a pre-Buddhist, animist Bon cho shrine and a Siva temple.

Chitkul Some 18 km from Barseri, at an altitude of 3450 m, is the furthest point foreigners can travel without special permits. With its typical houses, Buddhist temple and a small tower, it is worth the trip. The Kagyupa (Oral Transmission School) has a highly valued, old image of the Shakyamuni Buddha. There are four directional kings on either side of the door as well as a Wheel of Life. You can walk along the Baspa River which has paths on both sides. The rough path along the tributary starting at the bridge across the river, below the bus stand, is very steep in places with loose stones. Do not attempt it alone. A shop sells a few provisions.

Recong Peo and around

Recong Peo, also called 'Peo', at 2290 m, is the District HQ and a busy little market town. The Sub-Divisional Magistrate's office in a three-storey building below the bus stand deals with Inner Line Permits. Inner Line Permits are checked at **Jangi** and travellers without them may not be allowed any further. Contact SDM in Recong Peo a day ahead (see Permits, page 92).

A short walk above the town takes you to the Kalachakra Temple with a large Buddha statue outside and good views of Kinner Kailash. A

Tip...
Most Kinnauri Buddhist temples only accept visitors at around 0700 and 1900. You must wear a hat and a special belt available locally.

shop here sells provisions, medicines and has a telephone, but there's nowhere to change money. **Kothi village**, reached by a path from the Kalachakra Temple, has ancient Hindu temples associated with the Pandavas. One has a tank of sacred fish, 30 minutes' walk from the bazar.

Kalpa (Chini), 12 km from Recong Peo at 2960 m, is reached after a stiff climb. It has an interesting temple complex and Budh mandir and is surrounded by apple, *bemi* (wild apricot) and plum orchards and chilgoza pine forests, with striking views across to Kinner Kailash (6050 m).

A high road from Kalpa/Recong Peo with little traffic passes through Chilgoza pine forests, north to the hamlet of **Pangi**, 10 km away. Pangi is surrounded by apple orchards. The colourful Sheshri Nag temple at the top of the village has an inscription in a strange script above the entrance and standing stones in the courtyard. Apart from two Buddhist temples, the carved pagoda temple to Sheshri's mother encloses a huge boulder representing the Devi. The road then goes over bare and rugged hills beyond to **Morang** which has impressive monasteries with wood carvings and sculptures.

Listings Kinnaur and around *map p96*

Where to stay

Baspa Valley

$$$$ Banjara Camps
Barseri, 8 km beyond Sangla, T(0)9816-881936, www.banjaracamps.com.
Superb riverside site with impressive mountains looming above you. 18 twin-bed rooms and some 4-bed deluxe tents, delicious meals included, hot water bottles in the bed. Friendly staff, mountain biking, trekking and Lahaul, Spiti and Ladakh tours. Buses stop 2 km from the site, where the road drops down to the right. The car park at the foot of the hill is a 500-m walk from camp (a horn will summon porters). Highly recommended.

$$ Hotel River Rupin View
Rakcham Village, 12 km from Sangla, T(0)9816-686789.
Pretty little place well off the beaten track, set in a garden with basic rooms.

$$ Kinner Camp
Barseri, T(0)9769-375993, www.kinnerkamps.com.
Small tents with beds/sleeping bags and shared baths in a superb location. There's birdwatching, trekking and jeep safaris. Meals are available in the cafeteria.

$ Hotel Apple Pie
Sangla, T07186-226304.
Run by a veteran mountaineer.

$ Negi Cottage
Sangla, T(0)9418-904161.
The 3 rooms, all with bath, are brightly coloured inside and out so they have more character than most.

$ Shruti Guest House
Sangla, near market, www.shrutiguesthouse.com.
Comfortable, clean rooms with TV and attached bath. You get a friendly welcome,

and there is good home-cooked food as well as mighty Himalaya views.

Recong Peo and around

$$$-$$ Inner Tukpa
Between Kalpa and Recong Peo, T01786-223077, www.innertukpahotel.com.
Nestled in the woods between Kalpa and Recong Peo, there are spacious rooms here and even more spacious views.

$$ Monk Resort Roshi Rd
1.5 km from Kalpa, T(0)9816-737004, www.kinnaurgeotourism.com.
Set in pretty surroundings are these 4 spacious swiss cottage tents, huts and airy rooms. Recommended.

$$-$ Aucktong Guest House ('Aunties')
Near Circuit House, 1 km north on Pangi road, Kalpa, T(0)9816-179457.
Pleasant place offering 6 clean spacious rooms with large windows. There's also a restaurant. It's very friendly: "arrived for one night and stayed a week!".

$$-$ Kinner Kailash Cottage (HPTDC)
Kalpa, T01786-226159, www.hptdc.nic.in. May-Nov.
In a commanding position, this place has 5 rooms (bath tub Rs 1100) and camping. There's a limited menu.

$ Forest Rest House
Chini, 2 km from Kalpa.
In a modern building, camping is also available overnight (with permission) in the school grounds 1600-1000. The caretaker here can prepare meals.

Transport

Baspa Valley
Bus Twice daily between Karchham (0930) and Chitkul via **Sangla** (1100) and **Rakcham**. 4WD is recommended between Karchham and Chitkul in bad weather. Sangla to **Chitkul** (often 2-3 hrs late). Sangla to **Shimla** via **Tapri** (9 hrs). Sangla to **Recong Peo**, 0630. Tapri to **Chitkul**, 0930; Recong Peo to **Chitkul**, 0600 (prompt).

Recong Peo and around
Bus Reserve tickets from the booth shortly before departure. Bus to **Chandigarh**; **Delhi** 1030; **Kalpa**, occasional; **Kaza** (9 hrs), gets very crowded so reserve seat before 0700; **Puh**; **Rampur**, frequent (5 hrs); **Sangla/Chitkul** (4 hrs); **Shimla**; **Tabo**, via Kaza (9-10 hrs). There are buses from Kalpa to **Shimla**, 0730, and **Chitkul**, 1300. To get to Peo for the Kaza bus at 0730, walk down (40 mins) or arrange taxi from Peo.

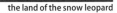

Spiti

the land of the snow leopard

From the checkpoint at Jangi the road goes to Puh, a steep climb with hairpin bends. The bridge at Khab, 11 km beyond Puh, marks the confluence of the Sutlej and Spiti rivers. The entry into the Spiti Valley at Khab is a rare example of crossing from the Himalaya to the Trans-Himalaya without going over a major pass. The Sutlej now disappears east towards the Tibet border, while the road follows the Spiti. Major deforestation of the mountain slopes has resulted in sections of the road being washed away. The new road, a remarkable feat of engineering, hairpins up to the village of Nako, with some basic guesthouses, and rejoins the river at Chango.

Sumdo, the last village of Kinnaur, has a border police checkpost and a tea shop, and is the starting point of State Highway 30, which passes through an arid valley with small patches

ON THE ROAD

The art of Chos Khor Gompa

Many of the colourful murals come close to the pure Indian style identified with Ajanta. The technique required the surface to be coated with several thin layers of lime and yak-skin glue and burnished vigorously to provide the 'ground' which was then smoothed and freshened with animal fat and butter. Natural vegetable dyes and powdered stone colours were mixed with *dzo* milk and yak urine for painting. The early Indian style murals used a profusion of reds and yellows with little stress on landscaping, the area around the principal figures being filled with small divinities. These images wear seraphic smiles and have half-shut dreamy eyes denoting introspective meditation. The later 17th-century paintings illustrate the Central Tibetan/Chinese art form where ultramarine takes over from the earlier dominance of reds and yellows, and landscapes become lively and vivid with the appearance of cliffs, swirling clouds, stylized flames, flora and fauna. Here the twists and turns of the limbs and the flowing elaborate drapery show great fluency. This is one of the few *gompas* in the Tibetan Buddhist-influenced areas of Ladakh, Lahaul and Spiti where the highly structured art of painting the complex Tibetan religious iconography is taught. What appears outwardly as a free art form is taught on lined paper where each shape and form is closely measured.

of cultivation of peas and barley near the snow melt streams. It is 31 km from Sumdo to Tabo. See also Trekking, page 15.

Tabo

At the crossroads of two ancient trade routes, Tabo (altitude 3050 m) was one of the great centres of Buddhist learning and culture. Founded in AD 996, the **Chos Khor Gompa** (see below) is the oldest living Buddhist establishment in this part of the world. Today, the small town is rapidly being modernized with paved streets and electric lights. Government offices have appeared alongside traditional mud homes and the local shops stock basic provisions for trekkers. There is a post office.

Chos Khor Gompa Founded in AD 996 as a scholastic institution, the monastery's original layout was planned as a *mandala* centred around a **Du khang** (Assembly Hall). The deodar wood used was imported from Kullu, Kinnaur, Chamba and Kashmir while the lack of quality structural stone resulted in the extensive use of earth, strengthened with gypsum for the high walls. Today the *gompa* is recognized as a historic Buddhist site. It comprises nine temples, four stupas and some cave shrines. The monastery houses 60 *lamas* and has a good collection of scriptures, *thangkas* and art pieces, including murals and frescos covering the walls. Carry a torch. No photography is allowed.

At the centre of the 'mandala' is the **Dri Tsang khang** (Inner Sanctum) and **Kora** (Circumambulatory Path). The five *Dhyani* Buddhas, escorted here by four Bodhisattvas, emerge from the darkness lit by a shaft of sunlight. The **Tsuglhakhang** (academy) features a 'resplendent' central *Mahavairochana*, a composite of four figures, each facing a cardinal direction, which represents the unity of all Buddhas. On the walls inside are stucco figures of different Buddhas and Bodhisattvas. The floral ceiling decorations are in the Ajanta style. Masks, weapons and ritual costumes are stored in the **Gon Khang,** which is closed to visitors. The **Zhalma** (Picture Hall) has a 17th-century entrance temple where the murals are recent and in pure Tibetan style. **Dromton Lhakhang Chenpo** (17th century) is dominated by Medicine Buddhas. The ceiling in high Tibetan style is exceptional, depicting *nagas*, titans, peacocks and parrots amongst rainbows. The walls of the **Ser Khang** (Golden Temple) were believed to have been coated with a layer of gold dust as thick as a yak's skin for painting the numerous larger-than-life figures. They were renewed in the 16th and 17th centuries. Dedicated to the Maitreya (Future) Buddha, **Chamba Chenpo La Khang** has a 6-m-high seated statue. The murals of the eight Buddhas here may be some of the earliest in Tabo.

To the north, the small natural caves above the road were an integral part of the monastic complex. **Pho Gompa**, the only surviving, with early murals showing pure Indian influence, has been restored. These post-Ajantan paintings, however, are already fading. On open ground to the east, on both sides of a dyke, there are pre-Buddhist rock carvings on metamorphosed igneous rocks showing ibex, swastikas, *yonis*, horses, panthers and human figures.

Dankar

Once the capital of Spiti, Dankar is a tiny village. The early 16th-century fort/monastery **Dankar Gompa** (3890 m), which once served as a jail, stands on an impressive overhang, perched on crumbling towers. Today it has more than 160 *lamas* in residence. The 'highest temple' has a collection of Bhotia Buddhist scriptures, a four-in-one *Dhyani Buddha* and interesting murals of Medicine Buddhas and protector deities. A large Mala (sacrificial wood) tree at the northwest corner of the monastery, the only one of four to survive, is held sacred by the villagers.

The *gompa* is a very steep two-hour climb from a point 2 km away, beyond Shichling on the main road. The 4WD road from the SH30, about 1 km west of Shichling, winds up 8 km to Dankar (a two-hour walk) and is easier. A beautiful large pond at just under 4100 m is reached by a 2.5-km track.

Lalung Gompa

Lalung Gompa, known for its carved wood panelling, is off the SH30, 22 km from Kaza, reached by 8-km narrow, drivable track. From Dankar Gompa this is a two-hour trek. Carry plenty of water as there are no streams and it can get very hot.

Pin Valley

About 5 km from Dankar is a sign for the Pin Valley National Park which is on the other side of the river. The Pin River joins the Spiti at Attargo. Above Attargo, 10 km along the Pin Valley, is the **Kungri Gompa** (circa 1330), which though not old is in an established monastic site with old carved wooden sculptures and is commonly understood to be a Bon monastery still practising elements of the pre-Buddhist Bon religion. The trek from the Bhabha Valley ends at the road head at Kungri, see page 30. See also Trekking, page 15. One bus a day departs from Kaza at 1200, goes along the Pin Valley as far as Mikkim and turns straight back at 1400, not allowing enough time to visit the *gompa*. You therefore face a long walk unless you can hitch a lift on a passing tractor, truck or yak.

At the confluence of the Pin River and one of its tributaries, 1 km from Mikkim, **Sangam** can be reached by car over a new iron bridge, or more adventurously by a

Fact...
Although rugged, the summer brings more rain here than the rest of Spiti resulting in a profusion of wild flowers.

pulley system with a person-sized bucket, 750 m west of the bus stop along the river. It requires a reasonable degree of fitness to negotiate, especially if crossing alone. The local greeting is *joolay, joolay*!

Pin Valley National Park is described as the "land of ibex and snow leopard" and was created to conserve the flora and fauna of the cold desert. It adjoins the Great Himalayan National Park (southwest), and Rupi Bhabha Sanctuary (south) with the Bara Shigri Glacier forming its north boundary. The park covers 675 sq km with a buffer zone of 1150 sq km mainly to its east where there are villages, and varies in altitude from 3600 m to 6630 m. The wildlife includes Siberian ibex, snow leopard, red fox, pika, weasels, lammergeier, Himalayan griffon, golden eagle, Chakor partridge, Himalayan snow cock and a variety of rose finches. The Siberian ibex can be sighted at high altitudes, beyond Hikim and Thango village. From July to September the young ibex kids need protection and so the females move up to the higher pastures near cliffs while the adult males concentrate on feeding lower down. The 60-km-long Lingti Valley is famous for its fossils.

Kaza

Kaza, at 3600 m, is 13 km from Lingti village and is the main town of the Spiti Valley. Old Kaza has village homes while New Kaza sports government offices. It is a busy bus terminus with plenty of hotels and homestays, a small market, a basic health centre and jeeps for hire. Inner Line Permits are issued by the **SDM's office** ⓘ *T01906-222202, open 1030-1700, closed 2nd Sat of each month*. Tourist facilities are open May to October. For an exceptional insight into the area, check out www.spitiecosphere.com with a focus on conservation.

There is an attractive one-day circular trek from here to **Hikim** and **Komik** villages visiting the monastery midway. **Hikim Gompa** (early 14th century), modelled on a Chinese castle, was built under Mongol patronage.

Kibber-Gete Wildlife Sanctuary

One of the world's highest wildlife sanctuaries, covering an area of 98 sq km, Kibber-Gete has **Mount Gya** (6754 m) to the north and **Kamelong** (5867 m) to the south. On the drive from Kibber to Tashigang, you may spot musk deer and bharal sheep but to see larger mammals (bear, wolf and the rare snow leopard) you would need to trek. Also to be seen are Himalayan birds of prey as well as snowcock and other high-altitude birds. Buses from Kaza take about an hour.

Tashigang

Tashigang, 18 km away, is one of the highest villages in the world connected by road. **Ki Monastery** on the way is the largest in Spiti and houses 300 *lamas*. Although it has suffered from wars, fires and earthquakes it still has a good collection of *thangkas* and *kangyurs* (scriptures). Although no permit is needed, the monks have instituted their private 'entrance fee' system which, by all accounts, appears quite flexible and linked to the visitor's perceived ability to pay. There are a few cheap guesthouses and camping is possible. If you cannot stay take a bus up and walk down via the Ki Monastery, 11 km from Kaza.

To Lahaul

Losar, at 4079 m, is the last village in Spiti, reached after driving through fields growing peas and cabbage among poplars, willows and apple orchards. There is a rest house and guesthouse and a couple of cafés serving Tibetan/Spitian food.

The road continues up for 18 km to the **Kunzum La** (Pass) at 4551 m. It means 'meeting place for ibex' and gives access to Lahaul and good views of some of the highest peaks of the Chandrabhaga group that lies immediately opposite the Kunzum La to the west. To the southeast is the Karcha Peak (6271 m). The pass has an ancient *chorten* marker. The temple to **Gyephang**, the presiding deity, is circumambulated by those crossing the pass; the giver of any offering in cash which sticks to the stone image receives special blessing.

The road descends through 19 hairpin curves to reach the rock strewn valley of the River Chandra at **Batal**, where a tea shop serves noodles and sells biscuits and bottled water. It continues to **Chhota Dhara** and **Chhatru**, with rest houses and eateries, and then **Gramphoo** joining the Manali–Keylong–Leh highway around three hours after leaving the pass. From Gramphoo to Manali is 62 km.

Listings Spiti

Where to stay

Tabo
Guesthouses in the village allow camping. There is a good list of homestays throughout Tabo and Spiti on www.spitiecosphere.com and www.himachaltourism.gov.in.

$$$ Dewachen Retreat
Tabo T(0)9459-566689, www. dewachenretreats.com.
Large comfortable cosy rooms with hot water and great views. They have another property in Rangrik, Kaza.

$$-$ Millennium Monastery Guest House
Run by monks in monastery complex.
13 colourful rooms, shared dirty toilets, hot water on request and meals available.

Dankar
$ The *gompa* has 2 rooms; only 1 has a bed.

$ Dolma Guest House
8 perfectly fine rooms.

Pin Valley
There is a **PWD** Rest House.

$ Norzang Guest House
Rooms for Rs 100.

Kaza
Kaza is ideal for camping and there are great opportunities for homestays in this area; for more information contact the fantastic **Spiti Ecosphere**, see What to do, below.

$$$ Kaza Retreat
T(0)9418-718123, www.banjaracamps.com.
11 clean, modern rooms with attached bathrooms. You can expect high standards here, good food and relaxing atmosphere, with stunning views a bonus. Recommended.

$$ Monk Resorts
Shego, 6 km from Kaza, T(0)9816-737004, www.kinaurgeo tourism.com.
Set in a pretty location surrounded by flowers are these 8 spacious Swiss cottage tents. They have other camps in Nako and Kalpa and can arrange homestays.

$$-$ Sakya's Abode
T(0)9418-208987, www.sakyaabode.com.
10 rooms in a fine-looking building with a wide range of rooms and a cheap dorm (Rs 80). It offers a friendly welcome and delicious home-cooked food. You can now book for 2 other local guesthouses through their website. Snow Lion has 8 large rooms and majestic views, while the cheaper **Kumphen Guest House** has simple rooms and delicious Tibetan food right inside the monastery compound.

Restaurants

Kaza
The fantastic **Spiti Ecosphere** (see What to do, below) has opened 2 exceptional cafés in Kaza. Check out www.spitiecosphere.com for more information on their work.

$$-$ Sol Café
Underneath the Spiti Ecosphere office, see What to do, below.
Sol Café focuses on great coffees, speciality teas, homemade chocolates and crêpes under the guidance of a French baker. The decor is influenced by Spitian and Tibetan culture. It's a travellers' café so a great place to meet people; there are movie nights, a book exchange and free water refills.

$$-$ Taste of Spiti
With stunning views and fantastic fusion food, Taste of Spiti serves up a healthy local grain pasta keu, black pea veggie burgers and hummus, as well as drinks with local crop seabuckthorn. They specialize in healthy heart-warming food and their proceeds go to fund various eco initiatives and work with local Spitian families. Highly recommended.

What to do

Kaza
Tour operators
Spiti Ecosphere, *www.spitiecosphere.com*. This is an exceptional project with a nod towards conservation, environmental and livelihoods; also volunteering projects, unique treks and promoting organic agriculture. They have an interesting range of tours including **Spiritual Sojourns** where you spend time with the Bhuchens, a rare sect of Tibetan Buddhist theatrical artists, and **Rustic Revelations** and **Spiti Kaleidoscope** where you get real insight into the lives and culture of these Himalayan peoples. There are also several **Carbon Neutral** volunteering projects. Ecosphere also put in 6 solar installations in 2013 as part of its initiative to provide reliable, green and decentralized energy to the Spiti valley. Highly recommended.

Transport

Tabo
Bus To **Chandigarh** via Kinnaur, 0900; **Kaza**, 1000.

Kaza
Bus Reserve a seat at least 1 hr ahead or night before. The road via Kunzum-La and Rohtang Pass can be blocked well into Jul. New bus stand, bottom end of village. In summer: from **Manali** (201 km), 12 hrs via Rohtang Pass and Kunzum La; **Shimla** (412 km) on the route described, 2 days. Approximate times shown: daily to **Chango**, 1400; **Kibber** 0900, **Losar** 0900; **Mikkim** (19 km from Attargo), in the Pin Valley, 1200 (2 hrs).

North of Shimla

high mountain passes and sacred lakes

Bilaspur and Bhakra-Nangal Dam
Bilaspur used to be the centre of a district in which the tribal Daora peoples panned in the silts of the Beas and Sutlej for gold. Their main source, the Seer Khud, has now been flooded by the Bhakra Nangal Lake and they have shifted their area of search upstream. For a bite to eat visit the **Lake View Café**.

The dam on the River Sutlej is one of the highest dams in the world at 225 m and was built as part of the Indus Waters Treaty between India and Pakistan (1960). The Treaty allocated the water of the rivers Sutlej, Beas and Ravi to India. The dam provides electricity for Punjab, Haryana and Delhi. It is also the source for the Rajasthan Canal project, which takes water over 1500 km south to the Thar Desert. There is accommodation should you wish to stay.

Mandi (Sahor)

Founded by a Rajput prince in circa 1520, Mandi (population 26,900, altitude 760 m) is held sacred by both Hindus and Buddhists. The old town with the main (Indira) bazar is huddled on the left bank of the Beas at the southern end of the Kullu Valley, just below its junction with the River Uhl. The Beas bridge – claimed to be the world's longest non-pillar bridge – is across Sukheti Khad at the east end of town. The main bus station is across the river, just above the open sports ground. It is worth stopping a night in this quaint town with 81 temples, a 17th-century palace and a colourful bazar. **For tourist information** ① *T01905-225036*.

Triloknath Temple (1520), on the riverbank, built in the Nagari style with a tiled roof, has a life-size three-faced Siva image (Lord of Three Worlds), riding a bull with Parvati on his lap. It is at the centre of a group of 13th- to 16th-century sculpted stone shrines. The Kali Devi statue which emphasizes the natural shape of the stone, illustrates the ancient Himalayan practice of stone worship.

Panchavaktra Temple, at the confluence of the Beas and a tributary with views of the Trilokinath, has a five-faced image (*Panchanana*) of Siva. The image is unusually conceived like a temple *shikhara* on an altar plinth. Note the interesting frieze of yogis on a small temple alongside.

Bhutnath Temple (circa 1520) by the river in the town centre is the focus at **Sivaratri Fair** (see page 108). The modern shrines nearby are brightly painted.

In lower Sumkhetar, west of the main bazar, is the 16th-century **Ardhanarishvara Temple** where the Siva image is a composite male/female form combining the passive Siva (right) and the activating energy of Parvati (left). Although the *mandapa* is ruined, the carvings on the *shikhara* tower and above the inner sanctum door are particularly fine.

From the old suspension bridge on the Dharamshala road, if you follow a narrow lane up into the main market you will see the slate roof over a deep spring which is the **Mata Kuan Rani Temple**, dedicated to the 'Princess of the Well'. The story of this Princess of Sahor (Mandi) and her consort **Padmasambhava**, who introduced Mahayana Buddhism in Tibet, describes how the angry king condemned the two to die in a fire which raged for seven days and when the smoke cleared a lake appeared with a lotus – Rewalsar or *Tso Pema* (Tibetan 'Lotus Lake').

Around Mandi

The small dark **Rewalsar Lake**, 24 km southeast, with its floating reed islands, is a popular pilgrimage centre. The colourful Tibetan Buddhist monastery was founded in the 14th century, though the pagoda-like structure is late 19th century. The Gurudwara commemorates Guru Gobind Singh's stay here. Start early for the hilltop temples by the transmission tower as it is a steep and hot climb. The **Sisu fair** is held in February/March. There are many buses to the lake from Mandi Bus Stand, one hour; you can also board them below the palace in Indira Bazar.

At **Prashar**, a three-tiered pagoda Rishi temple sits beside a sacred lake in a basin surrounded by high mountains with fantastic views of the Pir Panjal range. The rich woodcarvings here suggest a date earlier than the Manali Dhungri Temple (1553), which is not as fine. No smoking, alcohol or leather items are allowed near the temple or lake. There are basic pilgrim rest houses. A forest rest house is 1 km west of temple. To reach the temple, follow a steep trail from Kandi, 10 km north of Mandi, through the forest of rhododendron, oak, deodar and kail (three hours). After arriving at a group of large shepherd huts the trail to the left goes to the temple, the right to the forest rest house.

You can walk to **Aut**, see below, from Prashar in six to seven hours. A level trail east crosses a col in under a kilometre. Take the good path down to the right side of the *nullah* (valley) and cross the stream on a clear path. Climb a little and then follow a broad path on the left bank to the road. Turn right and down to **Peon village** in the *Chir nullah* and continue to Aut.

Tirthan Valley and Jalori Pass *For trekking information sees page 15.*

From Mandi the NH21 runs east then south along the left bank of the Beas, much diminished in size by the dam at **Pandoh**, 19 km from Mandi, from which water is channelled to the Sutlej. The dam site is on a spectacular meander of the Beas (photography strictly prohibited). The NH21 crosses over the dam to the right bank of the Beas then follows the superb **Larji Gorge**, in which the Beas now forms a lake for a large part of the way upstream to Aut. A large hydroelectric project is being constructed along this stretch. At **Aut** (pronounced 'out') there is trout fishing (season March to October, best in March and April); permits are issued by the Fishery Office in Largi, Rs 100 per day. The main bazar road has a few cheap hotels and eating places. It is also a good place to stop and stock up with trekking supplies such as dried apricots and nuts.

From Aut, a road branches off across the Beas into the **Tirthan Valley** climbing through beautiful wooded scenery up to the Jalori Pass. Allow at least 1½ hours by jeep to **Sojha**, 42 km from Mandi, and another 30 minutes to Jalori. Contact the tourist office in Kullu for trekking routes. One suggested trek is Banjar–Laisa–Paldi–Dhaugi/Banogi–Sainj, total 30 km, two days.

Banjar, with attractive wood-fronted shops lining the narrow street, has the best examples in the area of timber-bonded Himalayan architecture in the fort-like rectangular temple of **Murlidhar** (Krishna). Halfway to **Chaini**, 3 km away, the large **Shring Rishi Temple** to the deified local sage is very colourful with beautiful wooden balconies and an impressive 45-m-tall tower which was damaged in the last earthquake. The entrance, 7 m above ground, is reached by climbing a notched tree trunk. Such free-standing temple towers found in eastern Tibet were sometimes used for defence and incorporated into Thakur's castles in the western Himalaya. The fortified villages here even have farmhouses like towers.

From Banjar the road climbs increasingly steeply to **Jibhi**, 9 km away, where there are sleeping options and trekking. Two kilometres beyond is **Ghayaghi**, also with accommodation. A few kilometres on is **Sojha**, a Rajput village in the heart of the forest, which offers a base for treks in the Great Himalayan National Park.

Finally you reach the **Jalori Pass** (altitude 3350 m), open only in good weather from mid-April, which links Inner and Outer Seraj and is 76 km from Kullu. You may wish to take the bus up to the pass and walk down, or even camp a night at the pass. Check road conditions before travelling. A ruined fort, **Raghupur Garh**, sits high to the west of the pass and from the meadows there are fantastic views, especially of the Pir Panjal range. Take the path straight from the first hairpin after the pass and head upwards for 30-40 minutes. The road is suitable for 4WD vehicles. There is a very pleasant, gradual walk, 5 km east, through woodland (one hour), starting at the path to the right of the temple. It is easy to follow. **Sereuil Sar** (Pure Water) is where local women worship Burhi Nagini Devi, the snake goddess, and walk around the lake pouring a line of *ghee*. It is claimed that the lake is kept perpetually clear of leaves by a pair of resident birds. *Dhabas* provide simple refreshments and one has two very basic cheap rooms at the pass.

The Great Himalayan National Park and Tirthan Sanctuary

www.greathimalayannationalpark.com, foreigners Rs 200 per day, Indians Rs 50, students half price, video Rs 300/150.

The Great Himalayan National Park and Tirthan Sanctuary lies southeast of Kullu town in the Seraj Forest Division, an area bounded by mountain ridges (except to the west) and watered by the upper reaches of the rivers Jiwa, Sainj and Tirthan. The hills are covered in part by dense forest of blue pine, deciduous broadleaved and fir trees and also shrubs and grassland; thickets of bamboo make it impenetrable in places. Attractive species of iris, frittilaria, gagea and primula are found in the high-altitude meadows. Wildlife include the panther, Himalayan black bear, brown bear, tahr, musk deer, red fox, goral and bharal. The rich birdlife includes six species of pheasant. The park is 60,561 ha with an altitude of 1500-5800 m and the sanctuary covers 6825 ha; its headquarters are in Shamshi. Access is easiest from April to June and September to October.

Goshiani is the base for treks into the park. The first 3 km along the river are fairly gentle before the track rises to harder rocky terrain; there are plenty of opportunity to see birds and butterflies. The trout farm here sells fresh fish at Rs 150 per kg. Fishing permits, Rs 100, are obtainable from the Fisheries Department.

Listings North of Shimla

Where to stay

Mandi

$$$-$$ Raj Mahal
Lane to the right of the palace, Indira Bazar, T01905-222401, www.rajmahalpalace.com.
This former palace has character but is in need of attention. There are 14 rooms, including atmospheric deluxe rooms with bath (the sharpened sword in one might be mistaken for a towel rail). Rooms in the palace are charming whereas in the other block they are quite dull but cheap. There's a restaurant, bar and garden temple. You have to be persistent to book as they don't always answer the phone. Recommended.

$$$-$$ Visco Resorts
2 km south of Mandi, T01905-225057, www.viscoresorts.com.
In a modern resort by the river are 18 large rooms (some for 4). There's a good cheap vegetarian restaurant, and it's extremely well run.

$$ Hotel Regent Palms
Near Kargil Park, close to Raj Mahal, T01905-222777.

This bright newish hotel is centrally located and has all mod cons and attractive decor.

$ Hotel Lotus Lake
Rewalsar, above the lake, T01905-240239.
Run by the folks at Ziggar Monastery, this place has had a fresh lick of paint. If going to Rewalsar you can also stay by donation at the Sikh *gurudwara* (temple).

$ Rewalsar Inn (HPTDC)
Above the lake, T01905-240252, www.hptdc.nic.in.
There are good lake views from this hotel offering 12 reasonable rooms with bath, some with a TV and balcony. Dorm Rs 75.

Tirthan Valley and Jalori Pass

$$$$-$$$ Himalayan Trout House
Below Banjar, T01903-225112, www.mountainhighs.com.
All-weather eco-cabins, mud hut suites and stone cottage suites in a stunning location. Fine food is served, and there's great hospitality. Also here is an artist's studio, gazebo with fire and library. Trekking and

fishing can be arranged. A little shop sells organic wares. Highly recommended.

$$$ Banjara Sojha Retreat
Sojha, T01903-200070,
www.banjaracamps.com.
There are 5 basic double rooms and 4 lovely suites in this wooden lodge with fantastic views, good food and trekking information. You can see all the way to the mountains above Manali from here. Stunning.

$ Dev Ganga
9 km from Banjar in Jibhi, T(0)94181 54754.
8 comfortable double rooms, with exceptional views. Friendly staff.

$ Doli Guest house
Jhibi village, T01903-227034,
www.kshatra.com.
Good little rooms in a traditional building. There's also a sweet little café by the river in very pretty little village. Also ask about the cottages above the village with sitting rooms and woodburning stove. In tune with the local area and a growing number of backpackers, they are offering healthy retreats. Recommended.

$ Fort View Home Stay
Sojha, just by entrance to Banjara Camp,
T(0)9418-626634.
An atmospheric traditional building with 4 rooms inside and shared bathroom.

$ Raju's Place
Goshaini.
A family-run river-facing guesthouse, offering 3 rooms with bath. They provide great home-cooked food, treks and safaris. Access is by zip wire over the river.

Restaurants

Mandi
You can eat at **Raj Mahal Palace**; see Where to stay, above.

$$ Mayfair
Efficient and tasty North Indian food some continental and Chinese.

$ Gomush Tibetan Restaurant
Near gompa at Rewalsar Lake.
Excellent *momos*.

Festivals

Mandi
Feb/Mar Sivaratri Fair, a week of dance, music and drama as temple deities from surrounding hills are taken in procession with chariots and palanquins to visit the Madho Rai and Bhutnath temples.

Transport

Mandi
Bus Bus information T01905-235538. **Chandigarh** 1100 (203 km, 5 hrs). **Dharamshala** 1215, 6 hrs; **Kullu/Manali** every 30 mins, 3 hrs (Kullu), 4 hrs (Manali); **Shimla** (5½ hrs). Book private buses in town or opposite the bus stand at least 1 day in advance; they do not originate in Mandi. **Dharamshala**, 5 hrs; **Kullu/Manali**, 2 hrs (Kullu), 3½ hrs (Manali).

Taxi Rs 1500 to **Kullu**; Rs 2200 to **Manali**; Rs 2200 to **Dharamshala**.

Train Jogindernagar (55 km), easier to travel by road.

Tirthan Valley and Jalori Pass
Bus From **Jibli** the bus to **Jalori** can take 1 hr. Some go via **Ghayaghi** (approximate times): If heading for Shimla or Kinnaur, change buses at Sainj on NH22.

Bus from **Ani** and **Khanag** to the south, runs to **Jalori Pass** and back. 4 buses daily traverse the pass in each direction when it is open (8-9 months). Bus to **Sainj**, 3½ hrs, and on to **Shimla**, 5 hrs.

Taxi From **Banjar** to Jalori Pass costs Rs 800 (Rs 1200 return), to **Jibhi/Ghayaghi**, Rs 300, to **Kullu**, Rs 600, to **Manali**, Rs 1200, to **Mandi** Rs 700, to **Shimla**, Rs 3000. Buses are rare.

Kullu Valley

The Kullu Valley was the gateway to Lahaul for the Central Asian trade in wool and borax. It is enclosed to the north by the Pir Panjal range, to the west by the Bara Bangahal and to the east by the Parvati range, with the Beas River running through its centre. The approach is through a narrow funnel or gorge but in the upper part it extends outwards. The name Kullu is derived from Kulantapith 'the end of the habitable world'. It is steeped in Hindu religious tradition; every stream, rock and blade of grass seemingly imbued with some religious significance. Today, the main tourist centre is Manali, a hive of adventurous activity in the summer months, a quiet and peaceful place to relax in the winter snow.

Essential Kullu Valley

Finding your feet

Kullu-Manali (Bhuntar) airport, 10 km south of Kullu, has flights from Delhi, Shimla and Ludhiana; transfer by bus or taxi to Manali (Rs 750), Manikaran (Rs 650). If travelling on buses from the south, alight at Dhalpur Bus Stand in Kullu. Most buses to Kullu continue to Manali. See Transport, page 111.

When to go

Mid-September to mid-November is the best time to visit. May and June are hot but offer good trekking. March to mid-April can be cold with occasional heavy rain.

Where to stay

The choice of hotels is widening, with some good hotels in all ranges, though these are very full during Dasara. There are large off-season discounts (30-50%). Manali has a vast number of hotels catering mainly for Indian tourists and honeymooners.

Safety

Cases of Western travellers going missing in the Kullu Valley in recent years continue to be reported. They seem to have occurred mostly when trekking alone or camping. Some suggest that there have been genuine accidents in the mountains or that some drug users have 'opted out' and chosen to sever their ties and remain with *sadhus* in remote caves. However, the threat to personal safety is very real so if you're trekking beyond Manikaran, or from Naggar across the Chandrakhani Pass to the Malana Valley, you should not walk alone. Only use registered guides through local trekking agents.

ON THE ROAD

Dasara in Kullu

The festival of Dasara celebrates Rama's victory over the demon Ravana. From their various high mountain homes about 360 gods come to Kullu, drawn in their raths (chariots) by villagers to pay homage to Raghunathji who is ceremoniously brought from his temple in Kullu.

The goddess Hadimba, patron deity of the Kullu Rajas, has to come before any other lesser deities are allowed near. Her chariot is the fastest and her departure marks the end of the festivities. All converge on the Maidan on the first evening of the festival in a long procession accompanied by shrill trumpeters. Thereafter there are dances, music and a market. During the high point of the fair a buffalo is sacrificed in front of a jostling crowd. Jamlu, the village God of Malana, high up in the hills, follows an old tradition. He watches the festivities from across the river, but refuses to take part. On the last day Raghunathji's rath is taken to the riverbank where a small bonfire is lit to symbolize the burning of Ravana, before Ragunathji is returned to his temple in a wooden palanquin.

Kullu

busy Hindu temple town

Sprawling along the grassy west bank of the Beas, Kullu (population 18,300, altitude 1219 m), the district headquarters, hosts the dramatically colourful Dasara festival. Less commercialized than its neighbour Manali, it is known across India as the home of apple-growing and for the locally woven woollen shawls. There is little to occupy you here as a tourist.

The central area, including the main bus stand and Dhalpur (with ample hotels and restaurants) are close enough to cover on foot. Buses and taxis go to nearby sights.

Sights

Kullu's bulky curvilinear temples seem to have been inspired by the huge boulders that litter the riverbeds and hillsides outside town. A peculiar feature of the Nagari temples is the umbrella-shaped covering made of wood or zinc sheets placed over and around the *amalaka* stone at the top of the spire.

The **Raghunathji Temple** is the temple of the principal god of the **Dasara festival**. The shrine houses an image of Shri Raghunath (brought here from Ayodhya circa 1657) in his chariot. **Bhekhli**, a 3-km climb, has excellent views from the **Jagannathi Temple**. The copper 16th- to 17th-century mask of the Devi inside has local Gaddi tribal features. The wall painting of Durga is in traditional folk style. There are also superb views on the steep but poorly marked climb to the tiny **Vaishno Devi Temple**, 4 km north, on Kullu-Manali road.

Around Kullu

Bijli Mahadev, 11 km from Kullu at 2435 m, is connected by road most of the way with a 2-km walk up steps from the road head. The temple on a steep hill has a 20-m rod on top which is reputedly struck by *bijli* (lightning) regularly, shattering the stone *lingam* inside. The priests put the *lingam* together each time with *ghee* (clarified butter) and a grain mixture until the next strike breaks it apart again. Several buses until late afternoon from Left Bank Bus Stand, the road to Bijli is rough and the buses are in a poor state.

Bajaura Temple, on the banks of the Beas River, about 200 m off the NH21 at **Hat** (Hatta), is one of the oldest in the valley. The massive pyramidal structure is magnificently decorated with stone images of Vishnu, Ganesh and Mahishasuramardini (Durga as the Slayer of the Buffalo Demon) in the outer shrines. The slender bodies, elongated faces and limbs suggest East Indian Pala influence. Floriated scrollwork decorate the exterior walls.

Listings Kullu

Tourist information

Himachal Pradesh Tourism Development Corporation (HPTDC)
T01902-222349, near Maidan.
Open 1000-1700.
Provides maps and advice on trekking.

Where to stay

$$$-$$ Airport Inn
Next to Bhuntar airport, T01902-268286, airportinncomplex@gmail.com.
A convenient place to stay before travelling the 50 km to Manali.

$$$-$$ Shobla
Dhalpur, T01902-222800, www.shoblainternational.com.
25 rooms, flashy exterior, clean, pleasant atmosphere, airy restaurant, overlooking river.

$$ $ Sarwari (HPTDC)
10-min walk south of Dhalpur Bus Stand, T01902-222471.
Peaceful hotel with 16 simple but comfortable rooms (10 in more spacious new wing), 8-bed dorm (Rs 75), good-value restaurant, beer, pleasant gardens, elevated with good views.

$ Silver Moon (HPTDC)
Perched on a hill, 2 km south of centre, T01902-222488, www.hptdc.nic.in.
6 rooms with bath and heaters, each with small sitting room in traditional style, very clean, good food, has character (enhanced because Mahatma Gandhi stayed here).

Festivals

End Apr The colourful 3-day **Cattle Fair** attracts villagers from the surrounding area. Numerous cultural events accompany it.
Oct-Nov Dasara is sacred to the Goddess Durga which, elsewhere in India, tends to be overshadowed by **Diwali** which follows a few weeks later. In this part of the Himalaya it is a big social event and a get-together of the gods.

Shopping

Best buys are shawls, caps, *gadmas*. The state weaving cooperative, **Bhutti Weavers Colony**, 6 km south, has retail outlets; **Bhuttico**, is 1 store 2 km south of Apple Valley Resorts.

Akhara Bazar has a **Government Handicrafts Emporium**, **Himachal Khadi Emporium** and **Khadi Gramudyog**. **Charm Shilp** is good for sandals.

What to do

Tour operators
Look East, *c/o Bajaj Autos, Manikaran Chowk, Shamshi, T01902-065771.* Recommended for river rafting and bike hire.

Transport

Air Bhuntar Airport, T01902-265727. **Air India**, T1-800-180 1407, www.airindia.in.

Bus Most buses coming to Kullu continue to Manali. Most long-distance buses use the main bus stand, **Sarvari Khad**, with a booking office. For long distance and to **Manali**, left bank bus stand across the bridge: buses for **Naggar** (every 30 mins in summer) and **Bijli Mahadev**, and several to **Manali**; HPTDC deluxe bus to **Chandigarh** (270 km), 0800, 8 hrs; **Delhi**, 512 km, 15 hrs, extra buses during season, often better than private buses, you will pay more for a/c, the Volvo service is pricier; **Dharamshala**, 0800-0900, 8 hrs; **Shimla** (235 km), 0900, 8 hrs, Tickets from the tourist office; see under Tourist information, page 111.

Parvati Valley

orchards, hot springs and high peaks

The Parvati (Parbati) Valley runs northeast from Bhuntar. Attractive orchards and the fresh green of terraced rice cultivation line the route. Known for its hot springs at Manikaran, more recently the valley has become infamous for the droves of chillum-smoking Israelis and Europeans who decamp here in the summer months attracted by the intensive cultivation of narcotics.

Several local buses (and jeep taxis) travel daily to the valley from Kullu via Bhuntar, taking about two hours to Manikaran, which also has buses from Manali. The area is prone to landslides and flash floods; take special care. See Transport, page 113. For information on trekking, see page 15.

Jari

Jari is the point where the deep Malana Nala joins the Parvati River. It is a popular resting place for trekkers but also for drug users. The guesthouses vary; a few away from the village centre have better views.

Kasol

Kasol is the next village en route to Manikaran. The rapidly expanding village has spread on both sides of the road bridge which crosses a tributary that flows into the Parvati, not far from the village itself. About 500 m beyond the village, a narrow side road leads to the river and the location of a fine hot spring on the riverbank. Kasol is the main destination for long-stay visitors, many of whom sit in a haze of *charas* smoke by day and night.

Chhalal is a 20-minute walk from Kasol. It is a quiet village where families take in guests. A couple of guesthouses have also sprung up here.

Manikaran

Manikaran, 45 km from Kullu, is at the bottom of a dark gorge with **hot sulphur springs** emerging from the rock-strewn banks of the Parvati. A local legend describes how while Parvati bathed in the river, Naga, the serpent god stole her *manikaran* (earrings). At Siva's command Naga angrily blew them back from underground causing a spring to flow. Hindu and Sikh pilgrims come to the Rama temple and the *gurdwara* and gather to cook their food by the springs, purportedly the hottest in the world. There are separate baths for men and women.

Manikaran, though not attractive in itself, provides a brief halt for trekkers. Short treks go to Pulga and Khirganga beyond while a footpath (affected by landslips in places), leads to the Pin Valley in Spiti. If trekking this route, always go with a registered guide; do not attempt it alone. A road continues for 15 km to **Barseni**, which has become a popular place with long-term travellers.

Pulga and Khirganga

Pulga is in a beautiful location with some cheap guesthouses. It is a good four-hour walk east of Manikaran. Some long-stay travellers prefer the basic airy guesthouses outside the village which offer meals.

Khirganga is along the trek which winds through the lush Parvati Valley, east of Pulga. It is known for its sacred ancient hot springs marking the place where Siva is thought to have meditated for 2000 years. There is an open bathing pool for men and an enclosed pool for women, next to the humble shrine at the source. A few tents may be hired. *Dhabas* sell vegetarian food. This is the last village in this valley.

Listings Parvati Valley

Where to stay

Jari

$$$ The Himalayan Village
Doonkhara, between Jari and Kasol, T01902-276266, www.thehimalayanvillage.in.
Inspiring new construction based on traditional principles, in fact builders had to be trained in how to build this old-style property with layered wood and stone. Planning to expand with more rooms and tented area but seamlessly blending into the forest. Good restaurant and spa. Recommended.

$ Village Guest House
10-min walk beyond the village, follow signs, T(0)9805-190051.
One of several budget options that are springing up along the main road. This one is in the most peaceful setting and has 5 simple rooms with clean, shared hot bath and a restaurant. An excellent location on the edge of a traditional farming village, very friendly, good value.

Kasol

$ Alpine
T01902-273710, www.alpine guesthouse.net.
By far the best place in town right next to the river and deservedly popular. Friendly and welcoming with good clean rooms.

$ Panchali Holiday Home
T(0)98163 55095.
Good range of spacious rooms, many with balconies.

Manikaran

There are a large number of budget guesthouses but it is better to stay in Jari or Kasol and do a day trip.

$ Padha Family Guest House
Manikaran bazar, near Gurudwara, T(0)9817-044874.
Cheap rooms, super basic but clean with hot shower. Downstairs separate hot bathing room. **Moon Guest House** nearby offers much the same.

$ Parvati
Near the temple, T01902-273735.
10 simple rooms, sulphur baths, restaurant.

Transport

Parvati Valley

Bus There are frequent buses from **Bhuntar Bus Stand**, outside the airport, with many connections to/from **Kullu** and **Manali**. To **Manikaran**, 2½ hrs.

Kullu to Manali

magnificent views and Himachali castles

The NH21 continues north along the west side of the Beas. The older road to the east of the river goes through terraced rice fields and endless apple orchards, and is rougher and more circuitous but more interesting. Sections of both roads can be washed away during the monsoon.

Kullu to Katrain

As you wind out the centre of Kullu along the right bank you'll pass the **Sitaramata Temple** embedded in the conglomerate cliff and **Raison**, a grassy meadow favoured by trekkers. **Katrain**, in the widest part of the Kullu Valley, mid-way

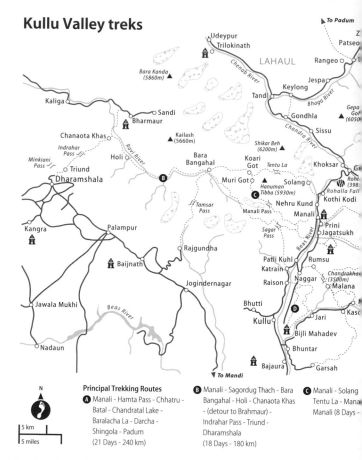

Kullu Valley treks

Principal Trekking Routes

A Manali - Hamta Pass - Chhatru - Batal - Chandratal Lake - Baralacha La - Darcha - Shingola - Padum (21 Days - 240 km)

B Manali - Sagordug Thach - Bara Bangahal - Holi - Chanaota Khas - (detour to Brahmaur) - Indrahar Pass - Triund - Dharamshala (18 Days - 180 km)

C Manali - Solang Tentu La - Mana Manali (8 Days -

between Kullu and Manali, is overlooked by **Baragarh Peak** (3325 m). There are plenty of options for an overnight stay. Across the bridge at **Patli Kuhl**, the road climbs through apple orchards to Naggar.

Naggar

Naggar's (Nagar) interesting castle sits high above Katrain. Built in the early 16th century, it withstood the earthquake of 1905 and is a fine example of the timber-bonded building of West Himalaya. It was built around a courtyard with verandas, from where there are enchanting views over the valley. With a pleasant, unhurried atmosphere, it is a good place to stop a while. It is also an entry for treks to Malana, see page 117.

The **castle**, probably built by Raja Sidh Singh, was used as a royal residence and state headquarters until the 17th century when the capital was transferred to Sultanpur (see Kullu, above). It continued as a summer palace until the British arrived in 1846, when it was sold to Major Hay, the first assistant commissioner, who Europeanized part of it, fitting staircases, fireplaces and so on. Extensive renovations have produced fine results, especially in the intricately carved woodwork. In the first courtyard are several black *barselas* (sati stones) with primitive carvings. Beyond the courtyard and overlooking the valley the **Jagti Pat Temple** houses a cracked stone slab measuring 2.5 m by 1.5 m by 2 m believed to be a piece of Deo Tibba, which represents the deity in 'the celestial seat of all the gods'. A priest visits the slab every day.

The small **museum** ⓘ *Rs 10*, has some interesting exhibits, including examples of local *pattu* and *thippu* (women's dress and headdress) and *chola* (folk dance costumes). There are also local implements for butter and tea making, and musical instruments like the *karnal* (broad bell horn) and *singa* (long curled horn).

Roerich Art Gallery ⓘ *Tue-Sun 0900-1300 (winter from 1000), 1400-1700, Rs 50*, a 2-km climb from the castle, is Nicholas Roerich's old home in a peaceful garden with excellent views. The small museum downstairs has a collection of photos and his distinctive stylized paintings of the Himalaya using striking colours. It's a beautiful collection from an inspiring family. Nicholas Roerich created the Roerich Pact in the 1930s in order to preserve culture and the arts in the wake of WWI. It was originally signed by 21 countries.

D Manali - Naggar - Malana - Manikaran - Kasol - Jari - Bijli Mahadev - Naggar - Manali. (9 Days - 140 km)

Uruswati Institute ① *uphill from the main house, Rs 15*, was set up in 1993. The **Himalayan Folk and Tribal Art Museum** is well presented, with contemporary art upstairs. One room upstairs is devoted to a charming collection of Russian traditional costumes, dolls and musical instruments.

There are a number of **temples** around the castle including the 11th-century Gauri Shankar Siva near the bazar, with some fine stone carving. Facing the castle is the Chaturbhuj to Vishnu. Higher up, the wooden Tripura Sundari with a multi-level pagoda roof in the Himachal style celebrates its fair around mid-May. Above that is the Murlidhar Krishna at Thawa, claimed as the oldest in the area which has a beautifully carved stone base. Damaged in the 1905 earthquake, it is now well restored. There are fine mountain views from here.

Listings Kullu to Manali

Where to stay

Katrain and Raison

$$$$ Neeralaya
Raison, T01902-245725, www.neeralaya.com.
Beautiful riverside cottages and villas made of stone and wood in the local *kathkuni* style with private kitchens and large verandas. Great local food. It's a sedate place here by the river with walks through the orchards, trout fishing possibilities and campfire suppers. Recommended.

$$$-$$ Ramgarh Heritage Villa
Near Raison between Kullu and Manali, T(0)9816-248514, www.ramgarhheritagevillamanali.com.
A farm since 1928, well-furnished rooms with TV and Wi-Fi, but beyond the front door there are orchards of pear, pomegranate and walnut trees and great views of the mountains. You can do trips to their kiwi plantation and they can organize paragliding, river rafting, yoga and picnics. Recommended.

$ Orchard Resorts
Dobhi, 2 km south of Katrain, T01902-240160.
Good off-season discount. 16 attractive wood-panelled 'cottages', with hot water, TV and heaters.

Naggar

Naggar is an atmospheric place to stay.

$$$-$ Castle
T01902-248316, www.hptdc.nic.in.
An absolutely beautiful property with an amazing temple. Castle was built in 1460 and has been a hotel since 1978. It has 13 rooms, which are stylish with traditional decor and furniture, comfortable beds, fireplaces and modernized baths. The best rooms (**$$**) overlook the valley, some share bath, and there's a very basic dorm (Rs 75). The restaurant, open May-Jun, has good service; add Rs 150 for vegetarian meals.

$ Alliance
200 m above the castle, T01902-248263, www.allianceguesthouse.com.
Run by French expat, this homely place has 6 very good value, clean, simple rooms, with hot water and meals available. Good for families.

$ Poonam Mountain Lodge
Close to Castle, T01902-248248, www.poonammountain.in.
6 spotless rooms, very good food, run by a friendly family. They also organize treks and jeep safaris and have a traditional cottage to rent.

$ Ragini
T01902-248185, raginihotel@hotmail.com.
16 smart rooms with modernized baths (hot water), large windows, good views from roof-top restaurant, excellent breakfasts, Ayurvedic massage and yoga, good value, friendly.

$ Sheetal
T01902-248250.
Overlooking valley, this clean and spacious place has 14 very pleasant rooms with bath, hot water (some tubs), TV and use of a kitchen.

$ Snow View
Down steps past Tripura Sundari Temple, T(0)98160 77132, snowviewhomestay@ gmail.com.
Weaving co-op outlet, with 7 rooms and a restaurant. Small and charming.

Restaurants

Naggar
There is also a *dhaba* up at the Jana waterfall recommended for trying real Himachal food – *dhal* made with sour milk, and cornflour *rotis*.

$$ Nightingale
200 m above bus stand.
Serves trout and Italian dishes.

$ German Bakery
Next to Ragini.
Sweet little café offering up the usual German bakery fare, and yak cheese sandwiches. Also beautiful photography on walls.

What to do

Naggar
Trekking
For trekking to **Malana**, it is best to employ a local guide. Pawan, from the old *chai* shop in the main village, is recommended.

Transport

Naggar
Bus The bus stop is in the bazar, below the castle. Several buses operate daily between **Kullu** and **Manali** via the scenic east bank route (1½ hrs). From Manali, more frequent buses to **Patli Kuhl** (6 km from Naggar, 45 mins), where you can get a local bus (half hourly in summer) or rickshaw.

Manali and around

mountain vistas and honeymooners

Set amidst picturesque apple orchards, Manali (population 30,000, altitude 1926 m) is a major tourist destination for Indian holidaymakers and adventure-seeking foreigners, attracted by the culturally different hill people and the scenic treks this part of the Himalaya offers. In summer months Manali is the start of an exciting two-day road route to Leh.

The town occupies the valley of the Beas, now much depleted by hydroelectric projects, with the once-unspoilt Old Village to the north and Vashisht up on the opposite hillside across the river. The town is packed with Pahari-speaking Kullus, Lahaulis, Nepali labourers and enterprising Tibetan refugees who have opened guesthouses, restaurants and craft shops. It's become increasingly built-up with dozens of new hotel blocks.

Essential Manali

Finding your feet

Kullu–Manali (Bhuntar) airport is 50 km away with bus and taxi transfers. The bus and taxi stands are right in the centre (though many private buses stop short of the centre) within easy reach of some budget hotels; the upmarket ones are a taxi ride away. See Transport, page 124.

Getting around

Manali, though hilly, is ideal for walking. For journeys outside the town taxi rates are high, so it is worth hiring a motorcycle to explore.

Best places to eat river trout
Smoked, baked or curried trout at Johnson Café
Trout cooked with almonds at La Plage
Korean trout sashimi at Café Yun
See page 122.

Sights

The **Tibetan Monastery**, built by refugees, is not old but is attractive and is the centre of a small carpet-making industry. Rugs and other handicrafts are for sale. The colourful **bazar** sells Kullu shawls, caps and Tibetan souvenirs.

Old Manali is 3 km away, across Manalsu Nala. Once a charming village of attractive old farmsteads with wooden balconies and thick stone-tiled roofs, Old Manali is rapidly acquiring the trappings of a tourist economy: building work continues unchecked in the lower reaches of the village, as ever more guesthouses come up to thwart those seeking an escape from the crowds of modern Manali, while the arrival of the drugs and rave scene in summer extinguishes most of Old Manali's remaining charm. The main road continues through some unspoilt villages to the modern **Manu Mandir**, dedicated to Manu, the Law Giver from whom Manali took its name and who, legend tells, arrived here by boat when fleeing from a great flood centuries ago. Aged rickshaws may not make it up the hill, so visitors might have to get off and walk.

Around Manali

Vashisht is a small hillside village that can be reached by road or a footpath, a 30- to 40-minute walk from the tourist office. Note the carvings on the houses of the wealthy farmers. **Vashist Temple** is very atmospheric and there are hot spring baths for men and women. The village, with its messy jumble of old village houses and newer buildings, has cheap places to stay which attract young travellers. A two-hour walk past the village up the hillside leads to a **waterfall**.

Hadimba Devi Temple

The Dhungri temple (1553), in a clearing among ancient deodars, is an enjoyable 2-km walk from the tourist office. Built by Maharaja Bahadur Singh, the 27-m-high pagoda temple has a three-tier roof and some fine naturalistic wood carving of animals and plants, especially around the doorway. The structure itself is relatively crude, and the pagoda is far from perfectly perpendicular. Massive deodar planks form the roof but in contrast to the scale of the structure the brass image of the goddess Hadimba inside, is tiny. A legend tells how the God Bhima fell in love with Hadimba, the sister of the demon Tandi. Bhima killed Tandi in battle and married Hadimba, whose spirituality, coupled with her marriage to a god, led to her being worshipped as a goddess. Today, she is seen as an incarnation of Kali.

The small doorway, less than 1 m high, is surrounded by wood-carved panels of animals, mythical beasts, scrolls, a row of foot soldiers and deities, while inside against a natural rock is the small black image of the Devi. To the left is a natural rock shelter where

Manali

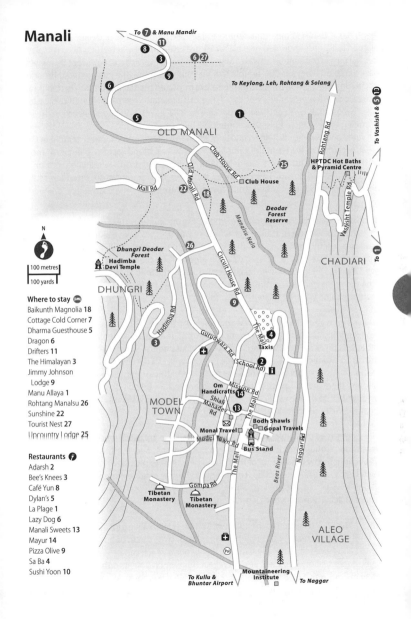

To **7** & Manu Mandir

8 **11**
3
6 **27**
9

To Keylong, Leh, Rohtang & Solang

To Vashisht & **5** **10**

6

5

1

OLD MANALI

25

Club House Rd

Rohtang Rd

HPTDC Hot Baths
& Pyramid Centre

Vashisht Temple Rd

To **1**

Mall Rd

Old Manali Rd

22 **18**

☐ Club House

Deodar
Forest
Reserve

Manalu Nala

CHADIARI

N

100 metres
100 yards

Dhungri Deodar
Forest
Ⓗ Hadimba
Devi Temple

26

Circuit House Rd

DHUNGRI

Hadimba Rd

3

9

Gurudwara Rd
(School Rd)

The Mall

4
Taxis

2
ℹ

MODEL
TOWN

Om
Handicrafts **14**
Shilali
Mahadev Rd

13
Manali Sweets

Monal Travel ☐

Model Town Rd

Mission Rd

The Mall

Bodh Shawls
☐ Gopal Travels

☐ Bus Stand

Beas River

Naggar Rd

Gompa Rd

Tibetan
Monastery

Tibetan
Monastery

The Mall

ALEO
VILLAGE

(Pol)

To Kullu &
Bhuntar Airport

Mountaineering
Institute
☐

To Naggar

Where to stay 🛏

Baikunth Magnolia **18**
Cottage Cold Corner **7**
Dharma Guesthouse **5**
Dragon **6**
Drifters **11**
The Himalayan **3**
Jimmy Johnson
  Lodge **9**
Manu Allaya **1**
Rohtang Manalsu **26**
Sunshine **22**
Tourist Nest **27**
Uncountry Lodge **25**

Restaurants 🍴

Adarsh **2**
Bee's Knees **3**
Café Yun **8**
Dylan's **5**
La Plage **1**
Lazy Dog **6**
Manali Sweets **13**
Mayur **14**
Pizza Olive **9**
Sa Ba **4**
Sushi Yoon **10**

legend has it that Hadimba took refuge and prayed before she was deified. The greatly enlarged footprints imprinted on a black rock are believed to be hers. Hadimba Devi plays a central part in the annual festival in May, at both Kullu and Manali. To prevent the master craftsman producing another temple to equal this elsewhere, the king ordered his right hand to be cut off. The artist is believed to have mastered the technique with his left hand and reproduced a similar work of excellence at Trilokinath (see page 128) in the Pattan Valley. Unfortunately, his new master became equally jealous and had his head cut off. It's a stunning temple, incredibly atmospheric.

A **feast and sacrifice** is held in mid-July when the image from the new temple in Old Manali is carried to the Hadimba Temple where 18 ritual blood sacrifices are performed. Sacrifices include a fish and a vegetable, and culminate with the beheading of an ox in front of a frenzied crowd. This ceremony is not for the faint-hearted. Pickpockets are known to take advantage of awestruck tourists, so take care.

Walks

Manali is the trail-head for a number of interesting and popular treks (see below). Beyond Old Manali, the **shepherd trail**, which winds its way up and down the hillside, allows you to capture a picture of Himalayan life as well as see some superb birdlife. The path starts at some concrete steps (after The Lazy Dog lounge/bar) on the first hairpin bend along the paved road to Old Manali (or you can pick it up where the road ends and taxis turn around at the top of the hill) and continues along the cemented path, which turns into a dirt trail. Return the same way, four to five hours.

Walk 1 This walk takes you towards Solang. In Old Manali Village take the right fork and then turn left in front of the new temple. This trail is a classic, following the right bank of the Beas River up towards the Solang Valley passing the villages of **Goshal, Shanag, Buruwa** to **Solang** (2480 m), a small ski resort with 2.5 km of runs. Solang is 14 km (five hours). You can get tea, biscuits, nuts and plates of steaming spicy noodles along the walk, and there are also places to stay (see Where to stay, below). To return to Manali it is a steady walk down the valley side to the main Rohtang Pass-Manali Highway where you can pick up a bus (Rs 5) or shared jeep (Rs 10).

Walk 2 This is an enjoyable three- to four-hour walk. Go prepared for cold for this walk as it takes you through woodland shading you from the sun. Keeping the **Hadimba Temple** on your right follow the contour of the hill and bear right to pick up a clear pack-horse trail which heads up the steep valley. This is a steady uphill climb through woodland giving superb views of the river below, abundant Himalayan birdlife and a chance to see all manner of activity in the woods, chopping, cutting and burning.

Walk 3 This walk takes you to the village of **Sethan** (12 km). Take a local bus to the Holiday Inn on the Naggar road. With the hotel behind you, cross the road and pass through the orchard and fields which have low mud walls all round which can be walked on. Bear east till you come to a disused track and then bear right and follow it to the once-untouched village of **Prini** which now has several five-star hotels. If you are lucky the *chai* shop will be open. Further east, the trail to Sethan village becomes somewhat indistinct, though local people are at hand to point you in the right direction. It is a superb three-hour hike up a wooded valley to Sethan (3000 m), which is well off the tourist trail.

Tourist information

HPTDC
Next to Kunzam Hotel, The Mall, T01902-253 351.
Helpful staff.

Where to stay

Hotels are often full in May and Jun so
it's better to visit off-season when most
places offer discounts. Winter heating
is a definite bonus.

In **Old Manali**, generally the further you walk,
the greater the reward. Those above the Club
House are almost out of Old Manali and are
in a great location overlooking the valley but
still close enough to town.

   Vashisht village is another popular choice.

$$$$ The Himalayan
Hadimba Rd, T01902-250999,
www.thehimalayan.com.
One Manali resident described this place as
a bit like Hogwarts, it's a new build echoing
a Gothic castle with turrets to boot. You can
expect rooms with 4-posters and fireplaces
and there is a magnificent view from the
Crow's Nest.

$$$$ Manu Allaya
Sunny Side, Chadiari, overlooking Old Manali,
T01902-252235, www.manuallaya.com.
53 smart, imaginative rooms, most done
in a contemporary design using wood and
marble, stunning views and good facilities,
a definite cut above the rest, ie an architect
has been involved. Recommended.

$$$ Baikunth Magnolia
Circuit House Rd, The Mall, T(0)9816-792888,
www.baikunth.com.
Definitely the most stylish place to stay
in Manali with beautiful decor, heavy
wooden doors and floors, and chic 4-posters.
Come in Apr to catch the magnolia tree in
bloom. A great place for a romantic getaway.
Highly recommended.

$$$ Jimmy Johnson Lodge
The Mall, T01902-253023, www.johnsonhotel.in.
12 very elegant rooms (cottages also
available), great bathrooms, pretty gardens,
great views and an outstanding restaurant.
Recommended.

$$$ Strawberry Garden Cottages
Below Sersai village on the Manali–
Nagar road, T(0)9218-924435,
www.strawberrygardenmanali.com.
Set in a stunning location, these 4 self-
contained, cute 2-floor cottages are in a
beautiful garden with great views. Friendly,
helpful English owner. Recommended.

$$ Himalayan Country House
Near Manu Temple, T01902-252294.
Popular place offering 15 smart double
rooms, with plenty of marble and pine,
and great views over Old Manali. Specializes
in trekking and motorbike safaris. Getting a
bit pricey though.

$$-$ Dharma Guest House
Above Vashist, T01902-252354,
www.hoteldharmamanali.com.
Perched high on the hill above Vashist,
this place has great views. Rooms are
clean and comfortable. Buns of steel
guaranteed climbing up there.

$$-$ Dragon
Old Manali, T01902-252290,
www.dragontreks.com.
This hardy perennial of the Old Manali scene
has had a chic facelift and offers a smarter
alternative in this part of town. Attractive
decor, lovely outdoor sitting areas and a
great vibe. There's also a good family suite.
Recommended.

$$-$ Drifters' Inn
Old Manali, T(0)9805-033127,
www.driftersinn.in.
In the heart of Old Manali, comfortable
rooms with TV, free Wi-Fi and a popular
café downstairs.

$$-$ Rohtang Manalsu (HPTDC)
Near Circuit House, The Mall, T01902-252332,
www.hptdc.nic.in.
27 large rooms, good restaurant, a garden
and superb views.

$ Cottage Cold Corner
Old Manali, T(0)98050 43677.
Strange name and certainly not the vibe,
with a very warm and friendly welcome
indeed. There are basic rooms, and a little
outdoor seating area.

$ Didi Guest House
Vashisht, T(0)78319 20896.
Through the village and above the school,
on the way to the waterfall. 10 wood-
panelled bedrooms. Cheap, chilled and
cheerful, with yoga and excellent views
up and down the valley.

$ Sunshine
The Mall, next to Leela Huts, T01902-252320.
There's lots of character at this friendly,
peaceful place, with 9 rooms in an old
traditional house, and others in a newer
cottage. Log fires, restaurant, lovely garden,
and a family atmosphere. It's such good
value you might need them to repeat the
price! Highly recommended.

$ Tourist Nest Guest House
Near Dragon, Old Manali, T(09816-266571.
Bright clean rooms with balconies; the top
floors still have views, whereas building
in front obscures views from lower floors.
There are now family rooms on the top floor.
Recommended.

$ Upcountry Lodge
Above Club House, Old Manali, T01902-252257.
In a quiet location in orchards, with 9 clean
rooms and attached hot bath, set in a
pleasant garden.

Restaurants

There are some great fine dining options.
In Old Manali there are plenty of Israeli
dishes and music which can range from
techno to Tibetan.

$$$ Johnson Café
Circuit House Rd, T01902-253023.
Elegant restaurant in a large garden,
specializing in trout – you can have it oven-
baked, curried, in masala or smoked. There are
also Western dishes, including excellent home-
made pasta, good filter coffee and delicious
ice creams. The beautiful lighting makes it
quite magical at night. Highly recommended.

$$$ La Plage
T(0)9805-340977, Old Manali.
Sister of the renowned La Plage from Goa,
this is a beautiful restaurant with divine
food. You can expect delicious trout cooked
with almonds, chicken in soy and sesame
with wasabi mash and amazing deserts. It's
a stunning location with amazing views,
attractive interiors and garden/terrace dining
and great service. Highly recommended.

$$$ The Lazy Dog
Old Manali, on left past shops going uphill
(before road swings to right).
Funky interior as well as excellent food,
good music, filter coffee, free Wi-Fi and
a lovely terrace overlooking the river.

$$ Adarsh
The Mall (opposite Kunzam).
One of many Punjabi places, but this one has
more style and a better menu than others.

$$ Café Yun
Opposite Drifters Inn, Old Manali.
Korean café with lovely vibe serving up
trout *sushi* and *sashimi*, as well as other
Korean delights and plenty of veggie
options. There is an amazing whole-
cooked trout on the menu too.

$$ Mayur
Mission Rd.
There's subdued decor and a great ambience
at this pleasant restaurant, with linen
tablecloths and candles on tables, Indian
classical music, a cosy wood-burning stove,
and a generator. Excellent food from a vast
international menu, served by smart and
efficient staff.

$$ Sa Ba
Nehru Park.
Excellent Indian dishes, snacks, pizzas and cakes, with some outdoor seating for people-watching. Recommended.

$$ Sushi Yoon
Vashist.
Chic little hole-in-the-wall café with just 12 seats serving up tasty sushi, delicious teas and coffees and the ultimate green tea ice cream. Highly recommended.

$$ Vibhuti's
The Mall, corner of Model Town Rd, up a short flight of steps.
South Indian vegetarian. Delicious *masala dosas*.

$ Bee's Knees
Old Manali.
Under the watchful eye of Avi, the man with the greatest smile, you can get big plentiful plates of Mexican food and all the usual Indian fare. Recommended.

$ Dylan's Toasted and Roasted
Old Manali, www.dylanscoffee.com.
The best coffee this side of Delhi, if not one of the best in India, served up by the affable Raj. The cookies are legendary as is his 'Hello to the Queen'; great atmosphere. Highly recommended.

$ Manali Sweets
Shiali Mahadev Rd.
Excellent Indian sweets (superb *gulab jamuns*); also good *thalis*.

$ Pizza Olive
Old Manali.
Very tasty wood-oven pizzas, a great range of pastas and even tiramisu. Recommended.

Festivals

Mid-Feb Week-long **Winter Sports Carnival**. **May** 3-day colourful **Dhungri Forest festival** at Hadimba Devi Temple, celebrated by hill women.

Shopping

Crafts and local curios
Bhutico Bodh, *by the Hindu temple.* A good range of shawls.
Great Hadimba Weaver's, *near Manu Temple, Old Manali.* Excellent value, hand-woven, co-op produced shawls/scarves and there is a little workroom to the side where you can watch them at work. Recommended.
Manushi, *in the market.* Women's co-op producing good quality shawls, hats, socks.
Shree-la Crafts, *near the main taxi stand.* Friendly owner, good value silver jewellery. Tibetan Bazar and Tibetan Carpet Centre.

Tailors
Gulati Traders, *Gulati Complex.* Sikh tailors, quick, good quality, copies and originals.

Trekking equipment
Ram Lal and Sons, *E9 Manu Market, behind bus stand.* Good range of well-made products, friendly, highly recommended.

What to do

From heli-skiing to rafting, mountain biking to paragliding and horse riding, there's a huge range of activities on offer in Manali.

Body and soul
Spa Magnolia, *at Johnson's Lodge Circuit House Rd, T(0)9816-100023.* Stylish spa with pricey treatments, but it's a bit of a treat. Ayurvedic and Western treatments available.
Yogena Matha Ashram, *Kanchani Koot, below Vashist, T(0)9418-240369, www.yogainmanali.com.* Swami Yogananda has a great following and offers down-to-earth spirituality with your downward dog. Recommended.

Skiing and mountaineering
Mountaineering and Allied Sports Institute, *1.5 km out of town, T01902-252342.* Organizes courses in mountaineering, skiing, watersports, high-altitude trekking and mountain rescue courses, as well as

5- and 7-day ski courses, Jan-Mar. There is a hostel, an exhibition of equipment and an auditorium.

Tour operators

Himalayan Adventurers, *opposite the tourist office, T01902-252750, www.himalayan adventurers.com.* Wide range of itineraries and activities from trekking and motorbiking to ski-touring and birdwatching.
HPTDC, *T01902-253531/252116.* Daily, in season by luxury coach (or car for 5): to Nehru Kund, Rahla Falls, Marhi, Rohtang Pass, 1000-1700, Rs 200 (car Rs 1200); to Solang, Jagatsukh and Naggar; 1000-1600, Rs 190 (car Rs 1200); to Manikaran, 0900-1800, Rs 250 (car Rs 1100).
Swagatam, *opposite Kunzam, The Mall, T01902-251073.* Long-distance buses, trekking, rafting; very efficient.

Trekking

Clarify details and the number of trekkers involved; shop around before making any decisions. For general trekking information, see page 15.
Above 14000ft, *log huts area, T(0)9816-632281, www.above14000ft.com.* Expert, environmentally conscious adventure organizers, specializing in treks, mountain biking, climbing expeditions and mountaineering courses throughout the region. Paperless office. Highly recommended.
Magic Mountain, *no office as such, but call Raju on T(0)9816-056934, www.magic mountainadventures.com.* Manali's most experienced cycling guide, Raju also offers trekking and jeep safaris, and is honest, friendly and reliable. Highly recommended.

Transport

Air Flights connect **Bhuntar Airport** near Kullu T01902-265037, with **Delhi**. Transport to town: taxi to Manali, Rs 1000 **Himachal Transport** (green) bus, every 15 mins (allow 2½ hrs travel time from Manali).

Bus Local bus stand, T01902-252323. Various state RTCs offer direct services to major towns. **HRTC Bus Stand**, the Mall, T01902-252116, reservations 1000-1200, 1400-1600. HPTDC coaches in season (fewer in winter); deluxe have 2 seats on either side: **Swagatam** (see Tour operators, above), run their own buses. **Chandigarh** 0700, 10 hrs, Rs 415; **Delhi** a/c 15 hrs, Rs 825; a/c sleeper Rs 1100; non a/c, Rs 425. **Dharamshala**, Rs 210, **Keylong**, 6 hrs, Rs 145. **Kullu** via **Naggar**: 2 daily, Rs 30, 1 hr; most Kullu buses go via the national highway and stop at **Patli Kuhl** (see Naggar, page 117). **Mandi**, Rs 112. **Rohtang Pass**, day trip with photo stops, striking scenery (take sweater/jacket), 1½ hrs at pass, Rs 120. **Shimla** (280 km), 0830, 1900, 9 hrs, Rs 415.

For details of transport to **Leh**, via the Rohtang Pass, Keylong and Sarchu, see Essential box, page 126.

Motorbike The uncrowded Kullu–Manali road via Naggar is an ideal place for a test ride. **Anu Auto Works**, halfway up the hill to Vashisht. Excellent selection; insurance and helmets provided. Mechanical support and bike safaris organized throughout the region. **Bike Point**, Old Manali. Limited choice of bikes in good condition, mechanical support and competitive rates. **Enfield Club**, Vashisht Rd, T(0)9418-778899. Enfields and Hondas for hire; reasonable charges, friendly, honest service.

Local taxi The local union is very strong, office near tourist office, T01902-265 8225. Fares tend to be high; from bus stand: Rs 50 for hotels (2-3 km). To Vashisht or top of Old Manali Rd, Rs 90; auto-rickshaws Rs 50.

Long-distance taxi Manali Taxi Services T(0)94181 83993. **Dharamshala**, Rs 3500; **Kaza**, Rs 6000; **Keylong**, Rs 4200; **Kullu**, Rs 700; **Mandi**, Rs 1500; **Naggar**, Rs 650; **Rohtang Pass**, Rs 1900.

Train Reservations at HPTDC office, T01902-251925.

Lahaul & the
Manali–Leh road

The stunningly beautiful road from Manali to Leh is one of the highest in the world and is currently the main route for foreigners into the regions of Lahaul and Ladakh.

Lying between the green alpine slopes of the Kullu and Chamba valleys to the south and the dry, arid plateau of Ladakh, the mountainous arid landscapes of Lahaul manage to get enough rain during the monsoon months to allow extensive cultivation, particularly on terraces, of potatoes, green peas and hops (for beer making). Lahaul potatoes are some of the best in the country and are used as seed for propagation. These and rare herbs have brought wealth to the area. Most people follow a curious blend of both Hindu and Buddhist customs though there are a few who belong wholly to one or the other religion.

Manali to Tandi

feel on top of the world

The first 52 km of this route runs up the Kullu Valley from Manali, then climbs through the Rohtang Pass.

Leaving Manali

From Manali the NH21 goes through the village of Palchan and then begins a sharp climb to **Kothi**, at 2530 m, set below towering cliffs. Beautiful views of coniferous hillsides and meadows unwind as the road climbs through 2800 m, conifers giving way to poplars and then banks of flowers. The 70-m-high **Rohalla Falls**, 19 km from Manali at an altitude of 3500 m, are a spectacular sight.

The landscape, covered in snow for up to eight months of the year, becomes totally devoid of trees above Marrhi, a seasonal settlement and restaurant stop, as the road climbs through a series of tight hairpins to the Rohtang Pass.

Essential Lahaul and the Manali–Leh road

Finding your feet

Lahaul can be approached by road from three directions: from Shimla via the Spiti Valley; from Manali over the Rohtang Pass (3985 m) into Upper Lahaul; from Zanskar (see page 177) over the Shingo La Pass, and from Ladakh over the Baralacha La Pass (4880 m). A much-delayed tunnel on the Manali–Leh road into Lahaul is currently scheduled to open in 2016. There is also a trekking route from Manali to Zanskar. No permits are necessary.

Best breathtaking moments

Spectacular view from Rohtang Pass,
page 127
Stunning Buddhist Khardong Monastery,
page 130
High-altitude desert camp at Jispa,
page 130

Getting around

The journey from Manali to Leh takes about 24-28 hours by bus, so if you leave at 0600, you'll arrive in Leh the next afternoon. HPTDC and private coaches run ordinary and luxury buses from Manali during the season, but these are usually based on demand and are not always daily. Seats should be reserved ahead. Front seats are best, though the cab gets filled by locals wanting a 'lift'. Those joining the bus in Keylong must reserve from Manali to be certain of a seat. Tickets cost Rs 1600 for the whole journey (including tent and meals); the usual overnight stop is at Sarchu where other cheaper tents may be available (some choose to sleep on the bus). There are reports of some bus drivers getting drunk or taking 'medicines' to keep them awake. For tips on travelling the road by motorbike, see box, page 129. Note that streams cross the Manali–Leh road at several places and may make the road impassable during heavy rain. Rockfalls are also a common hazard. See Transport, page 131.

When to go

The 530-km highway is usually open from July to September, depending on snowfall; most buses stop in mid-September. The Rohtang Pass itself normally opens at the end of May. Streams fed by snow-melt swell significantly during the day, making travel in the late afternoon more difficult than in the early morning when the flow is at its lowest.

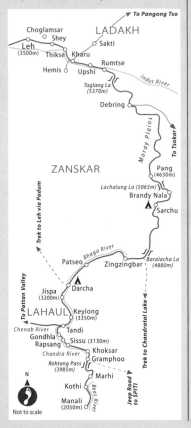

BACKGROUND
Lahaul

Historically there are similarities between this region and Ladakh since in the 10th century Lahaul, Spiti and Zanskar were part of the Ladakh Kingdom. The Hindu rajas in Kullu paid tribute to Ladakh. In the 17th century Ladakh was defeated by a combined Mongol-Tibetan force. Later Lahaul was separated into Upper Lahaul which fell under the control of Kullu, and Lower Lahaul which came under the Chamba rajas. The whole region came under the Sikhs as their empire expanded, whilst under the British Lahaul and Kullu were part of the administrative area centred on Kangra.

Rohtang Pass
From the pass you get spectacular views of precipitous cliffs, deep ravines, large glaciers and moraines. Buses stop for photos. From June until mid-October, when **Himachal Tourism** (HPTDC) runs a daily bus tour from Manali, the pass becomes the temporary home to a dozen or more noisy roadside 'cafés'.

The descent to **Gramphoo** (Gramphu), which is no more than a couple of houses at the junction of the road from Tabo and Kaza, offers superb views of the glaciated valley of the Chandra River, source of the Chenab. To the north and east rise the peaks of Lahaul, averaging around 6000 m and with the highest, Mulkila, reaching 6520 m. As the road descends towards Khoksar there is an excellent view of the Lumphu Nala coming down from the Tempo La glacier. An earlier glacial maximum is indicated by the huge terminal moraine visible halfway up the valley.

There is a police check post in **Khoksar**, at 3140 m, where you may be required to show your passport and sign a register. This can take some time if more than one bus arrives at the same time. About 8 km west of Khoksar work is in progress on the Rohtang tunnel, which will link the Solang Valley with the Chandra Valley. If you cross the bridge here you find an attractive waterfall.

Gondhla to Tandi
It is worth stopping here to see the 'castle' belonging to the local *thakur* (ruler), built around 1700. The seven-storey house with staircases made of wooden logs has a veranda running around the top and numerous apartments on the various floors. The fourth floor was for private prayer, while the Thakur held court from the veranda. There is much to see in this neglected, ramshackle house, particularly old weapons, statues, costumes and furniture. The 'sword of wisdom', believed to be a gift from the His Holiness the Dalai Lama, is of special interest. On close inspection you will notice thin wires have been hammered together to form the blade, a technique from Toledo, Spain. The huge rock near the Government School, which some claim to be of ancient origin, has larger-than-life figures of *Bodhisattvas* carved on it.

As the road turns north approaching **Tandi**, the Chandra rushes through a gorge, giving a superb view of the massively contorted, folded and faulted rocks of the Himalaya. Tandi itself is at the confluence of the Chandra and Bhaga rivers, forming the Chandrabhaga or Chenab. **Keylong** is 8 km from here, see page 130. At Tandi you can take a left turn and visit the Pattan Valley before heading to Keylong to continue on the journey.

The Pattan Valley has a highly distinctive agricultural system which despite its isolated situation is closely tied in to the Indian market. Pollarded willows are crowded together all around the villages, offering roofing material for the flat-roofed houses and fodder for the cattle during the six-month winter. Introduced by a British missionary in the 19th century to try and help stabilize the deeply eroded slopes, willows have become a vital part of the valley's village life, with the additional benefit of offering shade from the hot summer sun.

Equally important are the three commercial crops which dominate farming: hops, potatoes and peas, all exported, while wheat and barley are the most common subsistence grain crops.

Tandi to Trilokinath

Just out of **Tandi** after crossing the Bhaga River on the Keylong road, the Udeypur road doubles back along the right bank of the Chenab running close to but high above the river. The road passes through **Ruding**, **Shansha**, 15 km from Tandi, **Jahlma**, 6 km and **Thirot**, another 11 km on (rest house here). A bridge at **Jhooling** crosses the Chenab. Some 6 km further on, the road enters a striking gorge where a bridge crosses the river before taking the road up to **Trilokinath**, 6 km away.

Trilokinath

Trilokinath, at 2760 m, is approached by a very attractive road which climbs up the left bank of the Chenab. The glitteringly white-painted Trilokinath temple stands at the end of the village street on top of a cliff. The **Siva temple** has been restored by Tibetan Buddhists, whose influence is far stronger than the Hindu. Tibetan prayer flags decorate the entrance to the temple which is in the ancient wooden-pagoda style. In the courtyard is a tiny stone Nandi and a granite lingam, Saivite symbols which are dwarfed in significance by the Buddhist symbols of the sanctuary, typical prayer-wheels constantly being turned by pilgrims, and a 12th-century six-armed white marble Avalokiteshwara image (Bodhisattva) in the shrine, along with other Buddhist images. The original columns date from Lalitaditya's reign in the eighth century, but there has been considerable modernization as well as restoration, with the installation of bright electric lights including a strikingly garish and flickering *chakra* on the ceiling. Hindus and Buddhists celebrate the three-day **Pauri Festival** in August.

Udeypur

Some 10 km from the junction with the Trilokinath road is Udeypur (Udaipur). Visited in the summer it is difficult to imagine that the area is completely isolated by sometimes over 2 m of snow during the six winter months. It is supplied by weekly helicopter flights (weather permitting). The helipad is at the entrance to the village. Trekking routes cross the valley here and further west.

The unique **Mrikula** (Markula) **Devi temple** (AD 1028-1063) is above the bazar. The temple dedicated to Kali looks wholly unimposing from the outside with a battered-looking wood-tiled 'conical' roof and crude outside walls. However, inside are some beautiful, intricate deodar-wood carvings belonging to two periods. The façade of the shrine, the *mandapa* (hall) ceiling and the pillars supporting it are earlier than those beside the window, the architraves and two western pillars. Scenes from the *Mahabharata* and

ON THE ROAD
Motorcycling from Manali to Leh

Allow four days on the way up to help acclimatize, as the 500-km road will take you from 2000 m to 5420 m and down to 3500 m (Leh). The last petrol station is in Tandi, 7 km before Keylong. A full tank plus five to 10 litres of spare petrol will take you to Leh. Above 3500 m, you should open the air intake on your carb to compensate for the loss of power.

Apart from Keylong, there are no hotels, only a few tented camps, providing basic food and shelter from mid-June to mid-September. Some will be noisy and drafty. The lack of toilet facilities leads to pollution near the camps (don't forget your lighter for waste paper). A tent and mini-stove plus pot, soups, tea, biscuits, muesli, will add extra comfort, allowing you to camp in the wild expanses of the Moray Plains (4700 m).

Unless you plan to sleep in the camp there, you must reach Pang before 1300 on the way up, 1500 on the way down, as the police will not allow you to proceed beyond the checkpoint after these times. The army camp in Pang has helpful officers and some medical facilities.

the *Ramayana* epics decorate the architraves, while the two *dvarapalas* (door guardians), which are relatively crude, are stained with the blood of sacrificed goats and rams. The wood carvings here closely resemble those of the Hadimba Temple at Manali and some believe it was the work of the same 16th-century craftsman (see page 118). The silver image of Kali (*Mahisha-shurmardini*) 1570, inside, is a strange mixture of Rajasthani and Tibetan styles (note the *lama*-like head covering), with an oddly proportioned body.

Listings Pattan Valley

Where to stay

Udeypur
Camping is possible in an attractive site about 4 km beyond the town (with permission from the Forest Officer) but since there is no water supply, water has to be carried in from a spring about 300 m further up the road. You'll need to carry provisions too as there is little in the bazar.

$ Amandeep Guest House
T01909-222256.
7 semi-deluxe rooms with limited hot water. A decent *dhaba* opposite serves good Indian food.

$ Forest Rest House
Off the road in a pleasant raised position, T01900-222235.
2 rooms with bath, very basic; bring your own sleeping bag.

Keylong to Leh
high passes, tented camps and superlative views

The principal town of the district of Lahaul, Keylong (altitude 3350 m) is an increasingly widely used stopping point for people en route to Leh or for those trekking in the Lahaul/Spiti area. Beyond Keylong, the road passes through very high-altitude desert with extraordinary mountain vistas.

Keylong and around

Set amidst fields of barley and buckwheat surrounded by brown hills and snowy peaks, Keylong was once the home of Moravian missionaries. Only traders and trekkers can negotiate the pass out of season. Landslides on the Leh–Manali road can cause quite long delays and the town can be an unintended rest halt for a couple of days. There is a State Bank of India but no foreign exchange.

There is a pleasant circuit of the town by road which can be done comfortably in less than two hours. Tracks run down into the town centre. The **local deity** 'Kelang Wazir' is kept in Shri Nawang Dorje's home which you are welcome to visit. There is a **Tibetan Centre for Performing Arts**. A statue in the centre of Keylong commemorates the Indian nationalist **Rash Behari Bose**, born 15 May 1886 near Kolkata.

Khardong Monastery, 3 km away across the Chandra River up a steep tree-shaded path, is the most important in the area. It is believed to have been founded 900 years ago and was renovated in 1912. Nuns and monks enjoy equality; married *lamas* spend the summer months at home cultivating their fields and return to the monastery in winter. The monastery contains a huge barrel drum, a valuable library and collections of *thangkas*, Buddha statues, musical instruments, costumes and ancient weapons.

Sha-Shur Monastery, a kilometre away, was in legend reputedly founded as early as AD 17 by a Buddhist missionary from Zanskar, Lama Deva Tyatsho who was sent by the Bhutanese king. It has ancient connections with Bhutan and contains numerous wall paintings and a 4.5-m *thangka*. The annual **festival** is held in June/July.

Tayul Monastery, above Satingri village, has a 4-m-high statue of Padma Sambhava, wall paintings and a library containing valuable scriptures and *thangkas*. The *mani* wheel here is supposed to turn on its own marking specially auspicious occasions, the last time having been in 1986.

The road beyond Keylong

Jispa, 21 km on from Keylong at an altitude of 3200 m, has a hotel, a campsite, a few tea stalls and a mountaineering institute. About 2 km beyond Jispa is **Teh** which has accommodation. There is a 300-year-old palace, built in the Tibetan style, comprising 108 rooms over four storeys; apparently the largest traditional structure in Lahaul. It is 3.5 km off the main highway (turn off at Ghemur, between Keylong and Jispa) in a village called **Kolong**, and has recently been converted in to a heritage hotel. A museum has also been opened there, with some interesting exhibits depicting the traditional and ceremonial life of the local rulers, who still own the property.

All vehicles must stop for passport checks at **Darcha** checkpost where the Bhaga River is bridged. Tents appear on the grassy riverbank in the summer to provide a halt for trekkers to Zanskar. The road climbs to **Patseo** where you can get a view back of Darcha. A little further is **Zingzingbar**. Icy streams flow across the road while grey and red-brown scree reach down from the bare mountainside to the road edge.

The road then goes over the **Baralacha La** (54 km; 4880 m), 107 km from Keylong, at the crossroads of Lahaul, Zanskar, Spiti and Ladakh regions before dropping to **Sarchu** (on the state border). There are a dozen or so tented camps in Sarchu, some run by **Himachal Tourism** (HPTDC), mostly with two-bed tents (sometimes reported dirty), communal toilet tents, late-night Indian meal and breakfast; private bus passengers without reservations are accommodated whenever possible (Rs 150 per person); open mid-June to mid-September.

The road runs beyond **Brandy Nala** by the Tsarap River before negotiating 22 spectacular hairpin bends, known as the 'Gata Loops', to climb up to the **Nakli La**

(4950 m) and **Lachalung La** (5065 m). It then descends past tall earth and rock pillars to **Pang**, a summer settlement in a narrow valley where you can stop for an expensive 'breakfast' (usually roti, vegetables and omelettes to order). The camp remains open beyond 15 September; an overnight stop is possible in communal tents.

The 40-km-wide Moray plains (4400 m) provide a change from the slower mountain road. The road then climbs to **Taglang La** (5370 m), the highest motorable pass along this route and the second highest in the world; the altitude is likely to affect many travellers at this point.

You descend slowly towards the Indus valley, passing small villages, before entering a narrow gorge with purple coloured cliffs. The road turns left to continue along the Indus basin passing **Upshi** with a sheep farm and a checkpost, and then **Thikse**, before reaching **Leh**.

Listings Keylong to Leh

Where to stay

Keylong

$$-$ Chandrabhaga (HPTDC)
T01900-222247. Mid-Jun to mid-Oct.
3 rooms with bath, 2-bed tents, dorm (Rs 150), meals to order, and a solar-heated pool. Rates include vegetarian meals. Advance reservation is needed.

$ Dekyid
Below the police station, T01900-222217.
Quiet, friendly 3-storey hotel, with a helpful reception, decent-sized rooms with bath, excellent views over fields and a good restaurant, but service is very slow.

$ Gyespa
On main road, T01900-222207.
11 basic but adequate rooms plus a good restaurant.

$ Snowland
Above Circuit House, T01900-222219.
Modest but adequate 15 rooms with bath, and a friendly reception. Recommended.

$ Tashi Deleg
On main road through town, T01900-222450.
This place does well from being the first one you come to from Tandi, but it's slightly overpriced as a result. Rooms are comfortable

though, and the restaurant is one of the best in town. It's also has a car park.

The road beyond Keylong
There are summer tented camps at Jipsa, Darcha, Sarchu and Pang. Other accommodation is more limited. **Himachal Tourism** has a concrete 'lodge' in Jipsa with 3 basic rooms and toilets, and cheap camping in the yard.

$$ Ibex Hotel
Jispa, T01900-233204,
www.ibexhoteljispa.com.
In an impressive location is this glass and cement block housing 27 comfortable rooms and a dorm. Reserve ahead.

Transport

Keylong
Bus State and private luxury buses are the most comfortable but charge more than double the 'B'-class fare. To **Manali** (6-8 hrs); to **Leh** (18 hrs). To board deluxe buses to Leh in Keylong, reserve ahead and pay full fare from Manali (Rs 1300, plus Rs 300 for tent and meals in Sarchu).

Jeep To **Manali** by jeep, 4 hrs, weather permitting; **Sarchu** 6 hrs, **Leh** 14 hrs.

Northern
Himachal

Dominated by Dharamshala, this is a region replete with some of the most breathtaking mountain views imaginable. From Dalhousie eastwards there are tantalizing glimpses of snow-capped peaks, while McLeodganj has been attracting Western travellers for decades, coming in search of peace, tranquillity, the Dalai Lama and sometimes even themselves. The Kangra Valley sees far fewer visitors, but has an unhurried charm all of its own, epitomized by Pragpur, India's first heritage village.

Dharamshala and McLeodganj
magical atmosphere with the Dalai Lama presiding

Dharamshala (population 30,774) has a spectacular setting along a spur of the Dhauladhar range, from 1250 m at the 'Lower Town' bazar to 1768 m at McLeodganj. It is this 'Upper' and more attractive part of town that draws the vast majority of visitors.

Although the centre of McLeodganj itself has now become somewhat overdeveloped, it is surrounded by forests, set against a backdrop of high peaks on three sides, with superb views over the Kangra Valley and Shiwaliks, and of the great granite mountains that almost overhang the town.

Tsuglagkhang complex
This has been the home of the Dalai Lama and the religious focal point for exiled Tibetans in India since 1959. The *Tsuglagkhang* (main temple) opposite the Dalai Lama's residence resembles the sacred temple in Lhasa and is five minutes' walk from the main bazar. It contains large gilded bronzes of the Buddha, Avalokitesvara and Padmasambhava. The **Namgyal Monastery** ① *0500-2100*, within the complex has a Buddhist School of Dialectics, mostly attended by small groups of animated 'debating' monks, and is known as 'Little Lhasa'.

To the left of the Tsuglagkhang is the **Kalachakra Temple** with very good modern murals of *mandalas*, protectors of the Dharma, and Buddhist masters of different lineages of Tibetan Buddhism, with the central image of Shakyamuni. Sand *mandalas* (which can be viewed on completion), are constructed throughout the year, accompanied by ceremonies. The temple is very important as the practice of Kalachakra Tantra is instrumental in bringing about world peace and harmony.

Also within the complex is the **Tibetan Museum** ① T0189-222 2510, *Tue-Sun 0900-1700, Rs 10*, with an interesting collection of documents and photographs detailing Tibetan history, the Chinese occupation of Tibet and visions of the future for the country. It is an essential visit for those interested in the Tibetan cause.

McLeodganj

It is traditional to walk the **Kora** in McLeodganj, which is a ritual circuit of the temple complex and the Dalai Lama's residence. The Kora in McLeodganj replicates the ancient Lingkhor path around the Potala Palace in Lhasa. The beautiful walk is done clockwise, with stunning views of the mountains and numerous prayer wheels and prayer flags along the way; it finishes by the Namgyal Temple entrance.

The **Dalai Lama** ① *www.dalailama.com*, usually leads the prayers on special occasions – 10 days for **Monlam Chenmo** following **Losar, Saga Dawa** (May) and his own birthday (6 July). If you wish to have an audience with him, you need to sign up in advance at the Security Office (go upstairs) by **Hotel Tibet**. On the day, arrive early with your passport. Cameras, bags and rucksacks are not permitted. His Holiness is a Head of State and the incarnation of Avalokitesvara, the Bodhisattva of Love and Great Compassion; show respect by dressing appropriately (no shorts, sleeveless tops, dirty or torn clothes); monks may 'monitor' visitors.

Other sights in Dharamshala
Church of St John-in-the-Wilderness
① *open for Sun morning service.* Dating from 1860, this church with attractive stained-glass windows, is a short distance below McLeodganj. Along with other buildings in the area, it was destroyed by the earthquake of 1905 but has been rebuilt. In April 1998 thieves tried to steal the old bell, cast in London, which was installed in 1915, but could only move it 300 m. The eighth

Essential Dharamshala

Finding your feet

Flights to Gaggal Airport (13 km). Lower Dharamshala is well connected by bus with towns near and far. You can travel from Shimla to the southeast or from Hoshiarpur to the southwest along the fastest route from Delhi. The nearest station on the scenic mountain railway is at Kangra, while Pathankot to the west is on the broad gauge and is a three-hour drive away.

Tip...
A visitor's attempt to use a few phrases in Tibetan is always warmly responded to: *tashi delek* (hello, good luck), *thukje-chey* (thank you), *thukje-sik* (please), *gong-thag* (sorry), and *shoo-den-jaa-go* (goodbye).

Getting around

From Dharamshala, it is almost 10 km by the bus route to McLeodganj but a shorter, steeper path (3 km) takes about 45 minutes on foot. Local jeeps use this bumpy, potholed shortcut. Compact McLeodganj itself, and its surroundings, are ideal for walking. A ropeway (cable car) is being built between Lower Dharamshala and McLeodganj.

Best Tibetan experiences
Watch the Tibetan Monks debate at Namgyal Monastery, page 132
See handicraft traditions kept alive at Norbulingka, page 134
Watch Tibetan dance and culture at TIPA, page 141

Lord Elgin, one of the few viceroys to die in office, is buried here according to his wish as it reminded him of his native Scotland.

Tsechokling Monastery In a wooded valley 300 m below McLeodganj (down rather slippery steps), this little golden-roofed monastery can be seen from above. Built between 1984 and 1986, the monks here are known for their skill in crafting *tormas* (butter sculptures) and sand *mandalas*, which decorate the prayer hall (see Where to stay, below). Further down the 3-km steep but motorable road to Dharamshala is the Nechung Monastery in **Gangchen Kyishong** with the **Central Tibetan Administration (CTA)**, which began work in 1988.

Norbulingka Institute ⓘ *T01892-246405, www.norbulingka.org.* This institute is becoming a major centre for Buddhist teaching and the preservation of traditional crafts and techniques like sculpture and tangka painting. Named after the summer residence

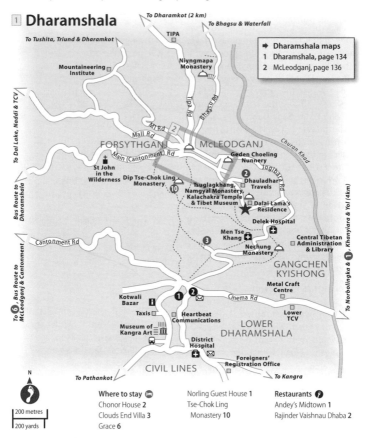

① Dharamshala

To Dharamkot (2 km)
To Bhagsu & Waterfall
To Tushita, Triund & Dharamkot
TIPA

> ➡ **Dharamshala maps**
> 1 Dharamshala, page 134
> 2 McLeodganj, page 136

Mountaineering Institute
Niyngmapa Monastery
Tipa Rd
Bhagsu Rd
To Dal Lake, Naddi & TCV
Mall Rd
Mt Rd
2
Churan Khad
FORSYTHGANJ
McLEODGANJ
Main (Cantonment) Rd
Geden Choeling Nunnery
St John in the Wilderness
Dip Tse-Chok Ling Monastery
10
Joghar Rd
Bus Route to Dharamshala
Tsuglagkhang, Namgyal Monastery, Kalachakra Temple & Tibet Museum
Dhauladhar Travels
Dalai Lama's Residence
Delek Hospital
Cantonment Rd
Men Tse Khang
3
Nechung Monastery
Central Tibetan Administration & Library
To Norbulingka & ①, Khanyiara & Yol (4km)
GANGCHEN KYISHONG
Bus Route to McLeodganj & Cantonment
Metal Craft Centre
Kotwali Bazar
1
2
Cinema Rd
Taxis
Heartbeat Communications
Lower TCV
To ⑥ Bus Route to McLeodganj & Cantonment
Museum of Kangra Art
LOWER DHARAMSHALA
District Hospital
N
Foreigners' Registration Office
CIVIL LINES
To Pathankot
To Kangra

200 metres
200 yards

Where to stay 🛏
Chonor House **2**
Clouds End Villa **3**
Grace **6**

Norling Guest House **1**
Tse-Chok Ling
Monastery **10**

Restaurants 🍴
Andey's Midtown **1**
Rajinder Vaishnau Dhaba **2**

BACKGROUND
Dharamshala

The hill station was established by the British between 1815 and 1847, but remained a minor town until His Holiness the **Dalai Lama** settled here after Chinese invasion of Tibet in October 1959. There is an obvious Tibetan influence in McLeodganj. The Tibetan community has tended to take over the hospitality business, sometimes a cause of friction with the local population. Now many Westerners come here because they are particularly interested in Buddhism, meditation or the Tibetan cause.

of the Seventh Dalai Lama built in 1754, it was set up to ensure the survival of Tibetan Buddhism's cultural heritage. Up to 100 students and 300 Tibetan employees are engaged in a variety of crafts in wood, metal, silk and metal, *thangka* painting (some excellent) and Tibetan language. The temple has a 4.5-m-high gilded statue of the Buddha and over 1000 painted images. There is a small **museum** of traditional 'dolls' made by monks and a **Tibetan Library** with a good range of books and magazines. You can attend lectures and classes on Tibetan culture and language and Buddhism or attend two **meditation** classes, free but a donation is appreciated.

Museum of Kangra Art ① *Main Rd, Tue-Sun 1000-1330, 1400-1700, free, allow 30 mins.* Near the bus stand in Lower Dharamshala, this museum includes regional jewellery, paintings and carvings; a reminder of the rich local heritage contrasted with the celebrated Tibetan presence. Copies of Roerich paintings will be of interest to those not planning to visit Naggar.

Around McLeodganj
Bhagsu, an easy 2-km stroll east, or Rs 40 auto-rickshaw ride, has a temple to Bhagsunath (Siva). The mountain stream here feeds a small pool for pilgrims, while there is an attractive waterfall 1 km beyond. Unfortunately this has resulted in it becoming very touristy, with increasing building activity and an influx of noisy day-trippers. The hill leading up the valley towards Dharamkot is known as Upper Bhagsu, and is lined with little shops, restaurants and guesthouses. It is a relaxing place with great views, and so attracts many backpackers for long stays here. Outside the rainy season lovely walks are possible.

Dharamkot, 3 km away (from McLeodganj by auto Rs 80, or on foot from Bhagsu), has very fine views and you can continue on towards the snowline. Villagers' homes and guesthouses are dotted up the hillside, accessible via pathways, and there is even a Chabbad House for the numerous Israeli tourists. In September, a fair is held at **Dal Lake** (1837 m), 3 km from McLeodganj Bus Stand; it is a pleasant walk but the 'lake', no more than a small pond, is disappointing.

Naddi Gaon, 1.5 km further uphill from the bridge by Dal Lake (buses from Dharamshala, 0800-1900), has really superb views of the Dhauladhar Range. **Kareri Lake** is further on. The TCV (Tibetan Childrens' Village) nearby educates and

> **Tip...**
> Lhamo Tso who runs **Lhamo's Croissant**, recommends tuning into the heart of McLeodganj and the Tibetan people by walking the Kora (see page 133) and buying the *Essence of the Heart Sutra* at **The Namgyal Bookshop** by the temple. It is a commentary by His Holiness the Dalai Lama on one of the Buddha's main teachings. She says "It is a book that can transform your life".

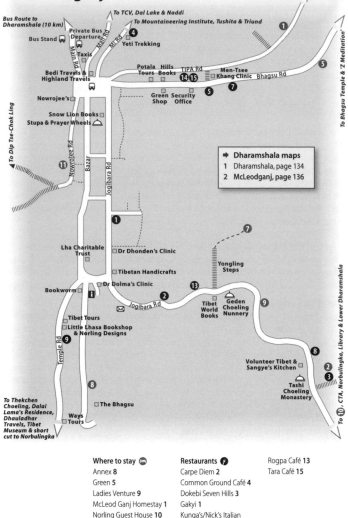

Dharamshala maps
1 Dharamshala, page 134
2 McLeodganj, page 136

Where to stay 🛏
Annex 8
Green 5
Ladies Venture 9
McLeod Ganj Homestay 1
Norling Guest House 10
Om & Namgyal Café 11
Pawan House 2
Sidharth House 7

Restaurants 🍴
Carpe Diem 2
Common Ground Café 4
Dokebi Seven Hills 3
Gakyi 1
Kunga's/Nick's Italian
  Kitchen 7
Lhamo's Croissant 5
Lung-Ta 8
Moonlight & Sunrise 14
Moonpeak Espresso
  & Thali 9

Rogpa Café 13
Tara Café 15

50 metres
50 yards

ON THE ROAD

Open your heart: volunteering in McLeodganj

There are many opportunities for volunteer work in and around Dharamshala, from English conversation to work at the hospital. Many offer a great insight into Tibetan culture and are key in empowering refugees.

Lha Charitable Trust (Temple Rd, T01892-220992, www.lhasocialwork.org, office open Monday-Saturday 0900-1700, lunch 1200-1300) needs volunteers for language classes, IT and web design, healthcare, fundraising, etc. Short-term or long-term placements are possible, or you can just drop in. They also offer Tibetan cooking classes, language, meditation, homestay, etc. Lha means 'innate goodness'.

Also look in at or check the free monthly magazine *Contact*, T(0)98161-55523, www.contactmagazine.net (also a useful resource for restaurant information and events in McLeodganj, Buddhist-related and otherwise). English-language teachers are in high demand to teach newly arrived refugees, for short- or long-term stints. There are a couple of places for teaching and conversation near Dokebi restaurant including Learning and Ideas for Tibet (www.learningandideasfortibet.org) who have conversation classes, movie parties and talks from ex-political prisoners. You can also volunteer with Rogpa (www.tibetrogpa.org) who provide free childcare for Tibetan people trying to juggle jobs and education – they run a lovely café on the Jogibara road too.

---

trains children in traditional handicrafts. Big hotels are rapidly appearing next to the traditional Naddi village. Most enjoy excellent views.

It is an 8-km trek to **Triund**, 2827 m, at the foot of the Dhauladhar where there is a Forest Lodge on a hill top. Some trekkers pitch tents, whilst others make use of caves or shepherds' huts. Take provisions and warm sleeping gear if planning to stay overnight. It's well worth the effort. A further 5 km, one-hour walk, brings you to **Ilaka**.

Listings Dharamshala and McLeodganj *maps p134 and p136*

Tourist information

HPTDC
Behind post office, McLeodganj, T01892-221205. Mon-Sat 1000-1700.
There are many opportunities for foreign volunteers (see box, above).

Where to stay

Dharamshala
Most visitors stay in McLeodganj (see page 138).

$$$$-$$$ White Haven Tea Estate
Below Dharamshala, T(0)86790 26162, www.hotelwhitehaven.in.
Charming working colonial tea estate set in 2.8 ha of beautiful gardens. 8 sumptuous rooms with creaking floorboards, log fires, lots of wood panelling and period antiques, exceptional service and tons of history. Recommended.

$$$ Clouds End Villa
North of Dharamshala, steep approach off Naoroji Rd, T01892-222109, www.cloudsendvilla.com.

7 rooms and 1 bungalow in Raja of Lambagraon's bungalow (Raj period), not luxurious but very clean, annexe has excellent valley views, authentic local cuisine (everything home-made), tours, peaceful, very friendly, excellent service.

$$$ Grace Hotel
558 Old Chari Rd, Kotwali Bazar, T01892-223265, www.welcomheritagegracehotel.com.
14 comfortable suites in a 200-year-old wooden manor, formerly the residence of India's first Chief Justice. Pleasantly situated slightly out of town, a good place to relax and admire the views. This is a stunning place with beautiful artefacts. There is a meditation room and do try the delicious Himachali food, it's exquisite with subtle spicing and yoghurt (sour milk). Highly recommended.

$$$-$$ Blossoms Village
Sidhpur, near Dharamshala, T01892-246 880, www.blossomsvillage.com.
19 lovely rooms including cottages and suites. Stylishly decorated using local timber. New spa in 2013, with treatments and wellbeing therapies. Lovely rooftop bar and restaurant.

$$$-$$ Norling Guest House
Norbulingka Institute, Gangchen Kyishong, T01892-246406, normail@norbulingka.org.
Clean, comfortable rooms, in modern facilities in a Tibetan-style house. Café accepts Master/Visa cards. Beautiful setting inside the Norbulingka Institute, so surrounded by art and meditative peace. Highly recommended.

$ Tsechokling Monastery
Camel Track Rd, 300 m below McLeodganj, down 300 steps, T01892-221726.
20 clean rooms, 3 attached, some singles, hot showers, breakfast and dinner at set times. 'Wonderfully peaceful'.

McLeodganj

$$$-$$ Chonor House
Thekchen Choeling Rd, T01892-221006, www.norbulingka.org.

11 very comfortable, stylish rooms furnished in Tibetan style (murals of lost monasteries and mythical beasts), good restaurant, clean, well-managed, popular with foreign diplomats, beautiful garden, a quiet and lovely place. Book ahead. Accepts credit cards. Highly recommended.

$$ Annex Hotel
Hotel Surya Rd, T01892-221002, 0941-8020814, www.annexhotel.in.
A short walk from the bus stand, all the rooms in this clean hotel have a balcony and are reached by the free Wi-Fi. Lounge and library, plus rooftop restaurant is excellent and has majestic sunset views.

$$ Pema Thang
Opposite Hotel Bhagsu, T01892-221871, www.pemathang.net.
15 rooms with a bit more character than the average, good views from private balconies (better from upper floors), wooden floors, quiet, friendly, hot water and Wi-Fi works in rooms, nice rooftop restaurant with good pizza and pasta. Yoga hall at the rear (see What to do, below).

$$-$ McLeod Ganj Homestay
Flourishing Flora, close to TIPA Gate, Dharamkot Rd, T(0)9736-083878, www.mcleodganjhomestay.net.
With 3 lovely rooms and 1 hillside hut, this is a short walk up the TIPA road towards Dharmkot and has a lovely family vibe. All the rooms have a little touch of Tibet, there's great Indian home-cooked food with as much organic as possible and cookery lessons with Nisha. Sometimes there is roast chicken on an open fire. Recommended.

$ Green Hotel
Bhagsu Rd, T01892-221200, www.greenhotel.in.
Popular with backpackers, 30 variable rooms (avoid ground floor ones near the noisy courtyard), restaurant with comfy sofas. Good internet.

$ Ladies Venture
Jogibara Rd, T01892-221559, www. ipcardesign.com/ladies venture.
Peaceful hotel with dorm and 13 clean rooms, cheapest with shared bath, standard rooms have bath and TV, while top category are huge with seating areas. Very popular (partly due to the helpful staff) and a good place to meet people. As they say, it's "just a name" and every body and soul is welcome. Small restaurant (good Chinese and Western food) and a terrace. Often full so book ahead.

$ Om
Western edge of bazar, T01892-221322, T(0)9857-632037.
Friendly hotel with 18 clean rooms, the en suite ones are excellent value, freshly painted and have consistent hot water, while cheap room share baths, great views at sunset from patio terrace and rooftop. Free Wi-Fi. The excellent **Namgyal** restaurant which used to be at the Temple has moved here, so expect the best pizza in northern India.

$ Pawan House
Next to Dokebi, Jogibara Rd, T01892-220069, www.pawanhouse.com.
Good views across the valley. Attractive spacious clean rooms with balconies; a good vibe. Recommended.

$ Sidharth House
Bottom of Yongling School Steps off Jogibara Rd, T(0)8679-591907.
Great guesthouse with conscious eco-vibe who established the 'Clean McLeodganj Project' and they have bins for compost as well as encouraging recycling. Highly recommended.

Around McLeodganj

$$$ Eagles Nest
Upper Dharamkot, T(0)9218-402822, www.hoteleaglesnest.com.
8 lovely themed rooms and suites in a beautiful old colonial house set in 20 ha of forest. Perched on top of the hill with spectacular views over Kangra and Kullu valleys. All inclusive, with excellent food and plenty of activities. Price includes all meals, horse riding and guides for trekking.

$$-$ Udechee Huts
Naddi Gaon, T01892-221781, www.udecheehuts.com.
Blending in with local style, 10 pleasantly furnished circular huts with bath (hot water), restaurant plus dining terrace, well kept, friendly hosts.

$ 9 Chimes
Upper Bhagsu, T(0)9736-130284, www.9chimes.com.
8 spacious rooms with balconies and good views and 1 apartment. Recommended.

$ DK House
Upper Bhagsu, T(0)94187 97494.
14 comfortable, spacious and clean rooms with big terrace and **Evergreen Restaurant** attached. Run by a friendly family.

$ Om Tara
Lower Dharamkot, T(0)981-6879749, www.houseomtara.com.
Keeping their eye on the environment and with friendly service, this is a popular little guesthouse among fruit trees. There are big verandas to enjoy the views. Recommended.

$ Shiv Shakti Guest House
Off Dharamkot Rd, T(0)9418-247776.
Run by friendly father and son, there are 18 basic rooms here with attached bath, plus a well-equipped cottage.

$ Trimurti Garden Café
Above Unity Pizza, Bhagsu, T(0)9816-869144, www.trimurtigarden.in.
A favourite haunt with simple rooms, café and numerous workshops, yoga classes and a music school.

$ ZKL Guesthouse
Above Bhagsu Rd, 500 m before Bhagsu itself, T01892-221581, www.zkl-monastery.com.
12 very basic but clean rooms in this charming monastery, with Buddhist teachings and a café in the summer. Outstanding value.

Restaurants

Most memorable food is in McLeodganj, as well as excellent Tibetan, there is also amazing Korean and Japanese food to be had.

McLeodganj

Enterprising Tibetans in the upper town offer good traveller favourites for those tired of curries; some serve beer. Try *thukpa* (Tibetan soups), noodle dishes, steamed or fried *momos* and *shabakleb*. Save plastic waste (and money) by refilling your bottles with safe filtered, boiled water at the eco-friendly **Green shop** on Bhagsu Rd, Rs 5 per litre; they also recycle used batteries.

$$ Café Illiterati Books and Coffee
LHS Jogiwara Rd, near Usho Institute.
This trendy mellow café has slate floors and wonderful views, full bookshelves on Buddhism, society or literature and coffee-table tomes, and an exciting menu (eg chilli ginger red-bean burger), including good salads.

$$ Carpe Diem
Past the Post Office, Jogibara Rd.
A Nepali-run joint with excellent Indian, Thai and continental flavours. Good vibe, appealing rooftop, beer under the table and open mic nights. Recommended.

$$ Dokebi Seven Hills
Near Lung Ta, Jogibara Rd.
Wonderful cosy restaurant with a delicious range of food including spicy hotpot-style soups, spicy kimchi and kimbap (Korean sushi); mainly vegetarian with some spicy chicken too. Upstairs there is lovely airy room with floor seating. Great fresh juices and smoky green tea. Highly recommended.

$$ Kunga's/Nick's Italian Kitchen
Bhagsu Rd.
Good vegetarian food, Italian including excellent pumpkin ravioli, plus quiches, pies, cakes and very good Tibetan food too.

With a huge terrace and great valley views, deservedly popular. Recommended.

$$ Namgyal
At Om Hotel, western end of bazar.
Open 1000-2200.
Cosy and welcoming venue with amazing pizzas like roquefort and walnut or smoked cheese and spinach; possibly best pizza in India! Good salads and Tibetan dishes too. Highly recommended.

$ Common Ground Café
Tushita Rd, above bus stand, behind Asian Plaza, www.commongroundsproject.org.
Serving up a Chinese-Tibetan food fusion, their menu underpins their ethos to foster shared understanding and respect between Chinese and Tibetans. It's a lovely place with great teas and desserts too.

$ Gakyi
Jogibara Rd.
Great range of Tibetan dishes, also excellent porridge and fruit muesli. Lovely lady owner.

$ Hotel Tibet
Bhagsu Rd behind the old bus stand.
Good Tibetan/Japanese restaurant and takeaway bakery. Very popular.

$ Lhamo's Croissant
Bhagsu Rd.
Beautiful café with furniture from **Norbulingka** offering tip-top cappuccino, healthy salads, monumental club sandwiches, home-made soups and outrageously good cakes and tarts, all served up by the eponymous Lhamo. They show films about the Tibetan cause every evening. Free Wi-Fi. Highly recommended.

$ Lung-Ta
Jogibara Rd. Mon-Sat 1200-2030.
Classy Japanese vegetarian restaurant, not for profit, daily set menu or à la carte, good breads and cakes, sushi on Tue and Fri. Try the *okononiyak* (Japanese veg omelette). Great value and very popular. There's a little shop on-site too. Highly recommended.

$ Snow Lion
Near the prayer wheels, T01892-221289.
Renowned for their Tibetan specialities, they also have Western meals and excellent cakes.

Cafés and snacks

Moonlight and Sunrise
Opposite Tibetan Welfare Office, Bhagsu Rd.
Small *chai* shops adjacent to each other with basic food. It's an excellent spot for meeting other travellers, especially in the evenings when overspill occupies benches opposite.

Moonpeak
Temple Rd, www.moonpeak.org.
Very atmospheric café where people spill out onto outside tables to enjoy great cappuccinos, sandwiches and fantastic cakes. The first of the many coffee shops. Holds photography and art exhibitions. Free Wi-Fi.

Moonpeak Thali
Next door to Moonpeak.
Has some Himachali dishes.

Rogpa
Jogibara Rd.
Tiny little café serving up lovely cakes and tasty coffee, all for charity. There's a little shop and second-hand stuff too. Recommended.

Tara Café
Bhagsu Rd.
Super-friendly place serving up huge pancakes.

Tenyang
Temple Rd.
Delicious coffee and cakes in a small cafe. Recommended.

Around McLeodganj

$$ Unity
Upper Bhagsu, on path to Dharamkot.
English owner creates amazing food, well presented and now a larger restaurant so more opportunity for wood oven pizzas.

$ Pachamama
Upper Bhagsu.
Great range of healthy global treats from a friendly team.

$ Singh Corner
Bhagsu.
Ah Bhagsu cake straight from the fridge; the original and best chocolate, caramel, biscuit combo. Beware of imitators!

$ Wa Blu
Upper Bhagsu.
Climb the steps for tempting Japanese food, miso soups and juices.

Entertainment

See *Contact*, a free monthly publication. With everyone travelling with laptops now, there is only 1 film club on the strip remaining on Jogibara Rd with a programme of Western films at a rather pricey Rs 150. **Lhamos Croissant** shows documentaries on Tibet. There are open mics at **Carpe Diem**. Indian classical music and Tibetan traditional music often at Yongling School and TIPA.

One Nest, *Lower Dharamkot*. Regular live music in the evenings (Indian Classical and Western nomads), contact dance and free dance sessions.
Tibetan Institute of Performing Arts (**TIPA**), *McLeodganj, www.tibetanarts. org*. Stages occasional music and dance performances; details at the tourist office (see under Tourist information, above).

Shopping

It is pleasantly relaxed to shop here, although competition and prices have increased in recent years. Many items on sale have been imported from the Tibetan market in New Delhi. McLeodganj Bazar is good for Tibetan handicrafts (carpets, metalware, jewellery, jackets, handknitted cardigans, gloves) and lots of Kashmiri items too; there's a special market on Sun.

Bookworm, *near Surya Resort*. Has a good selection of paperbacks, some second-hand. Recommended.

Dolls 4 Tibet is an initiative bringing together Tibetan refugees and local Indian women, making beautiful dolls together. 'We see our Doll Makers grow in confidence and their sense of self worth. Their eyes and smiles say it all when a doll they've finished is admired. The skills they learn are empowering, the money they take home spells a new-found independence and their social interactions across our diverse community benefits not only our team but the wider society.' You can buy them at **The Green Shop** and **Common Ground Café**.

Doritsang Tibetan Culture Centre, *Temple Rd, near SBBI*. Great range of books, CDs, clothes and Tibetan bits and pieces.

Green Shop, *Bhagsu Rd*. Sells recycled and handmade goods including cards and paper. Also sells filtered drinking water for half the price of bottled water.

Jewel of Tibet, *opposite prayer wheels*. Best selection of singing bowls, jewellery and Tibetan arts. Maybe not the cheapest, but certainly the best value.

Norbulingka Shop, *Temple Rd, close to Moonpeak*. Well-crafted bags, cushion covers and clothes from **Norbulingka** – preserving Tibetan cultural arts.

Rogpa, *Jogibara Rd*. Charity based shop selling great gifts, notebooks, cards, bags and wallets. And second hand clothes.

Tibet Book World, *Jogibara Rd, near Yongling School steps*. Best bookshop in town – great range of Buddhist and yogic titles as well as bestsellers.

Tibetan Children's Villages (**TCVs**), *main office on Temple Rd and workshops at various locations around town*. Fabrics and jewellery at fixed prices.

Tibetan Handicrafts Centre, *Jogibara Rd, near the tourist office*. Ask at the office for permission to watch artisans working on carpets, *thangkas*, etc. Reasonable prices.

What to do

Body and soul

McLeodganj and Dharmkot are a haven for all sorts of healing pursuits; check out One Nest and Body Temple in Dharmkot for yoga, massage trainings and courses. There are also several meditation intensive courses in the area.

Buddha Hall, *Main Rd, Bhagsu, T01892-221749*. Yoga, meditation and healing courses.

Himachal Vipassana Centre, *Dhamma Sikhara, next to Tushita, T(0)9218-414051, www.sikhara.dhamma.org. Donations only, reserve in advance, information and registration Mon-Sat 1600-1700*. 10-day retreat, meditation in silence.

Himalayan Iyengar Yoga Centre, *Dharamkot, www.hiyogacentre.com. Starting every Thu at 0830. Information and registration Mon 1330*. Offers 5-day course in Hatha yoga. Now has retreat centre too.

Tushita Meditation Centre, *Dharamkot village 2 km north of McLeodganj, T(0)8988-160988, www.tushita.info. Enquiries Mon-Sat 0930-1130, 1230-1600*. Quiet location, offers individual and group meditation; 10-day 'Introduction to Buddhism' including lectures and meditation (residential courses get fully subscribed, also drop-in guided meditation Mon-Sat 0915-1015 throughout the year, movies relevant to Buddhist interests Mon and Fri 1400, simple accommodation on site.

Z Meditation, *Kandi village, T(0)9418-036956, www.zmeditation.com*. Interesting course including yoga and meditation. Retreats offered in silence with separate discussion sessions, 5 days (Mon 1600-Sat 1100), includes a 'humble' breakfast; highly recommended for beginners, run by friendly couple in a peaceful location with beautiful views.

Tibetan cookery

Lhamo's Kitchen, *next to Green Shop, Bhagsu Rd T(0)9816-468719*. Runs 3 courses (soups, bread, *momos*), 1100-1300, 1700-1900, Rs 200 each. Friendly, fun, eat what you cook.

Tour operators

Dhauladhar Travels, *Temple Rd, McLeodganj, T01892-221158, dhauladhar@hotmail.com.* Agents for **Indian Airlines**.

HPTDC, *tickets from HPTDC Marketing Office, near SBI, Kotwali Bazar in Dharamshala, T018920-224928.* Luxury coach in season: Dharamshala to McLeodganj, Kangra Temple and Fort, Jawalamukhi, 1000-1900, Rs 200; Dharamshala to McLeodganj, Bhagsunath, Dal Lake, Talnu, Tapovan, Chamunda, 1000-1700, Rs 200.

Skyways Travels, *just off main square, Temple Rd, T(0)9857-400001.* Reliable travel agent who is a mine of knowledge and even has Paypal. Can make travelling in India a whole lot easier. Also for tours to Jammu and Kashmir, Rajasthan; trekking, camping and paragliding locally.

Summit Adventures, *main square, Bhagsu Nag, McLeodganj, T01892-221679, www.summit-adventures.net.* Specialist in trekking and climbing, also cultural trips and a yoga trekking tour.

Ways Tours & Travels, *Temple Rd, T01892-221775, waystour@vsnl.net.* Most reliable, Mr Gupta is very experienced, and provides professional service.

Trekking

The best seasons are Apr-Jun and Sep-Oct. Rates are upwards of Rs 1400 per person per day. See also **Summit Adventures**, above. For general trekking information, see page 15.

Highpoint Adventures, *Kareri Lodge, T01892-220931, www.trek.123himachal.com.* Organize treks for smaller groups and a range of tours.

Mountaineering Institute, *Mirza Ismail Rd, T01892-221787. Mon-Sat 1000-1700.* Invaluable advice on routes, equipment, accommodation, campsites, etc. Equipment and porters can be hired for groups of 8 or more, with reasonable charges. The deputy director (SR Saini) has described many routes in *Treks and Passes of Dhauladhar and Pir Pinjal* (Rs 150) although the scale of maps can be misleading. Consult the author for detailed guidance.

Transport

It is dangerous to drive at night in the hills.

Air Nearest airport is at Gaggal, T01892-232374, 13 km away (taxi Rs 650). To/from **Delhi** with **Air India** and **Spicejet**, www.spicejet.com.

Local bus Buses and share jeeps between Dharamshala and McLeodganj, 10 km, 30 mins, Rs 10/Rs 25.

Long-distance bus Most originate in Dharamshala, T01892-224903, but some super and semi-deluxe buses leave from below the taxi stand in McLeodganj. **HRTC** enquiries, T01892-221750. **HPTDC** run luxury coaches in season). **Delhi** (Kashmir Gate, 521 km), semi-deluxe coach departs McLeodganj 1700, 14 hrs; deluxe coach 1830, 1945; super deluxe coach, 1900 (Volvo). Prices vary – deluxe coach is around Rs 880 and some of the private companies charge Rs 1200. Avoid **Bedi Travels** with bad suspension. From Delhi at same times. 1930 arrives Lower Dharamshala 1000, recommended for best morning views of the foothills (stops en route). **Dalhousie** and **Chamba**, 8 hrs; **Manali**, 1700, Rs 400, 8 hrs; luxury coach, Rs 650, **Pathankot**, from Mcleod, Rs150. HRTC buses to **Baijnath**, 2½ hrs; **Chandigarh** (248 km), 9 hrs, via Una (overnight stop possible); also deluxe buses to **Dehra Dun**, Rs 410 and **Shimla** (from Dharamshala). **Kangra**, 50 mins, Rs 14; **Kullu** (214 km) 10 hrs; **Manali** (253 km) 11 hrs; best to travel by day (0800), fabulous views but bus gets overcrowded; avoid sitting by door where people start to sit on your lap! Always keep baggage with you; **Pathankot** (90 km), several 1000-1600, 4 hrs, connection for **Amritsar**, 3 hrs; **Shimla** (317 km, via Hamirpur/Bilaspur), 10 hrs.

There are also a range of **private bus services** to **Dalhousie**, **Delhi** (Connaught Pl), **Dehra Dun**, **Kullu Manali** and **Rishikesh** Several private agents, see **Skyway Travels**.

Local taxi Shared by 4, pick up shuttle taxi at Kotwali Bazar on its way down before it turns around at the bus stand, as it is usually full when it passes the taxi stand.

Long-distance taxi Can be hired from near the bus stands, T01892-221205. Between Dharamshala and McLeodganj,

Rs 150; to Pathankot around Rs 1500-2000 depending on size of vehicle.

Train The nearest broad-gauge railhead is at Pathankot. Booking office at the bus stand, below the tourist office, 1000-1100. For narrow-gauge railway, see page 146.

Kangra Valley

pretty valleys and paragliding opportunities

The Kangra Valley, between the Dhauladhar and the Shiwalik foothills, starts near Mandi and runs northwest to Pathankot. It is named after the town of Kangra but now the largest and main centre is Dharamshala. Chamba State, to its north, occupies part of the Ravi River Valley and some of the Chenab Valley.

Kangra

Kangra (altitude 615 m), 18 km south of Dharamshala, was once the second most important kingdom in the West Himalaya after Kashmir. Kangra town, the capital, was also known as Bhawan or Nagarkot. It overlooks the Banganga River and claims to have existed since the Vedic period with historical reference in Alexander's war records.

Kangra Fort ① *foreigners Rs 300, Indians Rs 150 (all admissions include audio guide), auto-rickshaw Rs 150 return, taxi Rs 250*, stands on a steep rock dominating the valley. A narrow path leads from the ticket office up steps to the fort, which was once protected by several gates (now reconstructed) and had the palace of the Katoch kings at the top. Just inside the complex is a small museum displaying Hindu and Jain stone statues, while further up the hill is an old Jain temple (still in use) and the ruins of a temple with exquisite carvings on its rear outer wall. At the very top, the remains of Sansar Chand's palace offer commanding views. The fort is worth the effort for these views alone. At its foot is a large modern Jain temple which has pilgrim accommodation (worth considering if you get stuck). There is also an overgrown British cemetery just next to the fort entrance.

Brajesvari Devi Temple, in Kangra Town, achieved a reputation for gold, pearls and diamonds and attracted many Muslim invaders from the 11th century, including Mahmud of Ghazni, the Tughlaqs and the Lodis, who periodically plundered its treasures and destroyed the idols. In the intervening years the temple was rebuilt and refurbished several times but in the great earthquake of 1905 both the temple and the fort were badly damaged. The Devi received unusual offerings from devotees. According to Abul Fazal, the pilgrims "cut out their tongues which grew again in the course of two or three days and sometimes in a few hours"! The present temple in which the deity sits under a silver dome with silver *chhatras* (umbrellas) was built in 1920 and stands behind the crowded, colourful bazar. The State Government maintains the temple; the priests are expected to receive gifts in kind only. The area is busy, atmospheric and rather dirty, with mostly pilgrim-oriented stalls. Above these is **St Paul's Church** and a Christian community.

Along the river between Old Kangra (where the main road meets the turning to the fort) and Kangra Mandir is a pleasant trail, mostly following long-disused roads past ruined houses and temples which evidence a once sizeable town. Kangra's bus stand is 1.5 km north of the temple.

BACKGROUND
Kangra Valley

In 1620 Shah Jahan captured Kangra fort for his father Jahangir, and Kangra became a Mughal province. Many of the court artists fled to neighbouring Chamba and Kullu as the Rajas submitted to Mughal rule. When Mughal power weakened, the 16-year-old **Sansar Chand Katoch II** (1775-1823) recaptured the fort and the rajas reasserted their independence. Under his powerful leadership, Kangra sought to extend its boundaries into the Chamba and Kullu Valleys but this was forestalled by the powerful Gurkhas from Nepal. With the rise of the Sikh empire, the valley was occupied until the Treaty of Amritsar. Then under the British, Dharamshala was made the administrative capital of the region which led to the decline of Kangra.

The **Kangra School of Painting** originated by virtue of Raja Goverdhan Singh (1744-1773) of Guler, who gave shelter to many artists who had fled from the Mughals, and during the mid-18th century a new style of miniature painting developed. Based on Mughal miniature style, the subject matter derived from Radha/Krishna legends, the rajas and gods being depicted in a local setting. Under Sansar Chand II the region prospered and the Kangra School flourished. Kangra fort, where he held court for nearly 25 years, was adorned with paintings and attracted art lovers from great distances. The 1905 earthquake damaged many of these buildings though you can still see some miniature wall paintings.

Masrur
A sandstone ridge to the northeast of the village of Masrur (altitude 800 m), 34 km southwest of Dharamshala, has 15 ninth- to 10th-century *sikhara* temples excavated out of solid rock. They are badly eroded and partly ruined. Even in this state they have been compared with the larger rock-cut temples at Ellora in Maharashtra and at Mamallapuram south of Chennai. Their ridge-top position commands a superb view over the surrounding fertile countryside, but few of the original *shikharas* stand, and some of the most beautifully carved panels are now in the State Museum, Shimla. There are buses from Kangra.

Jawalamukhi
This is one of the most popular Hindu pilgrimage sites in Himachal and is recognized as one of 51 *Shakti pitha*. The **Devi temple**, tended by the followers of Gorakhnath, is set against a cliff and from a fissure comes a natural inflammable gas which accounts for the blue 'Eternal Flame'. Natural springs feed the two small pools of water; one appears to boil, the other with the flame flaring above the surface contains surprisingly cold water. Emperor Akbar's gift of gold leaf covers the dome. In March/April there are colourful celebrations during the **Shakti Festival**; another in mid-October. There is accommodation here, and buses to/from Kangra.

Pragpur
Pragpur, across the River Beas, 20 km southwest of Jawalamukhi, is a medieval 'heritage village' with cobbled streets and slate-roofed houses. The fine 'Judges Court' (1918) nearby has been carefully restored using traditional techniques. A three- to four-day stay is recommended here and it is advisable to reserve ahead.

The little-known 'mountain' railway

A superb narrow-gauge railway links Pathankot in the west with Jogindernagar via Kangra (near Dharamshala) and Baijnath. The views of the Kangra Valley are quite spectacular. This is very much a working service and not a 'relic' (this train can be packed with ordinary users). Sadly, it is often very late as it is incredibly slow, and very uncomfortable because of the hard seats. 'Tourists' would do better to sample short sections of the line, and allow for delays – any purposeful journey is better done by bus. See Train, page 148, for an optimistic timetable.

Stops along the Kangra Valley Railway *See also box, above.*

Jogindernagar is the terminus of the beautiful journey by narrow-gauge rail (enquiries Kangra, T01892-252279) from Pathankot via Kangra. The hydro-power scheme here and at nearby Bassi channels water from the River Uhl. Paragliding and hang-gliding is possible at Billing (33 km), reached via Bir (19 km, see below).

Baijnath's temples are old by hill standards, dating from at least 1204. Note the Lakshmi/Vishnu figure and the graceful balcony window on the north wall. The **Vaidyanatha Temple** (originally circa 800), which contains one of 12 *jyotirlingas*, stands by the roadside on the Mandi-Palampur road, within a vast rectangular enclosure. Originally known as **Kirangama**, its name was changed after the temple was dedicated to **Siva** in his form as the Lord of Physicians. It is a good example of the Nagari style; the walls have the characteristic niches enshrining images of Chamunda, Surya and Karttikeya and the *sikhara* tower is topped with an *amalaka* and pot. A life-size stone Nandi stands at the entrance. There is a bus to and from Mandi taking 3½ hours.

Palampur, 16 km from Baijnath, 40 km from Dharamshala (via Yol), is a pleasant little town for walking, with beautiful snow views, surrounded by old British tea plantations, thriving on horticulture. It is a popular stop with trekkers. The Neugal Khad, a 300-m-wide chasm through which the Bandla flows is very impressive when the river swells during the monsoons. It holds a record for rainfall in the area.

Bir, 30 km east of Palampur, has a fast-growing reputation as one of the best paragliding locations in the world. Bordered by tea gardens and low hills, it also has four Buddhist monasteries worth visiting. Most prominent among these are Choling. You can also pick up fine Tibetan handicrafts from Bir, which has a large Tibetan colony. The village of Billing is 14 km up sharp, hair-raising hairpins and has the hilltop from where paragliders launch; see What to do, below. **Andretta** is an attractive village 13 km from Palampur. It is associated with **Norah Richards**, a follower of Mahatma Gandhi, who popularized rural theatre, and with the artist **Sardar Sobha Singh** who revived the Kangra School of painting. His paintings are big, brightly coloured, ultra-realistic and often devotional, incorporating Sikh, Christian and Hindu images. There is an art gallery dedicated to his work and memory; prints, books and soft drinks are sold in the shop. The **Andretta Pottery** (signposted from the main road), is charming. It is run by an artist couple (Indian/English), who combine village pottery with 'slipware'. The Sikh partner is the son of Gurcharan Singh (of Delhi Blue Pottery fame) and is furthering the tradition of studio pottery; works are for sale.

Where to stay

Kangra
Most hotels on the busy main road are noisy, even at night.

$$$$ Raas Kangra
20 km from Kangra aiport,
www.raashimalaya.com.
Boutique hotel with 41 suites all featuring balconies for panoramic views. It will bring innovative design together with natural beauty.

$ Jannat
Chamunda Rd, T01892-265479.
5 rooms with TV and hot water; there's also a restaurant. The closest to Kangra Mandir railway station.

Pragpur

$$$ Judge's Court (Heritage)
Set in a large orchard, T01970-245035,
www.judgescourt.com.
10 tastefully decorated rooms in a fine mansion, 1 in an annexe, 1 large private modernized suite with veranda. Family hospitality, home-grown vegetables and fruit, fresh river fish and authentic Himachali meals. Tours are available of Kangra Fort and other sights in this pretty village. Lovely atmosphere. Recommended.

Stops along the Kangra Valley Railway

$$$ Taragarh Palace
Al-hilal, 11 km southeast of Palampur,
T01894-242034, www.taragarh.com.
26 rooms in 1930s summer resort, period furniture and tasteful decor in public spaces, tennis, pool, lovely meandering gardens and mango orchards, and luxury Swiss tents in summer.

$$ Colonel's Resort
1 km out of Bir on the Billing road, T(0)9805-534220, www.colonelsresort.com.

8 doubles, 2 singles (simple, comfortable rooms) and 2 cottages, tents in garden (seasonal). Set in pear orchards and a working tea plantation, with sublime views down the valley and behind into Dhauladhar mountains. Its proximity to Bir makes it popular with paragliders, plus there's good hiking in the area.

$$ Darang Tea Estate
10 km from Palampur, T(0)9418-012565,
www.darangteaestate.com.
2 cottages and 1 room in the main house. A family-run homestay in a beautiful working tea estate. Exceptional food and warm hospitality. Recommended.

$$ The Tea-Bud (HPTDC)
2 km from bus stand, Palampur, T01894-231298, www.hptdc.nic.in.
A clean and quiet place in a beautiful setting, with 31 rooms. The deluxe category are in a newer block, while the older rooms are totally acceptable. There's hot water, restaurant, pleasant lawn, good service and ayurvedic treatments available.

$ Uhl (HPTDC)
Near Power House, on the hill outside Jogindernagar, T01908-222002,
www.hptdc.nic.in.
Unpretentious, clean and peaceful hotel offering 16 rooms with bath; the best are upstairs with a balcony. Restaurant. An eccentric though fairly clean little hut does chicken dinners.

What to do

Bir
Paragliding
Although unsuitable for beginners, there are courses available for intermediate fliers and a few residential pilots with tandem rigs. **Touching Cloud Base**, *www.touchingcloud base.com.* An excellent company offering great instruction and tandem flights.

Transport

Kangra

Air Gaggal Airport, see Dharamshala, page 143.

Bus To **Dharamshala**, Rs 20, under 1 hr.

Taxi A taxi to **Dharamshala** costs Rs 400.

Train Narrow-gauge **Kangra Valley Railway**, enquiries T01892-265026. From **Pathankot** to **Jogindernagar** (10 hrs) or **Baijnath**, reaching Kangra after 4½ hrs. **Jogindernagar to Pathankot**: reaches Kangra in 5-6 hrs; **Baijnath to Pathankot** arrives in Kangra in 3-4 hrs.

Chamba Valley

pretty temples and picturesque villages

Dalhousie

The spectacular mountain views in the hill station of Dalhousie (population 7400, altitude 2030 m) make it a popular bolt hole for tourists from the plains, but the main reason for its importance today is due to the number of good schools and the presence of the army.

The town was named after its governor-general (1848-1856) and was developed on land purchased by the British in 1853 from the Raja of Chamba. It sprawls out over five hills just east of the Ravi River. By 1867 it was a sanatorium and reached its zenith in the 1920s and 1930s as a cheaper alternative to Shimla, and the most convenient hill station for residents of Lahore. Rabindranath Tagore wrote his first poem in Dalhousie as a boy and Subhash Chandra Bose came secretly to plan his strategies during the Second World War. Its popularity declined after 1947 and it became a quiet hill station with old colonial bungalows, now almost hidden among thick pine forests interspersed with oak, deodar and rhododendron.

The three Malls laid out for level walks are around Moti Tibba, Potreyn Hill and Upper Bakrota. The last, the finest, is about 330 m above **Gandhi Chowk** around which the town centres. From there two rounds of the Mall lead to Subhash Chowk. The sizeable Tibetan community makes and sells handicrafts, woollens, jackets, cardigans and rugs. Their paintings and rock carvings in low relief can be seen along Garam Sarak Mall.

Echoes of the colonial past include five functioning churches: diminutive **St John's** (1863) on Gandhi Chowk is open for Sunday service (0930 summer, 1000 winter) and the large Catholic church of St Francis (1894) on Subhash Chowk is often open to visitors. The nostalgic **Dalhousie Club** (1895) displays old Raj-era photos and has preserved the original billiards table. The library contains bizarre English fiction and biographies, but sadly beer is not available in the bar.

Just over 2 km from Gandhi Chowk is the **Martyr's Memorial** at Panchpulla (five bridges), which commemorates Ajit Singh, a supporter of Subhash Bose and the Indian National Army during the Second World War. There are several small waterfalls in the vicinity, and on the way you can see the **Satdhara** (seven springs), said to contain mica and medicinal properties. **Subhash Baoli** (1.5 km from Gandhi Square), is another spring. It is an easy climb and offers good views of the snows. Half a kilometre away **Jhandri Ghat**, the old palace of Chamba rulers, is set among tall pine trees. For a longer walk try the Bakrota Round (5 km), which gives good views of the mountains and takes you through the Tibetan settlement.

Kalatope and Khajjiar

Kalatope Wildlife Sanctuary, 9 km from Dalhousie, with good mountain views, is a level walk through a forest sanctuary with accommodation in a pretty forest rest house bungalow (permission required from the DFO, Wildlife, Chamba, dfocha-hp@nic.in). There are good walking routes in the area, and wildlife includes black bears, leopards and serows. **Khajjiar**, 22 km further along the motorable road, is a long, wide glade ringed by cedars with a small lake and a floating island. Locals call it 'Mini Switzerland'. You can explore both areas in a pleasant three-day walk, alternatively a 30-km path through dense deodar forest leads from Khajjiar to Chamba. Buses to Khajjiar from Dalhousie take one hour.

Chamba

Picturesque Chamba (population 20,000, altitude 996 m) is on the south bank of the Iravati (Ravi), its stone houses clinging to the hillside. Some see the medieval town as having an almost Italian feel, surrounded by lush forests and with its Chaugan (or grassy meadow) in the centre. Although that's stretching it a little and recent developments have somewhat diminished its appeal, the warmer climes, unusual temples and mellow ambiance remain most attractive. Most hotels, temples and palaces are within walking distance of the bus stand.

Founded in the 10th century, Chamba State was on an important trade route from Lahaul to Kashmir and was known as the 'Middle Kingdom'. Though Mughal suzerainty was accepted by the local rajas, the kingdom remained autonomous but it came under Sikh rule from 1810-1846. Its relative isolation led to the nurturing of the arts – painting, temple sculpture, handicrafts and unique 'rumal'. These pieces of silk/cotton with fine embroidery imitate miniature paintings; the reverse is as good as the front.

The **Chaugan**, once almost a kilometre long, is the central hub of the town but sadly, over the last three decades, shops have encroached into the open space. There are several ancient Pahari temples in the town with attractive curvilinear stone towers. Follow the steep and winding road through the market to the **Lakshmi Narayana Temple Complex** (ninth to 11th centuries) containing six *sikhara* temples with deep wooden eaves, several smaller shrines and a tank. Three are dedicated to Vishnu and three to Siva, with some of the brass images inlaid with copper and silver. The **Hari Rai Temple**, next to the Chaugan (14th century), contains a fine 11th-century life-sized bronze Chaturmurti (four-armed Vishnu), rarely visible as it is usually 'dressed'; carved on the outer wall are Tantric couples. Close to the Aroma Hotel is the **Champavati Temple**, with carved wooden pillars, named after the daughter of Raja Sahil Varma who moved the capital here from Bharmour in AD 920 at her request. Others of note in the town centre are the Bansigopal, Sita Ram and Radha Krishna temples.

The 10th-century wooden **Chamunda Devi Temple**, 500 m uphill via steep steps from the bus stand, has some interesting wood carvings on its eaves and a square sanctum decked with bells. A further 500 m along the road to Saho is the elegantly slender **Bajreshwari Temple** with an octagonal roof, adjoined by a small, square unadorned temple.

The eye-catching **Akhand Chandi**, the Chamba Maharajas' palace, beyond the Lakshmi Narayan complex, is now a college. The old **Rang Mahal** (Painted Palace) in the Surara Mohalla was built by Raja Umed Singh in the mid-18th century. A prisoner of the Mughals for 16 years, he was influenced by their architectural style. The wall paintings in one room are splendid. The theme is usually religious, Krishna stories being particularly popular. Some of these were removed, together with carvings and manuscripts, to the Bhuri Singh Museum after a fire. The building now houses a sub-post office and a handicrafts workshop.

Bhuri Singh Museum ① *Museum Rd, Mon-Sat 1000-1700, Rs 100*, is a three-storey building (top floor currently closed) housing a heritage collection including some excellent *rumals*, carvings and fine examples of Chamba, Kangra and Basholi schools of miniature paintings. Archaeological finds include the remarkable 'fountain slabs' that adorned the spouts of village water sources. Dating from the 10th-18th centuries and hewn from local stone, these were memorials erected to the deceased; they are unique in Indian art. There are also many old photographs showing Chamba in its heyday. Opposite the museum is the finely built **St Andrew's Church**, belonging to the Church of Scotland and completed in 1905.

Bharmour

Capital of the princely state of Chamba for over 400 years, the tiny town of Bharmour (altitude 2130 m) is surrounded by high ranges and is snow-covered for six months of the year. It's 65 km from Chamba along a gruelling but incredibly scenic road, beset by landslides. Bharmour's ancient temples and its proximity to Manimahesh Lake and Manimahesh Kailash peak (5656 m) make it hallowed place, while alpine pastures in the region are home to Gaddi tribespeople (see below). The stone-built villages with slate-roofed houses adjoining Bharmour, and the snowy peaks all round, make it a beautiful spot.

The famous **Chaurasi** temple square has 84 shrines within, of varying architectural styles, built between the seventh and 10th centuries. The towering *sikhara* of **Manimahesh (Shiv) Temple** dominates the complex. Giant deodars flank the entrance, which is guarded by a life-size Nandi bull in polished brass; devotees whisper a wish in his ear and crawl under him for good health (a tight squeeze for some). The sanctum of the delicate **Lakshna Devi temple** (c 700 AD) houses a metre-high idol of the goddess cast in bronze. The wooden exterior, particularly the door jambs, is beautifully carved; a marvellous pair of un-eroded lions flank the door to the inner shrine.

Manimahesh, 34 km distant, has a lake in which pilgrims bathe during the Yatra (August-September) and worship at the lakeside temple. Shiva resides on the holy mountain of the same name. Helicopter flights go from the helipad above the Chaurasi complex in Bharmour to Gaurikund during the Yatra, return journey Rs 7000 (www.simmsammairways.com).

Bharmour is the centre of the **Gaddis**, shepherds who move their flocks of sheep and goats, numbering from a couple of hundred to a thousand, from lower pastures at around 1500 m during winter to higher slopes at over 3500 m, after snow-melt. They are usually only found in the Dhauladhar range which separates Kangra from Chamba. Some believe that these herdsmen first arrived in this part of Himachal in the 10th century though some moved from the area around Lahore (Pakistan) in the 18th century, during the Mughal period. Their religious belief combines animism with the worship of Siva; Bharmour's distinctive Manimahesh Temple is their principal centre of worship. In the winter the Gaddis can be seen round Kangra, Mandi and Bilaspur and in the small villages between Baijnath and Palampur. The men traditionally wear a *chola* (a loose white woollen garment), tied at the waist with a black wool rope and a white embroidered cap.

Tourist information

Dalhousie

Himachal Tourism
Near the bus stand, T01899-242 136.
Open 1000-1700.
Helpful for transport information, but
opening hours can be irregular out of season.

Chamba

Tourist Office
Hotel Iravati complex, see Where to stay,
below, T01899-222 671. Mon-Sat 1000-1630.

Where to stay

Dalhousie

$$$ Grand View
Near bus stand, T(0)86288 10659,
www.grandviewdalhousie.in.
53 spacious, well-equipped rooms (5 price
categories) in the best-preserved of
Dalhousie's many Raj-era hotels. The views
from the terrace are stunning, while the
restaurant and lounge bar (awaiting license
at the time of research!) are quintessentially
British. Gym and sauna and off-season
package deals are worth checking out.
Recommended.

$$$-$$ Silverton Estate Guest House
Near Circuit House, the Mall, T01899-240674,
www.heritagehotels.com/silverton. Closed
off season.
Old colonial building in large grounds,
5 rooms with dressing rooms, TV.

$$ Manimahesh (HPTDC)
Near the bus stand, T01899-242793,
www.hptdc.nic.in.
The 18 carpeted rooms are rather faded in
this typical tourist department hotel, which
has a cheap restaurant, bar with sofas and
good mountain views.

$ Crags
Off the Mall, T(0)89881 74574.
The 100 steps separating this place from
the Mall are the only disadvantage to this
excellent budget choice. The rooms are
dated but very clean with attached bath
(hot water) and a bell to ring for service.
Cheap and delicious meals are served, there
are good views east down the valley from
the huge (if not particularly attractive)
a terrace. Staff are very friendly, and the
elderly owner is pretty stylish and used to
catering to foreign travellers. A separate
cottage is a more recent addition for a
slightly higher price.

$ Geetanjali (HPTDC)
Thandi Sarak, steep 5-min climb from the bus
stand, T01899-242155.
10 huge rooms with bath (reliable hot water),
towels and clean sheets provided – but
expect mildew-scented air as it's a very
run-down colonial building.

$ Youth Hostel
Behind Manimahesh, T01899-242189,
www.youthhosteldalhousie.org.
Well-maintained modern building with
double rooms (Rs 300) and single sex dorms
(Rs 150). Internet, free Wi-Fi and dining hall.
Gets busy with groups so book ahead.

Kalatope and Khajjiar

$$$-$$ Mini Swiss
Khajjiar, T01189-923 6364, www.miniswiss.in.
Comfortable, very clean rooms in a 5-storey
building with great views, good restaurant
and bar, pool table and ping-pong.

$$ Devdar (HPTDC)
Khajjiar, T01899-236333, www.hptdc.nic.in.
Clean rooms (doubles and suites), dorm
(Rs 150) and a nice cottage (Rs 3000), simple
restaurant, horse riding, beautiful setting.
Free Wi-Fi.

Chamba

During Manimahesh Yatra in Sep hotels are often full.

$$ Iravati (HPTDC)
Court Rd, near bus stand, T01899-222671.
Friendly management, 19 variable rooms with bath and hot water. Regular rooms start at Rs 1500; they're spacious, nicely tiled, clean and overlook the Chaugan. The higher up the building, the better the views and the higher the prices. Decent restaurant.

$$-$ Aroma Palace
Near Rang Palace, Court Lane, T01899-225677, www.hotelaromapalacechamba.com.
Rooms range from economy to sumptuous honeymoon suite, which are all spotless, plus there's a restaurant and airy terrace. Breakfast is included and discounts are possible.

$$-$ Himalayan Orchard Huts
10 km out of town, T(0)94180 20401, www.himalayanlap.com.
Idyllic location, 20 mins' walk from nearest road, rooms in the guesthouse are set in a delightful garden with a spring-water pool, beautiful views from large terraces with hammocks, clean shared shower and toilets. Or you can pitch a tent in the garden. There's superb home cooking (a great all-inclusive deal), and it's run by a very friendly family. Recommended. They also own **Ridgemore Cottage**, a trekkers' hut atop a ridge, 4 hrs' walk from Orchard Hut. Highly recommended.

$ Chamba Guesthouse
Gopal Nivas, near Gandhi Gate, by the Chaugan, T01899-222564.
Simple lodgings with wooden floors and charm, this budget hotel almost hangs over the Ravi River with amazing views from the balcony. A popular choice, try to book ahead.

Bharmour

$ Him Kailash Homestay
Near the bus stop, T01895-225100.
Simple, friendly place with clean freshly painted rooms that have good valley views.

The cheapest rooms (Rs 500) don't have a TV or geyser, or even curtains; much larger rooms with proper amenities cost Rs 1000. There's not much English spoken.

Restaurants

Dalhousie

$$ Napoli
Near Gandhi Chowk.
Serving pizza, Indian and Chinese, meat and veg dishes in large portions. Very friendly and comfortable.

$ Friend's Dhaba
Subhash Chowk.
Good, unpretentious Punjabi, including *paneer burji* to die for.

Chamba
There are a number of atmospheric little *dhabas* in the alleys through Dogra Market.

$$-$ Copper Chimney
5th floor, White House Hotel.
Great tandoor over offerings and veg/non-veg Indian and Chinese food. Comfy a/c indoor section or 4 intimate tables on the roof terrace. It's a long slog up the stairs, however.

$ Jagaan
1st floor, Museum Rd.
Good selection served in a relatively calm atmosphere. *Chamba madhra* (Rs 90), a rich stew of kidney beans, ghee and curd, is a local speciality.

$ Ravi View Café
Next to Chaugan.
Reasonable snacks and Indian veg food plus beer. This HPTDC-run circular hut even has outside tables with killer views overlooking the river.

Festivals

Chamba
Apr Suhi Mela, lasts 3 days, commemorates a Rani who consented to be buried alive in

a dry stream bed in order that it could flow and provide the town with water. Women and children in traditional dress carry images of her to a temple on the hill, accompanied by songs sung in her praise. Men are strictly prohibited from participating.

Jul-Aug Gaddis and Gujjars take part in many cultural events to mark the start of harvesting. **Minjar** is a 7-day harvest festival when people offer thanks to Varuna the rain god. Decorated horses and banners are taken out in procession through the streets to mark its start. Sri Raghuvira is followed by other images of gods in palanquins and the festival ends at the River Irawati where people float *minjars* (tassels of corn and coconut).

Shopping

Dalhousie
Bhuttico, *The Mall (Garam Sarak), www. bhutticoshawls.com. Mon-Sat 0900-1930.* Fixed price shop, with branches nationwide, selling top quality Kullu shawls, socks and pullas (slippers with grass soles) that incorporate traditional designs.

Chamba
Handicrafts Centre, *Rang Mahal.* Rumal embroidery and leather goods.

Transport

Dalhousie
Air The nearest airport is at Gaggal; see Dharamshala, page 143.

Bus Dalhousie is on the NH1A. **Amritsar**, 7 hrs; **Delhi**, 12 hrs; To **Chamba** 4 buses daily, 2 go via Khajjiar, 2½ hrs; **Dharamshala**, 7 hrs; **Jammu**, 7 hrs. There's a regular service to **Pathankot** (change in Pathankot for frequent services to main towns/cities); **Shimla**, 1245, 14 hrs. Note that Banikhet village, 10 mins from Dalhousie, has many more bus options.

Jeep/Taxi From bus stand up to **Gandhi Chowk**, Rs 100, **Bakrota**, Rs 200.

Train Nearest station is at Pathankot, 2 hrs by taxi. There is a helpful Railway Out Agency close to the bus stand.

Chamba
Bus The hectic bus stand is at the south end of the Chaugan. To **Bharmour** (3 hrs, Rs 70); **Dalhousie** (2½ hrs, Rs 50); and to **Shimla** once per day.

Jeep hire is relatively expensive. Special service during **Manimahesh Yatra**.

Train Nearest station is at Pathankot, 120 km away.

Jammu
& Kashmir

The shimmering lakes, fertile valleys and remote, snow-covered peaks of Kashmir have had a magnetic appeal to rulers, pilgrims and humble travellers, from the Mughals onwards.

With levels of political violence going down in recent years, and the prominent marketing of houseboats, golf courses and ski resorts, Indian tourists are returning to Srinagar in large numbers. However, there remains an obvious military presence, and be aware that curfews or demonstrations might still occur. Trekking in the Vale of Kashmir should be undertaken only after careful research and with a reliable guide. Yet foreigners will find themselves warmly welcomed by the Kashmiris, and in Srinagar and the surrounding area there is plenty to see and do, not to mention to buy and to eat.

The state is equally famed for the magnificent realm of Ladakh and its capital, Leh, set in some of the world's most beautiful scenery. Here you can trek to your heart's content among some of the highest-altitude passes in the world, in one of India's remotest regions. The spectacular high-altitude deserts of Ladakh and Zanskar provide the setting for a hardy Buddhist culture whose villages and monasteries retain strong links with Tibet. Alchi, Hemis and Thiksey are just three of many striking monasteries clinging to mountainsides.

Essential Jammu and Kashmir

Finding your feet

The Himalayan states of Jammu and Kashmir comprise three regions of stark geographical and cultural diversity. Jammu, in the southwest, is a predominantly Hindu region bordering the Punjab, its foothills forming the transitional zone between the plains and the mountains. To the north the Shiwalik mountains give way to the Pir Panjal (5000 m). Between the Pir Panjal and the High Himalaya, around 1580 m, lies the largely Islamic Vale of Kashmir, where snow-capped peaks form a backdrop to the capital, Srinagar.

To the west and north are the Buddhist mountain provinces of Ladakh and Zanskar. The Zanskar River cuts an impressive course of 120 km before slicing through the mountains in a series of impressive gorges to join the Indus at Nimmu near Leh, the capital of Ladakh. During the winter months, the frozen Zanskar River provides the only access for Zanskaris into Ladakh. Combined with its two subsidiary valleys, the Stod (Doda Chu) and the Lung-Nak (Tsarap Chu or 'Valley of Darkness'), which converge below Padum, the main 300-km-long valley is ringed by mountains, so access to it is over one of the high passes. Ladakh also has the world's largest glaciers outside the polar regions, and the large and beautiful lake Pangong Tso, 150 km long and 4 km wide, at a height of over 4000 m. This makes for spectacular trekking country.

Getting around

Trains run as far as Jammu. Buses and jeeps go to Srinagar and on to Leh, which also has a spectacular road connection to Manali in Himachal Pradesh. There are domestic flights to Jammu, Srinagar and Leh.

When to go

Kashmir and Ladakh are best visited from May to October, unless you like freezing temperatures and harsh winter. The snow season in Gulmarg runs from December to April. Avoid the Vale of Kashmir on contentious dates such as Republic Day (26 January). Even in the Vale, the air in summer is fresh and at night can be quite brisk. The highest daytime temperatures in July rarely exceed 35°C but may fall as low as -11°C in winter. A short climb quickly reduces these temperatures. In Ladakh the sun cuts through the thin atmosphere, and daily and seasonal temperature variations are even wider. The rain-bearing clouds drifting in from the Arabian Sea never reach Ladakh, while Srinagar receives over 650 mm per annum, Leh has only 85 mm, much as snow. Over half Srinagar's rain comes with westerly depressions in the winter.

Time required

At least a week for the Vale of Kashmir and a houseboat stay; eight days in Ladakh to acclimatize and visit sights, more if you want to add in a trek or the Nupra Valley.

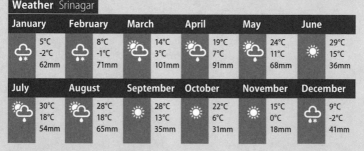

Weather Srinagar

January	February	March	April	May	June
5°C -2°C 62mm	8°C -1°C 71mm	14°C 3°C 101mm	19°C 7°C 91mm	24°C 11°C 68mm	29°C 15°C 36mm

July	August	September	October	November	December
30°C 18°C 54mm	28°C 18°C 65mm	28°C 13°C 35mm	22°C 6°C 31mm	15°C 0°C 18mm	9°C -2°C 41mm

Kashmir
Valley

The beauty of the Vale of Kashmir, with its snow-dusted mountains looming in shades of purple above serene lakes and wildflower meadows, still has the power to reduce grown poets to tears. Nonetheless, the reality of military occupation pervades many aspects of daily life, with army camps, bunkers and checkposts positioned every few hundred metres along the highways and throughout the countryside. Travellers can expect to encounter extremes of beauty and friendliness, not to mention hard salesmanship in an economy that was starved of tourist income for over 20 years.

Jammu and around

low-key winter capital with a strongly Hindu flavour

Jammu (population 951,373), the second largest city in the state, is the winter capital of government and main entry point for Kashmir by train. While it doesn't possess the charm of Srinagar, it is a pleasant enough city to spend a day. Built in 1730 by the Dogra rulers as their capital, Jammu marks the transition between the Punjab plains and the Himalaya hills.

Sights
Raghunath Temple ① *0600-2130, inner sanctum closes 1130-1800, museum 0600-1000, cloakroom for bags/cameras.* Raghunath Temple, in the old centre, is one of the largest temple complexes in North India, and dates from 1857. The temple, dedicated to Lord Rama, has a series of glittering gilded spires and seven shrines. The main shrine's interior is gold-plated, while surrounding shrines contain millions of 'saligrams' (mini-lingams fixed onto slabs of stone), most of which are fossils.

Rambiresvar Temple Centrally located on the Shalimar Road, **Rambiresvar Temple** (1883) is the largest Siva temple in North India. It is dedicated to Siva and named after its founder Maharaja Ranbir Singh. The 75-m orange tower is rather unattractive, but the

Safety warning for the Kashmir Valley

Many governments still advise against travel to the Kashmir Valley, with the exceptions of: the cities of Jammu and Srinagar; travel between these two cities on the Jammu-Srinagar highway; and the region of Ladakh. Take advice from your consulate, and be aware that travelling against their advice can render your travel insurance void. Most travellers report no problems, but it is essential to be careful and keep informed about the current political situation. For an on-the-ground perspective, check www.greaterkashmir.com and www.kashmirtimes.com.

Grenade attacks on army bunkers in the city used to be common and in the past, splinter groups took hostages as a means of putting pressure on the Indian government. Given the tensions between Kashmir and the government, Indian tourists are more likely to be directly targeted than foreigners. However, in recent years there has been a decline in violence overall and increasing numbers of Indian and Western tourists are visiting the valley.

If you are in town and see the shop shutters coming down before closing time, this is generally a sign that a protest is approaching. Either beat a hasty retreat in an auto-rickshaw, or take shelter in a shop until the demonstrators and police have passed. Always ask how the situation is before heading to the old city (Downtown) and don't go there on Fridays, when spontaneous demonstrations following afternoon prayers are more likely to occur. The Dal and Nagin lake areas are hardly affected on such occasions; at worst, you might not be able to get transport during a *bandh* (general shutdown). For background information on the political situation in Kashmir, see box, page 160.

central 2.3-m sphatik shivling is an extraordinary crystal lingam. A fine bronze Nandi bull watches the entrance to the shrine.

Mubarak Mandi About 700 m from the Rambiresvar Temple are the palace buildings of Mubarak Mandi. Dating from 1824, they blend Rajasthani, Mughal and baroque architectural elements. Within the dilapidated complex is the **Dogra Art Gallery** ① *Tue-Sun 1030-1630, foreigners Rs 5*, displaying royal memorabilia in the Pink Hall.

Amar Mahal Museum ① *Apr-Sep 0900-1300, 1400-1800, Oct-Mar 0900-1300, 1400-1700, foreigners Rs100, Rs 150 by auto-rickshaw from the centre of town, or take a minibus.* The Amar Mahal Museum is superbly sited on the bend of the Tawi, just off Srinagar Road, and has great views of the river. There is a maharajas' portrait gallery and 18th-century Pahari miniature paintings of *Mahabharata* scenes. The early 20th-century palace is a curiosity`; its French designer gave it château-like roofs and turrets. Look through a rear window to see Hari Singh's 100 kg golden canopied throne. Other rooms show modern art; admission to the library (with a fine collection of antique books) is only for researchers. The Hari Niwas Hotel is adjacent; the lawns are a welcome spot for refreshments when it's not too hot.

Bahu Fort Across the Tawi River lies the impressive **Bahu Fort**, thought to have a 3000-year history. The ramparts have been renovated and are now surrounded by a lush terraced garden, the Bagh-e-Bahu.

Vaishno Devi

The Vaishno Devi cave, 61 km north of Jammu, is one of the region's most important pilgrimage sites. As the temple draws near you hear cries of 'Jai Matadi' (Victory to the Mother Goddess). Then at the shrine entrance, pilgrims walk in batches through cold ankle-deep water to the low and narrow cave entrance to get a glimpse of the deity. Visitors joining the *yatra* find it a very moving experience. The main pilgrimage season is March to July.

The arduous climb along the 13-km track to the cave temple has been re-laid, widened and tiled, and railings provided. Another road from Lower Sanjichat to the Darbar brings you 2 km closer with 300 m less to climb. Ponies, *dandies* (a kind of local palanquin for carrying tourists) and porters are available from Katra at fixed rates. Auto-rickshaws and taxis can go as far as the Banganga.

Yatra slips are issued free of charge by the **Yatra Registration Counter (YRC)** in the bus stand in Katra. The slip must be presented at the Banganga checkpoint within six hours (or you face disciplinary action if caught). One slip can be used for up to nine people. If you are on your own or in a small group, you can usually avoid having to wait for a group if you present yourself at Gates 1 or 2, and smile.

Visitors should leave all leather items in a cloakroom at Vaishno Devi before entering the cave; take bottled water and waterproofs. Tea, drinks and snacks are available on the route.

The Jammu–Srinagar road

It's a stunning journey through the mountains as the bus winds its way up to the Jawahar tunnel that burrows through the Pir Panjal, with the jade-green Chenab river flowing hundreds of feet below. Emerging from the tunnel on the other side, high in the hills of south Kashmir, travellers are treated to a breathtaking view of the valley spread before out before them. Two new tunnels are being constructed, due to open in 2016/2017, which will cut the journey time to five hours, so now is the time to enjoy this road.

Essential Jammu

Finding your feet

The airport is within the city with prepaid taxis available to the centre (Ragunath Bazar). There are daily flights from Delhi, Mumbai and Srinagar, and twice-weekly flights to Leh (in high season). The railway station is in the New Town, across the Tawi River, a few kilometres from the old hilltop town where most of the budget hotels are located. The general bus stand, where inter-state buses arrive, is at the foot of the steps off the Srinagar Road in the old town. See Transport, page 162.

Getting around

The frequent, cheap city bus service or an auto-rickshaw come in handy, as the two parts of town and some sights are far apart.

When to go

The best time to visit is from November to March.

Safety

For safety information see box, opposite.

BACKGROUND
Recent history of the Kashmir conflict

Of the total area of Kashmir over which India continues to claim the legitimate right to govern, 78,000 sq km are currently controlled by Pakistan and a further 42,600 sq km by China. Kashmir has remained the single most important cause of conflict between India and Pakistan since 1949, while arguments for autonomy within the Kashmir Valley have periodically dominated the political agenda. The insurgency that started in the late 1980s has gone through several evolutions. Until the mid-1990s, it was overt and highly visible, with parts of Srinagar being held by the militants, openly carrying arms. Fierce counter-insurgency measures forced them underground, but the violence continued. Meanwhile, in May 1999, war broke out between Pakistan and India, in the Kargil area, lasting two months. The tension reached a peak in June 2002 after an attack on the Indian parliament in December 2001, allegedly carried out by Pakistan-based militants. Internationally, there were serious fears that the two countries were on the brink of nuclear war but thankfully the situation was wound down following a new agreement between India and Pakistan to try and find a peaceful solution to the problem.

On 8 October 2005 a massive 7.6 magnitude earthquake struck Kashmir, killing 73,000 people and injuring hundreds of thousands more on either side of the Line of Control. A Peace Bus (set up to enable Kashmiris to visit their relatives on the other side of the Line of Control, and as a 'confidence-building measure' between India and Pakistan) is still operational, despite frequent interruptions and suspensions to the service when tensions along the border are high.

Instability and the rise of the Taliban in Pakistan's Northwest Frontier, along with the holding of peaceful elections for the state assembly and the Lok Sabha in Indian-held Kashmir, have relegated Kashmir to the back pages, but a solution which meets with the full support of Kashmiris in both Indian and Pakistani Kashmir is still a distant prospect.

Listings Jammu and around

Tourist information

Jammu

Jammu and Kashmir Tourist Reception Centre
Vir Marg, T0191-254 8172, www.jktourism.org.
Has brochures.

JKTDC
T0191-257 9554, http://jktdc.co.in.

Where to stay

Jammu

$$$ Asia Jammu-Tawi
Nehru Market, north of town, T0191-243 5757, www.asiahotelsjammu.com.
The 44 rooms are beginning to show their age, but this Jammu stalwart has an excellent Chinese restaurant, bar, and a clean pool. Close to the airport.

$$$ Hari Niwas Palace
Palace Rd, T0191-254 3303, www.hariniwaspalace.in.

40 a/c rooms and suites in a heritage property with an elegant bar and classy restaurant. Meals and drinks are also served on the immaculate lawns, with a sweeping view. The cliff-top location next to Amar Mahal is the chief attraction. The Royal Deluxe rooms and Suites (**$$$$**) are huge, with wonderful views from either front or back. Heated pool and health club.

$$$ KC Residency
Vir Marg, T0191-252 0770, www.kcresidency.com.
Rising from the heart of Jammu, the KC tower has 61 good-quality a/c rooms, and a health club specializing in Ayurvedic massage, all crowned by a superb, multi-cuisine revolving restaurant.

$$ Jewel's
Jewel Chowk, T0191-2529801/2/3, www.jewelshotel.com.
Located in a busy, congested area, but the 18 a/c rooms are good value in an increasingly expensive city. There's a good fast-food restaurant and bar.

$$-$ Tourist Reception Centre
AKA Hotel Jammu Residency, Vir Marg, T0191-257 9554.
Set back from the main road, the TRC has 173 rooms with bath, arranged around well-kept gardens; price is dictated by size, quality and views. The restaurant has a good reputation, in particular for its Kashmiri food, and there's a bar.

$ Kranti Hotel
Near the railway station, T0191-247 0525.
One of the better budget hotels in the railway area with 45 clean rooms with attached bath and a restaurant.

Vaishno Devi
Katra is an attractive town at the foot of the Trikuta Hills where visitors to the Vaishno Devi cave can stay.

$$ Ambica
Katra, T01991-232062, www.hotelambika.com.
58 rooms, a/c, *puja* shop and health centre, spacious lawns.

$$ Asia Vaishnodevi
Katra, T01991-232061, www.asiavaishnodevi.in.
37 a/c rooms, restaurant, transport to Banganga.

$ Dormitories
At the halfway point to Vaishno Devi.
Simple rooms, provides sheets.

$ Prem
Main Bazar, Katra, T01991-232014.
Adequate rooms with hot water and a fire.

Restaurants

Jammu
The best eateries tend to be found in the upmarket hotels. However, there are some good snack places dotted around town, which can be fun to check out.

$$-$ Sagar Ratna
Hotel Premier, opposite KC Plaza, Residency Rd.
Vegetarian delights, both South and North Indian plus Chinese, at reasonable prices for smart-casual surrounds (a/c), and generous portions. Loud TV.

$$-$ Smokin' Joes Pizza
Bahu Plaza, near the railway station.
Very acceptable veg and non-veg pizza and pasta, but strictly no pork. Takeaway and home delivery are also available.

$ Barista
KC Cineplex and City Square Mall.
Popular Indian café chain, also sells sandwiches and cakes.

Vaishno Devi
Excellent vegetarian food is available; curd and *paneer* dishes are especially good. For non-*dhaba* food try the 2 vegetarian fast food places on the main street. Both are clean and good.

Shopping

Jammu

J&K Arts Emporium, *next to J&K Tourism, Residency Rd. Mon-Sat 1000-2000.* Good selection of cheap items.

Transport

Jammu

Air Rambagh Airport, 6 km. Transport to town: prepaid taxis and auto-rickshaws. Daily flights to **Delhi**, **Mumbai** and **Srinagar**; to **Leh** in high season on Mon and Fri (**Air India**, book well in advance).

Bus J&KSRTC, TRC, Vir Marg, T0191-257 9554 (1000-1700), general bus stand, T0191-257 7475 (0400-2000). To **Amritsar** (6 hrs) at least hourly via **Pathankot** (3 hrs); direct buses to **Srinagar** (9 hrs), **Katra** (for Vaishno Devi), and **Kishtwar**. To **Delhi** (12 hrs), hourly. **Srinagar** buses also leave from the railway station, usually 0600-0700.

Jeep *Sumos* to **Srinagar** leaving early morning (8-9 hrs).

Train 5 km from centre; allow at least 30 mins by auto. Enquiries T0191-245 3027. To **Delhi**: around 8 trains daily, taking 9-14 hrs. To **Amritsar**: 3 per day, taking 4½ hrs.

Srinagar

houseboats and Mughal gardens, against a backdrop of the Himalaya

Founded by Raja Pravarasen in the sixth century, ringed by mountains and alluringly wrapped around the Dal and Nagin lakes, Srinagar, meaning 'beautiful city', is divided in two by the River Jhelum.

Srinagar is the largest city in the state, with a population of 1,269,751, and the summer seat of government. Sadly the troubles of the past 25 years have scarred the town, leading to the desertion and neglect of many of its fine houses, buildings and Hindu temples. Older Srinagaris lament the passing of the formerly spruce city, yet Srinagar remains a charming place with a strong character, unique in India for its Central Asian flavour.

Devastating floods in 2014 saw the Jhelum burst its banks, causing much of the city to be submerged under water; many of the worst hit businesses, hotels and restaurants are yet to recover.

Dal Lake

Of all the city's sights, Dal Lake must be its trademark. Over 6.5 km long and 4 km wide, it is divided into three parts by manmade causeways. The small islands are willow covered, while round the lake are groves of *chinar*, poplar and willow. The Mihrbahri people have lived around the lakes for centuries and are market gardeners, tending the floating beds of vegetables and flowers that they have made and cleverly shielded with weeds to make them unobtrusive. Shikaras, the gondola-like pleasure boats that ply the lake, can be hired for trips around the Dal (the official rate Rs 300 per hour, but it's possible to bargain). The morning vegetable market is well worth seeing by boat: it starts around 0600 and a one-hour tour is adequate; it is in a Shi'ite area adorned with corresponding flags. At the end of the Boulevard in Nehru Park the tiny **Post Office Museum** ① *daily 1100-2000*, is unique in that it floats. You can also send your mail from here.

Hazratbal Mosque (Majestic Place) is on the western shore of Dal Lake, and commands excellent lake views. The modern mosque stands out for its white marble dome and has a special sanctity as a hair of the prophet Mohammad is preserved here. Just beyond is little **Nazim Bagh** (Garden of the Morning Breeze), one of the earliest Mughal gardens and attributed to Akbar.

Essential Srinagar

Finding your feet

The airport is 14 km south of town; a taxi to the main tourist areas takes 30-45 minutes. Srinagar has daily direct flights from Delhi, and weekly flights from Leh during the summer months. Direct buses from New Delhi take 24 hours, but this is an arduous trip. If you want to travel overland, it's more comfortable to take the train as far as Jammu (12 hours), stop for the night and then travel to the valley by jeep or bus the next day (eight to nine hours, including stops for lunch and tea). Srinagar is on NH1A linked to Jammu (293 km) by narrow 'all-weather' mountain road, through superb scenery. Often full of lorries and military convoys, the journey takes nine to 10 hours; few stops for food. Tourist buses from Jammu and Delhi arrive and leave from the Tourist Reception Centre, see page 168.

Tip...

Qayaam Chowk street, close to Dalgate, is known as 'the barbecue'. It's lined with small restaurants and stalls serving *sheesh* and *seekh* kebabs, accompanied by an array of delicious, home-made Kashmiri chutneys.

Best views

Sunset from Pari Mahal, page 164
From the top of Shankaracharya Temple, page 164
From the veranda of a houseboat, page 169

Getting around

There are government taxi stands with fixed rates at the Tourist Reception Centre (Residency Road), Dal Gate and Nehru Park, and an abundance of auto-rickshaws. Local buses are cheap, but can be crowded and slow. The days of dusk-to-dawn curfews are over, but even so, the city shuts down relatively early; by 2100 the streets are deserted and it can be tricky to find transport. See Transport, page 172.

Orientation

Once known as the city of seven *kadals* (bridges), there are now 12 that connect the two sides, the older ones giving their names to their adjoining neighbourhoods.

The city falls into three parts; the commercial area (**Uptown**), the old city (**Downtown**) and the area around the lakes (**Dalgate**, the Boulevard, **Nehru Park**). Uptown is the place for shopping, particularly Polo View and the Bund, which is a footpath that runs along the Jhelum, and Lal Chowk on the western side.

Mughal Gardens

Set in front of a triangle of the lake created by intersecting causeways (now demolished), with a slender bridge at the centre, lies the famous **Nishat Bagh** (Garden of Gladness) ① *Sat-Thu 0900-sunset, Rs 10.* Sandwiched between the hills and the lake, the steep terraces and central channel with fountains were laid out by Asaf Khan, Nur Jahan's brother, in 1632.

The **Shalimar Bagh** ① *Apr-Oct 0900-sunset, Nov-Mar 1000-sunset, Rs 10*, gardens are about 4 km away and set back from the lake. Built by Jahangir for his wife, Nur Jahan, the gardens are distinguished by a series of terraces linked by a water channel with central pavilions. These are surrounded by decorative pools, which can be crossed by stones. The uppermost pavilion has elegant black marble pillars and niches in the walls for flowers

ON THE ROAD
Choosing a houseboat

Houseboats are peculiar to Srinagar and can be seen moored along the busy shores of Dal Lake, the quieter and distant Nagin Lake and along the Jhelum River. They were originally thought up by the British as a ruse to get around the law that foreigners could not buy land in the state: being in the water, the boats didn't technically count as property. In the valley's heyday the boats were well kept and delightfully cosy; today, some are still lavishly decorated with antiques and traditional Kashmiri handicrafts, but others have become distinctly shabby.

Still mostly family-run, they usually include all meals and come in 5 categories: deluxe, A, B, C and D. The tariff for each category is given by the **Houseboat Owners Association**, www.houseboatowners.org, through whom you can also make bookings.

Most tourists enjoy their houseboat holidays; however, a significant number complain of being ripped off in various ways. It's better to spend extra on a boat with a good reputation than go for a bargain. If the deal sounds too good to be true, then it probably is and you will end up paying in other ways (ie by being coerced into shopping trips, from which your hosts will take a hefty commission). Try and find a boat with good references from other travellers, and look at sites such as www.tripadvisor.com. Also be aware that many boats in the Dal and Nagin lakes can only be accessed by *shikara*. While boat owners will always insist that a *shikara* will always be at your disposal, some tourists have found that this has not been the case and have found themselves marooned on boats with hosts they don't particularly like.

during the day and candles or lamps at night. The chinar (plane trees) have become so huge that some are falling down.

Chashma Shahi (Royal Spring, 1632) ① *0900-sunset, Rs 10*, is a much smaller garden built around the course of a renowned spring, issuing from a miniature stone dome at the garden's summit. It is attributed to Shah Jahan though it has been altered over the centuries. Nearby are the **Botanical Gardens** ① *Sat-Thu 0800-sunset, Rs 10*. Rather wilder than the other gardens, its tucked-away location makes it popular with runners.

West (2.5 km) of Chashmi Shahi, nestling in the hills, is the smallest and sweetest of the Mughal gardens, the charmingly named **Pari Mahal** (Fairy Palace) ① *sunrise-sunset, Rs 10*. Built in the 17th century by the ill-fated prince Dara Shikoh, who was later beheaded by his brother Aurangzeb, the garden has six terraces and the best sunset views of Srinagar. The terraced gardens, backed by arched ruins, are being restored and are illuminated at night.

Shankaracharya Temple
Set up on a hill, behind the Boulevard (known as Takht-i-Sulaiman or 'Throne of Soloman'), is the Shankaracharya Temple, with great views; it's a good place to orientate yourself. The temple was constructed during Jahangir's reign but is said to be on the same site as a second-century BC temple built by Asoka's son. The inelegant exterior houses a large lingum, while beneath is a cave where Shankaracharya is said to have performed a *puja*. The temple is 5.5 km up a steep road from the Boulevard; walking up the road is not permitted, although hitching a ride from the security check (open 0900-1700) at the

bottom is possible. There is an alternative rough path starting from next to the gate of the City Forest Hotel on Durganag Road (one hour up, 30 minutes down).

Sri Pratap Singh Museum

Lal Mandi, Tue-Sun 1030-1630, foreigners Rs 50.
....

South of the old city and the river is the dark and dusty Sri Pratap Singh Museum (1898). Kashmir's Hindu and Buddhist past stares you in the face as 1000-year-old statues of Siva, Vishnu and the Buddha, excavated from all over the valley, casually line the walls. One room houses an eclectic mix of stuffed animals, bottled snakes and birds' eggs, topped off by the dissembled skeleton of a woolly mammoth and looked down on by a collection of stags' heads, mounted on the papier-mâché walls. There are also miniature paintings, a selection of ancient manuscripts and coins, as well as weapons, musical instruments and an anthropology section. Look out for the extraordinary Amli shawl in the textiles room: an embroidered map of Srinagar, showing the Jamia mosque and the Jhelum dotted with houseboats (it took 37 years to complete). The museum suffered damage in the 2014 floods, and the collection will be reorganized when the museum extends into a larger building being constructed next door.

Old City

Srinagar's old city (known locally as Downtown) is a fascinating area to wander around with rather a Central Asian feel. Once the manufacturing and trade hub of Kashmir, each *mohalla* (neighbourhood) had its own speciality, such as carpet weaving, goldsmithery and woodcarving. It was said that you could find even the milk of a pigeon in the thriving bazars and its traders grew rich, building themselves impressive brick and wood houses, in a style that is a charming fusion of Mughal and English Tudor.

In the north of the Old City is the distinctive mound of **Hari Parbat Hill**, on which stands a fort built by Shujah Shah Durrani in 1808. You need permission from the TRC to visit the fort, which opened to the public in 2014. On the southern side of Hari Parbat, the **Makhdoom Sahib shrine** is dedicated to Hazrat Sultan and has wonderful views of the city. The actual shrine is off-limits to women and non-Muslims, but you can peek through the ornate, carved screen from outside and marvel at the fabulous array of chandeliers. The Makhdoom Ropeway, a **cable car** ① *tourists Rs 100*, goes up to the shrine giving fabulous views, although it often seems to close for maintenance. Alternatively, you can access the steps up the hill from near the Sikh Gurdwara **Chhatti Padshahi**, by the imposing **Kathi Darwaza** (gate) in the Old City walls. This arched gateway was the principle entrance to the fort; a Persian inscription states that it was built by Akbar in 1597-8. In the city wall on the opposite side of fort is the Sangeen Darwaza, which is more ornate.

From Makhdoom Sahib take an auto-rickshaw (or walk 15 minutes) to the **Jama Masjid** (1674). The mosque is notable for the 370 wooden pillars supporting the roof, each made from a single *deodar* tree. The building forms a square around an inner courtyard, with a beautiful fountain and pool at its centre. Its four entrance archways are topped by the striking, pagoda-like roofs that are an important

Tip...

Before entering a shrine or mosque, remove your shoes. Most places have a cloakroom where you can leave them for a few rupees. Women should put a scarf over their head and both sexes must cover arms and legs. You can put a donation for the shrine's upkeep in the green *tameer* (building) fund box, usually at the entrance.

architectural characteristic of the valley's mosques and shrines. The mosque was where the sacred hair of the Prophet Mohammed was kept before being moved to the Hazratbal Mosque.

About 10 minutes' walk to the southeast lies the 17th-century **tomb of Naqash Band Sahib**, a sufi saint. The interior of the shrine is covered with (modern) colourful papier-mâché flower designs; there is a women's section. The ornate mosque adjacent to the shrine is meticulously maintained, and is constructed of brick and wood alternate layers. Next to the shrine lie the graves of the 'martyrs' who died in the 1931 uprising against the Dogras. They are claimed as heroes by both the state government and the separatists – one of the few things both sides agree on.

Continue further in the same direction and you will reach the **Dastagir Sahib shrine**, which houses the tomb of Abdul Qazi Geelani. A fire in 2012 almost entirely destroyed the

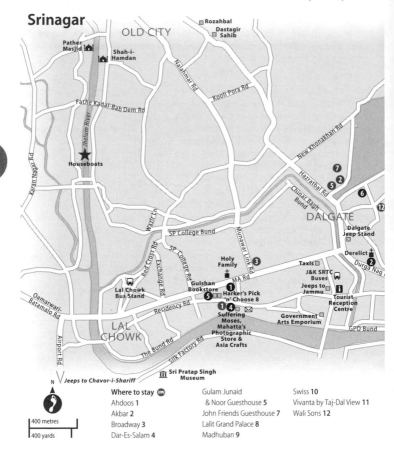

Srinagar

Where to stay 🏠
Ahdoos 1
Akbar 2
Broadway 3
Dar-Es-Salam 4

Gulam Junaid
 & Noor Guesthouse 5
John Friends Guesthouse 7
Lalit Grand Palace 8
Madhuban 9

Swiss 10
Vivanta by Taj-Dal View 11
Wali Sons 12

main structure, including antique chandeliers, exquisite papier mâché and carved wood decoration. The 300-year-old giant handwritten Qu'ran and the holy relic of the saint were saved, as they were in a fireproof vault. The shrine is to be rebuilt according to its original structural character, and many devotees still come to pray here. A minute's walk away is little **Rozahbal shrine**, which claims to contain the 'tomb of Jesus' (Holger Kersten's *Jesus Lived in India* recounts the legend; also see www.tombofjesus.com). The community here is sensitive about inquiring visitors: do not produce a camera, and don't be surprised if locals warn you away.

Head west towards the river for the beautiful **Shah-i-Hamdan Masjid**, the site of Srinagar's first mosque, built in 1395 by Mir Sayed Ali Hamadni. The original building was destroyed by fire and the current wooden structure dates back to the 1730s. The entrance is worth seeing for its exquisite papier-mâché work and woodcarving, but non-Muslims are not allowed inside the actual shrine. However, there is a women's section at the rear which female non-Muslims can enter and you can linger by the doorway with devotees, peeping inside to see the richly painted walls and chandeliers. Facing Shah-i-Hamdan, across the river is the limestone **Pathar Masjid** (1623), built for the Empress Nur Jahan and renamed Shahi Mosque.

Further up the river, on the same side as Shah-i-Hamdan, lies the 15th-century bulbous brick **Badshah Tomb of Zain-ul-Abidin's mother** ① *daily 0900-1700*, which is embellished with glazed turquoise tiles. The tomb adjoins a graveyard, containing the sultan Zain-ul-Abidin's grave and those of his wives and children, enclosed by an old stone wall that has been reused from an earlier Hindu temple. The area, Zaina Kadal, is interesting to walk around; carved copperwork is still produced here and you can see the craftsmen at work. It's the best place to buy your souvenir samovar.

Dachigam National Park
22 km east, past the Shalimar gardens.

This national park is home to the endangered Hangul deer as well as black and brown bears, leopards, musk deer and various migratory birds. Permits and further information about the best time to see the wildlife can be obtained from the TRC in Srinagar.

Restaurants
Café Robusta **1**
Krishna Dha ba **2**
Lhasa **3**
Mughal Darbar **4**

Shakti Sweets
& Modern Sweets **5**
Shamyana **6**

Tourist information

Tourist Reception Centre (TRC)
Residency Rd, T0194-245 2691,
www.jktourism.org. Open 24/7.
Houses the state department of tourism,
the **Jammu and Kashmir Tourism
Development Corporation (JKTDC)** (T0194-
2457927, http://jktdc.co.in), and **Adventure
Tourism** for booking accommodation
and tours. Also within the complex is the
J&K State Transport Corporation (T0194-
245 5107) for bus tickets. You can pick up
an excellent map showing both the city
and the whole state at the TRC.

Where to stay

Hotels on the Boulevard are popular –
particularly with Indian tourists – but tend
to be huge, impersonal and overpriced. The
Uptown area is good to stay in if you are
interested in exploring the city and prefer
to be away from the tourist rush. There are
also some houseboats on the Jhelum River,
with walk-on/walk-off access. You can hear
the noise of the traffic from these boats,
but there are no hawkers.

Hotels around Dalgate tend to offer more
budget options and can be very enjoyable.
Those on the lakeshore just opposite the
Boulevard (eg **Akbar**) are a good choice, as
the area is interesting and there is less hassle
from Shikara-men. The room costs quoted
reflect peak-season prices (Mar-Aug); if you
go in the winter, you can expect to get a
hefty discount. Be prepared to haggle.

$$$$ Broadway
Maulana Azad Rd, T0194-245 9001,
www.hotelbroadway.com.
One of Srinagar's best-known hotels, the
Broadway's original 1970s interior has
been well maintained. With lots of wood
panelling, rooms can be a little dark. Staff
are professional and polite, while the

comfortable, centrally heated rooms and
city location make it popular with business
travellers and journalists. It houses one of the
city's few drinking spots, has an outdoor pool
and is attached to the city's first coffee shop,
Café Arabica. Book online for discounts.

$$$$ The Lalit Grand Palace
Gupkar Rd, T0194-250 1001,
www.thelalit.com.
This former palace was the residence of
Kashmir's last maharajah, Hari Singh. Situated
on a hillside overlooking Dal Lake, it has
been tastefully kitted out with antiques
befitting its history, including India's largest
handmade carpet. One wing houses
enormous, classically styled suites, while the
other has 70 modern rooms. The restaurant,
bar and health club are open to non-guests.
It's a good place to go on a summer evening
for the alfresco buffet.

$$$$ Vivanta by Taj – Dal View
Kralsangri Hill, Brein, T0194-246 1111,
www.vivantabytaj.com.
All-out luxury in this sprawling elegant
resort, atop a peak with sublime Dal Lake
views. Rooms are chic without being
over-the-top, with Kashmiri details and
warm colours. 24-hr fitness suite, fantastic
restaurants and spa. A gorgeous place, worth
going for a meal if you can't afford a stay.

$$$ Ahdoo's
Residency Rd, T0194-247 2593,
www.ahdooshotel.com.
A Srinagar institution, Ahdoo's backs onto
the Jhelum river and is close to the city's
classiest handicraft and shawl shops around
Polo View. Deluxe rooms are huge with new
TVs, while standard rooms are not much
smaller, and all have marble bathtubs. Back
rooms have river views. It's a good place to
get a feel of the city, rather than the more
touristy area around the lake. The restaurant
is renowned for its Kashmiri (*Wazwan*) food,
chicken patties, and their tea.

$$$ Dar-Es-Salam
Rainawari, T0194-242 7803,
www.hoteldaressalam.com.
This white art deco ex-stately home is the
only hotel on Nagin Lake, with an established
garden and a sweep of lawn overlooking
houseboats. Mounted heads over the
entrance set the colonial tone, while period
furnishings in the 2 lounges include brass
antique pots and a Raj-era tiger's head. An
enclosed balcony surveys the lake. There are
modernized rooms (and $$$$ suites), central
heating, white duvets, and meals available in
the (formal) dining room.

$$$-$$ Hotel Akbar
Dalgate, Gate No 1, T0194-250 0507,
www.hotelakbar.com.
36 spacious rooms, some with balcony,
arranged around a pretty lawn with rose
arbours. Attractive lobby and restaurant
and it's a great location on the lakeside;
however, rooms are a little dated. Souvenir
shop and travel desk.

$$ Hotel Madhuban
Gagribal Rd, T0194-245 3800,
www.hotelmadhuban-kashmir.net.
The Madhuban has bags of character, with
a lot of wood going on in its homely rooms.
The restaurant has an attractive veranda
where guests can sit out in the summer
and there is a small but well-kept garden.

$$ Hotel Wali Sons
Boulevard Lane No 1, T0194-250 0345,
http://www.walisonshotelsandresorts.
com/boulevard.
A smart red-brick building, complemented
by white window frames and green roof.
The 17 spacious rooms have white duvets,
flatscreen TV, fan, clean carpets and huge
bathrooms with modern fixtures and decor.
Central location, and some public balconies
overlook Shankaracharya Hill. There's 24-hr
electricity and respectful staff.

$$-$ Swiss Hotel
Old Gagribal Rd, T0194-2500115,
www.swisshotelkashmir.com.
The Swiss has 35 clean rooms with attached
bath and hot water (morning and evening)
with greatly discounted rates for foreign
tourists. The attractive red-painted old house
has the best-value budget rooms in town.
In the annex, prices increase as you go up to
the 3rd floor, where rooms with coffee-table,
sofa and numerous lamps are immaculate.
There's a big garden. One of the few hotels
with a stated environmental policy.

$ John Friends Guesthouse
Pedestrian Mall Rd (opposite Ghat No 1),
Dalgate, T0194-245 8342.
Set back from Dal Lake, along walkways and
gangplanks, is this family guesthouse with
9 rooms in 2 buildings. Flowery garden with
seating, surrounded by poplars and willows,
with fairy lights at night. Decent budget
rooms, some with attached bath and TV,
24-hr hot water. A fascinating snapshot into
life on the lake.

$ There's a backpacker-conscious enclave
on the lake at Dalgate, where small and
simple guesthouses include **Gulam Junaid**
and **Noor Guesthouse**.

Houseboats
The following all quote **$$$$-$$**, but prices
are generally negotiable if you go in person.
See also box, page 164.

Athena Houseboats
Opposite Hotel Duke, Dal Lake, T(0)941
9063866, www.athenahouseboats.com.
One of the larger houseboat operators
with voluminous boats that can comfortably
sleep larger groups. Excellent service,
with real integrity: discourages hawkers
and tries to support only legitimate retail
and onward tourism.

Butt's Clermont Houseboats
West side of Dal Lake, T0194-241 5325,
www.buttsclermonthouseboat.com.
Moored by Naseem Bagh, 'Garden of
Breezes', shaded by chinar trees, by a
wall built by Emperor Akbar. Far from
the densely packed south side of Dal
Lake, 4 cream-painted boats feature
crewelwork on fabrics, carved cedar
panels, rosewood tables and a view of
Hazratbal mosque. In operation since 1940,
former guests include Lord Mountbatten,
George Harrison, PG Wodehouse,
Ravi Shankar and Michael Palin.

Gurkha Houseboats
Nagin Lake, http://welcomheritagehotels.in.
The Gurkha group are renowned for their
comfortable rooms and stylish boats on
peaceful Nagin Lake. Good service and food.

Mantana
Dal Lake, Gate 2, T0194-250 1488,
www.mantanatours.com.
A good choice to experience the old-style
opulence of a traditional Kashmiri houseboat.
As well as the carefully preserved,
sumptuous interiors, there is an ingeniously
constructed floating garden. Owned and
run by a reliable family.

Marguerite
The Bund, T0194-247 6699.
A charming boat with some lovely
woodcarving. The trustworthy Thulla family
are great fun and as the boat is moored to
the river bank, guests can come and go as
they please with no need to take a *shikara*.

Zaffer Houseboats
On Nagin Lake, T01954-250 0507,
www.zafferhouseboats.com.
Deluxe boats with a long history, panelled
walls, single-piece walnut tables, old writing
desks, backed onto the lake which means
the front terrace is delightful place to sit.
Peaceful and quiet despite the *sikhara*
salesmen. Excellent food, courteous
staff and interesting owners.

Restaurants

While Kashmiris generally prefer to eat at
home, being a tourist town, Srinagar has its
fair share of good restaurants catering for
all tastes. For a special treat, do the buffet at
the Lalit Grand or a meal at the Taj Vivanta
(with killer views). There are 3 wine shops
on the left side of the ground floor of the
Hotel Heemal building on the Boulevard.

Traditional Kashmiri food is centred around
meat, with mutton generally being the
favoured flesh. The traditional 36-course
banquet served at weddings is known as
a *wazwan* and you will find several of its
signature dishes on the menu in restaurants.
Yakhnee is a delicious mutton stew cooked in
a spiced curd sauce. *Goshtabas* and *rishtas* are
meatballs made from pounded (not ground)
meat, which makes a big difference in
consistency. *Goshtabas* come in a curd sauce;
rishtas in red sauce. *Roganjosh* is made with
chicken or mutton and is curd based, owing
its colour to red Kashmiri chilies. *Hakh* is the
Kashmiri version of spinach and *nadroo* are
lotuses, usually served in a *yakhnee* sauce.

$$ Char Chinar
Boulevard Rd, near Brein village.
You'll need to take a *shikara* to get to this
houseboat restaurant, moored on a tiny
island in Dal Lake. Named after the 4 giant
chinar trees that grow there, the food is
average, but it's a perfect place to sit in
peace with a good book on a sunny day.

$$ Lhasa
Boulevard Lane No 2. Daily 1200-2230.
Enjoy the lovely back garden with rose
bushes and well-spaced tables, each with its
own awning; the central fountain is defunct,
but old houses surround. The low-ceilinged
indoor area has fish-tanks and is cosy on
a cold night. They serve a varied menu of
excellent Chinese, Tibetan, and Indian non-
veg and veg food.

$$ Mughal Darbar
Residency Rd.
Popular with middle-class locals, the cosy
Mughal Darbar offers multi-cuisine fare,
specializing in Kashmiri *wazwan*. It's located
on the 1st floor, up the stairs.

$$ Shamyana
Boulevard Rd, www.shamyana.net.
Daily 1230-2230.
Consistently highly rated by locals and
popular with middle-class customers, this
restaurant serves high-quality Chinese and
Indian food (meat and veg, good tikka).
The calm front section is separated from
a funkier back room by wooden lattices.
Professional service.

$$-$ Café Robusta
Maulana Azad Rd, near Polo View.
Competes with nearby **Café Arabica** (in
the Broadway Hotel) to attract Srinagar's
latte lovers. Aside from pizza, kebabs and
cake, you can also sample a *shisha* (Middle
Eastern water pipe) with a range of flavoured
tobaccos on offer. Bring your laptop and
make use of the Wi-Fi.

$ Krishna Dhaba
Durga Nag Rd. Closed 1600-1900.
A haven for vegetarians in a city of meat-
eaters, the Krishna's canteen environment
gets the thumbs-up from fastidious Indian
tourists for its cleanliness and delicious pure
veg fare, the best in town.

$ Shakti Sweets and Modern Sweets
Residency Rd.
If you are invited to a Kashmiri home, a box
of *burfi* will go down well as a gift. Both serve
great snack food at rock-bottom prices, such
as *channa bhatura* and *masala dosa*, as well
as very popular chow mein.

Festivals

Apr Tulip Festival, Indira Gandhi Memorial
Tulip Garden. 1st 2 weeks of Apr, with over
1 million blooms.

Shopping

If you arrived in Srinagar without your
thermals or you're craving a bar of chocolate,
a bowl of cornflakes, Marmite on toast or just
about any other Western goods, then look
no further than **Harker's Pick 'n' Choose
Supermarket** on Residency Rd, for all your
expat needs.

Books
Gulshan Bookstore, *a few mins' walk from
Residency Rd, towards Lal Chowk.* Here you
will find all manner of books about Kashmir,
some of them extremely rare. It's an excellent
place for books on Kashmir's history and the
political situation.

Handicrafts
There are plenty of handicraft shops,
particularly around Dal Lake and Dalgate,
but beware of touts who are on commission.
Much of what is sold is not even Kashmiri:
inferior quality papier-mâché products from
Bihar and shawls from Amritsar have flooded
the market and are bought merrily by tourists
who don't know the difference. As a result,
along with the troubles of the past 25 years,
the valley's handicraft industry has been
tragically eroded. For a real understanding of
Kashmiri craftwork and to support the local
industry, call into any of the quality shops
on **Polo View** or the **Bund**. The prices may
seem high, but the quality and authenticity
are guaranteed. Shopkeepers here are rather
more restrained than the average Kashmiri
salesman making it a pleasant place to
wander around. .
Asia Crafts, *next to Suffering Moses (see
page 172).* Very fine embroidery and genuine

> **Fact...**
> All trade in shahtush and articles made
> from the wool of the *chiru* (Tibetan
> antelope) is banned, hence buying and
> exporting an article is illegal.

Kashmiri carpets, but much of its stock is now sold in New Delhi.

Habib Asian Carpets, *Zaldagar Chowk, Downtown, T0194-247 8640*. If you are serious about buying a genuine Kashmiri carpet, this is one of the few companies that has its workshop in the city.

Heritage Woodcrafts, *on the way to Shalimar gardens*. It's worth making the trip here for the carved walnut wood. Stuffed with fine pieces including some antiques, the authenticity of the work is guaranteed by the on-site workshop.

Kashmir Government Arts Emporium, *the Bund. Mon-Sat 1000-1800, closed for noon prayers*. In the old British Residency, a beautifully restored building with heritage gardens (and moth-eaten tigers lurking among the wares). Large showroom of fixed-price Kasmiri goods: rugs, papier mâché, crewel-work, furniture and more.

Suffering Moses, *next to Mughal Darbar restaurant*. Famous for its exquisite papier-mâché goods; really beautiful top-quality stock, and they ship overseas. The curious name was apparently awarded to the owner's father by the British, who were impressed by the amount of suffering that went into each work. **Sadiq's Handicrafts** is owned by the same family and is almost as much a museum as a shop; many of the antique treasures are not for sale and Mr Sadiq, a man passionate about art, will happily explain their history to you. Prices in both shops are fixed and there is no pressure to buy.

Photography

Mahatta's Photographic Store, *next to Suffering Moses (see above). Mon-Sat 1030-1830*. Worth a visit for its old-world charm, history and above all the priceless visual memory of old Srinagar it houses. Founded in 1918, this was once the place to have your portrait taken and was patronized by the elite of the day. The walls are lined with large prints of the city, taken up in the 1930s and 1940s. They are not for sale, but they have produced a booklet, Srinagar Views 1934-1965, and sell black and white postcards, and books.

Transport

Air Srinagar Airport, 14 km south. Taxi to town: Rs 500-600. Stringent security checks on roads plus 2 hrs' check-in at airport. Tight on hand luggage but you can generally get away with a laptop. Daily flights to **Delhi** and **Mumbai**; 1 direct flight per week to **Leh** with **Air India**.

Bus J&KSRTC, TRC, Srinagar, T0194-245 5107. Summer 0600-1800, winter 0700-1700. To **Kargil** (alternate days in summer), **Leh** (434 km). **Gulmarg**, daily bus at 0800 in ski season from TRC, returning in the evening. Taxis charge around Rs 3000 for same-day return. Or take **J&KSRTC** bus to **Tangmarg**, 8 km before Gulmarg and a *sumo* from there. To **Pahalgam** at 0830 (2-3 hrs).

Jeep Jeeps are faster than the bus and leave when full from various locations near Dalgate. To **Jammu**, 8-9 hrs. To **Yusmarg**, 2 hrs, at 1400. Shared jeeps to **Charar-i-Sharief**, 1 hr, leave when full from Iqbal Park, in west Srinagar.

Train The nearest railhead is **Jammu Tawi**.

Gulmarg

Some 56 km west of Srinagar, Gulmarg (altitude 2650 m) attracts a colourful mix of characters, from the off-piste powder-addict adventurers who stay for months to the coachloads of Indian tourists. Three times host of the country's annual Winter Games and India's premier winter sports resort, it is one of the cheapest places in the world to learn to ski, although there are only a few beginners' runs.

The season runs from December to April (best in January-February), and equipment is available for hire for around Rs 500 a day. Check with **Gulmarg J&K Tourism** ① *T01954-254439*, about opportunities for heli-skiing. Outside the winter season, Gulmarg is a popular day trip from Srinagar, with pony rides, walks and the world's highest green golf course being the main attractions.

The resort is served by three ski lifts and boasts the world's second highest **gondola** ① *daily 1000-1800, Rs 600/800 return*, which stops at the Kangdori mid-station before rising up to Apharwat Top (4000 m), from where you can ski the 5.2 km back to Gulmarg. Or in summertime, it's fun to take the cable car up to the top, then get off halfway back, to walk down the remaining distance (take a picnic). Be prepared for pushy touts and pony-men when trying to buy your ticket; unfortunately, the gondola system is chronically mismanaged.

Charar-i-Sharief

From Srinagar it's a scenic one-hour drive to Charar-i-Sharief (27 km), the last 10 km of road climbing through orchards and vales of willow. Spread over a series of ridges, the colourful roofs of modern houses date from a fire in 1995, when most of the town was burnt down – including the famed 700-year-old wooden **shrine and mosque** – during a battle between militants and Indian troops. The complex is now rebuilt as a grand tiered pagoda with carved walnut-wood screens. Entombed here is Sheikh Noor-u-Din Noorani, one of many names given to the great Sufi poet, seer, philosopher and saint who died in 1438. He preached peace, tolerance and non-violence, and his shrine attracts thousands of visitors both Muslim and Hindu. It's possible to combine a visit to the shrine and a day-trip to **Yusmarg** (45 minutes away); or there's a nice J&K bungalow on the edge of town, should you get stranded.

Yusmarg

A rolling meadowland 47 km southwest of Srinagar, surrounded by conifer forests and snowy peaks, Yusmarg (altitude 2400 m) is an up-and-coming tourist spot for Indian day-trippers. Pony rides are popular, and you will probably be inundated by horsemen on arrival (a board shows official rates). Views over **Nilnag Lake** are a pleasant one-hour walk (or pony ride) through undulating forest. The walk to **Doodh Ganga** river takes 30 minutes through the meadows; you can link Doodh Ganga and Nilnag for a longer day-trek. There's a tourist reception centre and JKTDC have huts and cottages (or locals will offer you cheaper accommodation); there are a couple of very simple eateries near the jeep stop.

Pahalgam

Ninety kilometres southeast of Srinagar, Pahalgam (altitude 2133 m), meaning 'village of shepherds', is the main base for the yearly **Amarnath Yatra** pilgrimage, which sees thousands of Hindu pilgrims climbing to a cave housing an 'ice lingam'. During the Yatra season, which runs from June to August, it gets very busy. Situated at the convergence of two dramatic river valleys, the town is surrounded by conifer forests and pastures.

Central Pahalgam is packed with shawl shops, eateries and hotels; there's a striking mosque and some pleasant parks (one of which surrounds the Pahalgam Club). The pointy-roofed **Mamleshwar Temple**, across Kolahoi stream, is devoted to Shiva.

There are many short walks you can take from Pahalgam and it is also a good base for longer treks to the **Suru Valley** and **Kishtwar**. A good day walk is the 12 km up the beautiful Lidder Valley to Aru; from there you can continue on to to **Lidderwat** (22 km) and **Kolahoi Glacier** (35 km). A wide selection of accommodation caters for all budgets; some of the best options are a couple of kilometres up the valley from the town centre.

Sonamarg

Literally meaning the 'golden valley', Sonamarg – 84 km northeast of Srinagar – gets its name from the yellow crocus blooms that carpet the valley each spring. At an altitude of 2740 m, it's the last major town in Kashmir before the Zoji La Pass – the gateway to Ladakh. Mountains and blankets of pine trees surround the village, and Indian tourists make pony trips to nearby **Thajiwas glacier**. It's also a start/end point for the **Amarnath Yatra** ⓘ www.amarnathyatra.org. The area is highly regarded for its trekking and fishing; trout were introduced here by the British in the 19th century.

Treks to high-altitude Himalayan alpine lakes, including Vishnasar (4084 m), Krishnasar (3810 m), Satsar, Gadsar, and Gangabal (3658 m), take eight days; the trekking season runs from July to October. Accommodation is available through JKTDC (see below) in the summer months and there are several hotels.

Listings Around Srinagar

Where to stay

Gulmarg

As with Srinagar, prices can be negotiated in the winter months, particularly for longer stays.

$$$$ Khyber Himalayan Resort & Spa
T01954-254666, www.khyberhotels.com.
Absolute luxury in a new resort with an Ayurvedic spa, gym, heated pool and amazing restaurants. Rooms are beautifully furnished with teak floors, silk carpets, walnut carving and rich Kashmiri fabrics. There are state-of-the-art bathrooms, while huge windows make the most of views. Also 4 cottages, some with own pool.

$$$ Hotel Highlands Park
T01954-254430, www.hotel highlandspark.com.
Oozing with old-world charm, rooms and suites are decorated with Kashmiri woodcraft

and rugs. Renowned for its atmosphere – the best bar in Gulmarg is here, a large yet cosy lounge, straight out of the 1930s – it's a wonderful place to unwind after a hard day on the slopes. Rooms have *bukharis* (wood stoves) to keep you warm and electric blankets are available on request. Also recommended for the food.

$$$ Nedou's Hotel
T01954-254428, http://nedous hotelgulmarg.com.
The oldest hotel in Gulmarg, the **Nedou's** has the same cosy colonial charm as **Highlands Park**. Its rooms and suites are comfortingly old-fashioned, with spotless bathrooms. The food isn't flash, but it's home-cooked, wholesome and delicious.

$$ Hotel Yemberzal
T01954-254523, www.yemberzalhotel.com.
Rooms are on the small side, but at least this means they heat up quickly. Each has its own

gas heater and the bathrooms have 24-hr running hot water. If you ask for the corner room, you can enjoy a panoramic view of the mountains. The restaurant is excellent and the management are extremely helpful. It's a 10-min walk to the lifts, but there's a taxi stand next door if you feel lazy.

$$-$ Green Heights
T01954-254404.
This wood-built hotel is slightly shabby, but the quirky staff more than compensate, making this a budget choice with character. The decent-sized rooms come with wood stoves and if you ask nicely, you might get a hot-water bottle. Close to the gondola.

$$-$ JK Tourism Huts
T(0)9419-488181, http://jktdc.co.in.
These comfortable huts come with 1-2 bedrooms, a living room and kitchen. Very good value and close to the drag-lift.

$ Raja's
T(0)9797-008107.
Buried in the woods, **Raja's** colourful shack consists of 3 rooms with shared bath and can accommodate up to 9 people. Popular with long-stayers.

Yusmarg

$$-$ J&KTDC Huts
T(0)9797-292001, http://jktdc.co.in.
Dotted around the centre of Yusmarg's meadow, connected by flagged paths, these comfortable huts are well-maintained and fresh, if simple. There are various configurations, some with pine walls, others whitewashed with pretty bedspreads, so check them all out. Basic doubles Rs 750; 30% discounts low-season.

Pahalgam

$$$$ Pahalgam Hotel
T01936-243252, www.pahalgamhotel.com.
Upper-end Raj-era hotel dating back to 1931, 4 buildings, with 36 of the 40 rooms enjoying splendid views of forested peaks across the River Lidder. Rooms are tasteful, centrally heated and very spacious. Some have been recently renovated but all are pleasing (18 suites). The pool is open in summer. Prices include all meals. There's an excellent shop (see Shopping, below).

$$-$ Brown Palace
T01936-243255, www.brownpalace.in.
A decent option with a range of rooms; all have attached bath with hot water. Wood panelling abounds, the lounge has bark walls and a fire, and there are 2 newer bungalows with living rooms at the rear.

$$-$ Himalaya House
3 km from the bus stand, 1 km from Laripora village, T01936-243072, http://himalayahouse.in.
A cosy hotel on the river with an enchanting island garden and a restaurant of repute. All rooms have attached bath and hot water, some with tubs and balcony, attractive crewelwork curtains and bedspreads. The comfortable lobby has a fireplace and is a good place to make friends. Free Wi-Fi. Cheaper older rooms are in a house across laneway. They can organize good tours and treks.

Sonamarg

$$ Snow Land Resorts
Mamman, www.snowlandresorts.com.
This is a good choice, well managed with cosy wood-panelled rooms. Those at the back are quieter and have great mountain views, but the vegetarian restaurant is merely average.

Restaurants

Gulmarg
Most hotels serve their own food but some close their kitchens in low season. In the bazar there is a row of *dhabas* serving a wide variety of Indian vegetarian food including *thalis*, *dosas* and Punjabi, with outside seating.

$$ Sahara Hotel
Next to Yemberzal Hotel.
Well worth venturing out in the cold for.
The owner spent 15 years working as a chef
in Saudi Arabia, Japan and China, so has a
wide repertoire. If you need a break from
Indian food, the continental choice here is
good, especially the chicken champion.

$ Lala's
*Close to the JK Tourism Huts (see Where to
stay, above).*
Good, honest home-cooked food.

Pahalgam
$$$-$ Trout Beat restaurant and the
welcoming **Café Log Inn**, both at the
Pahalgam Hotel. Serve the same menu
of vegetarian meals and snacks and, of
course, fish.

$ Nathu's Rasoi
Open 0800-2230.
You can't miss this self-service fast-food
vegetarian restaurant near the bus stand,
which serves excellent Indian and Chinese
dishes – most famed for its South Indian,
the best in Kashmir.

Shopping

Pahalgam
Almirah Books etc, *at Pahalgam Hotel*. An
average book selection and some tasteful
souvenirs. Also sell 'Shepherd's Craft' goods:
brightly decorated bags/purses, embellished
with the traditional designs of the Bakkarwala
nomadic shepherds (who embroider
saddlebags and hats with colourful threads).

Transport

Yusmarg
Jeep To Batmulla bus stand, **Srinagar**,
at 0800 (2 hrs). Or go via Charar-i-Sharief
(last *sumo* from Yusmarg 1630).

Kargil to the Zanskar Valley
the road route to an isolated valley of raw beauty and cultural integrity

Kargil
On the bank of the River Suru and with a largely Shi'ite population, Kargil
(population 119,307, altitude 2704 m) has a very different vibe to both Srinagar and Leh.
The town is considered grim by most visitors; however, it is the main overnight stop on the
Srinagar–Leh highway and provides road access to the Zanskar Valley.

Kargil was an important trading post on two routes, from Srinagar to Leh, and to Gilgit
and the lower Indus Valley. In 1999 the Pakistan army took control briefly of the heights
surrounding the town before being forced to retreat.

Centred around the busy main bazar are cheap internet cafés (unreliable), ATMs and
plenty of hotels (see page 177). There is a **tourist office** ① *behind the bus station, T01985-
232721, Mon-Sat 1000-1600.* Walking up the valley slope, perpendicular to the main bazar,
takes you past old village houses to finish at Goma Kargil (4 km) for excellent views.

Suru Valley
The motorable road extends from Kargil south to Padum through the picturesque
and relatively green Suru Valley, where willow trees dot a wide valley floor flanked by
mountain ridges. The valley's population has been Muslim since the 16th century, but
some ancient Buddhist monuments remain.

The first (and largest) settlement is **Sankoo**, 42 km from Kargil, which has a 7-m rock-
carved relief of the Maitreay Buddha and the ruins of Kartse Khar (a fort) 3 km distant. It's

also a bus rest-spot and place to pick up last-minute supplies. The road continues 15 km to **Purtikchay**, a lonely spot with just a scattering of houses but with stunning views down to the **Nun-Kun** peaks. A further 10 km on is **Panikhar**, set in an attractive agricultural bowl of the valley and where a glacier and Nun-Kun frame the horizon.

From Panikar you can trek (a hard day) over the Lago La to Parkachik, or take pleasant strolls around the hamlet and the neighbouring village of Te-Suru. It is also possible to cross the mountains to Pahalgam in Kashmir from here, and you should be able to find local guides and ponies to make the one-week trek. The regular bus from Kargil terminates at **Parkachik**, after which is Rangdum and the Zanskar Valley (see below). There are J&K tourist bungalows at settlements along the Suru Valley (see page 178 for details).

Rangdum

Making a convenient night's stop between Kargil and the Zanskar Valley, 130 km from Kargil, halfway to Padum, Rangum (altitude 3657 m) sits on a plateau of wild and incredible beauty. The isolated **Rangdum Monastery** perched on a hillock is particularly striking, and two Buddhist villages surrounded by *chortens* lie nearby.

Zanskar

Zanskar is a remote area of Ladakh contained by the Zanskar range to the north and the Himalaya to the south. It can be cut off by snow for as much as seven months each year when access is solely along the frozen Zanskar River. This isolation has helped Zanskar to preserve its cultural identity, though this is now being steadily eroded; a road is being currently being constructed to link Padum with Nimmu, on the Kargil–Leh highway.

Traditional values include a strong belief in Buddhism, frugal use of resources and population control: values which for centuries have enabled Zanskaris to live in harmony with their hostile yet fragile environment. The long Zanskar Valley was 'opened' up for tourism even later than the rest of Ladakh and quickly became popular with trekkers. There is river rafting on the Zanskar River, with trips up to 11 days. For trekking, see page 15.

Padum ⓘ *No permit needed.* About 40% of Padum (population 1300), the capital of Zanskar, are Sunni Muslim. The present king of the Zanskar Valley, Punchok Dawa, who lives in his modest home in Padum, is held in high regard. The ruined old town, palace and fort are 700 m from the rather uninspiring new town, which has transport, guesthouses and Internet. Access is by the Jeep road over the **Pensi La** (4401 m), generally open from mid-June to mid-October with a twice weekly bus service from Leh via Kargil (highly unreliable and crammed); the alternative method is to trek in. There is accommodation available (see Where to stay, below).

Listings Kargil to the Zanskar Valley

Where to stay

Kargil

Hotels are quite expensive, but bargaining is expected. On Hospital Rd, running uphill just off the Main Bazar, there's a further cluster of budget hotels (not listed here). Restaurants all serve meat; for vegetarian food look for signs advertising Punjabi meals. There's a little dairy outlet selling superb *lassi* near the J&K ATM off the Main Bazar (it's locally famous, ask around).

$$ Green Land
Signed down an alley off Main Bazar, T01985-232324, www.hotelgreenland kargil.com. Open all year round.

A popular and well-kept place, it's not cheap but prices reflect the standard of the rooms. Old block doubles are much cheaper, but the new block is much preferable with a range of rooms.

$$ PC Palace
Off Main Bazar, T(0)9906-356533, http://hotelpcpalacekargil.com.
Smart building with well-appointed rooms with flatscreen TV, fawn carpets, blankets and curtains, fancy lights and good bathrooms. Slightly smaller, darker rooms are at the rear, but they are also cheaper and quieter.

$ Tourist Marjina
Off Main Bazar, T09419-831517.
An ageing pink- and blue-painted building that is being encircled by high new hotels, making dark rooms even darker. It's a bearable budget option though, with reliable hot showers.

Suru Valley
J&K tourist bungalows, costing around Rs 200 per person, are found in villages along the Suru Valley. Sankoo also has plenty of shops and several *dhabas*, while the **Tourist Bungalow** in Panikhar enjoys remarkable views of Nun and Kun, but is isolated (take supplies). In Panikhar, the **Dak Bungalow** has 3 gloomy rooms and a better choice is **$ Khayoul Hotel** (T(0)9469-293976), with

2 sunny rooms in a family house, decked with cheerful fabrics and plants, meals are cheap.

Padum
Places to stay are limited, but there is a choice of 4 simple lodges. There is also a **tourist complex** with basic rooms and meals; you can camp there.

$ Ibex
Has the best rooms in town, a decent restaurant and a courtyard garden.

What to do

Most agents in Leh can arrange trekking expeditions to the Zanskar Valley.
Aquaterra Adventures, *www.aquaterra.in*. Have 12-day rafting trips down the Zanskar River every Aug.

Transport

Kargil
Bus To **Leh** at 0430 (7 hrs); to **Srinagar** at 2230-2300, some are deluxe (9 hrs). Buses to the Suru Valley leave from the crossroads of Main Bazar and Lal Chowk, to **Panikhar** daily at 0700 (4 hrs; return bus at 0600, 0800 and 1100) and to **Parkachik** at 1130 on alternate days (5 hrs, returning at 0700).

Jeep Shared jeeps to **Srinagar** leave from taxi stand on Lal Chowk, connected to the bus station by an alleyway, at 0400-0600 and 1300-1500 (6 hrs). Shared jeeps to **Leh** (7 hrs).

Srinagar to Leh road
one of the most fascinating journeys in the world

The road to Leh from Srinagar negotiates high passes and fragile mountainsides. There are dramatic scenic and cultural changes as you go from verdant Muslim Kashmir to ascetic Buddhist Ladakh.

When there is political unrest in Kashmir, the route, which runs very close to the Line of Control, may be closed to travellers. For more on the political situation, see box, page 160. For details about the monasteries and villages along the way, see page 195. The alternative route to Leh from Manali is equally fascinating, see page 125.

The route

After passing through **Sonamarg**, you reach the pass of **Zoji La** (3528 m). The pass is slippery after rains and usually closed by snow during winter months (November to April). From Zoji La the road descends to **Minamarg meadow** and **Dras** (3230 m). The winter temperatures have been known to go down to -50°C, and heavy snow and strong winds cut off the town. **Dras** has a spectacular setting and a scruffy centre with restaurants and shops; there's a TIC and decent enough J&K bungalows. The broad Kargil basin and its wide terraces are separated from the Mulbekh Valley by the 12-km-long **Wakha Gorge**.

From **Kargil** (see page 176) the road continues 30 km to **Shargol** – the cultural boundary between Muslim and Buddhist areas, with a very atmospheric and very tiny monastery located down a side-road – and then after another 10 km reaches **Mulbek**, a pretty village with a large (9 m) ancient Maitreya Buddha relief fronted by a *gompa* on the roadside. The ruins of **Mulbek Khar** (fort) sit atop a stalk of cliff next to two small *gompas*, a steep climb with fabulous views. Shortly after Mulbek is its larger sister village of **Wahka**, then the road crosses **Namika La**, at 3720 m (known as the 'Pillar in the Sky'). There is a tourist bungalow in tiny **Haniskut**, set in a pretty river valley marred by roads and pylons, where a very ruined fort lies on the northern side of the valley. The road then climbs to **Fotu La** at 4093 m, the highest pass on the route. From here you can catch sight of the monastery at Lamayuru. The road does a series of loops to descend to the ramshackle village of **Khaltse** with a couple of garden-restaurants, shops and lodges, where it meets the milky green Indus River.

Lamayuru, 10 km from Khaltse, with a famous monastery and spectacular landscapes, is worth a long lunch break or overnight stop (see Where to stay, below). There is a comfortable eco-camp in **Uletokpo**, just by the highway (see page 200). From Uletokpo village a 6-km track leads to dramatic **Rizong**, with a monastery and nunnery, which sometimes accommodate visitors. **Saspol** village marks the wide valley from which you can reach **Alchi** by taking a branch road across the Indus after passing some caves. **Lekir** is off the main road, 8 km after Saspol.

Further along the road you catch sight of the ruins of **Basgo** before it crosses the Chargyal Thang plain with *chortens* and *mani* walls and enters **Nimmu**. The road rejoins the Indus Valley and rises to a bare plateau to give you the first glimpse of Leh, 30 km away. **Phyang** is down a side valley, and finally **Spituk** is reached.

Listings Srinagar to Leh road

Where to stay

Mulbek

$ Karzoo Guesthouse
T(0)9419-880463.
In an impressive old Ladakhi building, with restaurant and camping space, conveniently located for walking to the monastery; all rooms share clean bathrooms, and the family are very hospitable. There are also a couple of other simple guesthouses and a J&K Tourist Bungalow. In Wakha, the sister village 3 km on the road towards Leh, there are a few *dhabas* and shops.

Ladakh

The mountains of Ladakh – literally 'many passes' – are not typical of the high Himalaya: the summits are often only 3000 m higher than the valleys, which themselves lie at an altitude of 3500 m. Because it is desert, there is little snow on the peaks, and they look like big brown hills, dry and dusty, with clusters of willows and desert roses along the streams. Bright blue skies are an almost constant feature, as the monsoon rains do not reach here, and the contrast with the dramatic landscape creates a beautiful and heavenly effect. For thousands of visitors Ladakh is a completely magical place, remote and relatively unspoilt, with delightful, gentle, ungrasping people.

Essential Ladakh

Finding your feet

Ladakh (population 280,000) is entirely mountainous. The mountains range from 2500 m to 4500 m, with passes from 4000 m to 6000 m, and peaks up to 7500 m. The main road routes to the capital, Leh, are from Srinagar in the west and Manali in the south, although for much of the year, the only access is by air.

Protected Area Permits (PAPs)

Foreign tourists require a **PAP** to visit the Nubra Valley, Dha-Hanu villages, Tso-moriri and Pangong Tso, for a maximum of seven days in each place. Permits are available from the District Commissioner's office in Leh (T01982-252010); you'll need to take your passport, and photocopy your visa and personal details pages, along with two photos. But all trekking/travel agents can also arrange them for you, which is a much easier option. Allow at least half a day for an agent to obtain a permit, officially given only for groups of two or more (although solo travellers rarely experience problems). Permits are not extendable, but can be post-dated. Many people opt for permits covering all restricted areas.

When to go

The temperature can drop to -30°C in Leh and Kargil and -50°C in Dras, remaining sub-zero from December to February. Yet on clear sunny days in the summer, it can be scorching hot and you can easily get sunburnt; take plenty of sun cream. Ladakh lies beyond the monsoon line so rainfall is only 50 mm annually and there are even occasional dust storms.

BACKGROUND

Ladakh

Until recently Ladakhi society has generally been very introverted and the economy surprisingly self-sufficient. An almost total lack of precipitation has meant that cultivation must rely on irrigation. The rivers have been harnessed but with difficulty as the deep gorges presented a problem. Altitude and topography determine the choice of crop and farming is restricted to the areas immediately around streams and rivers. Barley forms the staple food. Apricots are one of the most popular fruits and are dried for winter sustenance, while the kernel yields oil for burning in prayer lamps.

Livestock is precious, especially the yak which provides meat, milk for butter, hair and hide for tents, boots, ropes and dung for fuel. Goats, especially in the eastern region, produce fine *pashm* for export. Animal transport is provided by yaks, ponies, Bactrian camels and the broad-backed *hunia* sheep. The Zanskar pony is fast and strong and used for transport and
for the special game of Ladakhi polo. Travellers venturing out of Leh are likely to see villagers using traditional methods of cultivation with the help of *dzos* and donkeys and using implements that have not changed for centuries.

Cut off from the outside world for six months a year, Ladakh also developed a very distinct culture. Polyandry (where a woman has more than one husband) was common but many men became *lamas* (monks) and a few women *chomos* (nuns).

Most people depended on subsistence agriculture but the harsh climate contributed to very high death rates and a stable population. That is rapidly changing. Imported goods are now widely available and more and more people are taking part in the monetary economy. Ladakh and its capital Leh have been open to tourists since 1974, and some feel there are now far too many; the pitfalls of modern society are all too evident in the mounds of plastic rubbish strewn along the roadsides.

The population of Leh has increased by more than five times in the last decade, and during the summer months tourists descend in numbers that equal the local population. In winter, those who can, leave for the plains, so this is when a more traditional Leh experience can be had, if you can bear the cold and the inconvenience.

Leh

magical kingdom surrounded by mountains, palaces and stupas

Mysterious dust-covered Leh (population 147,104, altitude 3500 m) sits in a fertile side valley of the Indus, about 10 km from the river. Encircled by stark awe-inspiring mountains with the cold desert beyond, it is the nearest experience to Tibet in India. The old Palace sits precariously on the hill to the north and looms over Leh.

The city developed as a trading post and market, attracting a wide variety of merchants from Yarkand, Kashgar, Kashmir, Tibet and North India. Tea, salt, household articles, wool and semi-

Tip...

Carry your passport with you because Ladakh is a sensitive border region. It's also worth carrying multiple photocopies of your passport and permits, as some checkpoints demand a copy.

Essential Leh

Finding your feet

For seven to eight months in the year Leh is cut off by snow and the sole link with the outside world is by air. Tickets are in high demand so it is essential to book well ahead. From mid-June to the end of September (weather permitting) the Manali–Leh highway opens to traffic, bringing travellers to the New Bus Stand south of town. Taxis wait at both the airport and bus stand to take you to town.

> **Tip...**
> Given the darkness of many buildings in Leh, even at midday, it is worth taking a torch wherever you go. At night it is essential.

Getting around

Many hotels are within a few minutes' walk of the Main Bazar Street around which Leh's activities are concentrated. Most visitors prefer to stay on the outskirts of town, a short walk away, in guesthouses that have a more rural setting. All the places of interest in Leh itself can also be tackled on foot, though those arriving by air or from Manali are urged to acclimatize for 48 hours before exerting themselves. For visiting monasteries and spots out of town arrange a jeep or taxi, although there are some buses and hitchhiking is possible. See Transport, page 191.

> **Tip...**
> Use your own bags for shopping in Leh. Plastic bags are not allowed in the bazar, as they were finding their way into streams.

precious stones were traded in the market. Buddhism travelled along the Silk Road and the Kashmir and Ladakh feeder, which has also seen the passage of soldiers, explorers and pilgrims, forerunners of the tourists who today contribute most to the urban economy.

Sights

The wide Main Bazar Street dating from the 1840s, which once accommodated caravans, has a colourful vegetable market where unpushy Ladakhi women sell local produce on the streetside while they knit or chat. Makeshift craft and jewellery stalls are dotted around, along with plenty of shops run by Kashmiri shopkeepers. The Old Town, mainly to the east of the Main Street, with its maze of narrow lanes, sits on the hillside below the palace and is worth exploring.

Leh Palace ① *Sunrise to sunset, Rs 100.* Dun-coloured Leh Palace has been described as a miniature version of Lhasa's Potala Palace. Built in the mid-16th century, the palace was partly in ruins by the 19th century. It has nine storeys, sloping buttresses and projecting wooden balconies. From the town below it is dazzling in the morning sun and ghostly at night. Built by King Singe Namgyal and still owned by the royal family, it is now unoccupied – they live in the palace at Stok. Visible damage was caused during Zorawar Singh's invasion from Kashmir in the 1830s.

The palace is under restoration, with new window and door frames fitted, and structural improvements being made, but still be wary of hazardous holes in the floor. After a steep climb some find the palace disappointing, but the views from the roof are exceptional. Like the Lhasa Potala Palace it has numerous rooms, steps and narrow passages (take a torch). The central prayer room has religious texts lining the walls, and contains dusty deities and time-worn masks. The upper levels have some painted carved wooden lintels and old murals that give a hint of past splendours.

Central Asian Museum The new Central Asian Museum is housed in a beautifully constructed building in the Tsa Soma gardens, where camel caravans used to camp. The museum explores the history of the caravan trade that for centuries linked Ladakh, until its mid-20th century isolation, with Tibet, Afghanistan, Samarkand, Kashmir and other city states. The museum is shaped like a Ladakhi fortress tower, with four floors inspired by the architecture of Ladakh, Kashmir, Tibet and Baltistan. Exhibits, including metalware, coins and masks, reveal the cultural exchange throughout the region; a garden café and museum shop are planned.

A walking tour that includes the museum and visits restored buildings of the Old Town leaves from **Lala's Art Café** (see page 189) daily, 1000-1300.

Tsemo Gompa and Fort The 15th-century Tsemo Gompa ('Red' Temple) is a strenuous walk north of the city and has a colossal two-storey-high image of Maitreya, flanked by figures of Avalokitesvara (right) and Manjusri (left). It was founded in 1430 by King Graspa Bum-Lde of the Namgyal rulers and a portrait of Tashi Namgyal hangs on the left at the entrance.

Just above the *gompa* is **Tsemo Fort** ① *dawn-dusk, Rs 20*, the classic landmark above Leh which can be seen from miles around.

Leh Mosque ① *The inner section is not open to women visitors.* The striking Leh Mosque in the main bazar is worth visiting. The Sunni Muslim mosque is believed to stand on land granted by King Deldan Namgyal in the 1660s; his grandmother was the Muslim Queen of Ladakh.

Chokhang Gompa The Chokhang Gompa (New Monastery, 1957), off Main Bazar, was built to commemorate the 2500th anniversary of the birth of Buddha. The remains of the **Leh Gompa** houses a large golden Buddha.

Mani walls From the radio station there are two long *mani* walls. **Rongo Tajng** is in the centre of the open plain and was built as a memorial to Queen Skalzang Dolma by her son Dalden Namgyal. It is about 500 m long and was built in 1635. The stones have been meticulously carved. The other, a 350-m wall down the hill, is believed to have been built by Tsetan Namgyal in 1785 as a memorial to his father the king.

Sankar Gompa ① *3 km north of the centre, 0700-1000, 1700-1900, prayers at 1830 with chanting, drums and cymbals.* Sankar Gompa (17th-18th centuries) of the Yellow Hat Sect, is one of the few *gompas* built in the valley bottom; it's an enjoyable walk through fields from town. It houses the chief *lama* of Spituk and 20 others. The newer monks' quarters are on three sides of the courtyard with steps leading up to the *dukhang* (Assembly Hall). There are a number of gold statues, numerous wall paintings and sculptures including a large one of the 11-headed, 1000-armed *Avalokitesvara*. It's an atmospheric and beautiful enclave in the increasingly busy valley.

Shanti Stupa On Changspa Lane, across the stream from Sankar Gompa, you reach the start of the stiff climb up to the white Japanese **Shanti Stupa** (1989). This is one of a series of 'Peace Pagodas' built by the Japanese around the world. There are good views from the top where a café offers a welcome sight after the climb. There is also a road which is accessible by jeep. Below the *stupa*, the **New Ecology Centre**, has displays on appropriate technology, as well as a handicrafts centre, a technical workshop and an organic vegetable garden.

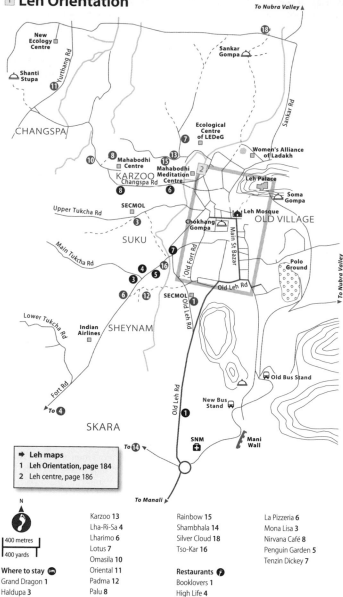

1 Leh Orientation

To Nubra Valley

New Ecology Centre

Yurthang Rd

Shanti Stupa 11

Sankar Gompa

CHANGSPA

Sankar Rd

Ecological Centre of LEDeG 7

Women's Alliance of Ladakh

Mahabodhi Centre 8

Mahabodhi Meditation Centre 15 13

Leh Palace

KARZOO

Changspa Rd 6

Soma Gompa

Upper Tukcha Rd

SECMOL

3

Leh Mosque

OLD VILLAGE

Chókhang Gompa

Main Tukcha Rd

SUKU

7

Main St Bazar

Old Fort Rd

4 16

3 5

6 12

SECMOL 1

Old Leh Rd

Polo Ground

To Nubra Valley

Lower Tukcha Rd

Indian Airlines

SHEYNAM

Old Leh Rd

Old Bus Stand

Fort Rd

To 4

SKARA

New Bus Stand

To 14

SNM

Mani Wall

➜ **Leh maps**
1 Leh Orientation, page 184
2 Leh centre, page 186

To Manali

N

400 metres
400 yards

Where to stay 🛏
Grand Dragon 1
Haldupa 3

Karzoo 13
Lha-Ri-Sa 4
Lharimo 6
Lotus 7
Omasila 10
Oriental 11
Padma 12
Palu 8

Rainbow 15
Shambhala 14
Silver Cloud 18
Tso-Kar 16

Restaurants 🍴
Booklovers 1
High Life 4

La Pizzeria 6
Mona Lisa 3
Nirvana Café 8
Penguin Garden 5
Tenzin Dickey 7

ON THE ROAD
Prepare for a different lifestyle in Leh

The whitewashed sun-dried brick walls of a typical two-storey, flat-roofed Ladakhi house, often with decorative woodwork around doors and windows and a carefully nurtured garden, look inviting to a traveller after a long hard journey. Many local families have opened up their homes to provide for the increasing demand for accommodation over a very short peak season, and new hotels are springing up everywhere.

On the whole, rooms are kept clean and the standard of budget hotels is better that you would expect elsewhere in India. There is usually a space for sitting out: a 'garden' with a tree or two, some flower beds and perhaps a vegetable patch.

Electricity is limited, so expect power cuts, which are random and unpredictable. Some hotels have generators. Those without may run out of tap water but buckets are always at hand. Hot water is a luxury, available only during mornings and evenings. Plumbing allows for flush WCs in most hotels, although compost toilets are the more ecological method. Guests are encouraged to economize on water and electricity; you will notice the low-power bulbs and scarcity of lights in rooms and public areas, so put away your reading material until sunrise.

Donkey Sanctuary ⓘ *Korean Temple Rd, www.donkeysanctuary.in*. One kilometre past Shanti Stupa, the Donkey Sanctuary, opened in 2008. This charity looks after around 40 donkeys at any one time and is well worth a visit.

Ladakh Ecological Development Group ⓘ *T01982-253221, www.ledeg.org, Mon-Fri 1000-1800*. The Ecological Centre of LEDeG and the **craft shop** opened in 1984 to spread awareness of Ladakhi environmental issues, encourage self-help and the use of alternative technology. It has a library of books on Ladakhi culture, Buddhism and the environment. Handicrafts are sold, and you can refill water.

Women's Alliance of Ladakh (WAL) ⓘ *Sankar Rd, Chubi, T01982-250293, www.women allianceladakh.org, video shown Mon-Sat 1500 (minimum 10 people)*. The Women's Alliance of Ladakh is an alliance of 5000 Ladakhi women, concerned with raising the status of traditional agriculture, preserving the traditionally high status of women and creating an alternative development model based on self-reliance for Ladakh. The centre has a café selling local and organic foods (see Restaurants, below), and a craft shop. They hold festivals, cultural shows, dances, etc, which are advertised around Leh; it's mainly aimed at local people, but all visitors are welcome.

Tourist information

J&K Tourism
2 km south on Airport Rd, T01982-252297, www.jktourism.org, or a more convenient office on Fort Rd, T01982-253462, 1000-1600.

➜ **Leh maps**
1 Leh Orientation, page 184
2 Leh centre, page 186

② **Leh centre**

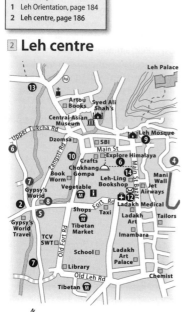

Not to scale

Where to stay 📍
Atisha **7**
Malpak **6**
Old Ladakh **4**
Tsomo-Ri **8**
Yak Tail **5**

Restaurants 📍
Chansa Traditional
  Ladakhi Kitchen **6**
Chopsticks **2**
Lala's Art Café **9**
Mentokling Apple
  Garden **13**
Open Hand Espresso Bar **7**
Pumpernickel **10**
Shubh Panjabi Dhaba **14**
Tibetan Friend's Corner **12**

Where to stay

There are now scores of guesthouses, often in traditional Ladakhi homes. Outside the peak period expect discounts (as much as 25-50%). Those in Karzoo and Changspa (some way from the bus stand) are quieter and more rural. Many hotels and guesthouses close during the winter months. There is lots of budget accommodation along Fort Rd and in the Changspa area; some are very basic and you might want to use your own sleeping bag. But generally you can find a clean simple room without needing to book in advance. For eco-conscious homestays in Ladakh, see www.himalayan-homestays.com.

$$$$-$$$ Grand Dragon
Old Leh Rd, Sheynam, T01982-257786, www.thegranddragonladakh.com.
Big hotel with all mod cons, Wi-Fi and great views. Stunning dining room and a nod to eco-tourism with double glazing, underfloor heating and solar panels.

$$$ Lharimo
Fort Rd, T01982-252101, www.lharimo.com.
An attractive central hotel with scarlet window frames and a whitewashed exterior. The large comfortable rooms have traditional bamboo ceilings and inoffensive ageing wooden furniture, TV and clean tiled bathrooms. The big grassy lawn is perfect for relaxing.

$$$ Lha-Ri-Sa
Skara, T01982-252000, www.ladakh-lharisa.com.
With a boutique vibe, they offer stylish rooms and the outside of the building is simply beautiful. The restaurant serves up flavours from all over India as well as traditional Ladakhi food. On the outskirts of town.

$$$ Lotus
Upper Karzoo, T01982-257265,
www.lotushotel.in.
High-spec rooms with quality furniture,
modern amenities, and a nod to traditional
Ladakhi decor. 24-hr hot water, central
heating and good multicuisine restaurant.
The views from the flowery garden look
straight onto the palace.

$$$ Shambhala
Skara, T01982-251100,
www.hotelshambhala.com.
Large airy rooms, an excellent restaurant
(often catering for German packages),
breakfast included, very pleasant, friendly
staff and lovely owners. Peaceful and
away from crowds, with an attractive
garden that has hammocks and fruit
trees. Free transport to centre.

$$$ Tso-Kar
Fort Rd, T01982-253071,
www.lehladakhhotel.com.
Very reasonably priced and well-maintained
rooms. The bathrooms are a little old but
clean, and there's TV and comfortable beds.
Astroturf, flowers, and cane chairs and tables
are in the courtyard.

$$$ Yak-Tail
Fort Rd, T01982-252118, www.hotel
yaktail.com. May-Oct.
One of Leh's oldest hotels, comfortable and
cosy (with decent heating). Some of the
30 rooms are 'houseboat style', others have
balconies, some have lots of patterns. The
restaurant is well-decorated with murals and
serves good Indian food. The courtyard has
been astro-turfed but swinging vines create
a pleasing greenhouse effect.

$$ Omasila
Changspa, T01982-252119,
www.hotelomasila.com.
A series of annexes around a pleasant
back lawn, plus a huge terrace and ornate
restaurant (serving their vegetables from the
garden). Rooms have TV and wooden floors;
it's worth paying a bit extra for the deluxe

rooms with seating areas. All have decent
tiled bathrooms and heating. Attracts a
more mature clientele. Free Wi-Fi.

$$ Oriental
Below Shanti Stupa, T01982-253153,
www.orientalguesthouse.com.
35 very clean rooms in a traditional
friendly family home, with good home
cooking served in the dining hall, great
views across the valley, and reliable treks
and travel arrangements.

$$ Shanti Guest House
Below Shanti Stupa, Changspa, T01982-
253084, http://shantihome.co.in.
A guesthouse with well-heated rooms, most
with great views. Excellent food, summer/
winter treks arranged with guide and free
Wi-Fi. Run by a friendly Ladakhi family.

$$ Tsomo-Ri
Fort Rd, T019822-252271,
www.ladakhtsomori.com.
15 rooms arranged around a central
whitewashed courtyard with trellises
of runner beans running up the stairs.
Surprisingly quiet, rooms have TV, carpets,
plain wood furniture, clean walls and plenty
of good bedding. There are wicker chairs
for relaxing in the courtyard.

$$-$ Padma Guesthouse & Hotel
Off Fort Rd down an alley, T01982-252630,
www.padmaladakh.net.
Clean, charming rooms with common bath
in a guesthouse in the old family home.
Upstairs, including a rooftop restaurant,
has mountain views, plus there are hotel-
style rooms in the newer block. There's a
beautiful and peaceful garden, a Buddhist
chapel/meditation room, solar panels and
a good library, but they are mostly known
for their outstanding hospitality.

$$-$ Silver Cloud
By Sankar Gompa, 15 mins' walk from
centre, T01982-253128, http://silvercloud
guesthouse.blogspot.co.uk. Open during
the winter months.

Ladakhi guesthouse with a rural homestay atmosphere offering a wide range of spotless rooms and dorm, run by a friendly helpful family. Free Wi-Fi, excellent food and a large garden.

$ Atisha
Malpak, off Fort Rd, T09906-992187, atisha_leh@rediffmail.com.
This place is not much to look at on arrival, but simple rooms are spotless with bright paint and shiny tiled bathrooms. Prices increase as you go up from ground to 3rd floor. The rooftop terrace is lovely, and although there's not much of an aspect it feels rural and a burbling brook surrounds. Very pleasant low-key family.

$ Haldupa
Upper Tuckha Rd, Malpak, T01982-251374.
Cheapest rooms in the old building share (smelly) bathrooms, hot buckets available, and a memorable shrine is in the same building. The new 2-level wing is swish and there's a delightful garden with plenty of seating. Organic food is available.

$ Karzoo
Karzoo Lane, T01982-252324.
The usual flowery garden; very cheap rooms with shared bath in an old Ladakhi house and modern clean rooms in the new annex (still waiting for the upper storey to be built), but very relaxed and helpful staff. Omelettes are served for breakfast. Recommended.

$ Malpak
Upper Tuckha Rd, Malpak, T01982-257380, dollayleh@yahoo.co.in.
Quaint 6-room guesthouse in an old building, all rooms with attached bath. Shady outdoor tables next to a luxuriant flower and vegetable garden, and a convenient yet peaceful location. A recommended budget choice.

$ Old Ladakh
In the Old Town, T01982-252951.
8 rooms around an inner courtyard (varying in comfort), has bags of character with red

lacquered windows and door frames, the odd cracked window and great views from top floor. Pleasant atmosphere (old-school vibes).

$ Palu Guest House
Changspa, T(0)9419-218674.
This sweet family home is secluded and set back from Changspa Rd. The spacious rooms have clean sheets, carpets and big windows; some have private bath and TV, others share a bathroom, all have working geysers. There's a particularly attractive flowery garden and veg patch, with shady seating.

$ Rainbow
Karzoo, T01982-252332, http://rainbowghleh.com.
Big clean rooms, some with wonderful views of mountains and Shanti Stupa, hot water in the morning, great hospitality, and lovely garden with restaurant. Rooms in the old house share baths, or the new wing has en suite ones.

Restaurants

$$ Chopsticks Noodle Bar
Fort Rd.
Great East Asian, Tibetan and regional food in a clean and attractive restaurant. Deservedly popular and worth at least one visit when in Leh.

$$ Penguin Garden
Just off Fort Rd.
Good garden café with a pleasant atmosphere, care of Nepali owners.

$$-$ Booklovers' Retreat
Changspa.
A perennial favourite as a cosy place for food and hanging out. There's a roof terrace.

$$-$ La Pizzeria
Changspa Rd, Changspa.
Pretty authentic pizza, very pleasant ambiance, some mattress seating, and soft lantern light at night.

$$-$ Mona Lisa
Fort Rd.
International food covers all bases (pizzas, *momos*, garlic cheese bread), and is particularly recommended for the tandori selection. Lovely atmosphere under lamps on the terrace.

$$-$ Nirvana Café
Live music after 2100. Indoor and outdoor seating under lanterns and fairy lights, some Sinai-style slouching areas. Laid-back vibe and varied menu of South Asian, Asian and lots of Italian, prices slightly higher than average. No alcohol.

$$-$ Open Hand Espresso Bar & Bistro
Off Fort Rd, www.openhand.in.
A chic retreat, with loungers and seating on decking by a vegetable garden, chunky wood furniture inside, great cakes, cappuccinos and home-cooked meals, healthy smoothies and more. Ethical shopping – clothes, silks, cushions, gifts etc – plus Wi-Fi.

$ Chansa Traditional Ladakhi Kitchen
Next to Chokhang Vihara, off Main Bazar.
A chance to try traditional Ladakhi cuisine (vegetarian); simple indoor seating, or outside under the shade of a parachute. Whiteboard shows the day's dishes, such as *sku* – a delicious chunky wholewheat pasta and veg broth, plus limited offerings of Chinese, Indian (great mushroom masala) and Western food. Cheap and tasty.

$ High Life Tibetan Restaurant
Fort Rd.
Exceptional range of high quality Tibetan food, plus good salads and Western dishes, inviting indoor seating with gingham tablecloths or big outdoor area.

$ Lala's Art Café
Off Main Bazar, Old Town.
Quaint restored Ladakhi house in the Old Town with a roof terrace, and a shrine on the ground floor. Coffee and cakes are the order of the day.

$ Local Food Café
Mon-Sat 1100-1630.
Serves good Ladakhi snacks, while promoting traditional farming methods threatened by the modern cash economy, run by the Women's Alliance.

$ Mentokling Apple Garden
Changspa Rd, Zangsti.
Great *paratha* breakfasts, good menu generally, with Indian and Thai dishes. Lovely garden.

$ Shubh Panjabi Dhaba
Main Bazar.
Typical Sikh-style *thalis* and cheap dishes in a basic restaurant; half-plates available, great *lassis* and good *paratha* breakfasts.

$ Tenzin Dickey
Fort Rd.
Delicious *kothay* (fried *momos*), soups, and other Tibetan/Chinese dishes, some western food, all veg, and the Tibetan herbal tea is good. Simple and neat little place with checked tablecloths.

$ Tibetan Friend's Corner
Main St, Bazar.
Clean and cheerful, *kothay* and a wide menu of Tibetan/Chinese veg and non-veg, thick pancakes and great hot drinks, locally popular.

$ Also recommended are the kebab stalls near the mosque.

Bakeries
Several German bakeries sell good bread (trekking bread keeps for a week) and excellent cakes and muesli.
Pumpernickel, *Zangsti Rd.* The original German bakery is the best and friendliest, with indoor/outdoor seating, excellent apricot and apple crumble/pie and a message board for trekkers. There are also traditional ovens turning out delicious local bread in the lane next to the museum, behind the mosque.

Entertainment

Dancing and singing
Ladakhi dancing and singing, below entrance to the palace, by Soma Gompa, 1730 (1 hr), Rs 200.

Festivals

Dates vary depending on the lunar calendar.
Apr-May Buddha Purnima marks the Buddha's birth, at full moon.
Sep Ladakh Festival. The main events are held in the Leh polo grounds with smaller events in other districts. Usually during the first 2 weeks in Sep, there are dances, displays of traditional costumes, handicrafts, Ladakhi plays, archery and polo matches.
Dec Celebration of Losar which originated in the 15th century to protect people before going to battle.

Shopping

In **Dzomsa** you can get water bottles refilled, dispose of batteries, get laundry done and there are organic goods available. At the **Ecological Shop for Organic Products** you can stock up on local produce including apricot jam, fruit and nuts in season, and bottled juice.

Leh Bazar is full of shops and market stalls selling curios, clothes and knick-knacks. Tea and *chang* (local barley brew) vessels, cups, butter churns, knitted carpets with Tibetan designs, Tibetan jewellery, prayer flags, musical bowls and pashminas are all available. Prices are high especially in Kashmiri shops so bargain vigorously. There are tight restrictions on the export of anything over 100 years old. However, even though most items are antique-looking, they are, in fact, fresh from the backstreet workshops. If you walk down the narrow lanes, you will probably find an artisan at work from whom you can buy direct.

Books
Book Worm. Second-hand books, coffee table books and fiction.
Leh-Ling Bookshop, *near the Post Office, Main Bazar*. Good selection, especially on trekking in the region.

Tailors
There are many tailors lining Nowshara Gali.

What to do

Archery
The **Archery Stadium** is nearby where winter competitions attract large crowds; the target is a hanging white clay tablet.

Meditation
Mahabodhi Meditation Centre, *Changspa Lane, off Changspa Rd, www.mahabodhi-ladakh.org. Closed in winter*. Enquire about short courses and yoga classes. Also a centre in Chogsalmar, open all year.

Polo
Polo, the 'national' sport, is popular in the summer and is played in the polo ground east of the city. The local version which is fast and rough appears to follow no rules! The **Polo Club** is the highest in the world.

Tour operators
There are dozens of trekking agents in Leh town, and it's no problem to turn up in high season and get organized in a day or 2.
K2, *Hill Top Building, Main Bazar, T01982-253980, www.k2adventureleh.com*. Good rates for treks (Markha Valley); very friendly, environment conscious.
Rimo Expeditions, *Kang-lha Chen Hotel, T01982-253348, www.rimoexpeditions.com*. Insightful and informative about the local area, running a whole host of treks, as well as mountain biking, mountaineering, river rafting, cultural tours and family holidays.
Shakti Experiences, *Gurgaon, Delhi, www.shaktihimalaya.com*. Sensitively run sustainable tours and personalized treks

to remote villages in the rugged high mountains. Luxurious but understated. **Yama Treks**, *Leh, T01982-250833 www. yamatreks.com*. Efficient, run by the very personable Mr Rinchen Namgial; cultural tours as well as treks.

Whitewater rafting and kayaking

Possible on the Tsarap Chu, Indus and Zanskar rivers from mid-Jun; the upper reaches of the former (Grade IV rapids) are suitable for experienced rafters only, though the remaining stretch can be enjoyed by all. Along the Indus: Hemis to Choglamsar (easy, very scenic); Phey-Nimmu (Grade III); Nimmu-Khaltse (professional). Ensure that life jackets and wet suits are provided. Half- to full-day trips possible, including transport and lunch.

Transport

Air The small airport is 5 km away on Srinagar Rd. It is surrounded by hills on 3 sides and the flight over the mountain ranges is spectacular. Transport to town by taxi is around Rs 200.

Allow 2 hrs for check in. Weather conditions may deteriorate rapidly even in the summer resulting in flight cancellations (especially outside Jul and Aug) so always be prepared for a delay or to take alternative road transport out of Ladakh. Furthermore, the airlines fly quite full planes into Leh but can take fewer passengers out because of the high-altitude take-off. This adds to the difficulty of getting a flight out. Book your tickets well in advance.

To Delhi daily, throughout the year (weather permitting). **Srinagar**, direct on Wed with **Air India**. For **Jammu**, connections via Delhi, or direct with **Air India** on Mon and Fri.

Bus Local buses leave from the **stand** near the cemetery. The vehicles are ramshackle but the fares are low. See under relevant monasteries for details of timings. Enquiries **J&KSRTC**, T01982-252285.

> **Tip...**
> If you have already spent some time in the Himalaya, you may be better acclimatized, but a mild headache is common and can be treated with aspirin or paracetamol. Drink plenty of fluids on journeys.

Long distance Leh is connected to Manali via Keylong and to Srinagar, via Kargil, by state highways. Both roads can be seriously affected by landslides, causing long delays. The Leh–Srinagar road is also often blocked by army convoys.

Himachal Tourism runs regular deluxe buses between Leh and Manali, 530 km, usually mid-Jun to end Sep. Book at HPTDC Office, 1st floor, Fort Rd, T(0)9622-374300, a/c Volvo, leaves alternate days at 0500 from opposite the J&K Bank, Fort Rd, overnight in Keylong. **J&K SRTC** run cheaper ordinary/ deluxe buses, a gruelling journey departing at 0430, booked at bus stand, stop overnight at Keylong.

J&K SRTC bus to **Kargil**, 230 km, 0430, 10 hrs, bus to **Srinagar** 434 km, 0800 (and 1400 if passengers), overnight stop in Kargil.

Shared jeeps or **minibuses** Make the journey to **Manali** in 1 day, leaving at between 2400-0200 taking 22-24 hrs, costing about Rs 1800 per seat. Jeeps leave from the Old Bus Station, to **Srinagar** at 1700, 15 hrs; to **Kargil** at 0700, 8-9 hrs. Book seats a day in advance; it's worth paying extra for front seats.

The road to Manali This route crosses some very high passes and is open mid-Jun/ Jul until late Sep (depending on the weather), taking 2 days by bus. Road conditions may be poor in places. Departure from Leh can be early (0400) with overnight stop in Keylong; next day to Manali. Alternatively, camp in Sarchu (10 hrs from Leh), or Jespa; next day 14 hrs to Manali. Roadside tents provide food en route during the tourist season; carry snacks, water and a good sleeping bag when planning to camp. Many travellers find the mountain roads extremely frightening and they are comparatively dangerous. Some are cut out of extremely unstable hillsides, usually with nothing between the road's edge and the near-vertical drop below; parts remain rough and pot-holed and during the monsoons, landslides and rivers can make it impassable for 2-3 days. It is also a long and uncomfortable journey, but there is some spectacular scenery. See also page 125.

Taxi Tourist taxi and jeep Ladakh Taxi Operators' Union, 1st floor at bus stand, T01982-252723, 0700-1900 daily, with fixed-rate fares. A day's taxi hire to visit nearby *gompas* can also be arranged through travel agents. Private 4WD between Leh and Manali is expensive, but recommended if you want to stop en route to visit monasteries on a 2-day trip.

Southeast of Leh

vast monastery complexes and tiny gompas within easy reach of Leh

South and east of Leh is an amazing stretch of road with some fascinating monasteries strung along it. Many of these make good day trips from Leh, and are possible excursions by bus and hitching. If you hire a car or jeep (which is good value when shared by four), you can see several places in a single day.

Choglamsar

The road between Leh and Choglamsar is now quite built up and at times clogged with traffic. On the east bank of the Indus, 7 km south of Leh, Choglamsar is a green oasis with poplars and willows where there are golf links and a polo ground as well as horticultural nurseries. The Central Institute of Buddhist Studies is here with a specialist library. Past the Tibetan refugee camps, children's village and the arts and crafts centre, the Choglamsar Bridge crosses the Indus. The **Chochot Yugma Imambara** ⓘ *a few minutes' walk from the bridge*, is worth a visit. Buses depart Leh hourly from 0800-1800.

Stok

Across Choglamsar Bridge, 16 km south of Leh, is **Stok Palace**, dating from the 1840s when the King of Ladakh was deposed by the invading Dogra forces. The royal line continues till today, and the present king lives in a private wing of the palace with his wife and son. The palace is a rambling building and the family use only a dozen of the 80 rooms. The small **Palace Museum** ⓘ *May-Oct 0900-1300 and 1400-1900, Rs 50*, with three rooms, is a showpiece for the royal *thangkas*, many 400 years old, crown jewels, dresses, coins, *peraks* (headdresses) encrusted with turquoise and lapis lazuli as well as religious objects. There's also a rather lovely café, which has superb views.

The **gompa**, a short distance away, has some ritual dance masks. **Tsechu** is held for two days in February and there is an **archery contest** in July. A three-hour walk up the valley behind Stok takes you to some extraordinary mountain scenery dominated by the 6121-m-high Stok Kangri. There are at least three simple guesthouses in town, of which the Yarsta is most comfortable. Buses to Stok leave Leh at 0730 and 1700, or taxis from the Leh central taxi stand are available at fixed rates.

Shey

Palace open all day; try to be there 0700-0900, 1700-1800 when prayers are chanted, Rs 20.

Until the 16th century, Shey was the royal residence, located at an important vantage point in the Indus Valley. Kings of Leh were supposed to be born in the monastery. The royal family moved to Stok in order to escape advancing Dogra forces from Kashmir who came to exploit the trade in pashmina wool. Shey, along with Thiksey, is also regarded as an auspicious place for cremation.

Most of the fort walls have fallen into disrepair but the palace and its wall paintings have now been restored. The

Tip...
Camera flash is usually not allowed in monasteries to reduce damage to wall paintings and *thangkas*, carry a torch.

palace gompa with its 17.5-m-high blue-haired Maitreya Buddha, imitating the one at Tsemo Gompa, is attended by Drukpa monks from Hemis. It is made of copper and brass but splendidly gilded and studded with precious gem stones. Paintings in the main shrine have been chemically cleaned by the Archaeological Society of India. The large victory **stupa** is topped with gold. Extensive grounds covering the former lake bed to the east contain a large number of *chortens* in which cremated ashes of important monks, members of the royal family and the devout were buried. A newer temple houses another old giant Buddha statue. There are several **rock carvings**; particularly noteworthy is that of five *dhyani* Buddhas (circa eighth century) at the bottom of the hill. The small hotel below the *gompa* has spartan but clean rooms. It is 15 km southeast of Leh on the Indus River or can be reached along a stone path from Thiksey. Hourly buses depart Leh 0800-1800.

Thiksey
Rs 30, hourly buses from Leh 0800-1800.

Situated 25 km south of Leh on a crag overlooking the flood plain on the east bank of the Indus, Thiksey Monastery is one of the most imposing monasteries in Ladakh and was part of the original Gelugpa order in the 15th century. The 12-storey monastery, with typical tapering walls painted deep red, ochre and white, has 10 temples, a nunnery and 80 *lamas* in residence whose houses cling to the hillside below. The complex contains numerous *stupas*, statues, *thangkas*, wall paintings (note the fresco of the 84 Mahasiddhas, high above) swords and a large pillar engraved with the Buddha's teachings.

The new temple interior is dominated by a giant 13-m-high Buddha figure near the entrance. The principal **Dukhang** (assembly hall) at the top of the building has holes in the wall for storing religious texts and contains the guardian deities. At the very top, the Old Library has old wooden bookcases with ancient texts and statues; adjacent is the tiny **Chamsing Lhakhang**. Views from the roof are staggeringly good. The slightly creepy **Gonkhang** has Tibetan-style wall paintings. The **museum** ① *0600-1800, closed 1300-1330*, is near the entrance, and also sells souvenirs. There's a restaurant and guestrooms, below the museum.

Thiksey is a popular place to watch religious ceremonies, usually at 0630 or 1200. An early start by taxi makes even the first possible, or it's possible to stay overnight (see page 195). They are preceded by the playing of large standing drums and long horns similar to *alpenstock*. Masked dances are performed during special festivals.

Stakna
Across the valley on a hill, Stakna is the earliest Drukpa monastery, built before Hemis though its decorations are not as ancient. It is also called 'Tiger's nose' because of the shape of the hill site. This small but well-kept monastery has a beautiful silver-gilt *chorten* in the assembly hall, installed around 1955, and some interesting paintings in the dark temple at the back. No need for a local guide as the *lamas* are always willing to open the doors. There are excellent views of the Indus Valley and the Zanskar range.

Hemis Monastery
0800-1300, 1400-1800.

On the west bank of the Indus, 45 km southeast of Leh, Hemis Monastery, built on a green hillside surrounded by spectacular mountain scenery, is tucked into a gorge. The **Drukpa monastery** was founded by Stagsang Raspa during the reign of Senge Namgyal (circa 1630). It is the biggest (350 lamas) and wealthiest in Ladakh and it's a 'must', thus is busy with tourists.

Pass by *chortens* and sections of *mani* walls to enter the complex through the east gate which leads into a large 40 m by 20 m courtyard. Colourful flags flutter in the breeze from posts, and the balconied walls of the buildings have colourfully painted door and window frames. On the north side are two assembly halls approached by steps. The large three-tiered *Dukhang* to the right used for ceremonies is old and atmospheric; the smaller *Tshogskhang* (main temple) contains three silver gilt *chortens* and is covered in murals. The murals in the verandas depict guardian deities, the *kalachakra* (wheel of life) and 'Lords of the four quarters' are well preserved.

A staircase alongside the *Tshogskhang* leads to a roof terrace where there are a number of shrines including a bust of the founder. The *Tsom Lakhang* (chapel) has ancient Kashmiri bronzes, a golden Buddha and a silver *chorten*. The largest of the monastery's prized possession is a heavy silk *thangka*, beautifully embroidered in bright coloured threads and pearls, which is displayed every 12 years (next time in 2016). The museum contains an important library of Tibetan-style books and an impressive collection of *thangkas*.

Not many people make the walk to the new golden Buddha on a nearby cliff, and there is also a pleasant 3-km walk uphill to another *gompa*. A stay in Hemis overnight enables you to attend early morning prayers, a moving experience and recommended. Bus services make a day trip possible.

Chemrey
Picture-perfect Chemrey is a short way off the main road, walkable from where the bus drops passengers. Perched on a little peak above encircling barley fields is **Thekchok Gompa**, home to 70 monks. A road winds to the top, but it's nicer to walk up the steep steps through traditional homesteads. The wonky prayer hall has countless murals of the Buddha, and there are three further *lhakhang* (image halls) to visit; a museum on the roof contains *thangkas* and statues. The beautiful setting and relative lack of visitors makes Chemrey a very worthwhile stop.

Sakti and Takthok
The road continues through a sloping valley to Takthok, first passing Sakti village with the dramatic ruins of a fortress by the roadside. At ancient **Takthok Gompa** ① *Rs 30*, there is a holy cave-shrine in which the sage Padmasambhava meditated in the eighth century. The walls and ceiling are papered with rupee notes and coins, numerous statues are swathed in prayer scarves, and centuries of butter lamps have left their grime. A highly colourful *dukhang* hall contains three beautiful statues. It is the only monastery in Ladakh belonging to the Nyingma sect of Buddhism; about 60 lamas reside here, and at the new *gompa* constructed nearby in 1980. It's possible to take a morning bus from Leh to Takthok and walk the 5 km back down the valley to Chemrey. Should you get stranded in Takthok, a **Tourist Bungalow** ① *opposite the Gompa, T(0)9622-959513*, has four jaded but sunny rooms, some with squat toilets.

Where to stay

Thiksey

$ Chamba
T01982-267385.
Basic chalet rooms with Indian toilets lie next to a scruffy yard, or the main building has more comfortable rooms. The garden restaurant makes for a good lunch break after exploring the monastery.

Festivals

Hemis

Jun Hemis Tsechu is perhaps the biggest cultural festival in Ladakh. It commemorates the birth of **Guru Padmasambhava** who is believed to have fought local demons to protect the people. Young and old of both sexes join *lamas* in masked dance-dramas, while stalls sell handicrafts A colourful display of Ladakhi Buddhist culture, lasting 3 days, it attracts large numbers of foreign visitors.

Along the Srinagar road

staggeringly located monasteries, fascinating overnight stops

The Srinagar road out of Leh passes through a flat dusty basin mostly occupied by army encampments with mile after mile of wire fencing. The scenery is stunning and, as with the Leh–Manali Road, is punctuated with monasteries. A bus leaves Leh each afternoon for Alchi (see page 197), allowing access to most of the sites described in this section. A few places make for interesting and peaceful overnight stops.

Spituk

Standing on a conical hill, some 8 km from Leh, **Spituk Monastery** was founded in the 11th century. The buildings themselves, including three chapels, date from the 15th century and are set in a series of tiers with courtyards and steps. The Yellow-Hat Gelugpa monks created the precedent in Ladakh for building on mountain tops rather than valley floors. You can get good views of the countryside around.

The long 16th- to 17th-century **dukhang** (assembly hall) is the largest building and has two rows of seats along the length of the walls to a throne at the far end. Sculptures and miniature *chortens* are displayed on the altar. Spituk has a collection of ancient Jelbagh masks, icons and arms including some rescued from the Potala Palace in Lhasa.

Also 16th- to 17th-century, the **Mahakal Temple**, higher up the hill, contains a shrine of Vajrabhairava, often mistaken for the Goddess Kali. The terrifying face is only unveiled in January, during the **Gustor festival**.

Phyang

Phyang Gompa, 16 km from Leh, dominates a beautiful side valley dotted with poplars, homesteads and *chortens* with a village close by. It belongs to the Red-Hat Kagyupa sect, with its 16th-century Gouon monastery built by the founder of the Namgyal Dynasty which is marked by a flagstaff at the entrance. It houses 60 lamas and hundreds of statues including some Kashmiri bronzes (c14th century), *thangkas* and manuscript copies of the Kangyur and Tengyur.

The temple walls have colourful paintings centred on the eight emblems of happiness. The walls in the main prayer hall are covered with ancient smoke-blackened murals, and a giant rolled-up *thangka* hangs from the ceiling. The faces of the statues in the Protector's Hall have been covered. A grand new wing has been constructed, with rather gawdy paintings by the artists (many of whom came from Bhutan). Morning prayers take place 0600-0730. Phyang is the setting for a spectacular July Tseruk festival with masked dancing.

There are three buses daily (0900, 1400 and 1630, 45 minutes; return to Leh at 0800, 1000, 1300 from the monastery, 1600 and 1730); the morning bus allows you to explore the valley and walk back to Leh. However, it is worth overnighting in Phyang as there is a pleasing guesthouse (see page 199), good walks around the traditional village and dramatic valley up to the fort, as well as stunning views to the pyramid-peak of Stok Kangri.

Phyang to Nimmu

About 2 km before Nimmu the Indus enters an impressive canyon before the Zanskar joins it, a good photo opportunity. As the road bends, a lush green oasis with lines of poplars comes into view. The mud brick houses of Nimmu have grass drying on the flat rooftops to provide fodder for the winter. A dry stone *mani* wall runs along the road; beyond Nimmu the walls become 2 m wide in places with innumerable *chortens* alongside. The rocky outcrops on the hills to the right appear like a natural fortress. Nimmu serves mainly as a bus rest-stop, but there are a couple of small hotels (Nilza Guesthouse is most acceptable) and a collection of *dhabas* and shops.

Basgo

The road, lined by *mani* walls and *chortens*, passes through Basgo Village with the ruins of a Buddhist citadel impressively sited on a spur overlooking the Indus Valley. It served as a royal residence for several periods between the 15th and 17th centuries. The **fort palace** was once considered almost impregnable having survived a three-year siege by Tibetan and Mongol armies in the 17th century.

Among the ruins two temples have survived. The higher **Maitreya Temple** (mid-16th century) built by Tashi Namgyal's son contains a very fine Maitreya statue at the rear of the hall, flanked by *bodhisattvas*. Some murals from the early period illustrating the Tibetan Buddhist style have also survived on the walls and ceiling; among the Buddhas and *bodhisattvas* filled with details of animals, birds and mermaids, appear images of Hindu divinities.

The 17th-century **Serzang Temple** (gold and copper), with a carved doorway, contains another large Maitreya image whose head rises through the ceiling into a windowed box-like structure. The murals look faded and have been damaged by water. The fort is very photogenic, particularly so in the late afternoon light. The Chamba View guesthouse and restaurant is by the road, as you exit the village.

Lekir (Likir)

Some 5.5 km from Basgo, a road on the right leads up to **Lekir Monastery** via a scenic route. Lower Lekir, a scattering of houses where most accommodation is found, is about 1 km off NH1 accessed by confusing unpaved tracks. You can walk from Lower Likir up to the monastery, about 5 km on the road, or via short-cuts crossing the river. The picturesque whitewashed monastery buildings rise in different levels on the hillside across the Lekir River. A huge gold-coloured Maitreya Buddha flanks the complex.

Lekir was built during the reign of Lachen Gyalpo who installed 600 monks here, headed by Lhawang Chosje (circa 1088). The *gompa* was invested with a collection of fine images, *thangkas* and murals to vie with those at Alchi. The present buildings date mainly from the 18th century since the original were destroyed by fire. A path up leads to the courtyard where a board explains the origin of the name: Klu-Khyil (snake coil) refers to the *nagas* here, reflected in the shape of the hill. Lekir was converted to the Gelugpa sect in the 15th century. The head *lama*, the younger brother of the Dalai Lama, has his apartments here, which were extended in the mid-1990s.

The **Dukhang** (assembly hall) contains large clay images of the Buddhas (past, present and future), *thangkas*, and Kangyur and Tengyur manuscripts, the Kangyur having been first compiled in Ladakh during Lachen Gyalpo's reign. The **Nyenes-Khang** contains beautiful murals of the 35 confessional Buddhas and 16 arahats. Wooden steps lead up to the **Gon-Khang** housing a statue of the guardian deity here, as well as *thangkas* and murals. Further steps lead to a small but very interesting **museum** ⓘ *Rs 20, opened on request (climb to a hall above, up steep wooden stairs)*, displays *thangkas*, old religious and domestic implements, costumes, etc, which are labelled in English.

Village craftsmen produce *thangkas*, carved wooden folding seats and clay pottery. If you wish to stay overnight, the monastery has guestrooms which share bathrooms (by donation); for further accommodation options in the villages, see page 199. A bus goes to Leh at 0730 from the monastery.

Alchi
0800-1300, 1400-1800, Rs 50, www.achiassociation.org.

The road enters Saspol, 8 km after the Lekir turn-off. About 2 km beyond the village, a link road with a suspension bridge over the river leads to Alchi, which is hidden from view as you approach. As the road enters the village, impressive old houses in various states of repair can be seen. It's possible to climb up the small rocky peak behind these, to a square white turret with graves around, for good views up the Indus valley and of the village. A patchwork of cultivated fields surrounds the monastery complex.

A narrow path from the car park winds past village houses, donkeys and apricot trees to lead to the **Dharma Chakra monastery**. You will be expected to buy a ticket from one of the three *lamas* on duty. The whole complex, about 100 m long and 60 m wide, is enclosed by a whitewashed mud and straw wall. Alchi's large temple complex is regarded as one of the most important Buddhist centres in Ladakh and a jewel of monastic skill. Founded in the 11th century by Rinchen Zangpo, the 'Great Translator', it was richly decorated by artists from Kashmir and Tibet. Paintings of the *mandalas*, which have deep Tantric significance, are particularly fine; some decorations are reminiscent of Byzantine art. The monastery is maintained by monks from Lekir and is no longer a place for active worship.

A path on the right past two large prayer wheels and a row of smaller ones leads to the river which attracts deer down to the opposite bank in the evenings. At the rear, small *chortens* with inscribed stones strewn around them, line the wall. It is worth walking around the exterior of the complex, and you'll get a beautiful view of the Indus River with mountains as a backdrop. For accommodation options, see Where to stay, page 200.

The temple complex The entrance *chortens* are worth looking in to. Each has vividly coloured paintings within, both along the interior walls as well as in the small *chorten*-like openings on the ceilings. The first and largest of these has a portrait of the founder Rinchen Zangpo (closed at the time of research).

The first temple you come to is the **Sum-stek**, the three-tier temple with a carved wooden gallery on the façade and triple arches. Inside are three giant four-armed, garlanded stucco figures of *Bodhisattvas*: the white *Avalokitesvara* on the left, the principal terracotta-red *Maitreya* in the centre at the back, and the ochre-yellow *Manjusri* on the right; their heads project to the upper storey which is reached by a rustic ladder (inaccessible). The remarkable features here are the brightly painted and gilded decorations on the clothing of the figures which include historical incidents, musicians, palaces and places of pilgrimage. Quite incongruous court scenes and Persian features appear on *Avalokitesvara* while the figures on *Maitreya* have Tantric connotations illustrating the very different styles of ornamentation on the three sculptures. The walls have numerous *mandalas* and inscriptions, as well as thousands of tiny Buddhas.

The oldest temple is the **Dukhang**, which has a covered courtyard (originally open to the sky) with wooden pillars and painted walls; the left wall shows two rowing boats with fluttering flags, a reminder perhaps of the presence in ancient times of lakes in this desert. The brightly painted door to the *dukhang*, about 1.5 m high, and the entrance archway has some fine woodcarving. The subsidiary shrines on either side of the doorway contain *Avalokitesvaras* and *Bodhisattvas* including a giant four-armed Maitreya figure to the extreme right. This main assembly hall, which was the principal place of worship, suffers from having very little light so visitors need a good torch. The 'shrine' holds the principal gilded *Vairocana* (Resplendent) Buddha (traditionally white, accompanied by the lion) with ornate decorations behind, flanked by four important Buddha postures among others. The walls on either side of the main hall are devoted to fine but damaged *Mandala* paintings illustrating the four principal manifestations of the *Sarvavid* (Omniscient) Buddha – *Vairocana*, *Sakyamuni* (the Preacher), *Manjusri* (Lord of Wisdom) and as *Prajna Paramita* (Perfection of Wisdom). There are interesting subsidiary panels, friezes and inscriptions. On exiting, note the terrifying figure of *Mahakala* the guardian deity above the door with miniature panels of royal and military scenes. The one portraying a drinking scene shows the royal pair sanctified with haloes with wine-cups in hand, accompanied by the prince and attendants – the detail of the clothing clearly shows Persian influence.

The **Lotsawa** (Translator's) and **Jampang** (Manjusri) *lhakhangs* were built later and probably neglected for some time. The former contains a statue of Rinchen Zangpo along with a seated Buddha, while the latter has a finely carved doorway and exterior lintels. Ask for the lights to be switched on.

Lhakhang Soma (New Temple) is a square hall used as a meditation centre with a *chorten* within; its walls are totally covered with *mandalas* and paintings portraying incidents from the Buddha's life and historic figures; the main figure here is the preaching Buddha. There is an interesting panel of warriors on horseback near the door. Ask for the temple to be opened if it is locked. **Kanjyur Lhakhang** in front of the Lhakhang Soma houses the scriptures.

Lamayuru

In Lamayuru, 10 km before Khaltse, the famous **Yungdrung Gompa** is perched on a crag overlooking the Indus in a striking lunar landscape between a drained lake and high mountains. Little medieval houses nestle on the steep slope beneath the monastery, and the effect is dramatically photogenic.

The monastery complex, which includes a library thought to be the oldest in the region, was founded in the 11th century and belongs to the Tibetan Kagyupa sect. The present monastery dating from the 16th century was partly destroyed in the 19th. You can still see some of the murals, along with the redecorated **Dukhang** (assembly hall). A small glass panel in the right hand wall of the *dukhang* protects a tiny holy cave, and there are many beautiful bronzes displayed. In a small temple, below the monastery, is an 11-headed and 1000-armed Avalokiteshvara image; the walls here are coated with murals – you will need to ask someone to get the key. Some of the upper rooms are richly furnished with carpets, Tibetan tables, statues, silver *stupas* and butter lamps.

In June/July the monastery holds the famous **Yuru Kabgyat** festival, with colourful masked dancing, special prayers, and burning of sacrificial offerings. There are several guesthouses strung along the road and up the hillside (see Where to stay, below); it's also possible to camp near the stream in a willow grove. There are daily buses from Leh at 0800; buses to Leh and Kargil leave Lamayuru at around 0930, and to Chitkan at 1000.

Wanla

Shortly after Lamayuru, a jeep road leaves the highway heading south down the Yapola Valley to **Wanla** which has a beautiful *gompa*, from the same era as Alchi and decorated by same artists. It has been recently restored, see www.achiassociation.org, and is adjoined on a dramatic ridge by a ruined fort. In Wanla village there are guesthouses. The next village is **Phanjila**, and further along there is a homestay in the delightful village of **Hinju**, from where the track peters out into a fantastic trekking route.

Drokhpa area

Dha and **Biama** (Bema) are two Drokhpa (aka Brokpa) villages where the so-called pure Aryan tribe speak a distinct dialect and live in a fair degree of isolation; Buddhism here is mixed with animist practices. You may reach these Indus Valley villages from **Khaltse** on the Leh–Srinagar road via the scenic villages of Dumkhar, Tirit, Skurbuchan and Hanu. There are homestays and a campsite at Biama, but Dha (3 km further) is the more popular option for overnight stays.

Listings Along the Srinagar road

Where to stay

Phyang

$ Hidden North Guesthouse
T(0)9906-999950, http://ladakhtrek.com/ accommodation-in-ladakh/.
This attractive guesthouse, set on a hillside, has marvellous views. There are 7 unfussy clean rooms, one with private terrace, some with private bath; run by a nice Ladakhi-German couple. There's a huge shared terrace and garden and meals are available. It's perched at the top end of the village, a 5-min uphill walk from the last bus stop. Treks can also be arranged by their responsible outfit.

Lekir

The bus directly to the monastery facilitates staying in 1 of 4 options near the monastery. Or, if you are dropped off on NH1, there are half a dozen choices in Lower Lekir, about 1 km walk on dirt tracks from NH1. Hotels all provide dinner and breakfast. Just below the monastery gate is the **Gonpa Restaurant** (0630-2030) for breakfast and reasonably priced Tibetan and Chinese food.

$$ Lhukhil
T01982-253588, www.ladakhpackages.com.
Grand gateway and luxuriant garden, although outdoor seating is on patchy grass next to scary statues and dragon-wrapped pillars. 24 rooms are well-fitted out and comfortable, with towels, toiletries, and some views. Meals are included.

$ Lotos Guesthouse
T01982-227171, T(0)9469-297990, opposite Hotel Lhukhil, Lower Lekir.
3 clean modern rooms with mats over the floor and plenty of warm bedding, sharing a

bathroom, attractive front garden and fruit trees, food costs extra. Cheap and cheerful.

$ Norboo Lagams Chow Guesthouse and Camp
Lower Lekir.
A bit of a building site, set at the back of a long scruffy orchard (camping possible) with small uncurtained rooms, one with (unfinished) bath, others using the traditional Ladakhi toilet in the house behind. It's cheap and dinner is served in the traditional kitchen-cum-dining room, surrounded by pots of all shapes and sizes.

$ Norboo Spon Guesthouse and Camping
Lower Lekir.
Signposted off the road to the monastery, or a 300-m walk from Lower Likir on the way to the monastery. In a large Ladakhi house, roof decked with prayer flags, bright white paint and red trims, set among trees in a large garden with plenty of seating. Dining seating area of little tables, rugs and cushions with the odd decorative mask is homely; there's a shared balcony. Rooms upstairs have good views, wicker chairs and a decent shared bathroom. Charming and kind family.

$ Old Likir Guesthouse
A 10-min walk downhill through the fields from the monastery (signposted).
Only 3 very simple rooms (the 2 upstairs one are best) in a farming family's home. There are mattresses on the floor and little else, but fabulous views either of the valley below or the Buddha's back and monastery above. Very cheap rates include breakfast and dinner.

$ A short walk up from the monastery are **Dolker Tongol** and **Chhuma** guesthouses; both are basic, but have views.

Alchi
Alchi has a several guesthouses, some are not great value, but the ones listed here are well-priced for what they offer. It is a pleasant little village with some shops, *dhabas*, hotel restaurants and souvenir stalls, none of which are a long walk from the bus stop or the monastery.

$$ Alchi Resort
T(0)9419-218636, http://alchiresort.com.
Cross a little bridge after the unattractive main building (restaurant downstairs) to a flowery fruit-filled garden edged by whitewashed cottages in adjoining pairs; those at the end, around a central gazebo, enjoy more privacy. Well-appointed motel-layout rooms differ slightly in configuration, all have flatscreens, laminate wood floors or carpets, and plain tiled bathrooms.

$$ Ule Ethnic Resort
Uletokpo, next to the highway, 10 km past Saspol, T01982-253640, www.uleresort.com.
15 cottages and 31 posh canvas tents in a well set up eco-resort. It caters mainly to groups, but is an alternative night's stop to Alchi village.

$$-$ Zimskhang Holiday Home
On the lane to the monastery, T01982-227086, www.zimskhang.com.
Some pricier rooms in a large building that is more attractive outside than in, with an appealing public balcony upstairs, spacious rooms with flatscreen TVs, bathrooms with marble basin-tops and floors, but by no means swanky. Cheaper clean rooms in an older building share bathrooms and are good value, overlooking the open-air restaurant.

$ Choskor
15-min walk back along the road towards Leh, T01982-227084.
Set in a lovely garden, this colourful guesthouse has rooms ranging from simple doubles with shared baths, to great-value upstairs rooms with attached bath. A roof terrace has rural views; eat in the garden or inside the restaurant with painted motifs on the wall. Cheap for pitching your own tent. Taxi and laundry services are available, and they pride themselves on their clean sheets.

$ Heritage Home
*Right next to the monastery entrance,
T(0)9419-811535.*
A very pleasant and convenient choice.
Rooms are large, carpeted, freshly painted,
en suite (hot water in the evening), with
soap and clean towels. Upstairs is more
expensive, and there's a decent restaurant
out front with apricot trees.

Lamayuru
Most guesthouses are on the NH1 in the
lower village, with a couple of homestays
on the hill towards the monastery. They all
provide food, and little **Zambala Restaurant**,
on the highway opposite the Dragon Hotel,
does surprisingly good chai and *aloo paratha*.

$$ Fotola
T(0)9469-048470, http://hotelfotola.com.
12 plain rooms, slightly set back from the
road facing the rocky valley wall, with
attached bath, towels provided. There's no
garden as such, but a bonus is the upstairs
restaurant serving a variety of Indian and
Italian food.

$ Dragon
*Lower Rd, T01982-224501, dragon_skyabu@
yahoo.com.*
A range of spacious carpeted rooms, 4 with
en suite by the garden restaurant, 8 with
shared bath in the building to the rear.
Most are south-facing, and room 10 has
attractively painted walls. There are clean
sheets and it's very reasonably priced. The
restaurant serves up excellent Indian meals.
Internet available (during the 3 hrs of power
in the evenings), as is hot water.

$ Lion's Den
*300 m from the village centre, T01982-224542,
liondenhouse@gmail.com.*
Ignore the unfinished concrete ground floor,
as the upstairs rooms are given warmth
by colourful walls, rugs and bedding
(shared bath). Good views of the weird rock
formations in the valley from the 2 corner

rooms with attached bath. The little outdoor
restaurant with checked cloths has shade or
there's a Ladakhi dining room.

$ Niranjana Hotel
T01982-224555.
Next to the monastery, this institutional-
looking hotel has 20 rooms on 3 levels with
excellent valley views. Rooms are plain but
comfortable, they take the time to turn
down the sheets. All share modern, clean
communal bathrooms, with hot showers
available in the evenings. Downstairs
restaurant is good.

$ Tharpaling
*100 m past the village centre on main road,
T01982-224516.*
The warm family atmosphere is what appeals
most to visitors to this simple guesthouse.

Restaurants

Alchi
$$-$ Zimskhang and **Heritage** both have
good drop-in restaurants, other hotels
provide meals when there are guests.

$ Golden Oriole German Bakery
Good cake selection but they don't
always have bread. They serve Chinese
and Indian dishes and pizza, and are a
good place for breakfast. Same menu as
Zimskhang but at lower prices. The terrace is
a nice place to sit and watch folks pass
on their way to the monastery.

There are a couple of *dhabas* near the bus
stop; **Dil Dil Restaurant** is kept clean and
does cheap dal, veg and rice. Most shops
near bus stop also serve omelettes, dal
and chai, and sell strong beer.

Transport

Alchi
Bus 1 daily direct bus from **Leh** in summer,
1500, 3 hrs, returns around 0700. **Srinagar**-
bound buses stop at **Saspol**, from there it is
a 2.5-km walk across the bridge.

These once-restricted areas are open to foreign visitors with a PAP (see box, page 180). Travel to the valleys and lakes is far easier by jeep, although twice-weekly buses go to Panamik and Pangong-Tso in summertime, and hitching is not impossible in the Nubra valley. There are guesthouses in villages throughout the Nubra-Shyok valleys, and temporary tented camps are occasionally set up by tour companies during the season, but it's still a good idea to take a sleeping bag.

Nubra Valley

For an exhilarating high-altitude experience over possibly the highest motorable pass in the world, travel across the Ladakh range over the 5600-m **Khardung La**. This is along the old Silk Route to the lush green Nubra Valley up to **Panamik**, 140 km north of Leh. Camel caravans once transported Chinese goods along this route for exchanging with Indian produce. The relatively gentle climate here allows crops, fruit and nuts to grow, so some call it 'Ldumra' (orchard).

It is possible to visit the Nubra-Shyok valleys over two days, but it's much preferable (and much the same cost) to make the journey over three. After crossing the Khardung La, the first village is **Khardung**, 42 km later, in a majestic setting. The road continues down the Shyok Valley to **Deskit**, which has an old and a new (less appealing) town centre and several places to stay. On a hill above the old village is a Gelugpa sect **monastery** (the largest in Nubra) built by the Ladakhi king Sohrab Zangpo in the early 1700s. There is large statue of Tsongkhapa, and the Rimpoche of Thiksey monastery south of Leh oversees this monastery also. A further 10 km past Diskit is the village of **Hunder**, probably the most popular place to stay overnight, with several garden-guesthouses to choose from. Highly prized double-humped camels can occasionally be seen on the sand dunes near Hunder, allegedly descendants of the caravan-camels that used to ply the Silk Route, and it is possible to take a 15- to 30-minute camel ride (on a tame beast). Past Hunder the road continues to **Turtuk**, opened to tourists in 2010. The scenery is impressive and the tiny settlements here are culturally Balti and practice Islam.

The second biggest monastery in Nubra is near **Tiger** village along the road to Panamik in the Nubra Valley. Called the **Samtanling** *gompa*, it was founded in 1842 and belongs to the Gelugpa sect. **Panamik** has several guesthouses and reddish, sulphurous hot springs nearby. The ILP allows travel only up **Ensa Gompa**, included on some itineraries, and approached by foot for the last 30 minutes.

Traffic into and out of the Nubra Valley is controlled by the army at Pulu. From Leh there are two buses per week from June to September; a few have tried by bike, which can be put on the roof of the bus for the outward journey.

Pangong-Tso

A popular excursion from Leh is to the narrow 130-km-long Pangong-Tso, a lake at 4250 m, the greater part of which lies in Tibet. The road, which is only suitable for 4WD in places, is via **Karu** on the Manali–Leh Highway, where the road east goes through **Zingral** and over the Chang La pass. Beyond are **Durbuk**, a small village with low-roofed houses, and **Tangste**, the 'abode of Chishul warriors' with a Lotswa Temple, which is also an army base with a small bank. The rough jeep track takes you through an impressive rocky gorge which opens out to a valley which has camping by a fresh water stream in the hamlet of **Mugleb** and then on to

Lukung and finally **Spangmik**, 153 km from Leh. On the way you will be able to see some Himalayan birds including *chikhor* (quail) which may end up in the cooking pot.

Tip...
Always carry multiple photocopies of your passport and PAP with you, to facilitate the crossing of checkpoints.

An overnight stop on the lake shore allows you to see the blue-green lake in different lights. You can walk between Lukung and Spangmik, 7 km, on the second day, passing small settlements growing barley and peas along the lake shore. You return to Leh on the third day. There are tented camps at Durbuk, Tangtse and Lukung. At Spangmik there is a wider choice of accommodation, in the form of homestays (mats on floor) or in the rather pricey Pangong Tso Resort (rooms have attached bath). Buses go from Leh at 0630 on Saturdays and Sundays, but almost everyone makes the journey by private jeep.

Tso-Moriri

The Rupshu area, a dry, high-altitude plateau to the east of the Leh–Manali Highway, is where the nomadic Changpas live, in the bleak and windswept Chamathang highlands bordering Tibet. The route to the beautiful Tso-Moriri (*tso* – lake), the only nesting place of the bar-headed geese on the Indus, is open to visitors. It is 220 km from Leh; jeeps make the journey. To the south of the 27-km-long lake is the land of the Tibetan wild ass.

You can travel either via **Chhumathang**, 140 km, visiting the hot spring there or by crossing the high pass at Taglang La, leaving the Manali–Leh Highway at Debring. The route takes you past the **Tsokar** basin, 154 km, where salt cakes the edges. A campsite along the lake with access to fresh water is opposite **Thukje** village which has a *gompa* and a 'wolf-catching trap'. The road then reaches the hot sulphur springs at **Puga** before arriving at the beautiful Tso-Moriri, about four hours' drive from Tsokar. You can follow the lake bank and visit the solitary village of **Karzog**, at 4500 m, north of the lake, which also has a *gompa*. There are some rest houses and guesthouses at Chhumathang and Karzog and camping at Tsokar and Karzog as well as a tent camp at Chhumathang.

Listings North and east of Leh

Where to stay

Nubra valley

There are lots of little guesthouses springing up in the Nubra Valley, mainly located around the village of Hunder.

$$ Yarab Tso
Tiger, T(0)9622-820661,
www.hotelyarabtso.com.
Carpeted rooms with private baths and attractive furnishings; in an idyllic setting with large garden, plus very good food.

$ Olgok
Hunder, T01980-221092.
Large simple rooms are very clean and neat in this homely guesthouse where the owners go out of their way to be helpful. Fresh food from the quaint garden; located in the centre of Hunder and close to the sand dunes.

Make sure your trekking guide is experienced and competent. A detailed book, although dated, is the Trailblazer guide *Trekking in Ladakh*, which can be bought in bookshops in Leh. Some treks, eg Spituk to Hemis and Hemis High Altitude National Park, charge a fee of Rs 25 per person per day or Rs 10 for Indians. For trekking, July and August are pleasant months. Go earlier and you will be trudging through snow much of the time. September and October are also good months, though colder at night.

Markha Valley Trek, Spituk to Hemis
Both places are in the Indus Valley, just 30 km apart. A very satisfying nine to 10 days can be undertaken by traversing the Stok range to the Markha Valley, walking up the valley and then back over the Zanskar range to Hemis. The daily walking time on this trek is five to six hours so you must be fit. Places to camp are highlighted below, but there are also basic homestays or guesthouses in the villages if you don't want to carry equipment.

There is an interesting monastery at **Spituk**, a short drive from Leh (see page 195). From Spituk proceed southwest of the Indus along a trail passing through barren countryside. After about 7 km you reach the **Zingchen Valley** and in a further five hours, the beautiful village of **Rumbak**. Camp below the settlement. You can also trek here from Stok which takes one-two days and a steep ascent of the **Namlung La** (4570 m).

From Rumbak it is a five-hour walk to **Utse** village. The camp is two hours further on at the base of the bleak **Gandha La** (4700 m), open, bare and windswept. To go over the pass takes about three hours, then the same time again to negotiate the wooded ravine to **Skiu**. Here the path meets the Markha Valley. You can make a half-day round trip from Skiu to see the impressive gorges on the Zanskar River. The stage to **Markha**, where there is an impressive fort, is a six-hour walk. The monastery, while not particularly impressive from the outside, has some superb wall paintings and *thangkas*, some dating from the 13th century. You need to take a torch.

The next destination is **Hankar** village, whose ruined fort forms an astonishing extension of the natural rock face, an extremely impressive ruin. From here the path climbs quite steeply to a plateau. There are good views of Nimaling Peak (6000 m) and a number of *mani* walls en route. From **Nimaling** it is a two-hour climb to **Gongmaru La** (5030 m) with views of the Stok range and the Indus Valley. The descent is arduous and involves stream crossings. There is a lovely campsite at **Shogdu** and another at **Sumda** village, 3 km further on. The final stage is down the valley to **Martselang** from where you can walk down 5 km to **Karu** village on the Leh–Manali road or take a 2-km diversion to visit **Hemis** monastery.

Hemis High Altitude National Park
Set up in 1981, the park adjoining the monastery comprising the catchments of Markha, Rumbak and Sumda *nalas*. The reserve area has been expanded a couple of times, and now covers 4400 sq km making it the largest national park in South Asia. The rugged terrain with valleys often littered with rocks and rimmed by high peaks (some over 6000 m), supports limited alpine vegetation but contains some rare species of flora and fauna, including the ibex, Pallas' cat, *bharal* and *shapu*. It is the habitat of the endangered and elusive snow leopard, now numbering around 200 (mainly in the Rumbak area, best

ON THE ROAD
Taking a walk on the wild side

The Himalayan range is the longest and the highest mountain range in the world. The sheer diversity of the topography makes it one of the best places to spot some of the rarest wildlife and birds. The forested regions offer a large variety of birds. You might see Himalayan griffons, crested serpent eagles, lamagiers, forest owlets, common flamebacks, golden orioles, scarlet minivets, rose finches, chukors, snow cocks, pigeons, Himalayan blue magpies, monals, khaleej pheasants, the critically endangered western tragopans, or black-necked cranes around Tso Kar. In fact, the flatlands around Tso Kar in Ladakh is one of my favourite places to see birds. Another great place to venture to in order to see birds and wildlife is the Great Himalayan National Park, in Himachal Pradesh. The park is a habitat to 375 fauna species, which includes 31 mammals, 181 birds and 127 insects.

In my 18 odd years of trekking in the western Himalaya the sighting that has had me the most excited is seeing a snow leopard for the first time in Rumbak valley of Ladakh in 1995. Watching a snow leopard was awe-inspiring. Once I was even offered a chanko cub, which is a Tibetan wolf. I was camped in the village of Rumtse where I met a villager from the Khanag valley who had a three-month-old cub that he had found and was not sure what to do with.

My work as a trekking and climbing guide takes me to some remote parts and over the years I have seen dramatic changes in not just glaciers receding due to global warming but also extensive deforestation because of many hydroelectric projects. This has affected carnivores like the snow leopard and the chanko due to the loss of prey caused by habitat destruction. A positive development is the increase in snow leopard tourism in Ladakh which has prompted the locals to stop viewing the big cat as an enemy and has opened doors to alternative income generation.

Kaushal Desai, tour guide at **Above 14000ft**, www.above14000ft.com.

spotted in winter). It is hoped that the activities of local villagers, who graze livestock within the park, can be restricted to a buffer zone so that their animals can be kept safe from attack by wolves and snow leopards. Villages used to trap the leopard, but now they are reimbursed for any livestock lost to snow leopard attacks.

There are camping sites within the park, which can be reserved through the Wildlife Warden in Leh. There are also homestays, see www.himalayan-homestays.com, run in conjunction with the **Snow Leopard Conservancy India Trust (SNC-IT)** ⓘ *www.snowleopardconservancy.org*. SNC-IT also run 10-day winter expeditions.

Ripchar Valley Trek
This is a shorter trek of four to five days; however, the average daily walking time is seven hours so don't think that the shortness of the trek means less effort. A guide is recommended.

The first stage involves transport from Leh (five to six hours), then an hour's walk to **Hinju** (3750 m); camp or homestay overnight at the village. Stage two continues up through the Ripchar Valley to cross the **Konze La** (4570 m), from where you will see the Zanskar River and gorge and the Stok range. Then descend to **Sumdo Chenmo**, quite a treacherous route as it involves river crossings. There is a monastery here with an impressive statue of the

Buddha and some attractive wall paintings. A campsite lies just beyond the village. The next day takes you from Sumdo Chenmo to **Lanak** (4000 m), a walk of five to six hours. The final stage, about seven hours, from Lanak to **Chilling**, is over the **Dungduchan La** (4700 m) with excellent views. The path continues down the valley following a stream to Chilling. Overnight in Chilling or do the two-hour drive back to Leh. Some agents also offer the option of rafting back to Leh from Chilling along the Zanskar River.

Trekking in Zanskar

Trekking here is not easy. The paths are often rough and steep, the passes high and the climate extreme. Provisions, fuel and camping equipment should be bought in advance from Kishtwar, Manali or Leh. You can get necessities such as dried milk, biscuits, noodles and sugar from Padum, though supplies are scare at the beginning of the season. In Padum the Tourism Officer and Government Development Officer will be able to advise and maybe even assist in hiring horses. Porters can be hired at **Sani** village for the traverse of the **Umasi La** into Kishtwar. Horses cannot use this pass. In Padum you may be able to hire porters with whom you can cover rougher terrain. It is best to contact a trekking agent in advance. See What to do, page 178.

Pensi La to Padum You can trek this three-day route before the road opens (June-October) when it is free of vehicles.

Karsha to Lamayaru This is a demanding nine-day trek which includes seven passes, five of which are over 4500 m. The highest is the Singi La (5060 m). It is essential to be very fit before starting the trek. Each day's walking should take under six hours, but with time for rests and lunch this adds up to a full day. An extra day allows for flexibility.

The 16th-century monastery of the Tibetan Gelugpa (Yellow Hat) sect at **Karsha** is the largest and wealthiest in the Zanskar Valley and is occupied by nearly 200 monks. Karsha has an inn with dormitory beds and a vegetarian canteen.

Padum to Leh This is another demanding trek which also takes about 10 days. Some are through the spectacular gorges between Markha and Zangla. A local guide is recommended as this is truly a wilderness area. The trek involves walking along stream beds and in July there is still too much snow melt to allow safe crossings. Recommended only for August/September.

It is seven hours' walking from Padum to Zangla and this includes crossing the Zanskar River by a string and twig bridge that spans over 40 m. Ponies are not allowed on it and if it is windy sensible humans don't cross. You can now start your trek at Zangla as there is a motorbike route from Padum to Zangla. At **Zangla** you can see the King's Palace, which has a collection of *thangkas* painted by the king's son (who was once a monk). The third stage takes you over the **Cha Cha La** (5200 m). On the next stage river crossings are again necessary. This is time consuming and if you are travelling in mid-summer, an extra day may be called for.

You then follow the **Khurna River** to a narrow gorge that marks the ancient border between Zanskar and Ladakh, and end up below the **Rubarung La**. When you cross this you get good views of the Stok range. You then descend into the Markha Valley and from here you can reach Leh in six stages by heading west into the heart of the valley and then crossing the Ganda La to Spituk, or in three stages by crossing the Gongmaru La and descending to Martselang and nearby Hemis.

ON THE ROAD
In search of the snow leopard

My work as a trekking and climbing guide in the western Himalaya takes me to some really remote parts. In my 16 years of trekking and wanderings, the one sighting that had me the most excited has catching sight of a snow leopard for the first time in the Rumbak Valley of Ladakh. I stood mesmerized watching the big cat walk along a mountain slope just 100 m from where I was standing. It is hard to express in words the feeling of seeing such a magnificent creature.

Strange as it might sound, on a trip a few years back I was camped in the village of Rumtse, also in Ladakh, where I met Changpa from the Khanag Valley, who had a three-month-old *chanko* (Tibetan wolf) cub – he even offered to give it to me. He said he had found the cub somewhere on the plateau and was not sure what to do with it.

Sightings of snow leopard and *shankhoo* are pretty rare, but animals I have regularly seen on my treks in Himachal and Ladakh include: Himalayan ibex, blue sheep (*bharals*), Himalayan thar, musk deer, Himalayan black and brown bears, Tibetan antelope, kiyangs or the Tibetan wild asses, marmots, hares and pikas.

The Human/animal conflict has increased for the carnivores like the snow leopard and the *chanko*, due to the loss of prey because of the increasing destruction of their habitat. However, the increase in 'snow leopard tourism' in Ladakh, has prompted the locals to stop viewing the big cat as an enemy and has opened doors to alternative income generation in various valleys of Ladakh.

Kaushal Desai, Above 14,000ft

Although set on the Nepal side of the Himalaya, *Snow Leopard* by Peter Matthiessen is a wonderfully evocative nature and travelogue dating back to the 1970s, offering great insights not only into the Himalaya, but also into Buddhism.

Padum to Darcha This is a week-long trek and starts with a walk along the Tsarap Chu to **Bardan**, which has *stupas* and interesting idols, and **Reru**. There is a now a motorable road till Mune from where the trek starts towards Darcha.

After two stages you reach **Purni** (with a couple of shops and a popular campsite), where you can stay two nights and make a side trip to the impressive 11th-century **Phugtal monastery** (a two-hour walk). On a spectacular site, it has been carved out of the mountainside round a limestone cave. Usually there are about 50 monks in attendance. From Purni you continue on to Kargiakh, the last village before the **Shingo La**. It's another day's walk to the camp below this high pass (5200 m).

The mountain scenery is stunning with 6000-m-plus peaks all around. Once over the pass you can stop at **Rumjack** where there is a campsite used by shepherds or you can continue to the confluence of the **Shingo** and the **Barai** rivers where there is now a bridge. From here the trail passes through grazing land and it is about 15 km to **Darcha**, the end of the trek. Keen trekkers can combine this with a trek from Darcha to **Manali**. The average daily walking time of the Padum-Darcha trek is six hours so you have to be very fit. There is now a motorable road from Darcha all the way to Zanskar Sumdo which is after the Shingo La Pass.

Trekking in the Nubra and Shyok valleys

The easing of controls to visit the Nubra-Shyok valleys has made possible treks that start from points in the Indus Valley not far from Leh, cross the Ladakh Range to enter the Shyok River valley and then re-cross the Ladakh range further to the west to re-enter the Indus Valley near Phyang monastery. Ask a good local trekking agent for advice on how to get the required 'Restricted Area Permits'.

Day 1 Drive from Leh south along the Manali road to Karu, near Hemis, where you turn left and drive about 10 km to the roadhead at the village of Sakti, just past **Takthak monastery**. Trek about 90 minutes to **Chumchar** and camp.

Day 2 Cross the Ladakh range at the **Wari La** (4400 m) and descend to Junlez on the northern flank.

Day 3 Walk downhill to **Tangyar** (3700 m) with a nice *gompa*.

Days 4, 5, 6 A level walk along the **Shyok River** valley takes you to **Khalsar** from where you follow the military road west to the confluence of the Shyok and Nubra rivers at **Diskit** (see Nubra Valley, above).

Days 7, 8, 9 Three days to gradually ascend the northern flanks of the Ladakh Range passing the hamlets of **Hunder**, **Wachan** and **Hunder Dok** to the high pastures of **Thanglasgo** (4700 m).

Days 10, 11 Trek back over the Ladakh Range via the Lasermo La pass (5150 m) to a campsite on the southern base of the pass.

Day 12 Camp at Phyang village about 1 km above Phyang monastery before driving back to Leh.

Practicalities

Getting there

Air

India is accessible by air from virtually every continent. Most international flights arrive in Delhi or Mumbai; Delhi is the most convenient entry point for northwest India though internal flights are easy and cheap. Some carriers permit 'open-jaw' travel, arriving in and departing from different cities in India. Some (**Air India**, **Jet Airways** or **British Airways**) have convenient non-stop flights from Europe eg from London to Delhi, takes only nine hours.

On arrival, you can fly to numerous destinations across India with **Jet Airways**, **Indigo** or **Spicejet**. The prices are very competitive if domestic flights are booked in conjunction with **Jet** on the international legs. In 2015/2016 the cheapest return flights to Delhi from London started at around £500, but increased to £900+ during the high seasons of Christmas, New Year and Easter.

From Europe Despite the increases to Air Passenger Duty, Britain remains the cheapest place in Europe for flights to India. From mainland Europe, major European flag carriers, including **KLM** and **Lufthansa**, fly to Delhi from their respective hub airports. In most cases the cheapest flights are with Middle Eastern or Central Asian airlines, transiting via airports in the Gulf. Several airlines from the Middle East (eg **Emirates**, **Gulf Air**, **Kuwait Airways**, **Qatar Airways** and **Oman Air**) offer good discounts to Indian regional capitals from London, but fly via their hub cities, adding to the journey time. Consolidators in the UK can quote some competitive fares, such as: www.skyscanner.net, www.ebookers.com; and **North South Travel** ⓘ *T01245-608291, www.northsouthtravel.co.uk (profits to charity).*

From North America From the east coast, several airlines, including **Air India**, **Jet Airways**, **Continental** and **Delta**, fly direct from New York to Delhi and Mumbai. **American** flies to both cities from Chicago. Discounted tickets on **British Airways**, **KLM**, **Lufthansa**, **Gulf Air** and **Kuwait Airways** are sold through agents although they will invariably fly via their country's capital cities. From the west coast, **Air India** flies from Los Angeles to Delhi and Mumbai, and **Jet Airways** from San Francisco to Mumbai via Shanghai. Alternatively, fly via Hong Kong, Singapore or Bangkok using one of those countries' national carriers. **Air Canada** operates between Vancouver and Delhi. **STA** ⓘ *www.statravel.com*, has offices in many US cities as well as Toronto. Student fares are also available from **Travel Cuts** ⓘ *www.travelcuts.com*, in Canada.

From Australasia Qantas, Singapore Airlines, Thai Airways, Malaysian Airlines, Cathay Pacific and Air India are the principal airlines connecting the continents, although **Qantas** is the only one that flies direct, with services from Sydney to Mumbai. **Singapore Airlines**, with subsidiary **Silk Air**, offers the most flexibility. Low-cost carriers including **Air Asia** (via Kuala Lumpur), **Scoot** and **Tiger Airways** (Singapore) offer a similar choice of arrival airports at substantially lower prices, though long stopovers and possible missed connections make this a slightly more risky venture than flying with the mainstream airlines. **STA** and **Flight Centre** offer discounted tickets from their branches in major cities in Australia and New Zealand. **Abercrombie & Kent** ⓘ *www.abercrombiekent.co.uk*, **Adventure World**

ⓘ *www.adventureworld.com*, **Peregrine** ⓘ *www.peregrineadventures.com*, and **Travel Corporation of India** ⓘ *www.tcindia.com*, organize tours.

Airport information The formalities on arrival in India have been increasingly streamlined during the last few years and the facilities at the major international airports greatly improved. However, arrival can still be a slow process. Disembarkation cards, with an attached customs declaration, are handed out to passengers during the inward flight. The immigration form should be handed in at the immigration counter on arrival. The customs slip will be returned, but must be handed over to customs on leaving the baggage collection hall. You may well find that there are delays of over an hour at immigration in processing passengers who need help with filling in forms. When departing, note that you'll need to have a printout of your itinerary to get into the airport, and the security guards will only let you into the terminal within three hours of your flight.

Departure tax This is normally included in your international ticket; check when buying. (To save time 'Security Check' your baggage before checking in on departure.) Some airports have also begun charging a Passenger Service Fee or User Development Fee to each departing passenger. This is normally included in international tickets, but some domestic airlines have been reluctant to incorporate the charge. Keep some spare cash in rupees in case you need to pay the fee on arriving at the terminal.

Getting around

Air

India has a comprehensive network linking the major cities of the different states. Deregulation of the airline industry has had a transformative effect on travel within India, with a host of low-budget private carriers offering sometimes unbelievably cheap fares on an ever-expanding network of routes in a bid to woo the train-travelling middle class. Promotional fares as low as Rs 9 (US$0.20) are not unknown, though such numbers are rendered somewhat meaningless by additional taxes and fuel charges – an extra US$30-50 on most flights. Booking a few days in advance, you can expect to fly between Delhi and Leh for around US$120 one way including taxes.

Within northwest India there are many regional airports offering daily services, weather permitting. There are daily flights from Delhi to both Amritsar and Chandigarh. Bhuntar Airport (also known as Kullu Airport) in Himachal Pradesh provides good access to Manali and is served by Air India. There are frequent flights from Delhi to Leh's Kushok Bakula Rimpochee Airport with Air India, Jet Airways and Go Air. You can fly from Delhi to Kangra Airport, 14 km southwest of Dharamsala, with Air India and Spicejet. There are regular flights to Jammu and Srinagar (Kashmir) airports with Indigo, Air India, Spicejet and Go Air.

Competition from the efficiently run private sector has, in general, improved the quality of services provided by the nationalized airlines. It also seems to herald the end of the two-tier pricing structure, meaning that ticket prices are now usually the same for foreign and Indian travellers. The airport authorities, too, have made efforts to improve handling on the ground.

Although flying is comparatively expensive and has a larger environmental impact, for covering vast distances or awkward links on a route it is an option worth considering, though delays and re-routing can be irritating.

The best way to get an idea of the current routes, carriers and fares is to use a third-party booking website such as www.cheapairticketsindia.com (toll-free numbers: UK T0800-101 0928, USA T1-888 825 8680), www.cleartrip.com, www.makemytrip.co.in, or www.yatra.com. Booking with these is a different matter: some refuse foreign credit cards outright, while others have to be persuaded to give your card special clearance. Tickets booked on these sites are typically issued as an email ticket or an SMS text message – the simplest option if you have an Indian mobile phone, though it must be converted to a paper ticket at the relevant carrier's airport offices before you will be allowed into the terminal. Makemytrip.com and Travelocity.com both accept international credit cards.

Rail

Trains can still be the cheapest and most comfortable means of travelling long distances saving you hotel expenses on overnight journeys. Rail travel also gives access to station Retiring Rooms, which can be useful from time to time. Above all, you have an ideal opportunity to meet local travellers and catch a glimpse of life on the ground. See also www.indianrail.gov.in and www.erail.in. A very useful website offering an insight into how to book and navigate the Indian rail network is www.seat61.com.

High-speed trains There are several air-conditioned 'high-speed' services: **Shatabdi** (or 'Century') **Express** for day travel, and **Rajdhani Express** ('Capital City') for overnight journeys. These cover large sections of the network but due to high demand you need to book them well in advance (up to 90 days). Meals and drinks are usually included. The *Shatabdi* runs services to Chandigarh and Amritsar.

Tip...

You can only travel by train from Delhi as far as Chandigarh, Amritsar, Pathankot (for access to Dharamsala) and Jammu. It is only road access around eastern Himachal, up to Manali and beyond to Leh.

Royal trains You can travel like a maharaja on the **Palace on Wheels** ⓘ *www.palace onwheels.net*, the famous seven-nighter which has been running for many years and gives visitors an opportunity to see some of the 'royal' cities in Rajasthan during the winter months for around US$2500 and affords some special privileges such as private fine dining at Mehrangarh Fort in Jodhpur. **Classes A/c First Class**, available only on main routes, is very comfortable with two- or four-berth carpeted sleeper compartments with washbasin. As with all air-conditioned Sleeper accommodation, bedding is included, and the windows are tinted to the point of being almost impossible to see through. **A/c Sleeper**, two and three-tier configurations (known as 2AC and 3AC), are clean and comfortable and popular with middle-class families; these are the safest carriages for women travelling alone. **A/c Executive Class**, with wide reclining seats, are available on many Shatabdi trains at double the price of the ordinary **a/c Chair Car**, which are equally comfortable. **First Class (non-a/c)** is gradually being phased out, and is now restricted to a handful of routes in the south, but the run-down old carriages still provide a pleasant experience if you like open windows. **Second Class (non-a/c)** two- and three-tier (commonly called **Sleeper**), provides exceptionally cheap and atmospheric travel, with basic padded vinyl seats and open windows that allow the sights and sounds of India (not to mention dust, insects and flecks of spittle expelled by passengers up front) to drift into the carriage. On long journeys Sleepers can be crowded and uncomfortable, and toilet facilities can be unpleasant; it is nearly always better to use the Indian-style squat loos rather than the Western-style ones as they are better maintained. At the bottom rung is **Unreserved Second Class**, with hard wooden benches. You can travel long distances for a trivial amount of money, but unreserved carriages are often ridiculously crowded, and getting off at your station may involve a battle of will and strength against the hordes trying to shove their way on.

Indrail passes These allow travel across the network without having to pay reservation fees and Sleeper charges but you have to spend a high proportion of your time on the train to make it worthwhile. However, the advantages of pre-arranged reservations and automatic access to 'Tourist Quotas' can tip the balance in favour of the pass for some travellers.

Tourists (foreigners and Indians resident abroad) may buy these passes from the tourist sections of principal railway booking offices and pay using foreign currency, major credit cards, travellers' cheques or rupees with encashment certificates. Fares range from US$57 to US$1060 for adults or half that for children. Combined rail and air tickets are also to be made available.

Indrail passes can also conveniently be bought abroad from special agents. For people contemplating a single long journey soon after arriving in India, the Half- or

One-day Pass with a confirmed reservation is worth the peace of mind; two- or four-day passes are also sold.

The UK agent is **SDEL** ① *103 Wembley Park Dr, Wembley, Middlesex HA9 8HG, UK, T020-8903 3411, www.indiarail.co.uk*. They make all necessary reservations and offer excellent advice. They can also book **Air India** and **Jet Airways** internal flights. Alternatively, check out www.indianrail.gov.in.

Cost A/c First Class costs about double the rate for two-tier shown below, and non-a/c Second Class about half. Children (aged five to 12) travel at half the adult fare. The young (12-30 years) and senior citizens (65 years and over) are allowed a 30% discount on journeys over 500 km (just show your passport).

Period	US$ A/c 2-tier	Period	US$ A/c 2-tier
½ day	26	21 days	198
1 day	43	30 days	248
7 days	135	60 days	400
15 days	185	90 days	530

Fares for individual journeys are based on distance covered and reflect both the class and the type of train. Higher rates apply on the *Mail* and *Express* trains and the air-conditioned *Shatabdi* and long-distance *Rajdhani* expresses.

Internet services Much information is available online at www.railtourismindia.com, www.indianrail.gov.in, www.erail.in and www.trainenquiry.com, where you can check timetables (which change frequently), numbers, seat availability and even the running status of your train. Internet e-tickets can be bought and printed on www.irctc.co.in – a great time-saver when the system works properly, though paying with a foreign credit card is fraught with difficulty. If you plan to do a lot of train travel it might be worth the effort to get your credit card recognized by the booking system. This process changes often, so it's good idea is to consult the very active India transport forums at www.indiamike.com. Another good option is to seek a local agent who can sell e-tickets (though some agents charge up to Rs 150 a ticket) and can save hours of hassle; simply present the print-out to the ticket collector. However, it is tricky if you then want to cancel an e-ticket which an agent has bought for you on their account.

Tickets and reservations It is now possible to reserve tickets for virtually any train on the network from one of the 1000 computerized reservation centres across India. It is always best to book as far in advance as possible (usually up to 60 days). To reserve a seat on a particular train, note down the train's name, number and departure time and fill in a reservation form while you line up at the ticket window; you can use one form for up to four passengers. At busy stations the wait can take an hour or more. You can save a lot of time and effort by asking a travel agent to get your tickets for a fee of Rs 50-150. If the class you want is full, ask if special 'quotas' are available. **Foreign Tourist Quota (FTQ)** reserves a small number of tickets on popular routes for overseas travellers; you need your passport and either an exchange certificate or ATM receipt to book tickets under FTQ. The other useful special quota is **Tatkal**, which releases a last-minute pool of tickets at 1000 on the day before the train departs. If the quota system can't help you, consider buying a 'wait list' ticket, as seats often become available close to the train's departure time; phone the station on the day of departure to check your ticket's status. If you don't have a reservation for a particular train but carry an Indrail Pass, you may get one by arriving three hours early. Be wary of touts at the station offering tickets, hotels or exchange.

Timetables Regional timetables are available cheaply from station bookstalls; the monthly *Indian Bradshaw* is sold in principal stations. The handy *Trains at a Glance* (Rs 30) lists popular trains likely to be used by most foreign travellers and is available at stalls at Indian railway stations and in the UK from SDEL (see page 215).

Road

Road travel is sometimes the only choice for reaching many of the mountain regions of India. some of the more remote places of interest, particularly national parks or isolated tourist sites. For the uninitiated, travel by road can also be a worrying experience because of the apparent absence of conventional traffic regulations. Vehicles drive on the left – in theory. Routes around the major cities are usually crowded with lorry traffic, especially at night, and the main roads are often poor and slow. There are a few motorway-style expressways, but most main roads are single track. Some district roads are quiet, and although they are not fast they can be a good way of seeing the country and village life if you have the time. In eastern Himachal and other remote Himalayan regions, landslides are common, disrupting travel.

Bus

Buses reach virtually every part of India, offering a cheap, if often uncomfortable, means of visiting places off the rail network. Very few villages are now more than 2-3 km from a bus stop. Services are run by the State Corporation from the State Bus Stand (and by private companies, which often have offices nearby). The latter allow advance reservations, including booking printable e-tickets online (check www.redbus.in and www.viaworld.in) and, although tickets prices are a little higher, they have fewer stops and are a bit more comfortable. There are some sleeper buses (a contradiction in terms) – if you must take a sleeper bus, choose a lower berth near the front of the bus. The upper berths are almost always really uncomfortable on bumpy roads.

Bus categories Though comfortable for sightseeing trips, apart from the very best 'sleeper coaches' even **air-conditioned luxury coaches** can be very uncomfortable for really long journeys. Often the air conditioning is very cold so wrap up warm. Journeys over 10 hours can be extremely tiring so it is better to go by train if there is a choice. **Express buses** run over long distances (frequently overnight); these are often called 'video coaches' and can be an appalling experience unless you appreciate loud film music blasting through the night. Ear plugs and eye masks may ease the pain. They rarely average more than 45 kph. **Local buses** are often very crowded, quite bumpy, slow and usually poorly maintained. However, over short distances, they can be a very cheap, friendly and easy way of getting about. Even where signboards are not in English someone will usually give you directions. Many larger towns have **minibus** services which charge a little more than the buses and pick up and drop passengers on request. Again very crowded, and with restricted headroom, they are the fastest way of getting about many of the larger towns.

Bus travel tips Some towns have different bus stations for different destinations. Booking on major long-distance routes is now computerized. Book in advance where possible and avoid the back of the bus where it can be very bumpy. If your destination is only served by a local bus you may do better to take the Express bus and 'persuade' the driver, with a tip in advance, to stop where you want to get off. You will have to pay the full fare to the first stop beyond your destination but you will get there faster and more comfortably. When an unreserved bus pulls into a bus station, there is usually an unholy scramble for seats, whilst those arriving have to struggle to get off! In many areas there is an unwritten 'rule of reservation' using handkerchiefs or bags thrust through the windows to reserve seats. Some visitors may feel a more justified right to a seat having fought their way through the crowd, but it is generally best to do as local people do and be prepared with a handkerchief or 'sarong'. As soon as it touches the seat, it is yours! Leave it on your seat when getting off to use the toilet at bus stations.

Car

A car provides a chance to travel off the beaten track, and gives unrivalled opportunities for seeing something of India's great variety of villages and small towns. Until recently, the most widely used hire car was the Hindustan Ambassador. However, except for the newest model, they are often very unreliable, and although they still have their devotees, many find them uncomfortable for long journeys. Ambassadors are gradually giving way to more efficient (and boring) Tata and Toyota models with mod-cons like air conditioning – and seat belts. A handful of international agencies offer self-drive car hire (**Avis**, **Sixt**), but India's majestically anarchic traffic culture is not for the faint-hearted. It's much more common, and comfortable, to hire not just the car but someone to drive it for you.

Car hire Hiring a car and driver is the most comfortable and efficient way to cover short to medium distances, and although prices have increased sharply in recent years car travel in India is still a bargain by Western standards. A car shared by three or four people can be very good value. Even if you're travelling on a modest budget a day's car hire can help take the sting out of an arduous journey, allowing you to go sightseeing along the way without looking for somewhere to stash your bags. Local drivers often know their way around an area much better than drivers from other states, so where possible it is a good idea to get a local driver who speaks the state language, in addition to being able to communicate with you. The best way to guarantee a driver who speaks good English is to book in advance with a professional travel agency, either in India or in your home country. You can, if you choose, arrange car hire informally by asking around at taxi stands, but don't expect your driver to speak anything more than rudimentary English. **Metropole Travel Services** ⓘ *www.metrovista.in*, based in Delhi are exceptionally good.

On pre-arranged overnight trips the fee you pay will normally include fuel and interstate taxes – check before you pay – and a wage for the driver. Drivers are responsible for their own expenses, including meals (and the pervasive servant-master culture in India means that most will choose to sit separately from you at meal times). Some tourist hotels provide rooms for drivers, but they often choose to sleep in the car overnight to save money. Urge them to use the drivers' rooms so they are fresh for the road ahead. In some areas drivers also seek to increase their earnings by taking you to hotels and shops where they earn a handsome commission; these are generally hugely overpriced and poor alternatives to the hotels recommended in this book, so don't be afraid to say no and insist on your choice of accommodation. If you feel inclined, a tip at the end of the tour of Rs 100 per day is perfectly acceptable. Be sure to check carefully the mileage at the beginning and end of the trip. Check that your car/driver are suitable for mountain journeys.

	Tata Indica non-a/c	Tata Indigo non-a/c	Hyundai Accent a/c	Toyota Innova
8 hrs/80 km	Rs 1200	Rs 1600	Rs 2200	Rs 2500
Extra km	Rs 8	Rs 10	Rs 15	Rs 15
Extra hour	Rs 80	Rs 100	Rs 180	Rs 200
Out of town				
Per km	Rs 8	Rs 10	Rs 15	Rs 15
Night halt	Rs 200	Rs 200	Rs 250	Rs 300

Taxi

Taxi travel in India is a great bargain, and in most cities you can take a taxi from the airport to the centre for under US$10. Yellow-top taxis in cities and large towns are metered, although tariffs change frequently. These changes are shown on a fare chart which should be read in conjunction with the meter reading. Increased night-time rates apply in most cities, and there might be a small charge for luggage. Insist on the taxi meter being flagged in your presence. If the driver refuses, the official advice is to contact the police. This may not work, but it is worth trying. When a taxi doesn't have a meter, you will need to fix the fare before starting the journey. Ask at your hotel desk for a guide price. As a foreigner, it is rare to get a taxi in the big cities to use the meter – if they are eager to, watch out as sometimes the meter is rigged and they have a fake rate card. Also, watch out for the David Blaine-style note shuffle: you pay with a Rs 500 note, but they have a Rs 100 note in their hand. This happens frequently at the pre-paid booth outside New Delhi train station too, no matter how small the transaction.

At stations and airports it is often possible to share taxis to a central point. It is worth looking for fellow passengers who may be travelling in your direction and sharing a pre-paid taxi. At night, always have a clear idea of where you want to go and insist on being taken there. Taxi drivers may try to convince you that the hotel you have chosen 'closed three years ago' or is 'completely full'. Say that you have a reservation.

Rickshaw

Auto-rickshaws (autos) are almost universally available in towns across North India and are the cheapest and most convenient way of getting about. It is best to walk a short distance away from a hotel gate before picking up an auto to avoid paying an inflated rate. In addition to using them for short journeys it is often possible to hire them by the hour, or for a half- or full-day's sightseeing. In some areas younger drivers who speak some English and know their local area well may want to show you around. However, rickshaw drivers are often paid a commission by hotels, restaurants and gift shops so advice is not always impartial. Drivers generally refuse to use a meter, often quote a ridiculous price or may sometimes stop short of your destination. If you have real problems it can help to note down the vehicle licence number and threaten to go to the police. Beware of some rickshaw drivers who show the fare chart for taxis.

Cycle-rickshaws and **horse-drawn tongas** are more common in small towns or on the outskirts of a large one. You will need to fix a price by bargaining. The animal attached to a tonga usually looks too undernourished to have the strength to pull the driver, let alone passengers.

Essentials A-Z

Accident and emergency

Contact the relevant emergency service (police T100, fire T101, ambulance T102) and your embassy. Make sure you obtain police/medical reports required for insurance claims.

Drugs

Be aware that the government takes the misuse of drugs very seriously. Anyone charged with the illegal possession of drugs risks facing a fine of Rs 100,000 and a minimum 10 years' imprisonment. Several foreigners have been imprisoned for drugs-related offences in the last decade.

Electricity

India's supply is 220-240 volts AC. Some top hotels have transformers. There may be pronounced variations in the voltage, and power cuts are common. Power back-up by generator or inverter is becoming more widespread, even in humble hotels, though it may not cover a/c. Socket sizes vary so take a universal adaptor; low-quality versions are available locally. Many hotels, even in the higher categories, don't have electric razor sockets. Invest in a stabilizer for a laptop.

Embassies and consulates

For information on visas and immigration, see page 228. For a comprehensive list of embassies (but not all consulates), see www.immihelp.com or http://embassy.goabroad.com. Many embassies around the world are now outsourcing the visa process which might affect how long the process takes.

Health

Local populations in India are exposed to a range of health risks not encountered in the Western world. Many of the diseases are major problems for the local poor and destitute and, although the risk to travellers is more remote, they cannot be ignored. Obviously 5-star travel is going to carry less risk than backpacking on a budget.

Healthcare in the region is varied. There are many excellent private and government clinics/hospitals. As with all medical care, first impressions count. It's worth contacting your embassy or consulate on arrival and asking where the recommended (ie those used by diplomats) clinics are. You can also ask about locally recommended medical dos and don'ts. If you do get ill, and you have the opportunity, you should also ask your medical insurer whether they are satisfied that the medical centre/hospital you have been referred to is of a suitable standard.

Before you go

Ideally, you should see your GP or travel clinic at least 6 weeks before your departure for general advice on travel risks, malaria and vaccinations. Make sure you have travel insurance, get a dental check (especially if you are going to be away for more than a month), know your own blood group and if you suffer a long-term condition such as diabetes or epilepsy make sure someone knows or that you have a **Medic Alert** bracelet/necklace with this information on it. Remember that it is risky to buy medicinal tablets abroad because the doses may differ and India has a huge trade in false drugs.

Vaccinations

If you need vaccinations, see your doctor well in advance of your travel. Most courses must be completed at least 4 weeks before you go. Travel clinics may provide rapid courses of vaccination, but are likely to be more expensive. The following vaccinations are recommended: typhoid, polio, tetanus, infectious hepatitis and diptheria. For details of malaria prevention, contact your GP or local travel clinic.

The following vaccinations may also be considered: rabies, possibly BCG (since TB is still common in the region) and in some cases meningitis and diphtheria (if you're staying in the country for a long time). Yellow fever is not required in India but you may be asked to show a certificate if you have travelled from Africa or South America. Japanese encephalitis may be required for rural travel at certain times of the year (mainly rainy seasons). An effective oral cholera vaccine (Dukoral) is now available as 2 doses providing 3 months' protection.

If you get ill

Contact your embassy or consulate for a list of doctors and dentists who speak your language, or at least some English. Good-quality healthcare is available in the larger centres but it can be expensive, especially hospitalization. Make sure you have adequate insurance. You can also ask at your hotel for good local doctors.

Medical services
Chandigarh
General Hospital, T0172-266 301. There are also 24-hr chemists.

Delhi
For hospitals, embassies and high commissions have lists of recommended doctors and dentists. Doctors approved by IAMAT (International Association for Medical Assistance to Travellers) are listed in a directory. Casualty and emergency wards in both private and government hospitals are open 24 hrs. All hospitals listed have 24-hr chemists. **Apollo Hospital**, Indraprastha, T011-269 5858. **Ram Manohar**

Lohia, Willingdon Crescent, T011-2336 5525, 24-hr A&E. **Bara Hindu Rao**, Sabzi Mandi, T011-2391 9476. **JP Narayan**, J Nehru Marg, Delhi Gate, T011-2323 0733. **Safdarjang General**, Sri Aurobindo Marg, T011-2616 5060. **S Kripalani**, Shaheed Bhagat Singh Mg, Connaught Pl, T011-2336 3728. **Chemists**: In Connaught Pl: **Nath Brothers**, G-2, off Marina Arcade; **Chemico**, H-45. There are branches of **Apollo Pharmacy** dotted throughout city.

Dharamshala and McLeodganj
Delek Hospital, T01892-220053/223381, often foreign volunteer doctors, good for dentistry. **Men Tse Khang** (Tibetan Medical Institute) T01892-222484, Gangchen Kyishong, for Tibetan herbal medicine. **Zonal Hospital**, T01892-222133. **Dr Dolma's** and **Dr Dhonden's** clinics, near McLeodganj Bazar for Tibetan treatment.

Jammu
Hospital, T0191-254 7637.

Leh
SNM Hospital, T01982-252014, open 0900-1700, is well-equipped (also for advice on mountain sickness), after hours, T01982-253629.

Manali and around
Lady Willingdon Hospital, T01902-252379.

Mandi
Zonal Hospital, T01905-222177.

Shimla
Tara Hospital, The Ridge, T0177-280 3275. **Dr Puri**, Mehghana Complex, The Mall, T0177-280 1936, speaks fluent English, is efficient, and very reasonable.

Websites
Blood Care Foundation (UK), **www.bloodcare.org.uk** A Kent-based charity 'dedicated to the provision of screened blood and resuscitation fluids

in countries where these are not readily available'. They will dispatch certified non-infected blood of the right type to your hospital/clinic. The blood is flown in from various centres around the world.

British Global Travel Health Association (UK), www.bgtha.org This is the official website of an organization of travel health professionals.

Fit for Travel, www.fitfortravel.scot. nhs.uk This site from Scotland provides a quick A-Z of vaccine and travel health advice requirements for each country.

Foreign and Commonwealth Office (FCO) (UK), www.fco.gov.uk A key travel advice site, with useful information on the country, people, climate and lists the UK embassies/consulates. The site also promotes the concept of 'know before you go' and encourages travel insurance and appropriate travel health advice. It has links to Department of Health travel advice site.

The Health Protection Agency, www.hpa. org.uk Up-to-date malaria advice guidelines for travel around the world. It gives specific advice about the right drugs for each location. It also has useful information for those who are pregnant, suffering from epilepsy or planning to travel with children.

Medic Alert (UK), www.medicalalert.com This is the website of the foundation that produces bracelets and necklaces for those with existing medical problems. Once you have ordered your bracelet/necklace you write your key medical details on paper inside it, so that if you collapse, a medic can identify you as having epilepsy or a nut allergy, etc.

World Health Organisation, www.who.int The WHO site has links to the *WHO Blue Book* on travel advice. This lists the diseases in different regions of the world. It describes vaccination schedules and makes clear which countries have yellow fever vaccination certificate requirements and malarial risk.

Language

Hindi, spoken as a mother tongue by over 400 million people, is India's official language. The use of English is also enshrined in the constitution for a wide range of official purposes, notably communication between Hindi and non-Hindi speaking states. The use of English is also enshrined in the Constitution for a wide range of official purposes, notably communication between Hindi and non-Hindi speaking states. The most widely spoken Indo-Aryan languages are: Bengali (8.3%), Marathi (8%), Urdu (5.7%), Gujarati (5.4%), Oriya (3.7%) and Punjabi (3.2%). Among the Dravidian languages Telugu (8.2%), Tamil (7%), Kannada (4.2%) and Malayalam (3.5%) are the most widely used. Hindi is the official language of Himachal Pradesh, but *pahari* or other local dialects are often spoken, while around McLeodganj, home of His Holiness the Dalai Lama, you will hear a lot of Tibetan spoken. In Ladakh, they speak Ladakhi otherwise known as Bhoti. While although there is a Kashmiri language, most people speak Urdu in Kashmir. It is possible to study a number of Indian languages at language centres.

English is widely spoken in towns and cities; even in quite remote villages it is usually not difficult to find someone who speaks at least a little English. Outside of major tourist sites, other European languages are almost completely unknown. The accent in which English is spoken is often affected strongly by the mother tongue of the speaker and there have been changes in common grammar, which sometimes make it sound unusual. Many of these changes have become standard Indian English usage, as valid as any other varieties of English used around the world. Outside of major tourist sites, other European languages are almost completely unknown. It is possible to study a number of Indian languages at language centres.

WARNING

Price increases

The price of admission to historic monuments throughout India is set to rise drastically. As of March 2016, admission to 'Category A' monuments (World Heritage Sites such as the Taj Mahal) increased from Rs 250 to Rs 750 per person per day (Rs 10 for Indians), while fees at lesser monuments have risen from Rs 100 to Rs 300. Indian tourism bodies such as the IATO have protested the changes, and at time of writing were negotiating with the Tourism Ministry to reverse or reduce the price hikes. Nevertheless, it's quite possible that admission fees will be double or more the prices listed in this edition of the guide by the time you visit.

Money

US$1= Rs 67.89, €1=Rs 73.95, £1= Rs 97.58 (Feb 2016). Indian currency is the Indian Rupee (Re/Rs). It is not possible to purchase these before you arrive. If you want cash on arrival it is best to get it at the airport bank, although see if an ATM is available as airport rates are not very generous. Rupee notes are printed in denominations of Rs 1000, 500, 100, 50, 20, 10. The rupee is divided into 100 paise. Coins are minted in denominations of Rs 10, 5, Rs 2, Rs 1 and (the increasingly uncommon) 50 paise. **Note** Carry money in a money belt worn under clothing but keep a small amount in an easily accessible place.

ATMs

By far the most convenient method of accessing money, ATMs can be found all over India, usually attended by security guards, with most banks offering some services to holders of overseas cards. ATMS are springing up in even the most remote locations, but if travelling off the beaten track arrange money beforehand. Banks whose ATMs will issue cash against Cirrus and Maestro cards, as well as Visa and MasterCard, include **Bank of Baroda**, **Citibank**, **HDFC**, **HSBC**, **ICICI**, **IDBI**, **Punjab National Bank**, **State Bank of India (SBI)**, **Standard Chartered** and **UTI**. A withdrawal fee is usually charged by the issuing bank on top of the conversion charges applied by your own bank. Fraud prevention measures quite often result in travellers having their cards blocked by the bank when unexpected overseas transactions occur; advise your bank of your travel plans before leaving.

Credit cards

Major credit cards are increasingly acceptable in the main centres, though in smaller cities and towns it is still rare to be able to pay by credit card. Payment by credit card can sometimes be more expensive than payment by cash, whilst some credit card companies charge a premium on cash withdrawals. **Visa** and **MasterCard** have an ever-growing number of ATMs in major cities and several banks offer withdrawal facilities for Cirrus and Maestro cardholders. It is however easy to obtain a cash advance against a credit card. Railway reservation centres in major cities take payment for train tickets by Visa card which can be very quick as the queue is short, although they cannot be used for Tourist Quota tickets.

Currency cards

If you don't want to carry lots of cash, pre-paid currency cards allow you to preload money from your bank account, fixed at the day's exchange rate. They look like a credit or debit card and are issued by specialist money changing companies, such as **Travelex** and **Caxton FX**. You can top up and check your balance by phone, online and sometimes by text.

Changing money

The **State Bank of India** and several others in major towns are authorized to deal in foreign exchange. Some give cash against Visa/MasterCard (eg **ANZ**). American Express cardholders can use their cards to get either cash or TCs in Delhi. The larger cities have licensed money changers with offices usually in the commercial sector. Changing money through unauthorized dealers is illegal. Premiums on the currency black market are very small and highly risky. Large hotels change money 24 hrs a day for guests, but banks often give a substantially better rate of exchange. There is a bank at the airport as well as a Thomas Cook counter. Many international flights arrive during the night and it is generally far easier and less time consuming to change money at the airport than in the city. You should be given a foreign currency encashment certificate when you change money through a bank or authorized dealer; ask for one if it is not automatically given. It allows you to change Indian rupees back to your own currency on departure. It also enables you to use rupees to pay hotel bills or buy air tickets for which payment in foreign exchange may be required. The certificates are only valid for 3 months.

Opening hours

Banks are open Mon-Fri 1030-1430, Sat 1030-1230. Top hotels sometimes have a 24-hr money changing service. **Government offices** open Mon-Fri 0930-1700, Sat 0930-1300 (some open on alternate Sat only). **Post offices** open Mon-Fri 1000-1700, often shutting for lunch, and Sat mornings. **Shops** open Mon-Sat 0930-1800; bazars keep longer hours.

Public holidays

The Hindu calendar

Hindus follow 2 distinct eras: The **Vikrama Samvat** which began in 57 BC and the Salivahan Saka which dates from AD 78 and has been the official Indian calendar since 1957. The Saka new year starts on 22 Mar and has the same length as the Gregorian calendar. The 29½-day lunar month with its 'dark' and 'bright' halves based on the new and full moons, are named after 12 constellations, and total a 354-day year. The calendar cleverly has an extra month (*adhik maas*) every 2½ to 3 years, to bring it in line with the solar year of 365 days coinciding with the Gregorian calendar of the West.

Some major national and regional festivals are listed below. A few count as national holidays: **26 Jan**: Republic Day; **15 Aug**: Independence Day; **2 Oct**: Mahatma Gandhi's Birthday; **25 Dec**: Christmas Day.

Major festivals and fairs

Jan

New Year's Day (1st) is accepted officially when following the Gregorian calendar but there are regional variations which fall on different dates, often coinciding with spring/harvest time in Mar and Apr. **Losar Festival** (date changes depending on lunar calendar) dates back to the pre-Buddhist Bon era in Tibet and is widely celebrated in Ladakh. People make offerings of incense at gompas and family shrines and there is dancing and celebrations in the most popular festival of the region.

Feb

Vasant Panchami, the spring festival when people wear bright yellow clothes to mark the advent of the season with singing, dancing and feasting.

Feb/Mar

Maha Sivaratri marks the night when Siva danced his celestial dance of destruction (Tandava), which is celebrated with feasting and fairs at Siva temples, but preceded by a night of devotional readings and hymn singing.

Mar

Holi, the festival of colours, marks the climax of spring. The previous night bonfires are lit symbolizing the end of winter (and conquering of evil). People have fun throwing coloured powder and water at each other and in the evening some gamble with friends. If you don't mind getting covered in colours, you can risk going out but celebrations can sometimes get very rowdy (and unpleasant). Some worship Krishna who defeated the demon Putana.

Apr

Baisakhi (13/14th) is celebrated both as the beginning of the solar year and as a harvest festival across the Punjab and Haryana. It is especially cherished by the Sikhs as the 10th Guru, Guru Gobind Singh, developed the order of the Khalsa on this date; it is an auspicious time to visit grudwara (Sikh temple). There are also a lot of colourful wedding celebrations around this time.

Apr/May

Buddha Jayanti or Vesak, the first full moon night in Apr/May marks the birth of the Buddha. It is worth timing your visit to McLeodganj around this time.

Jul

His Holiness, the Dalai Lama's Birthday (5th) is celebrated enthusiastically around McLeodganj.

Jul/Aug

Raksha (or Rakhi) Bandhan symbolizes the bond between brother and sister, celebrated at full moon. A sister says special prayers for her brother and ties coloured threads around his wrist to remind him of the special bond. He in turn gives a gift and promises to protect and care for her. Sometimes rakshas are exchanged as a mark of friendship.

Aug

Independence Day (15th), a national secular holiday, is marked by special events.

Aug/Sep

Janmashtami, the birth of Krishna is celebrated at midnight at Krishna temples.

Sep/Oct

Dasara has many local variations and is the most popular festival in the Kullu Valley. In this region, it celebrates Lord Rama killing the demon king Ravana and is marked with **Ramlila**, various episodes of the Ramayana story are enacted with particular reference to the battle between the forces of good and evil. In some parts of India it celebrates Rama's victory over the Demon King Ravana of Lanka with the help of loyal Hanuman (Monkey). Huge effigies of Ravana made of bamboo and paper are burnt on the 10th day (Vijaya dasami) of **Dasara** in public open spaces.

Oct

Gandhi Jayanti (2nd), Mahatma Gandhi's birthday, is remembered with prayer meetings and devotional singing.

Oct/Nov

Navratri, also known as the **Nine Night festival of the Goddess**, is most popular in Gujarat but also widely celebrated in Kashmir at Katra, the base camp of the Mata Vaishno Devi Temple.

Diwali/Deepavali (Sanskrit ideepa lamp), the festival of lights. Some Hindus celebrate Krishna's victory over the demon Narakasura, some Rama's return after his 14 years' exile in the forest when citizens lit his way with oil lamps. The festival falls on the dark chaturdasi (14th) night (the one preceding the new moon), when rows of lamps or candles are lit in remembrance, and rangolis are painted on the floor as a sign of welcome. Fireworks have become an integral part of the celebration and are often set off days before Diwali. Most people wear new clothes; some play games of chance.

Nov

Guru Nanak Jayanti (24th) is the most popular of the Sikh holy days and commemorates the birth of Guru Nanak. **Akhand Path** (unbroken reading of the holy book) takes place and the book itself (Guru Granth Sahib) is taken out in procession.

Dec

Christmas Day (25th) sees Indian Christians celebrate the birth of Christ in much the same way as in the West; many churches hold services/Mass at midnight. There is an air of festivity in city markets which are specially decorated and illuminated.
New Year (31st) sees hotel prices peak and large supplements are added for meals and entertainment in the upper category hotels. Some churches mark the night with a Midnight Mass.

Muslim holy days

These are fixed according to the lunar calendar. According to the Gregorian calendar, they tend to fall 11 days earlier each year, dependent on the sighting of the new moon.

Ramadan, known in India as 'Ramzan', is the start of the month of fasting when all Muslims (except young children, the very elderly, the sick, pregnant women and travellers) must abstain from food and drink, from sunrise to sunset.
Id ul Fitr is the 3-day festival that marks the end of Ramzan.
Id-ul-Zuha/Bakr-Id is when Muslims commemorate Ibrahim's sacrifice of his son according to God's commandment; the main time of pilgrimage to Mecca (the Hajj). It is marked by the sacrifice of a goat, feasting and alms giving.
Muharram is when the killing of the Prophet's grandson, Hussain, is commemorated by Shi'a Muslims. Decorated tazias (replicas of the martyr's tomb) are carried in procession by devout wailing followers who beat their chests to express their grief. Shi'as fast for the 10 days.

Safety

Personal security

In general the threats to personal security for travellers in India are remarkably small. However, incidents of petty theft and violence directed specifically at tourists have been on the increase so care is necessary in some places, and basic common sense needs to be used with respect to looking after valuables. Follow the same precautions you would at home. There have been much-reported incidents of severe sexual assault in Delhi, Kolkata and some more rural areas in the last few years. Avoid wandering alone outdoors late at night in these places. During daylight hours be careful in remote places, especially when alone. If you are under threat, scream loudly. Be cautious before accepting food or drink from casual acquaintances, as it may be drugged – though note that Indians on a long train journey will invariably try to share their snacks with you, and balance caution with the opportunity to interact. As a general rule, travellers are advised to be vigilant in the lead up to and on days of national significance, such as Republic Day (26 Jan) and Independence Day (15 Aug) as militants have in the past used such occasions to mount attacks.

Following a major explosion on the Delhi to Lahore (Pakistan) train in Feb 2007 and the Mumbai attacks in Nov 2008, increased security has been implemented on trains and at stations. Similar measures at airports may cause delays for passengers so factor this into your timing. Also check your airline's website for up-to-date information on luggage restrictions. In Delhi, you even find x-ray machines at the metro stations. That said, in the great majority of places visited by tourists, violent crime and personal attacks are extremely rare.

Travel advice

It is better to seek advice from your consulate than from travel agencies. Before you travel you can contact: **British Foreign & Commonwealth Office Travel Advice Unit**, T020 7008 1500 (Pakistan desk T020-7270 2385), www.fco.gov.uk. **US State Department's Bureau of Consular Affairs**, Overseas Citizens Services, Room 4800, Department of State, Washington, DC 20520-4818, USA, T202-501 4444, http://travel.state.gov. **Australian Department of Foreign Affairs Canberra**, Australia, T02-6261 3305, www.smartraveller.gov.au. Canadian official advice is on www.voyage.gc.ca.

Theft

Theft is not uncommon. It is best to keep TCs, passports and valuables with you at all times. Don't regard hotel rooms as being automatically safe; even hotel safes don't guarantee secure storage. Avoid leaving valuables near open windows even when you are in the room. Use your own padlock in a budget hotel when you go out. Pickpockets and other thieves operate in the big cities. Crowded areas are particularly high risk. Take special care of your belongings when getting on or off public transport.

If you have items stolen, they should be reported to the police as soon as possible. Keep a separate record of vital documents, including passport details and numbers of TCs. Larger hotels will be able to assist in contacting and dealing with the police. Dealings with the police can be very difficult and in the worst regions, even dangerous. The paperwork involved in reporting losses can be time consuming and irritating and your own documentation (eg passport and visas) may be demanded.

In some states the police occasionally demand bribes, though you should not assume that if procedures move slowly you are automatically being expected to offer a bribe. The traffic police are tightening up on traffic offences in some places. They have the right to make on-the-spot fines for speeding and illegal parking. If you face a fine, insist on a receipt.

If you have to go to a police station, try to take someone with you.

If you face really serious problems (eg in connection with a driving accident), contact your consular office as quickly as possible. You should ensure you always have your international driving licence and motorbike or car documentation with you.

Confidence tricksters are particularly common around railway stations or places where budget tourists gather. A common plea is some sudden and desperate calamity; sometimes a letter will be produced in English to back up the claim. The demands are likely to increase sharply if sympathy is shown.

Telephone

The international code for India is +91.
Mobile phones

Practically all business in India is now conducted via mobile phone. Calls and mobile data are incredibly cheap by global standards – local calls cost as little as half a rupee per min – and if you're in the country for more than a couple of weeks and need to keep in touch it can definitely be worth the hassle to get a local SIM card. Arguably the best service is provided by the government carrier **BSNL/MTNL** but connecting to the service is virtually impossible for foreigners. Private companies such as **Airtel**, **Vodafone**, **Idea** and **Tata Indicom** are easier to sign up with, but the deals they offer can be befuddling and are frequently changed. To get the connection you'll need to complete a form, have a local address or receipt showing the address of your hotel, and present photocopies of your passport and visa plus 2 passport photos to an authorized reseller – most phone dealers will be able to help, and can also sell top-up. **Univercell**, www.univercell.in, and **The Mobile Store**, www.themobilestore.in, are widespread and efficient chains selling phones and SIM cards. Naturally reception can be patchy in some remote locations and valleys.

India is divided into a number of 'calling circles' or regions, and if you travel outside the region where your connection is based, you will pay higher 'roaming' charges for making and receiving calls, and any problems that may occur – with 'unverified' documents, for example – can be much harder to resolve.

Landlines

You can still find privately run phone booths, usually labelled on yellow boards with the letters 'PCO-STD-ISD'. You dial the call yourself, and the time and cost are displayed on a computer screen. Cheap rate (2100-0600) means long queues may form outside booths. Telephone calls from hotels are usually more expensive (check price before calling), though some will allow local calls free of charge.

A double ring repeated regularly means it is ringing; equal tones with equal pauses means engaged (similar to the UK). If calling a mobile, you're as likely to hear devotional Hindu music or Bollywood hits coming back down the line as a standard ringtone.

One disadvantage of India's tremendous rate of growth is that millions of telephone numbers go out of date every year. Current telephone directories themselves are often out of date and some of the numbers given in this book will have been changed even as we go to press. **Directory enquiries**, T197, can be helpful but works only for the local area code.

Time

India doesn't change its clocks, so from the last Sun in Oct to the last Sun in Mar the time is GMT +5½ hrs, and the rest of the year it's +4½ hrs (USA, EST +10½ and +9½ hrs; Australia, EST -5½ and -4½ hrs).

Tipping

A tip of Rs 10 to a bellboy carrying luggage in a modest hotel (Rs 20 in a higher category) would be appropriate. In upmarket restaurants, a 10% tip is acceptable when service is not already included, while in places serving very cheap meals, round off the bill with small change. Indians don't normally tip taxi drivers but a small extra is welcomed. Porters at airports and railway stations often have a fixed rate displayed but will usually press for more. Ask fellow passengers what a fair rate is.

Tourist information

There are **Government of India** tourist offices in the state capitals, as well as state tourist offices (sometimes **Tourism Development Corporations**) in the Delhi and some towns and places of tourist interest. They produce their own tourist literature, either free or sold at a nominal price, and some also have lists of city hotels and paying guest options. The quality of material is improving though maps are often poor. Many offer tours of the city, neighbouring sights and overnight and regional packages. Some run modest hotels and midway motels with restaurants and may also arrange car hire and guides.

Tour operators

UK

Ace Cultural Tours, T01223-841055, www.aceculturaltours.co.uk. Expert-led cultural study tours.

Explorations Company, T01367-850566, www.explorationscompany.com. Bespoke holidays, including to the Andaman Islands and Rajasthan.

Colours Of India, T020-8347 4020, www.partnershiptravel.co.uk. Tailor-made cultural, adventure, spa and cooking tours.

Cox & Kings, T020-7873 5000, www.coxandkings.co.uk. Offers high-quality group tours, private journeys and tailor-made holidays to many of India's regions, from the lavish to the adventurous, planned by experts.

Dragoman, T01728-861133, www.dragoman.com. Overland, adventure, camping.

Exodus, T0845-287 7408, www.exodus.co.uk. Small group overland and trekking tours.

Greaves Tours, T020-7487 9111, www.greavesindia.com. Luxury, tailor-made tours using only scheduled flights. Traditional travel such as road and rail preferred to flights between major cities.

Master Travel, T020-7501 6741, www.mastertravel.co.uk. Organizes professional study tours in fields including education and healthcare.

Steppes Travel, T01285-787557, www.steppestravel.co.uk. Wildlife safaris, tiger study tours and cultural tours with strong conservation ethic.

India

Above 14,000ft, Manali, www.above14000ft.com. See pages 124 and 205.

Ecosphere Spiti, Kaza, www.spitiecosphere.com. See page 104.

The Blue Yonder, T0413-450 2218, www.theblueyonder.com. India's pioneers in responsible travel run wonderful half-day to multi-day trips in Puducherry, Kerala, Sikkim and Rajasthan. Enthusiastic guides and unusual destinations.

Ibex Expeditions, New Delhi, T011-2646 0244, www.ibexexpeditions.com. Responsible tourism company for tours, safaris and treks. Founding member of the Ecotourism Society of India and award-winner for the most innovative tour operator in India.

Indebo India, New Delhi, T011-4716 5500, www.indebo.com. Customized tours and travel-related services throughout India.

Indiabeat, B-4 Vijay Path, Tilak Nagar, Jaipur, T0141-651 9797, www.indiabeat.co.uk. Specializing in dream trips and once-in-a-lifetime experiences, this British team decamped to Jaipur have great insider knowledge and insight into India.

Paradise Holidays, New Delhi, T011-4552 0735, www.paradiseholidays.com. Wide range of tailor-made tours, from cultural to wildlife.**Royal Expeditions**, New Delhi, T011-2623 8545, www.royalexpeditions.com. Specialist staff for customized trips, knowledgeable about options for senior travellers. Owns luxury 4WD vehicles for escorted self-drive adventures in the Himalaya, and offers sightseeing tours in classic cars in Jaipur.

North America

Relief Riders International, T1-413-329 5876, www.reliefridersinternational.com. Unique horseback tours through the Thar Desert of Rajasthan, with guests working as support staff to a full-scale aid mission.

Visas and immigration

Virtually all foreign nationals, including children, require a visa to enter India. The rules regarding visas change frequently and arrangements for application and collection also vary from town to town so it is essential to check details and costs with the relevant embassy or consulate. These remain closed on Indian national holidays.

As of 2015 India has brought 113 countries into its visa-on-arrival scheme, which after several bizarre false starts is – at time of writing – almost as simple as it sounds. An "e-Visa" costs US$60 and is valid for a stay of up to 30 days; the visa cannot be extended, and only permits travel for tourism purposes. Apply at www.indianvisaonline.gov.in, no later than 4 days before your arrival. For up-to-date information on visa requirements visit www.india-visa.com.

No foreigner needs to register within the 180-day period of their tourist visa. If you have a 1-year visa or as a US citizen a 10-year visa and wish to stay longer than 180 days you will need to register with the Foreign Registration Office. For up-to-date information on visa requirements visit www.india-visa.com.

Index

Entries in bold refer to maps

Credits

Footprint credits
Editor: Nicola Gibbs
Production and layout: Emma Bryers
Maps: Kevin Feeney
Colour section: Angus Dawson

Publisher: Felicity Laughton
                Patrick Dawson
Marketing: Kirsty Holmes
Sales: Diane McEntee
Advertising and content partnerships:
Debbie Wylde

Photography credits
Front cover: Curioso/Shutterstock.com
Back cover top: Anthon Jackson/
Shutterstock.com
Back cover bottom: Elena Mirage/
Shutterstock.com
Inside front cover: Tim Graham/SuperStock.
com; designbydx/Shutterstock.com;
Mikadun/Shutterstock.com

Colour section
Page 1: Zzvet/Shutterstock.com
Page 2: Annop Itsarayoungyuen/
Shutterstock.com
Page 4: MOLPIX/Shutterstock.com;
Gritsana P/Shutterstock.com
Page 5: Luciano Mortula/Shutterstock.com;
Sam Dcruz/Shutterstock.com; Rafal Cichawa/
Shutterstock.com
Page 7: Gritsana P/Shutterstock.com;
Daniel Prudek/Shutterstock.com;
Panom/Shutterstock.com
Page 8: worldswildlifewonders/
Shutterstock.com

Duotones
Page 24: Don Mammoser/Shuttersock
Page 64: Aleksei Sarkisov/Shutterstock
Page 154: OlegD/Shutterstock

Printed in Spain by GraphyCems

Publishing information
Footprint Delhi & Northwest India
2nd edition
© Footprint Handbooks Ltd
March 2016

ISBN: 978 1 910120 86 6
CIP DATA: A catalogue record for this book
is available from the British Library

® Footprint Handbooks and the
Footprint mark are a registered
trademark of Footprint Handbooks Ltd

Published by Footprint
6 Riverside Court
Lower Bristol Road
Bath BA2 3DZ, UK
T +44 (0)1225 469141
F +44 (0)1225 469461
footprinttravelguides.com

Distributed in the USA by
National Book Network, Inc.

Every effort has been made to ensure that
the facts in this guidebook are accurate.
However, travellers should still obtain advice
from consulates, airlines, etc about travel
and visa requirements before travelling.
The authors and publishers cannot
accept responsibility for any loss, injury
or inconvenience however caused.

All rights reserved. No part of this
publication may be reproduced, stored
in a retrieval system, or transmitted, in
any form or by any means, electronic,
mechanical, photocopying, recording,
or otherwise without the prior permission
of Footprint Handbooks Ltd.